THE NEW POLITICAL ECONOMIES:

A Collection of Essays
from Around the World

THE NEW POLITICAL ECONOMIES:

A Collection of Essays from Around the World

Edited by

**Laurence S. Moss,
Babson College**

Blackwell
Publishing

Blackwell Publishers, Inc.
350 Main Street
Malden, MA 02148 USA

Blackwell Publishers, Ltd.
108 Cowley Road
Oxford, OX4 1JF
United Kingdom

Library of Congress Cataloging-in-Publication Data is located at the Library of Congress.
   Includes bibliographical references and index.
ISBN 0-631-234969 (case: alk. paper)
ISBN 0-631-234977 (pbk: alk. paper)

ISBN 0-631-234969
ISBN 0-631-234977 (P)
ISSN 0002-9246

CONTENTS

The New Political Economies:
A Collection of Essays from Around the World

Editor's Introduction

THE MAJORITY OF THE AUTHORS who have contributed articles to this volume believe that the "new political economies" are offshoots of neoclassical economics. This means that the stock of any particular type of new political economy rises or falls according to what each author thinks of the neoclassical research program. Those who like neoclassical economics tend to also like one or more versions of the new political economies. The opponents of neoclassical economics tend to also oppose and criticize the new political economies.

The American Journal of Economics and Sociology sets no ideological standards for its collaborators or contributors and tries to encourage authors of differing perspectives to share their thoughts in a scholarly and responsible manner. The readers of this volume must serve as the ultimate judges of the usefulness of this volume. Its essays cluster around five principal subject headings:

- Fiscal Sociology
- Constitutional Economics
- Austrian School Perspectives
- New Perspectives on Transition Economies
- Radical Criticisms and Reflections

The lead article, by the historian A. M. C. Waterman, traces the term "political economy" back to the opening decades of the seventeenth century. At that time, several European authors wanted to extend the "household management" literature of ancient Greece to the emerging nation-states of Europe. The economists/advisors wished to use any knowledge about the polity and its attendant institutions to advise kings about what should be done.

American Journal of Economics and Sociology, Vol. 61, No. 1 (January, 2002).

Waterman suggests that a body of knowledge that might qualify as the "science" of political economy only emerged in the nineteenth century when the Poor Laws were attacked by David Ricardo, Thomas Malthus, and others. These critics explained how the rational eligible agent (the welfare recipient) would behave when subsidized by the state and feared that such laziness as was expected to occur would make the Poor Laws a prescription for social disaster. This was economic reasoning as we recognize it today, complete with the *homo economicus* assumption.

Waterman's survey highlights the development of the various analytic structures that subsequent generations of economists used to provide advice to governments. In the late eighteenth and early nineteenth centuries, the dominant collection of recommended policies was loosely termed "free trade liberalism." By the end of the nineteenth century, and especially after John Maynard Keynes published his seminal book in 1936 (Keynes 1936), economic policy had morphed into the famous "neoclassical synthesis." An important part of this synthesis was the central importance of the twisting and turning of those notorious "steering wheels" of fiscal and monetary policies to provide macro stability (Lerner 1942). By the middle of the twentieth century, a veritable "democratic socialism" had become the policy rhetoric of most of the profession—a volte-face from the free trade liberalism of a hundred years earlier. But this romance with interventionism did not last very long.

As early as 1967 and most dramatically during the 1970s, economics turned another sharp corner. A large section of the economics profession concluded that government fine-tuning did more to *destabilize* the economy than to provide positive coordinative benefits. Waterman insists that among contemporary economists

> [t]he "new political economies" of the late twentieth and early twenty-first centuries have been powerfully corrosive of those collectivist or at any rate *dirigiste* doctrines taken for granted by [prior economists]. *Oeconomie politique* has been rolled back again. The onus of proof has been shifted, and now lies with those who wish to assert a more important part for the state in the economic life of a nation. (see below, Waterman:37–38)

Perhaps things were different in the German-speaking nations. Part II of this volume includes an interesting discussion of another subfield of neoclassical economics known as Fiscal Sociology (FS).

Fiscal Sociology, like political economy, takes its name from developments in the seventeenth century. At that time, the modern nation-state began to regularize taxation and renounce the use of surprise plunder and confiscation as fiscal devices. In the first part of the twentieth century, Rudolf Goldscheid and Joseph A. Schumpeter grasped this historical development and explained its significance to the social sciences. The subfield of FS languished for reasons that had little to do with the merits of the program and more to do with world-shattering events in Germany, especially during the tumult of the two world wars. In this volume, Backhaus calls for a rehabilitation of FS from A to Z and, by using an A to Z list of topics, contributes mightily to his cause. According to him, FS belongs among the new political economies. In this day and age of globalized trade and mass culture, Backhaus calls for a renewal of FS as the most promising thread of a revitalized political economy.

Next, Dr. Jan-Peter Olters reminds us that any discussion of tax policy and the financing of the modern democratic state must take notice of the reality of political parties and the competition that exists between them. Olters rehabilitates some of the tools of analysis that the field of political economy inherited from the writings of Anthony Downs and others in the 1960s (Downs 1967). He applauds the efforts of the economists who, as Professor Gary J. Miller pointed out, finally got around to "studying voters as rational maximizers" and then proceeded to "sublimate political science to economics" (Miller 1997). Olters brilliantly extends the Downs approach by offering the "first building block toward a more comprehensive description of the intricate, multi-tiered political processes characterizing democracies" (see below, Olters:96).

Households consult their income and what they know about the income of others in the community before they consider how to finance a given level of public goods. They are motivated to join political parties and in some cases help determine that party's platform agenda. Down's median voter theorem is in this way extended to the party system and helps explain the shifts in income redistribution associated with the financing of public goods. On balance, these redistributive shifts are a profound source of social stability in modern democracies.

Part III covers the subject of "constitutional economics," which is another rapidly evolving subfield of public choice economics. Neoclassical welfare economics as it emerged and was presented in the leading texts, especially from 1930 to 1960, claimed that the state could intervene into the market system for the purpose of choosing different allocations of resources without in any way altering the basic legal rules that characterize the economy and help it function in the first place. In his contribution, Professor Richard Wagner explains that every single change in economic policy will itself be an instrument for changing the "rules of the game." Wagner goes on to explain that

> [a]ll economic policy is constitutional policy in that it is centrally involved in shaping the character of the regime that will govern our relationships with one another. Economic policy does not truly make direct choices among alternative allocative outcomes. It makes choices regarding the framework of rules that govern human relationships. In making policy choices we constitute the principles by which our relationships with one another are governed. (see below, Wagner:108)

Professor Peter Kurrild-Klitgaard's article complements Wagner's. He offers an answer to the question as to why government structures function in different ways than ordinary markets. The principal difference centers on "opting out." In a typical market for a product or service, a disgruntled purchaser can withdraw his or her demand and leave that market. In modern political life a disgruntled citizen cannot cast off and leave the polity. Kurrild-Klitgaard wants to know "why not"? More often than not, the dissenting household is simply forced to go along with the majority.

By reconstructing the logical arguments of the seventeenth-century contractarian writers Thomas Hobbes and John Locke, Kurrild-Klitgaard shows how the addition of the "exiting" option changes or at least helps to modify the traditional textual interpretations of these classic works. Indeed, in Locke's case, the additional strategy of opting out of the political community actually helps clarify his writings. From these reconstructions of celebrated texts, Kurrild-Klitgaard advances the discussion and suggests that, from the modern public choice framework, the very "possibility of exit creates a guarantee for the individual player against excessive high . . . costs" imposed by other members of the community. Such an option may in the end actually promote the "general good of all players" in the community (see below, Kurrild-Klitgaard:145–146).

As we have read in Waterman's opening contribution, the modern Austrian school challenged modern socialist thinking on a variety of levels and for a variety of reasons. But the Austrian school was not entirely subsumed within neoclassical thought, as Waterman's terse discussion might lead some readers to believe. Indeed, modern Austrian scholars continue to assert their independence and list their differences with the central paradigm of modern economic analysis. One difference that is of some interest to our study of the "new" political economies has to do with the proper understanding of *homo economicus*. For modern Austrians, economic man is always and everywhere a social actor. Human action is embedded in history, and history consists of economic, social, and governmental processes. These processes are not separate and distinct; the three spheres of action interlock and overlap.

In Professors Peter J. Boettke and Virgil Henry Storr's coauthored chapter, economic man is clarified in relation to Mark Granovetter's popular claim that all economic action is embedded in social norms and customs and that the study of society is always prior to the study of economic markets (Granovetter 1985). According to Boettke and Storr, Granovetter's claim is misleading. It is as misleading as saying that society is embedded in the economy and therefore it is only necessary to study economics. The truth, they state, is that the modern Austrian school follows the direction of Max Weber's mode of thinking and in so doing provides "a richer conception of embeddedness than is commonly articulated" (see below, Boettke and Storr:172). Some types of economic action are embedded in social structures and some types are not. It just depends!

Unlike Boettke and Storr, Schnellenbach's stimulating paper strikes hard at the bold claims of modern public choice economics and its various subdiciplines. Since public choice economics informs many of what are called the "new political economies," Schnellenbach offers an Austrian school critique of these developments. Let us sketch the argument.

The great Austrian scholar and Nobel laureate Friedrich A. Hayek coined the terms "scientism" to refer to those futile efforts intellectuals make to extend the methods of the natural sciences to the social sciences (Hayek 1955). What Schnellenbach terms the Hayekian "knowledge-related research program" is presented as the polar opposite of the neoclassical policy approach that searches for some final rational allocation or distribution of scarce resources that can be described as "efficient." According to Schallenbach, all such approaches are suspicious because they "use the yardstick of Pareto-efficiency" (see below, Schnellenbach: 192).

Schnellenbach prays for a new political economy that will really be "new," perhaps one that appreciates the contribution of spontaneously formed rules (Hayek's approach), and is ferociously skeptical of plans to "design rules [that will govern] the political process" (see below, Schnellenbach:195). This author sees little worth celebrating in the modern public choice approach. While not all modern Austrians reject the neoclassical concept of efficiency and even Hayek may not have rejected the concept entirely, it is clear that Schnellenbach does.

Fully one-third of this essay collection is given over to a series of writers who probe the new political economies of the world to learn about the political and economic life of a specific nation-state. Dr. Vladimir Kollontai's piece teaches us that in Russia there is no single "new" political economy. Russian economic life throughout most of the twentieth century has consisted of a rush to decide which social or economic goal should receive priority over others. The formal modeling of economic life typically fell on deaf ears, especially after 1992, when both Russia and the Republics hurried down the road toward some variant of the market system and sharply away from central planning. Professor Andrew Savchenko compares the reforms in Belarus with the reforms in the Baltic countries following the collapse of the USSR a decade ago. His main point is that observable differences are better explained by political and social factors than by economic considerations.

Professor John Marangos hurls still another batch of rotten tomatoes at the neoclassical approach to political economy. According to Marangos, whether we consider Jeffrey Sachs' ideas about "shock therapy" or the ideas of the so-called gradualist school, a thoroughgoing political economy should incorporate both "institutional and political structure into the transition analysis" (see below, Marangos:256). After all, how can an economy of state-owned enterprises be transformed into an economy of the free market if the government must intervene in some major way? Once the massive intervention of government is admitted, in what sense can we speak of free trade liberalism?

Professor Shuntian Yao's contribution reminds us that where there is massive government intervention and regulation there is necessarily corruption. In modern China, he states, corruption is all-encompassing. The top jobs go to those connected to the ruling powers, and the holders of these jobs then accept bribes and apply the law selectively. Yao insists that, in China, government salaries bear little or no relationship to what economists call "marginal productivity." High-ranking officials are typically paid far beyond their marginal products, and this is an important source of inefficiency. Anyone wishing to start a project must obtain the necessary permits and licenses, which means dealing with corrupt officials. All categories of corruption work together to make Chinese society far from efficient and a far cry from what can in any sense be termed a fair distribution of wealth. Yao uses neoclassical economics to present his excellent analysis.

Yao's chapter is followed by Professors Warren Young and Joris Meijaard's attempt to extend the Laffont-Tirole model of regulatory capture to the nuclear power industry. A comparison is offered between the manner in which nuclear crises are managed in the United States and how they are managed in Japan. Although these two countries differ enormously with regard to cultural norms, the insights of modern economic analysis still seem to apply to both. This chapter strikes a chord in favor of neoclassical economics.

The African continent is far behind Europe and Asia when it comes to living standards. Economic development can and does occur, but these welcome developments are often stalled or even cut short by the ubiquitous military coup d'etat, especially in sub-Saharan Africa. Professor Augustin Kwasi Fosu of the African Economic Research Consortium in Nairobi offers a prescient analysis of the connection between economic variables and the particular type of coup that has occurred. Some coups, especially the successful ones, do correlate with subsequent developmental goals. Fosu establishes the correlation with statistical tools but concludes that the "peaceful transition of regimes would be most preferable" to all the turmoil that we have seen in sub-Saharan Africa (see below, Fosu: 341).

Our special invited issue ends with two strongly worded papers that both sound warning notes. The coauthored paper by Professors Jonathan Michie, Christine Oughton, and Frank Wilkinson argues that what are presently called the "new" political economies are really just variants of neoclassical economics. This is the same conclusion that Professor Schnellenbach reached in his contribution, approaching the problem from a neo-Austrian perspective, while these authors furnish us with a radical perspective.

In the last chapter, Professors Donald Clark Hodges and Larry Lustig examine the new political economies in terms of human capital, one tool of the modern neoclassical school (although they do not identify the human capital idea as "Chicago-school neoclassical economics"). The human capital approach leads them to appreciate the role of the modern "expert class" or "expertoisie." We are advised to compare the experts with the workers and in so doing radically "recast Marx's model" (see below, Hodges and Lustig:375). The authors allege that the experts have become the new exploiting class. Such a rehabilitation of the nineteenth-century socialist would give us a truly "new" political economy, but so far no generally-accepted rehabilitation of Marx appears to have taken place.

If Hodges and Lustig's recommendation were to prove fruitful, we would have a stark contrast to Waterman's opening chapter. According to Waterman, the "new" political economy—the one bequeathed to us in these early years of the twenty-first century—is a variant of nineteenth-century free trade liberalism. Hodges and Lustig write of a post-capitalist age and conclude that we are living in that age. Our age therefore cannot be described as Waterman has done; such an approach misses its conflict and strife.

There we have it. Fifteen interesting papers by authors from around the globe. All the essays have something to say about the "new" political economies, and what they say ranges from favorable or mildly critical in the cases of Backhaus, Olters, Wagner, Kurrild-Klitgaard, Boettke, Storr, Yao, Young, and Meijaard to highly unfavorable views by Schnellenbach, Kollantai, Marangos, Michie, Oughton, Wilkinson, Hodges, and Lustig.

However, it is not so simple to group the papers according to their authors' attitudes toward neoclassical orthodoxy. Often, the very expression "new political economies" means something entirely different as we travel from one writer to the next. If the diversity of usage in this collection is representative of the state of social science in the twenty-first century, then we are in store for more than a globalized discussion of the common problems of social and economic life. The pages of *The American Journal of Economics and Sociology* may indeed serve as one of the important platforms on which this debate takes place, as has been done in this instant volume.

References

Downs, Anthony. (1957). *An Economic Theory of Democracy*. New York: Harper & Row.

Granovetter, Mark. (1985). "Economic Action and Social Structure: The Problem of Embeddedness," *American Journal of Sociology* 91: 481–510.

Hayek, Friedrich. (1955). *The Counter Revolution of Science*. New York: Free Press.

Keynes, John Maynard. (1964 [1936]). *The General Theory of Employment, Interest and Money*. New York: Harcourt Brace, Inc.

Lerner, Abba P. (1983 [1942]). "The Steering Wheel," *University Review* (June) in Idem, *Selected Economic Writings of Abba P. Lerner*. New York: New York University Press.

Miller, Gary J. (1997). "The Impact of Economics on Contemporary Political Science," *Journal of Economic Literature* 35 (September): 1173–1204.

PART I

Historical Perspectives

American Journal of Economics and Sociology, Vol. 61, No. 1 (January, 2002).

"New Political Economies" Then and Now

Economic Theory and the Mutation of Political Doctrine

By A. M. C. WATERMAN*

ABSTRACT.   . . . the private interests and prejudices of particular orders of men . . . have given occasion to very different theories of political œconomy . . . These theories have had a considerable influence, not only upon the opinions of men of learning, but upon the public conduct of princes and sovereign states. (Smith, *Wealth of Nations* [1776]1976, p.11)

I

Introduction

THE TERM "POLITICAL ECONOMY" seems to have entered modern discourse for the first time in 1611 in a treatise on government by L. de Mayerne-Turquet (Groenewegen 1987, pp. 904–906). Four years later a fellow "Consultant Administrator," Antoyne de Montchrétien, Sieur de Watteville (c.1575–1621), published his *Traicté de l'œconomie politique* ([1615] 1889), which though "a mediocre performance and completely lacking in originality" (Schumpeter 1954, p. 168), marks the beginning of an intellectual enterprise that has continued—with some large ups and downs—to this day. The object of that enterprise is to generalize Aristotle's οικονομικη ("economics") to the level of the πολιτεία ("commonwealth" or "state"). For in Aristotle's *Politics* (1967, pp. 31–32) "economics" is to be construed as "the art of household management" where "household" means a more or less self-sufficient, manorial estate. Hence at the outset "political economy"

* A. M. C. Waterman is a Fellow of St. John's College, Winnipeg and Professor of Economics in the University of Manitoba. He wishes to thank all who have read and commented on drafts of this paper, which was originally presented at the Department of Economics annual conference, October 2000, especially Fletcher Baragar, Geoffrey Brennan, Mark Blaug, Jim Dean, Nancy Folbre, Laurence Moss and Jim Stanford. He alone is responsible for all remaining errors of fact and interpretation.

American Journal of Economics and Sociology, Vol. 61, No. 1 (January, 2002).
© 2002 American Journal of Economics and Sociology, Inc.

was an attempt to extend the art of estate management to the needs and resources of a modern nation state, of which France was in the 1600s the foremost example.

It was in this way that Sir James Steuart employed the term in his *Inquiry into the Principles of Political Œconomy* ([1767] 1966). Although Adam Smith rejected the enterprise as futile and harmful, he accepted the usage, but introduced an important analytical distinction between two senses of "political economy." In the *normative* sense understood by Smith's predecessors and contemporaries (i.e., prescriptions for running France like a manorial fief) the term signifies some "system" of public policy designed to "increase the riches and power" of a country ([1776] 1976, paras. I.xi.n.1; II.5.31; IV.1.3). But in the *positive* sense that is now orthodox though often contested, "what is *properly* called Political Œconomy" is "a branch of the science of a statesman or legislator": namely "an inquiry," which is in principle disinterested and open-ended, into "the nature and causes of the wealth of nations" (IV.intro; IV.ix.38; emphasis added).

In this article I shall be concerned with the positive sense of "political economy": that is, as a *body of theory* that purports to explain economic phenomena. For whatever else has changed, one element of continuity that runs from the political economy of Montchrétien and before to that of Joseph Stiglitz and beyond is its inescapable dependence upon theory of some kind.

Another element of continuity is the two-way street that runs between economic theory and political thought and action. In one direction, the "private interests and prejudices of particular orders of men"—not to mention the social and economic circumstances of their time and place—"have given occasion to very different theories of political œconomy." In the other, "[t]hese theories have had a considerable influence, not only upon the opinions of men of learning, but upon the public conduct of princes and sovereign states" (Smith [1776] 1976, p. 11).

A complete intellectual history of the relation between economic and political ideas would look carefully in both directions: to the "context" of the conversation, as well as to the "text" of its recorded exchanges (Skinner 1969). However, I have argued elsewhere that a merely "internalist" attention to "text" can be justified for some purposes (Waterman 1998a, pp. 303–304, 312–313). In this article, there-fore, I shall look in one direction only. I shall adopt a rigorously internalist approach, averting my eyes from wars, slumps, classes and cultures, and keeping them fixed on the logic of the ongoing eco-nomic-theory conversation. My purpose in so doing is to propose the following strong thesis for debate: *The " 'new' political economies" of the present day differ sharply in their ideological implications from those of 50 years ago*. Neoclassical orthodoxy provided the intellectual foundations of a collectivist—or at any rate an interventionist and *diri-giste*—political consensus. But the new political economies have de-stroyed those foundations, and have replaced them with economic theories far more congenial to an earlier, *laissez-faire* consensus born in the European Enlightenment.

The thesis calls for a three-part division of the history of political economy. My story must begin with the "new" political economy of Adam Smith and his successors: a brief reminder of their decisive re-jection of the original *œconomie politique* of such as Montchrétien and Steuart, and of their powerful and influential arguments for wide-spread *laissez-faire*. It must continue with the long and gradual retreat from *laissez-faire* associated with the emergence and development of "neo-classical," marginalist economics after 1870. For as Joan Robin-son once said, "neo-classical economics is the economics of social-ism." Many of its leading practitioners believed they had discovered a scientific basis for "economic control": the management of a national economy by enlightened administrators acting in the public interest—a sophisticated recrudescence of seventeenth-century *œconomie politique*. The story must conclude with a summary of those develop-ments in economic theory in the last 50 years that have destroyed the rational basis of "economic control," and that now predispose the ed-ucated public to a favorable reconsideration of Adam Smith's "natural system of perfect liberty and justice" (Smith [1776] 1976, p. 606).

II

"The Natural System of Perfect Liberty and Justice"

SHORTLY BEFORE HIS DEATH in 1797 the great Whig statesman Edmund Burke, who once said that *Wealth of Nations* was "probably the most important book ever written" (O'Brien 1993, p. 144, n. 1), could boldly declare that "the laws of commerce, which are the laws of nature, [are] consequently the laws of God" (Burke 1781–1797, IX, p.125).

Some conception of "nature" is central to all eighteenth-century social theory (Waterman 1991, pp. 28–37). Human nature is part of nature, and is that which explains the structure and functioning of society. Human nature is characterized by dominance of the "passions" over "reason," by ignorance of the present and by inability to know the future. Of the passions that drive human action, "self-love" is the most constant and therefore normally determinative. Because human knowledge is so limited and fallible, the order we perceive in society would seem to be an unintended consequence of private decisions driven by self-love. Somehow or other, the institutions of any viable society must have evolved so as to harness the self-regarding acts of individuals to the common good (at best), or at any rate to prevent them from destroying the social fabric (at worst). Interference with this "spontaneous order" (Hayek 1960, pp. 160–161; cf. Mill [1874] 1969, p. 381) by central authority is at least as likely to do harm as good. *Économie politique* is both futile and mischievous. Not even *le roi soleil* himself is well served by it. Yet social viability under *laissez-faire* depends on the willingness of individuals to observe natural justice: to play the game according to the rules even when the referee is not looking.

These were the presuppositions of Anglophone social thought in the eighteenth century, as collected and developed from Mandeville, Bishop Butler and David Hume by historians and philosophers of the Scottish Enlightenment (Hamowy 1987). Economic theorizing in Britain by the end of the eighteenth century took these thoughts for granted, and developed their implications for public policy in a commercial society.

It is sufficient for my purposes to treat *Wealth of Nations* (Smith [1776]1976) as a paradigm. Smith owed much to Cantillon, Hume, Josiah Tucker and Quesnai; pointedly ignored Steuart's analytically sound but politically unacceptable contributions; was on friendly terms with Turgot;[1] seems to have been unaware, like most other economists then and later, of Condillac's remarkable achievement; and appeared in print before Paley, whose lectures were delivered at Cambridge between 1766 and 1776 but published only in 1785.

The central feature of the pre-classical analytical tradition is a two-sector, "food" and "luxuries" macro-model (Waterman 1996, 2001), with "Malthusian" population adjustment in response to any change in capital stock, the latter—given the relative size of the putatively "unproductive" public sector—determined by the "parsimony" of a capitalist class driven by "the natural effort of every man to better his condition" (Smith [1776]1976, IV.v.b.43). All market prices "gravitate" to a "natural" level determined by long-period costs of production (I.vii.12–26); in seeking "only his own gain" each capitalist directs his capital to the most profitable outlet, equalizes the profit rate and so "labours to render the annual revenue of society as great as he can" (IV.ii.9); for any state of the taste for "luxuries," the "natural" wage rate is an increasing function of the rate of capital accumulation (I.viii.43–45); but parametric increases in the taste for "luxuries" causes production and population to grow, and may permanently increase the real wage. In Smith's version of the model, increasing returns to scale in the "luxuries" sector will amplify the effect upon population and production of any increase in the taste for "luxuries."

Because the interest of "labourers" is "strictly connected with the interest of the society," and because "no society can surely be happy, of which the greater part of the members are poor and miserable" (I.ix.p.9; I.viii.36), high and rising wages ought to be a prime object of public policy. Hence economic growth should be maximized and the taste for "luxuries" encouraged. The more parsimonious are capitalists and the smaller the share of government in national expenditure, the higher the rate of economic growth. The "natural" propensity of capitalists to better their condition through parsimony will flourish best when they are left completely free to pursue their own interest. Both domestic and foreign trade will then grow and diversify, and it is particularly through the latter—as Hume ([1752]1994, essays 13 and 14) had argued powerfully—that the taste for luxuries is developed. Hence both factors that cause high and rising wages, growth and taste, are interconnected with, and optimally related to, the greatest possible freedom of private enterprise and trade, and the smallest possible participation of government in the economy.

In pre-classical economic theory the primary constraint upon growth was capital. Land was generally treated as abundant. But when the concept of diminishing returns in the agricultural sector gradually became clear to the next generation of economists as an implication of Malthus's first *Essay on Population* (1798), land displaced capital as the chief constraint. Because there is no lasting remedy for land shortage, the so-called "classical" political economy of the new century replaced Adam Smith's "chearful" study of growth and development with a Dismal Science of scarcity. Malthus, West, Torrens, Ricardo, Chalmers, M'Culloch and James Mill viewed the turbulent economy of post-1815 England with the aid of a common model of growth and distribution (Samuelson 1978). It was now profits and wages, rather than prices, which "gravitate" to a "very low rate" at which "all accumulation" and population growth are "arrested": in stationary state wages and profits are minimal, "and almost the whole produce of the country . . . will be the property of the owners of land and the receivers of tithes and taxes" (Ricardo [1817] 1911, pp. 71–72).

Notwithstanding this drastic change in analytical focus, the policy implications of the "new" political economy of that day remained very much as before. That the welfare of the laboring poor was and ought to be the prime object of public policy was corroborated by the utilitarian principle of the "greatest good for the greatest number" distilled from the ethical theory of Paley and Bentham. That high wages depended in part on rapid growth, and that the latter was fostered by freedom to employ capital and by the smallest possible share of government in the economy remained uncontested. That a growing taste for "luxury" among the laboring class would increase the stationary-state real wage was strongly reinforced by the distribution-theoretic features of the new model, which demonstrated that a parametric increase in the target ("subsistence") real wage not only increases the absolute but also the relative share of labor income by transferring part of the surplus from landlords to capitalists and laborers (Waterman 1995). A general predilection for *laissez-faire* that Adam Smith shared with the Physiocrats (who invented the slogan) was given a rigorous justification by Ricardo's new theory of comparative advantage: any duty or bounty on a traded product "causes a pernicious distribution of the general funds of society—it bribes a manufacturer to commence or continue in a comparatively less profitable employment" (Ricardo [1817]1911, p. 210).

Perhaps the most striking political implication of the "new political economy" was the attack on the Poor Laws mounted by Malthus and Chalmers, strongly supported by Ricardo and all the Philosophic Radicals. Adam Smith had criticized the Poor Laws because they interfered with the mobility of labor (Smith 1976, I.x.c.45–59). But the classical objection was more sophisticated. Because the condition of the poor could only be permanently improved if they themselves sought to achieve higher family incomes by deferring marriage (and therefore procreation), it was essential to harness their self-interest in this cause. Institutions became crucially important, and for the first time in the history of our discipline, rational choice—already taken for granted in the analysis of capitalist behavior—was applied to the behavior of the poor. The Elizabethan Poor Law made it rational for the poor to marry early and maintain a low or zero saving rate.

> The comforts and well-being of the poor cannot be permanently secured without some regard on their part, or some effort on the part of the legislature, to regulate the increase of their numbers, and to render less frequent among them early and improvident marriages. The operation of the system of the poor laws has been directly contrary to this. (Ricardo [1817]1911, p. 61)

Savings banks, parochial education and abolition of the Poor Laws would provide the opportunities and incentives to the poor to develop the habits of independence and self-help essential to their "improvement."

By the mid-1820s classical political economy presented a coherent and powerful body of analysis, building on and refining the work of Adam Smith and his contemporaries, the seeming implications of which supplied the rational basis of a non-interventionist, pro-free-trade, anti-Poor-Law consensus that informed political thinking in Britain and America for most of the nineteenth century. Malthus had his doubts about unemployment and "stagnation," and he broke ranks by defending agricultural protection; but in each of these respects he was viewed as a heretic by the profession and his theories ignored for more than a century. John Stuart Mill ([1848]1909, p. 922) allowed the "infant industry" exception to free trade pioneered by Alexander Hamilton (1791). Mill also wrote encouragingly about socialism in 1852.[2] But his posthumous second (actually third) thoughts of 1869 were far more cautious (Mill [1848]1909, pp. 984–989). Karl Marx was the last of the classical economists and is commonly thought of as a socialist author. But there is far less advocacy of socialism in *Das Kapital* than there is in the 1852 edition of Mill's *Principles*; and only few and scattered allusions to any possible socialist economy. Marx's model is basically Smithian, with certain key assumptions modified so as to predict the spontaneous *disorder* and eventual collapse of capitalism, brought about by the self-interested acts of individual capitalists—as if led by an invisible hand.

Save for the almost entirely neglected contributions of Thünen (1783–1850), Cournot (1801–1877) and Dupuit (1804–1866), the intellectual or at any rate the social-scientific landscape of the English-speaking world was filled from 1800 to the mid-1870s with developments of, and variations on, Adam Smith's "natural system of perfect liberty and justice."

III

The Economics of Control

WHAT HAPPENED NEXT was the belated assimilation of some insights of Condillac, Thünen, Cournot, Dupuit and Gossen during the so-called "marginal revolution"; the application of marginal concepts to welfare theory; a deployment of neo-classical production and welfare concepts in the theory of "market socialism"; a revival of macroeconomics resulting from the so-called Keynesian revolution; and a grand combination of all these in what Samuelson described as "the neo-classical synthesis." The neo-classical synthesis provided a conceptual framework for yet another "new political economy," which gradually came to replace the presupposition of *laissez-faire* among the educated classes of Britain and America by the middle of the twentieth century. For by 1950 it was taken for granted by all—save a tiny minority of ignored and/or derided dissidents—that modern, technical economic theory had supplied the tools for implementing democratic socialism without the need of revolution. The mood of the time is perfectly captured by Abba Lerner's *The Economics of Control*:

> The fundamental aim of socialism is not the abolition of private property but the extension of democracy. This is obscured by dogmas of the right

and of the left. The benefits of both the capitalist economy and the collectivist economy can be reaped in the controlled economy. The three principal problems to be faced in a controlled economy are employment, monopoly, and the distribution of income. Control must be distinguished from regulation. Liberalism and socialism can be reconciled in welfare economics (Lerner 1944, p. xi).

Even those such as Joseph Schumpeter, who disliked the prospect of socialism, feared it was probably inevitable. "Marx's vision was right," for "the capitalist process not only destroys its own institutional framework but it also creates the conditions for another"; "The March into Socialism" has already begun; "Can socialism work? Of course it can" (Schumpeter [1943] 1987, pp. 162, 421–431, 167).

To the neoclassical building-blocks of scientific socialism we now turn.

III A. Neo-Classical Production and Distribution Theory

The classical concept of diminishing returns to a variable factor of production as applied to the fixed factor, land, was well known to Turgot ([1768] 1970), Steuart ([1767] 1966, I: pp. 130–131) and others long before its rediscovery by Malthus, West, Torrens and Ricardo in 1815. But the first to generalize the principle to any or all factors—and to formalize it by means of that differential calculus the theory cries out for—was J. H. von Thünen (1783–1850), the first volume of whose *Isolierte Staat* appeared in 1826; who seems to have invented the term "marginal" (Marshall [1890] 1952, p. viii); and whom Marshall much later claimed to have "loved above all my other masters" (Schumpeter 1954, pp. 465). When production takes place under constant returns to scale (CRS), marginal-product factor pricing exactly exhausts the total product, so generalizing the Malthus-Ricardo theory of income distribution. The classical and pre-classical concept of an aggregate "surplus" of production that Malthus, Ricardo and Marx shared with Petty, Quesnai and Smith is thereby shown to be redundant and misleading.

Thünen's "treatment of distribution anticipated the whole of what later came to be known as the marginal productivity theory of distribution and in some respects he improved even on the presentation of John Bates Clark, which came almost fifty years later" (Blaug 1997, p.

308). Economists reinvented the wheel as usual, and definitive treatments were duly supplied by P. H. Wicksteed (1894), J. B. Clark (1899) and Knut Wicksell ([1901] 1935), assisted by A. W. Flux's ([1894] 1968) demonstration of product-exhaustion by means of Euler's theorem on homogeneous functions.[3]

It is obvious that the concept of a marginal product implies continuous factor substitutability over the relevant range of the production function. Moreover, the requirement of CRS implied by Euler's theorem can only be met, for any firm with a U-shaped long-run average-cost curve, at the minimum point of the latter. But at long-run equilibrium of a perfectly competitive industry each firm produces at that point, and industry production varies in response to any change in demand by the entry or exit of firms. Hence a CRS set of *industry* production functions may be deemed to exist that—for any given set of factor endowments and for any given state of technique—determine the complete range of production possibilities in a perfectly competitive market economy at full, long-period equilibrium for every possible assignment of factors to industries.

It is equally obvious that these new technical developments, though based on a classical insight, diverge sharply from classical economics in two important respects. In the first place, product exhaustion, normal profits and long-period equilibrium imply precisely that "stationary state" that Ricardo and his friends hoped they would never see. Neo-classical production theory is "static" or timeless, abstracting from accumulation, population growth and technical progress. Secondly, the logical requirement of CRS rules out increasing returns to scale that for Adam Smith and Marx, if not for Malthus and Ricardo, were characteristic of an industrializing economy. As always in any science, growth of knowledge is purchased at a cost.

III B. Neo-Classical Utility and Welfare Theory

That value is determined by "subjective" utility rather than by "objective" cost is an idea that goes back to the Scholastics (Schumpeter 1954, p. 175). In 1776 Étienne Bonnot, abbé de Condillac (1714–1780), explained value in terms of marginal utility in *Le Commerce et le*

Gouvernement ([1776] 1997, pp. 83–84). According to a recent Nobel Prize winner, Condillac developed in that work "a general theory of the generation of surpluses, of general economic equilibrium, and of maximal efficiency" (Allais 1992, p. 174). However, Condillac's work was totally ignored for a century; the concept of marginal utility was successively rediscovered by W. F. Lloyd (1834), Jules Dupuit (1844), H. H. Gossen (1854) and W. S. Jevons (1862), each in seeming ignorance of his predecessors.

Though Malthus had formulated a demand function as early as 1800 (Waterman 1998b, pp. 579–580), "subjective" value theory was resisted for so long because it denied the core of the classical research program: Ricardo's labor theory of value. The logjam finally broke in the early 1870s with important publications by Jevons ([1871] 1957), Carl Menger ([1871] 1950) and Léon Walras ([1874] 1954), a period now canonized in textbooks as the "marginal revolution." In various ways these authors and their successors constructed the components of what eventually became a complete model of the general interdependence of prices and production in a market economy driven by agents who maximize their own satisfaction by equalizing marginal benefits and costs over all possible activities. When agents maximize subject to constraint, demand curves are negatively sloped because "marginal utility" declines; supply curves are positively sloped because "marginal cost" increases.[4] The congruence, indeed the isomorphism, of a marginal analysis of value and demand with a marginal analysis of cost and supply soon became apparent. By 1937 Paul Samuelson was able to demonstrate in his Harvard doctoral dissertation that "the theory of maximizing behavior" is one of "the foundations of economic analysis" (Samuelson 1947).

It is obvious (if not tautologous) that diminishing marginal utility must imply gains from bilateral trade; and easy to show that in multilateral market exchange both demanders and suppliers enjoy an access of utility: "consumers' surplus" and "producers' surplus," respectively. It is also obvious in a CRS world that where imperfect competition keeps price above marginal cost, the total surplus is both reduced and redistributed in favor of suppliers. Hence perfectly competitive markets may be conceived to maximize "economic welfare."

Alfred Marshall ([1890] 1952) and many others drew inferences for redistributive taxation and other welfare-policy measures from these deceptively simple[5] propositions. A. C. Pigou (1920) analyzed externalities and the resulting "market failures" and defined an aggregate welfare maximum as that state in which the "marginal social product" of all resources in all alternative uses is equalized. But all these attempts at normativity eventually foundered on the rock of interpersonal comparisons of utility. It was left to Vilfredo Pareto (1896, [1906] 1971) to formulate the only welfare criterion to survive L. Robbins's (1932) influential attack on interpersonal comparisons nearly 40 years later.

Pareto rejected cardinal utility and worked strictly with ordinal utility, which he renamed "ophelimity." He also rejected Marshall's partial equilibrium analysis in favor of the Walrasian model of general interdependence. Making use of the indifference-curve analysis pioneered by F. Y. Edgeworth (1881), Pareto was able to provide a convincing demonstration of the most important theorem of neo-classical economics: in a world of strictly private goods, general equilibrium of a perfectly competitive economy defines a welfare optimum—in the sense that it is impossible to make any individual better off without making at least one other worse off *as these individuals perceive their own welfare*. Because of the insularity and chauvinism of the Anglo-American world, Pareto's results and their significance, and the Walrasian framework within which they were presented, were neither known nor understood by most English-speaking economists until Robbins, the "market socialists" and J. R. Hicks (1939a) had digested and republished them in the 1930s.

III C. "Socialist Calculation"

"The nomenclature of utility and disutility . . . leads one immediately to ask whether a free enterprise system represents such a use of satisfying wants as to insure society the greatest surplus of utility over disutility" (Blaug 1997, p. 286). Except in Austria, socialist or, at any rate, reformist sympathies were normal among the first two or three generations of neo-classical economists. The new tools of analysis seemed to afford the possibility of a rational approach to social reform. Wicksell was a life-long socialist who exercised an enduring influence over his younger colleagues of the Stockholm school. Pigou's work has been described as "virtually a blue-print for the welfare state" (Backhouse 1985, p. 166). Pareto's *Cours d'Economie Politique* (1896) examined the allocation of resources to be pursued by a socialist state in achieving "the maximum well-being of its citizens." His compatriot Enrico Barone demonstrated the formal equivalence of the welfare optimum under either capitalism or socialism in his famous article, "The Ministry of Production in the Collectivist State" (Barone [1908] 1935).

Friedrich von Wieser, Menger's successor at the University of Vienna, had noted as early as 1893 that a socialist economy would require a complete set of "natural values" (which might be approximated by market prices under competitive capitalism with equal wealth endowments); and that the task of calculating these correctly would be formidable (Wieser [1893] 1971). Wieser's most famous pupil, Ludwig von Mises, made this the basis of a frontal attack on socialism launched in 1920 (Mises [1920] 1935), which inaugurated the celebrated "socialist calculation" debates (O'Neill 1996) of the inter-war years. Several distinguished neo-classical economists took up the challenge. Fred M. Taylor (1929) chose "The Guidance of Production in the Socialist State" as the subject of his presidential address to the American Economic Association of 1928. Oskar Lange thanked Mises for drawing attention to an important practical consideration[6] and recommended that "[a] statue of Professor Mises ought to occupy an honourable place in the great hall of the . . . Central Planning Board of a socialist state" (Lange 1936, p. 53). In a series of influential publications from 1929 to 1937, Taylor, Lange and A. P. Lerner established the orthodox, neo-classical theory of socialism (Hoff [1938]1949, pp. 392–394). A central planning board can function like Walras's auctioneer, generating a set of resource prices by trial and error. Managers of state enterprises set product prices at marginal cost and adjust the scale of production by reinvesting any surpluses. At equilibrium, the first-order marginal conditions exist for Pareto optimality: the equality of subjective and objective marginal rates of substitution among all goods, products and factors.

It was only in Lerner's articles on the economics of socialism that the conditions of a welfare optimum in the general equilibrium model were fully specified for the first time. Important contributions by A. Bergson (1938) and Hicks (1939b) set the seal of professional approval on the "new welfare economics." Though the collectivist and free-market versions of the theory are formally equivalent, most orthodox, mainstream economists of the 1930s and 1940s preferred the former. This is because the analysis of increasing returns to scale and the consequent breakdown of competition—pioneered by J. A. Hobson (1909), Piero Sraffa (1926) and A. A. Young (1928) and made canonical by Joan Robinson (1933) and E. H. Chamberlin (1933)—showed convincingly that there is no theoretical reason to doubt that price will normally exceed marginal cost in a free-market economy; whereas the putative benefits of perfect competition, unobtainable under capitalism, can be simulated under socialism. Many would have agreed with Paul Sweezy that "Marxian economics is essentially the economics of capitalism, while 'capitalist' economics is in a very real sense the economics of socialism" (1935, p. 79). Joan Robinson (1964b) was an astute critic of the Lange-Lerner-Taylor prescription, but as late as 1980 she could write (with probable allusion to Kantorovitch) that

> there is an important area where neo-classical theory comes into its own. The concept of a production possibility surface and of the distribution of scarce means between alternative uses are the very foundation of economic planning. While the theory of allocation is withering in the free-market world, it is blossoming afresh in socialist economies. (Robinson 1980, p. xvi)

III D. Full Employment

For economists of Joan Robinson's generation it was the theoretical inability of market forces to determine output at *any* point on the "production possibility surface" (save by chance), even more than the impossibility of perfect or even "pure" competition, that was decisive in their rejection of the free-market version of general equilibrium.

Say's law is implicit in the Walrasian model. Unemployment can only exist in general disequilibrium. Excess supply in factor markets is matched by excess demand in some other market or markets, such as the money market. But the putative remedy, falling money-prices in factor markets, is unavailable. Walras's *tâtonnement* and Samuelson's dynamic stability analysis that formalizes *tâtonnement* (1947, Part II) correctly rule out transactions in disequilibrium. This is because any "false trading" would falsify expectations and therefore change agents' evaluations of their assets. And that in turn would cause supply and demand curves to shift before equilibrium was attained. As a matter of mere logic—in economics though not in mechanics—"it is impossible for a system to get into a position of equilibrium, for the very nature of equilibrium is that the system is already in it, and has been in it for a certain length of past time" (Robinson [1953–1954] 1964a, p. 120).

When the *General Theory* appeared in 1936, therefore, Keynes's ruthless disregard of the Walrasian model was received by many as a theoretical breakthrough of the first magnitude.[7] By locating his story in the Marshallian short period and implicitly assuming that with massive underemployment of productive factors all supply curves are horizontal, Keynes could use Marshall's quantity adjustment ([1890]1952, pp. 287–288), rather than Walras's operationally useless price adjustment, to analyze the consequence of a change in "effective demand" (a concept resurrected from Malthus) and so leave all absolute *and relative* prices unchanged. Aggregation is therefore logically admissible (Hicks 1939a, p. 33; 1965, p. 78) and "macroeconomics" legitimated. In a closed economy aggregate supply is the same as aggregate income. And if aggregate demand is an increasing, non-homogeneous function of income with non-unitary slope, equality of aggregate supply with aggregate demand will determine a unique level of output and employment at which what Keynes misleadingly called "equilibrium" (e.g., 1936, p. 28) will exist. If the slope is less than unity, this quasi-equilibrium will be "stable" in an operational sense. For at any state of expectations, quantity adjustment with unchanged prices affects asset values in a manner that reinforces the adjustment.[8]

"Keynes denies that there is an *invisible hand* channelling the self-centred action of each individual to the social optimum. That is the sum and substance of his heresy" (Samuelson [1946] 1966, p. 1523). But since aggregate demand can be managed or at least manipulated by government through its control over the banking system and the national budget, an *ex post facto* theoretical justification was provided for the unvarnished empiricism of many national governments during the great depression of the 1930s. More importantly for the new political consensus, a theoretical rationale was supplied for the "full-employment" policies announced with much fanfare by the governments of Britain, Canada, Australia and the United States from 1944 to 1946.

III E. The Neo-Classical Synthesis and Mathematical Economics

Figure 1 represents the production possibilities *AB* of a closed economy with two goods, *Y* and *X*, a social indifference curve *CD* that touches *AB* in *E,* and a possible position of general underemployment, *U*. *AB*, drawn for given factor endowments and a given state of technique, summarizes neo-classical production theory. *CD*, drawn for given asset endowments and a given state of taste, summarizes the preferences of "society," either as revealed by individual market behavior or as discovered by the managers of a collectivist state.

Suppose production takes place at *U*. According to neo-classical assumptions this implies general disequilibrium. Market forces must then be able to perform two functions: (1) to move production to some point on *AB*, such as *F*; and (2) to determine that point at *E* where the marginal conditions for Pareto optimality are satisfied. "Right-wing Keynesians" such as Keynes himself rejected (1) but accepted (2). Moreover, they defended economic "individualism" on ethical grounds as "the best safeguard of personal liberty" (Keynes 1936, pp. 378–381). "Left-wing Keynesians" such as Joan Robinson ([1953]1973, p. 264), Lerner and many others of that generation rejected both (1) and (2). Moreover, they were sceptical about the value of "personal liberty" under capitalism.

By far the most influential of all Keynesians after 1946 was Paul Samuelson. With quasi-liturgical symbolism, his world-famous *Economics: An Introductory Analysis* (1948) bore on its front cover a version of the "Keynesian cross": a rising saving function of national income intersecting an horizontal investment function. Samuelson agreed with Keynes that markets might function adequately provided that government stabilize the economy at full employment. But he noted with approval that "nations all over the world [are] moving to-

Figure 1

The Neo-Classical Synthesis

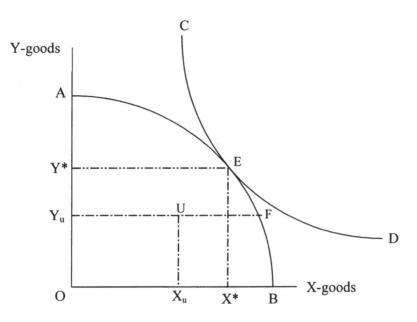

wards a planned state," disparaged *laissez-faire,* and held that Adam Smith's ideas "have done almost as much harm as good in the past century and a half" (Samuelson 1948, pp. 421, 436).

A recent commentator (Nelson 2001) has observed that Samuelson is an American Progressive in the political tradition of Richard T. Ely, J. R. Commons and Thorstein Veblen. But by replacing their theoretically degenerate "institutionalism" with the neo-classical synthesis of Paretian socialism and Keynesian macroeconomics, he "adapted the basic progressive scheme for the scientific management of American society . . . to the circumstances of the post-World War II setting" (Nelson 2001, pp. 50, 52). The neo-classical synthesis provided a "left-of-centre Keynesian" model that made the economics of control obvious to the meanest intelligence. Not only in the United States, but in many countries and in many languages millions of undergraduates during the next three decades and more assimilated its underlying message: *The eco-nomic activity of a human society is a rational system that can be suffi-ciently comprehended by economic scientists, who may therefore be trusted to design and implement measures to control economic activity so as to achieve politically determined collective goals.* The "new politi-cal economy" of Samuelson and his associates, *mutandis mutatis*, is none other than that French *œconomie politique* that Adam Smith and his followers hoped they had stamped out once and for all.

Powerful and sophisticated mathematical analyses by Samuelson himself and by many others bolstered, for "men of learning," the sci-entific authority of the economics of control. Frank Ramsey's (1927, 1928) pioneering work on dynamic optimization set the tone for a large literature on public planning of intertemporal resource allocation through the 1970s and beyond (e.g., Sen 1967; Arrow and Kurz 1970; Forster 1980; and so on). Influential contributions to mathematical economics were made by Soviet mathematicians during this period (e.g., Kantorovich [1939]1960, [1942]1965; Pontryagin et al. 1962). Wassily Leontief's (1936) input-output analysis was used as a planning tool in the Soviet Union. John von Neumann's ([1938] 1945–1946) model of "general economic equilibrium" inaugurated two decades of investigation by the best brains in our profession into the existence and stability of equilibrium in Leontief-type multisectoral models, ex-panding optimally in "time" with Pareto-efficient accumulation (Hahn and Matthews 1964, pp. 853–888).

When the economy is conceived as a machine (Kuenne 1968, pp. 5–10), in one case indeed as a "sausage machine" (Samuelson and Solow 1953; see Hahn and Matthews 1964, p. 872), the economics of control looks easy. For most of the century after 1870, there is a rough but detectable correlation between a left-wing political commitment to "social engineering" (e.g., Veblen [1921]1965, pp. 64, 144, 157–158, etc.) and mathematical economics. Among the few to dissent from the *dirigiste* consensus were those who rejected or were sceptical of mathematical economics on strictly theoretical grounds, such as Mises, Hayek and Frank Knight.

The "natural system of perfect liberty and justice," being founded on an *ecological* rather than a *mechanical* view of the economy, was banished from polite society for nearly a century.

IV

"New" Political Economies in the Twenty-First Century

THE ECONOMICS OF CONTROL has been subjected in the last 50 years to a rigorous scrutiny from which little of it, if any, has been left standing. Though in Milton Friedman's sense "we are all Keynesians now," the development of macroeconomic theory since the mid-1950s increasingly has tended to cast doubt on its relevance for discretionary demand management. The neo-classical model of general equilibrium, brought to its highest perfection in the work of K. J. Arrow and G. Debreu (1954, among other works), is now regarded as useless, whether as a source of welfare-policy prescriptions, or as a rationale either of capitalism or of socialism (Stiglitz 1994). Save under dictatorship, the possibility of determining collective goals through the political process currently seems remote. And even if collective goals could be determined democratically—and even if economic tools were available to implement those goals—it is today well understood that agents in the public sector can normally be expected to place their own private goals first, and that these may be in conflict with collective goals.

By undermining the intellectual foundations of a pro-socialist political consensus in these ways, the "new political economies" of the past 20 years or so have produced a detectable ideological effect. Though external factors such as the collapse of the Soviet empire have compelled "men of learning" to re-examine their political assumptions, there can be little doubt that new and very "different theories of political œconomy" have "had a considerable influence" not only upon them, but upon "public conduct" of the present-day equivalents of "princes and sovereign states." It is no longer fashionable for an economist or a politician to be a socialist.

IV A. Macroeconomics

Keynes's novel but somewhat incoherent theorizing was eagerly tidied up by the younger generation.[9] Mathematical models were constructed, the variables of which corresponded with the categories in newly collected national accounts that had been inspired to some extent both by the *General Theory* itself (Patinkin 1976) and by Jan Tinbergen's (1935) path-breaking econometrics. The most influential of these models was Hicks's (1937) elegant compression of Keynes's sprawling masterpiece into the Walrasian framework of *Value and Capital* (1939a). It was a small matter thereafter to disaggregate by sector; add equations for the labor market; and generalize for the income-expenditure and monetary effects of interaction with the rest of the world (Meade 1951; Swan 1960; Mundell 1961). Given constant-price national accounts, reasonably honest balance of payments estimates, monetary data from the central bank, price indices and official labor force surveys, all relevant magnitudes are in principle observable;[10] and the way opened for the elaboration of large-scale econometric income-expenditure models comprising several hundred equations that proliferated in the 1960s and 1970s (e.g., Klein and Goldberger 1955; Bank of Canada 1976).

"Keynesian" models were and are typically fixprice (Hicks 1965, pp. 76–83). Therefore, the discovery of the "Phillips Curve" (Phillips 1958; Lipsey 1960) presented a major theoretical and policy challenge to the "new political economy" of the 1950s. Samuelson and Solow (1960) "roughly" estimated the Phillips Curve for the United States, transformed it into a relation between unemployment and price inflation, and presented it as a "menu of choice" for policy makers, soon to be widely known as the "trade-off." The trade-off quickly entered the vocabulary of macroeconomics and was canonized in the sixth edition of Samuelson's textbook ([1948]1964). It was soon noted that a stable trade-off would destroy economic control in an open economy under fixed exchange rates, for both the world inflation rate and the world unemployment rate must then rule (Waterman 1966; cf. Swan 1960). But a more general, and far more radically subversive, attack on economic control through demand management was launched at that time by E. S. Phelps (1967) and M. Friedman (1968).

Milton Friedman was one of the very few leading economists of his generation to have resisted the "disease" that struck down Samuelson and so many others; and had produced important theoretical studies critical of the Keynesian framework (see, for example, Friedman 1956, 1957, 1961). Friedman's presidential address to the American Economic Association of 1967[11] exploited the expectational instability of the Phillips Curve recognized by Samuelson and Solow (1960, p. 193) to show that with adaptive expectations, the long-run trade-off is vertical at what he called the "natural rate of unemployment" (Friedman 1968).

Though the profession eventually rejected Friedman's provocatively Smithian terminology in favor of the uneuphonious "NAIRU," the idea itself immediately became embedded in the core of macroeconomic theory. The fuzzy concept of "involuntary unemployment," always suspect (see, for example, Samuelson [1946]1966, p. 1520), ceased to be theoretically interesting; more importantly, so did the correlative concept of "full employment," central to the economics of control. The level of employment became instead a topic in the microeconomics of labor markets with costly information (Phelps 1970). A. A. Alchian (1970) showed that temporary unemployment is a matter of rational choice for a worker expecting a better position, and is therefore "productive." It is now customary to analyze the unemployment level in terms of separation and hiring rates of flow, determined exogenously by such factors as productivity, the minimum wage and the extent of unemployment insurance (Hall 1979; Ramaswami 1983; Darby, Haltiwanger and Plant 1985; Barro and Lucas 1994).

Friedman's dramatic result was based upon the *ad hoc* assumption of adaptive expectations, which implies that agents are irrational. But real human beings learn from experience (Arrow 1962) and form their expectations probabilistically on the basis of all available information (Muth 1961). Before long, therefore, the next generation of young turks replaced Friedman's rough-and-ready expedient with the theoretically impeccable assumption of rational expectations (Sargent 1973; Sargent and Wallace 1976; Lucas 1975; and so forth). Combined with the theoretically appealing but empirically implausible assumption of instantaneous market clearing, this so-called New Classical macroeconomics generates the notorious "policy-ineffectiveness proposition" (McCafferty 1990, pp. 343–345). Not only can discretionary demand management have no permanent or long-run effect, it can have no transitory or short-run effect either. All Keynesian "multipliers" are always and everywhere zero, which is thus the *ne plus ultra* of the anti-Keynesian reaction against the economics of control.

As might be expected, this unwelcome result was vigorously contested by even younger turks, and "New Keynesian" models have proliferated that incorporate rational expectations but reject instantaneous market-clearing, and in a variety of ways purport to justify those wage and price rigidities that enable Keynesian models to produce real effects in the short run (e.g., Mankiew and Romer 1991). Meanwhile, a "Post-Keynesian" tradition that originated with Joan Robinson and other "left-wing Keynesians" has persisted, united in little except a general predilection for a Sraffian rather than a Marshallian explanation of relative prices (Harcourt 1987) and a dislike of mainstream economic theorizing, from which it has become increasingly cut off. In either the "New Keynesian" or "Post-Keynesian" case it turns out that "virtually every practical theory of macroeconomics" must be based at least in part on "hypotheses other than rationality" (Arrow 1987, p. 202).

So far as the macroeconomic half of the economics of control is concerned, agreement is possible on one matter only. Consensus is dead.

IV B. Information, Prices and Markets

In the world of the Arrow-Debreu model, every good is a dated, contingent commodity, and all agents have full information about the present and a complete set of futures and insurance markets to protect them against uncertainty. No "decisions" have to be made. The market is a "human-link analogue computer" that grinds out the only information required by the system: a complete set of prices that correspond with the "shadow prices" required for socialist production (Goodwin 1970, pp. 11–12, 24–28). Production managers simply find "in the book of blueprints the appropriate page corresponding to current (and future) factor prices" (Stiglitz 1994, p. 6) and could be replaced by robots. Therefore, "in Samuelson's classic textbook" and in all its many imitators, the economic problem was summarized in three questions about total production: "What?" "How?" and "For whom?" The important theoretical "question about who decides or how decisions are to be made" was ignored. "While decision makers in the socialist economies paid more attention to these questions, they had neither the information nor the incentives to make good decisions" (Stiglitz 1994, p. 201). Most microeconomic theorizing of the past 50 years has therefore been addressed to some of the more interesting questions posed by the Arrow-Debreu model. What are the welfare implications when Pareto optimality requires a shift along the production-possibility frontier, or when some of the marginal conditions are not satisfied, or when some of the markets are missing? How useful is the model when the assumptions of perfect information and perfectly competitive equilibrium are relaxed, as they must be if transactions costs are to be admitted into the analysis? What becomes of the model when because of informational constraints it is more efficient for some production to be coordinated by entrepreneurs making real decisions than by relative prices; and how is this "hands-on" coordination affected by the "principal-agent" problem and by "bounded rationality"—limitations on our merely human capacity to receive and process information? What are the implications of the answers to these questions for the relative efficiency of socialist and market economies?

Early discussion of the first of these sets of questions took place in the context of Hecksher-Ohlin trade theory. A change in trade policy (for example) that increases national income might be supposed Pareto-superior if the gainers could compensate the losers and remain better off (Pareto 1896; Barone [1908]1935; Kaldor 1939; Hicks 1939b). But Scitovsky (1941) showed that this result could be reversed with a different income distribution, thereby undermining the comforting distinction that originated with J. S. Mill between the "laws of Production," which are scientific, and "those of Distribution," which are at least in part political ([1848] 1909, p. 21). Further analysis by Samuelson (1947, Ch.VII; 1950) showed that "we cannot even be sure that group A is better off than group B even if A has collectively more of everything" (Boulding 1952). It was also originally in the context of trade theory that a different question arose for welfare economics: If the conditions of Pareto optimality are violated in some parts of the economy, are they sufficient welfare criteria elsewhere? The "general theory of second best" of R. G. Lipsey and K. Lancaster (1956) showed that they were not. A "second best," such as lowering import duties without perfect competition, may be no better than a third-best option. Since the existence of government virtually necessitates second-best policies, the marginal conditions can be no guide for intervention in a mixed economy. A more general formal objection to the usefulness of the Arrow-Debreu model arises from its multidimensional conception of a "commodity," which almost guarantees the impossibility of a complete set of futures and insurance markets; and that, more seriously, must undermine the assumption of perfect competition (Stiglitz 1994, pp. 16–18, 34, 38).

Incompleteness of the market arises from transactions costs, for markets require resources in order to function (even Walras's auctioneer may expect to be paid) and some are too costly to be worthwhile. The existence and significance of transactions costs was pioneered by Ronald Coase (1937, 1960), who showed that they can explain why some economic activity is coordinated by firms rather than by markets and, more generally, why economic institutions exist. A "new institutional economics" (Furobotn and Richter 1997) that developed from these ideas has focused on imperfect information in a variety of ways: asymmetric information; the "principal-agent problem," which is a special case of the former (Ross 1973; Sappington 1991); "strategic intelligence" (Greenwald and Stiglitz 1986); and "bounded rationality" (Simon 1959, 1978). Much of this has been brought together by Oliver Williamson (1975, 1985, 1986) who has shown that hierarchical business organization is more efficient than atomistic markets in a world of limited information.

Coase, or at any rate those who developed his ideas in the "law-and-economics" branch of economic theorizing, analyzed the efficiency of various institutional arrangements and argued that private property rights are crucial in providing incentives to efficient resource allocation and use. This doctrine and the presupposition in favor of privatization that it justifies have been contested by Joseph Stiglitz (1994, Ch.10) who observes—ironically, in view of Coase's own original contribution—that it ignores the pervasiveness of transactions and information costs. In a world of perfect information, public and private ownership are equally efficient. However, "neither the model of the market economy nor the [equivalent] model of the market socialist economy provided a good description of the markets they were supposed to be characterizing" (Stiglitz 1994, p. 195). The economic (as distinct from the merely political) arguments for privatization rather are based upon the inability of governments to make and keep commitments to reward the efficient and punish the inefficient, the more powerful incentives to innovation and risk-taking in the private sector, and the ultimate sanction of bankruptcy (Stiglitz 1986, Ch. 7; Sappington and Stiglitz 1987). These arguments, like the "new institutionalism" noted above, take imperfect competition for granted and formalize it as an efficient response to imperfect information.

Friedrich von Hayek was perfectly aware, in his original attack upon socialism, that information is the heart of the matter, and believed that only a regime of private property and free markets could generate the information necessary to coordinate production and distribution in a complex, industrial society (Hayek 1935). The counter-attack of Taylor, Lange and Lerner was apparently successful because of the suitability of neo-classical price and welfare theory for their model of market socialism. Hayek and Mises did not believe in neo-classical economics. They rejected the mechanistic concept of static equilibrium and preferred to study economic agents in real time, engaging in a continual process of learning, not only about means but also about ends. Therefore, it seemed to them at the time—as it still seems to their neo-Austrian school successors (Vaughn 1994)—that it is unhelpful to model market processes formally, and is merely obfuscating to use mathematics. They were thus at a disadvantage in controversy, and the socialists were deemed for a generation and more to have won the high ground. Though Hayek later published important work on knowledge in economic theory (see, for example, Hayek 1937, 1945, 1978) and was duly awarded a Nobel Prize, his ideas were long ignored by the profession, and lately he has been criticized by Stiglitz—who agrees with his general conclusions about socialism—for his unwillingness to use the language of his fellow economists. Because "Hayek . . . failed to develop formal models of the market process, it is not possible to assess claims concerning the efficiency of that process" (Stiglitz 1994, pp. 24–25). Following the lead of George Stigler (1961) and George Akerlof (1970), Stiglitz and his collaborators rejected Austrian methodological defeatism[12] and began in the 1970s to construct "a number of such simple models" (Stiglitz 1994, p. 26). Their results confirm the uselessness of the Walras-Pareto-Arrow-Debreu model considered above, either as "the economics of socialism" or as a rationale of Adam Smith's "invisible hand." While generally corroborating the Austrian belief in the superiority of free markets over central planning and control, they encourage a pragmatic, piecemeal view of the public sector in a mixed economy. "The socialist-versus-market debate posed the question the wrong way. The correct question is not which mode of production is superior, but what are the comparative advantages of each sector, what should be the appropriate scope of each?" (Stiglitz 1994, p. 247).

IV C. Collective Decision

Even if a well-defined production-possibility hyper-surface existed, and even if national governments possessed the power—through skillful use of macroeconomic analysis and econometric modeling—to determine aggregate production on that hyper-surface, the fourth textbook question posed by Stiglitz would remain: "Who decides, and how?" Without a complete set of perfectly competitive markets, the question applies *a fortiori* to necessarily political determination of the socially optimum point on that hyper-surface.

One of the "presuppositions of Harvey Road . . . may perhaps be summarised in the idea that the government of Britain was and would continue to be in the hands of an intellectual aristocracy using the method of persuasion . . . Keynes tended till the end to think of the really important decisions being reached by a small group of intelligent people" (Harrod 1952, pp. 192–193). The high tradition of disinterested duty that distinguished the British civil service in Keynes's day guaranteed that the "intelligent people" would seek the common good. But in countries such as the United States where democracy—not to say populism—was more obtrusive, it was feared by many that monetary and fiscal policy formulated by government for short-term political gain would have an inflationary bias. It was also increasingly recognized that demand management is subject to long lags and therefore likely to be destabilizing. These considerations induced Friedman (1948, 1951) to recommend that the objective of "full employment" be abandoned, that government eschew discretionary demand management, and that rules be designed and followed to ensure that monetary and fiscal changes act as automatic stabilizers.

Friedman's distrust of "Keynesian" policy was congruent in various ways with a large body of theoretical analysis on the relation between political motivation and macroeconomic instability (e.g., Kalecki 1943; Akerman 1947; Downs 1957; Nordhaus 1975; MacRae 1977; and so forth). It should be noted that these objections to discretionary policy would remain even if New Keynesians should eventually be success-ful in establishing a generally acceptable theoretical framework for de-mand management.

But even if discretionary demand management were efficacious, and even if democratic governments could be trusted to employ it, the problem would remain of just where to be on the production-possibil-ity hyper-surface. How can we know the socially optimal composition of output? Why should we suppose that agents in the public sector would act so as to achieve it?

Bergson (1938) and Samuelson (1947) devised a social welfare function as a positive study of "the consequences of various value judgments" (Samuelson 1947, p. 220) and were able to demonstrate that many of the Paretian conditions hold regardless of value judg-ments. But no unambiguous criteria of social welfare emerged. For any set of factor endowments and individual tastes, there is an infinite number of Pareto-optimum outcomes depending on asset endow-ments; and explicit value judgments are required in order to rearrange the latter. A different approach was taken by Kenneth Arrow (1951), who analyzed voting procedures as a means of determining collective preferences, building on recent psephological work (Bowen 1943; Black 1948; Arrow 1950) and bringing to its highest development a line of inquiry going back to Lewis Carroll (Black 1958). As is well known, Arrow concluded that "if we exclude the possibility of inter-personal comparisons of utility, then the only method of passing from individual tastes to social preferences which will be satisfactory and which will be defined for a wide range of sets of individual orderings are either imposed or dictatorial" (1951, p. 59). The seeming impossi-bility of truly collective choice did not deter a tradition of analysis based upon Bowen (1943), according to which, "one can induce the median-voter's preferences for public policies from the policies that actually emerge under majority rule" (Brennan and Lomasky 1993, p. 76). But H. G. Brennan and L. Lomasky (1993) have shown that neither the "median voter" model nor the belief that an invisible hand operates in voting so as to bring about a socially beneficent outcome from narrowly interested voting is tenable. Voting is an "expressive" act, like cheering at a football match; and "fully rational voters will not reliably vote for the political outcomes they prefer." "Democracy is flawed as a mechanism for making social decisions and, on occasion, may produce genuinely disastrous results" (Brennan and Lomasky 1993, p. 197).

Secure in the selfless devotion of a noble army of upper-class statesmen, bureaucrats and colonial administrators, British economists from Jevons to Joan Robinson—almost all of whom were themselves drawn from that class—ignored the problems of political process and political agency. It was otherwise in less favored lands. Mathematical models of the economics of smuggling, law enforcement and bribery appeared in Italy before the end of the eighteenth century (Theocharis 1961, pp. 22–27). By the 1880s Italian economists such as Mazzola and Pantaleoni had begun to investigate the public economy within an exchange framework (Buchanan 1975, p. 384). In Sweden, starting in the early 1900s, Wicksell and Erik Lindahl studied "just taxation" in the theoretical context of politically determined budgeting (Musgrave and Peacock 1958). In the United States, as in Sweden, what became known as "Public Choice" theory grew out of the study of public finance, with seminal papers by R. A. Musgrave (1938), H. R. Bowen (1943), J. M. Buchanan (1949)—who received a Nobel Prize for his many contributions to this field—and Samuelson (1954). The importance of this branch of economic theorizing lies in "the elementary fact that collective or public-sector decisions emerge from a political process rather than from the mind of some benevolent despot" (Buchanan 1975, p. 385). Political process includes the "supply-side" actions of bureaucrats, who may be taken to be rational maximizers pursuing private goals (Mises 1944; Tullock 1965; Niskanen 1971; and so forth). Bureaucrats, and all others in a political process, compete in "rent-seeking." Public regulation of the private sector is the outcome of competing attempts by powerful interests to "capture" rents (Stigler 1971), as Adam Smith ([1776]1976, IV.i–viii) well understood. Yet another "New Political Economy" has emerged from this tradition in the past 15 years that aims at *explaining* economic policy rather than designing or recommending it, and that rejects the "conventional assumption that policy is determined by maximizing a social welfare function" (Saint-Paul 2000, p. 915).

Little if anything remains of "the presuppositions of Harvey Road." Neither political procedures nor bureaucrats, it would seem, can do much either to identify collective preferences or—if they could somehow be discovered—to satisfy them.

V

The Bottom Line

HALF A CENTURY AGO an almost unbroken consensus existed among "intelligent people" to the effect that the state can and ought to manage, regulate or control economic activity in the public interest. "Intelligent people" were sustained in this conviction by "state-of-the-art" economic theory, which proved that it was so. Adam Smith ([1776]1976, IV.ix.51) had warned that "the duty of superintending the industry of private people, and directing it towards employments most suitable to the interest of the society" was one "for the proper performance of which no human wisdom or knowledge could ever be sufficient." But the "neo-classical synthesis" showed he was wrong and his warning went unheeded.

In the last quarter of the twentieth century this consensus has collapsed. Left-wing governments in New Zealand, Australia and many other countries compete in their zeal for deregulation, privatization and rolling back the welfare state. The Labour Prime Minister of Great Britain calls himself in all sincerity a "Thatcherite." No doubt the reasons for this are complex and many, and include the rapid and unexpected withering away of socialism in the Soviet empire. If any new, "neo-conservative" consensus is emerging it would seem to be based on a superstitious veneration of "market forces" somewhat similar, *mutatis mutandis*, to that blind faith in "economic control" that characterized the old consensus.

Insofar as "neo-conservatism" has any genuine intellectual foundations, however, these are to be sought, in part, in the present state of economic theory. The "new political economies" of the late twentieth and early twenty-first centuries have been powerfully corrosive of those collectivist or at any rate *dirigiste* doctrines taken for granted by Knut Wicksell and Thorstein Veblen, Beatrice Webb and Harold Laski,

Fred M. Taylor and Abba Lerner. *Œconomie politique* has been rolled back once again. The onus of proof has been shifted, and now lies with those who wish to assert a more important part for the state in the economic life of the nation.

Notes

1. "[T]heir opinions on the most essential points of political economy were the same" (Stewart [1794] 1980, p. 304).

2. "The restraints of Communism would be freedom in comparison with the present condition of the majority of the human race" (Mill [1848] 1909, p. 210).

3. Enrico Barone pointed out in 1895 that product exhaustion was implied by Walras's (1874) cost-minimization equations with no mention of marginal product, but his submission to the *Economic Journal* reporting this result was rejected by Edgeworth who was then the editor (Blaug 1997, p. 435).

4. The assumption that all choice and production sets are convex was later made explicit (Debreu 1959).

5. See Blaug 1997, pp. 342–349.

6. Which consideration was well known to Trotsky (1933)—see Hoff ([1938]1949, pp. 263–264)—but anathema to Soviet authority.

7. "The *General Theory* caught most economists under the age of thirty-five with the unexpected virulence of a disease first attacking and decimating an isolated tribe of south sea islanders" (Samuelson [1946] 1966, p. 1517).

8. That the logical impossibility of such a quasi-equilibrium when saving is non-zero was formally remedied by R. F. Harrod's "warranted rate of growth" (1939, p. 16). For Joan Robinson ([1953] 1973, p. 263) the necessary instability of warranted growth was yet another nail in the orthodox coffin.

9. As Robinson writes, "Your genius wears seven-league boots, and goes striding along, leaving a paper-chase of little mistakes behind him" (Robinson 1973, p. 266).

10. Provided we can assume that we observe variables in the neighborhood of their equilibrium values (Hicks 1965, p. 16).

11. Later this was called "easily the most influential paper on macroeconomics published in the post-war era" (Blaug 1997, p. 678).

12. "[T]he fact that the real world is more complicated than any model which we might construct does not absolve us of the need for testing our ideas out using simple and understandable models."

References

Akerlof, George A. 1970. "The Market for 'Lemons': Quality Uncertainty and the Market Mechanism," *Quarterly Journal of Economics* 86: 488–500.

Akerman, J. 1947. "Political Economic Cycles," *Kyklos* 1: 107–117.

Alchian, Armen A. (1970). "Information Costs, Pricing, and Resource Unemployment," in *Microeconomic Foundations of Employment and Inflation Theory* (ed. E. S. Phelps). New York: Norton.

Allais, Maurice. (1992). "The General Theory of Surpluses as a Formalization of the Underlying Theoretical Thought of Adam Smith, his Predecessors and his Contemporaries," in *Adam Smith's Legacy* (ed. M. Fry). London: Routledge.

Aristotle. (1967). *The Politics, with an English Translation by H. Rackham.* Cambridge: Harvard University Press.

Arrow, K. J. (1950). "A Difficulty in the Concept of Social Welfare," *Journal of Political Economy* 56: 328–346.

———. (1951). *Social Choice and Individual Values.* New York: Wiley.

———. (1962). "The Economic Implications of Learning by Doing," *Review of Economic Studies* 29: 155–173.

———. (1987). "Rationality of Self and Others in an Economic System," in *Rational Choice: The Contrast between Economics and Pysychology* (eds. R. W. Hogarth and M. W. Reder). Chicago: University of Chicago Press.

Arrow, K. J. and Debreu, G. (1954). "Existence of an Equilibrium for a Competitive Economy," *Econometrica* 22: 265–290.

Arrow, K. J. and Kurz, M. (1970). *Public Investment, the Rate of Return and Optimal Fiscal Policy.* Baltimore, MD: Johns Hopkins Press.

Backhouse, Roger. (1985). *A History of Modern Economic Analysis.* Oxford, UK: Blackwell.

Bank of Canada. (1976). *The Equations of RDX2.* Technical Report No. 5. Ottawa.

Barone, Enrico. ([1908] 1935). "The Ministry of Production in the Collectivist State," tr. in Hayek (1935).

Barro, Robert J. and Lucas, Robert F. (1994). *Macroeconomics.* First Canadian ed. Burr Ridge IL: Irwin.

Bergson, A. (1938). "A Reformulation of Certain Aspects of Welfare Economics," *Quarterly Journal of Economics* 52: 310–334.

Black, Duncan. (1948). "On the Rationale of Group Decision-Making," *Journal of Political Economy* 56: 23–34.

———. (1958). *The Theory of Committees and Elections.* London: Cambridge University Press.

Blaug, Mark. (1997). *Economic Theory in Retrospect.* Fifth ed. Cambridge: Cambridge University Press.

Boulding, K. E. (1952). "Welfare Economics," in *A Survey of Contemporary Economics* (ed. B. F. Haley) vol. 2. Homewood IL: Irwin.

Bowen, H. R. (1943). "The Interpretation of Voting in the Allocation of Resources," *Quarterly Journal of Economics* 58: 27–48.

Brennan, H. G. and Lomasky, L. (1993). *Democracy and Decision: The Pure Theory of Electoral Preferences.* Cambridge: Cambridge University Press.

Buchanan, J. M. (1949). "The Pure Theory of Government Finance: A Suggested Interpretation," *Journal of Political Economy* 57: 496–505.

———. (1975). "Public Finance and Public Choice," *National Tax Journal* 28: 383–394.

Burke, Edmund. (1981–1997). *The Writings and Speeches of Edmund Burke* (eds. P. K. Langford et al.) 12 vols. Oxford: Oxford University Press.

Chamberlin, E. H. (1933). *The Theory of Monopolistic Competition: A Re-Orientation of the Theory of Value*. Cambridge MA: Harvard University Press.

Clark, J. B. (1899). *The Distribution of Wealth*. New York: n.p.

Coase, R. H. (1937). "The Nature of the Firm," *Economica* 4: 386–405.

———. (1960). "The Problem of Social Cost," *Journal of Law and Economics* 1–44.

Condillac, Etienne Bonnot, abbé de. ([1776] 1997). *Le Commerce et le Gouvernement considérés relativement l'un à l'autre*. Paris. Transl (S. Eltis) as *Commerce and Government Considered in their Mutual Relationship*. Cheltenham, UK: Elgar.

Darby, M. R., Haltiwanger, J. C., and Plant, M. W. (1985). "Unemployment Rate Dynamics and Persistent Unemployment under Rational Expectations," *American Economic Review* 75: 614–637.

Debreu. G. (1959). *The Theory of Value*. New York: Wiley.

Downs, A. (1957). *An Economic Theory of Democracy*. New York: Harper.

Dupuit, Jules. (1844). "On the Measurement of the Utility of Public Works," transl. R. H. Barback from *Annales des Ponts et Chaussés*, in *International Economic Papers*, No. 2. London: Macmillan, 1952.

Edgeworth, F. Y. (1881). *Mathematical Psychics*. London: Macmillan.

Forster, B. A. (1980). "Optimal Energy Use in a Polluted Environment," *Journal of Environmental Economics and Management* 321–333.

Flux, A. W. ([1894] 1968). "Review of Wicksteed (1894)," reprinted in *Precursors in Mathematical Economics* (eds. W. A. Baumol and S. M. Goldfeld). London: London School of Economics.

Friedman, Milton. (1948). "A Monetary and Fiscal Framework for Economic Stability," *American Economic Review* 37: 245–264.

———. (1951). "Les Effets d'une Politique de Plein Emploi sur la Stabilité Économique: Analyse Formelle," *Économie Appliquée* 4: 441–456; (tr.) in Friedman (1953).

———. (1953). *Essays in Positive Economics*. Chicago: University of Chicago Press.

———. (1956). "The Quantity Theory of Money: A Restatement," in *Studies in the Quantity Theory of Money* (ed. M. Friedman). Chicago: University of Chicago Press.

———. (1957). *A Theory of the Consumption Function*. Princeton, NJ: Princeton University Press.

————. (1961). "The Lag in Effect of Monetary Policy," *Journal of Political Economy* 69: 193–238.

————. (1968). "The Role of Monetary Policy," *American Economic Review* 68: 1–17.

Furobotn, E. G. and Richter, R. (1997). *Institutions and Economic Theory: The Contribution of the New Institutional Economics.* Ann Arbor: University of Michigan Press.

Gossen, H. H. (1854). *Entwickelung der Gesetze des menschlichen Verkehrs, und der daraus fleissenden Regeln für menschliches Handeln.* Braunschweig: Vieweg.

Goodwin, R. M. (1970). *Elementary Economics from the Higher Standpoint.* Cambridge: Cambridge University Press.

Greenwald, B. and Stiglitz, J. E. (1986). "Externalities in Economies with Imperfect Information and Incomplete Markets," *Quarterly Journal of Economics* 101: 229–264.

Groenewegen, Peter. (1987). "'Political Economy' and 'Economics,'" in *The New Palgrave: A Dictionary of Economics* (eds. J. Eatwell, M. Milgate, P. Newman), 4 vols. London: Macmillan.

Harrod, R. F. (1952). *The Life of John Maynard Keynes.* London: Macmillan.

Hahn, F. H. and Matthews, R. C. O. (1964). "The Theory of Economic Growth: A Survey," *Economic Journal* 74: 779–902.

Hall, Robert E. (1979). "A Theory of the Natural Unemployment Rate and the Duration of Unemployment," *Journal of Monetary Economics* 5: 153–170.

Hamilton, Alexander. (1791). *Report on Manufactures.* Reprinted, Washington: Government Printer's Office, 1913.

Hamowy, Ronald. (1987). *The Scottish Enlightenment and the Theory of Spontaneous Order.* Carbondale, IL: Southern Illinois University Press.

Harcourt, C. G. (1987). "Post-Keynesian Economics," in *The New Palgrave: A Dictionary of Economics* (eds. J. Eatwell, M. Milgate, and P. Newman). London: Macmillan.

Harrod, R. F. (1939). "An Essay in Dynamic Theory," *Economic Journal* 49: 14–33.

————. (1952). *The Life of John Maynard Keynes.* London: Macmillan.

Hayek, F. A. von. (1935) (ed.) *Collectivist Economic Planning.* London: Routledge.

————. (1937). "Economics and Knowledge," *Economica* 4: 33–54.

————. (1945). "The Use of Knowledge in Society," *American Economic Review* 35: 519–530.

————. (1960). *The Constitution of Liberty.* Chicago: University of Chicago Press.

————. (1978). "Competition as a Discovery Procedure," in *New Studies in Philosophy, Politics, Economics and the History of Ideas.* London: Routledge and Kegan Paul.

Hicks, J. R. (1937). "Mr Keynes and the Classics: A Suggested Interpretation," *Econometrica* 5: 147–159.

———. (1939a). *Value and Capital*. Oxford: Oxford University Press.

———. (1939b). "Foundations of Welfare Economics," *Economic Journal* 49: 696–712.

———. (1965). *Capital and Growth*. Oxford: Oxford University Press.

Hobson, J. A. (1909). *The Industrial System*. London: Longmans, Green.

Hoff, T. J. B. ([1938] 1949). *Economic Calculation in the Socialist Society* (tr. M. A. Michael). London: Hodge.

Hume, David. ([1752] 1994). *Political Essays* (ed. K. Haakonssen). Cambridge: Cambridge University Press.

Jevons, W. S. (1862). "Brief Account of a General Mathematical Theory of Political Economy," in Jevons [1871].

———. ([1871] 1957). *The Theory of Political Economy*. New York: Kelley and Millman.

Kaldor, N. (1939). "Welfare Propositions of Economics and Interpersonal Comparisons of Utility," *Economic Journal* 49: 549–552.

Kalecki, M. (1943). "Political Aspects of Full Employment," *Political Quarterly* 14: 322–330.

Kantorovich, L. V. ([1939] 1960). "Mathematical Methods of Organizing and Planning Production" (tr.), *Management Science* 6: 363–422.

———. ([1942] 1965). *The Best Use of Economic Resources* (tr. P. K. Knightsfield, ed. G. Morton). Oxford: Pergamon.

Keynes, J. M. (1936). *The General Theory of Employment, Interest and Money*. London: Macmillan.

Klein, L. R. and Goldberger, A. S. (1955). *An Econometric Model of the United States, 1929–52*. Amsterdam: North-Holland.

Kuenne, Robert E. (1968). *Microeconomic Theory of the Market: A General Equilibrium Approach*. New York: Macmillan.

Lange, Oskar. (1936). "On the Economic Theory of Socialism," *Review of Economic Studies* 4: 123–142.

Leontief, Wassily. (1936). "Quantitative Input-Output Relations in the Economic System of the United States," *Review of Economics and Statistics* 18: 105–125.

Lerner, Abba P. (1944). *The Economics of Control: Principles of Welfare Economics*. New York: Macmillan.

Lipsey, R. G. and Lancaster, K. (1956). "The General Theory of Second Best," *Review of Economic Studies* 24: 11–32.

Lipsey, R. G. (1960). "The Relation between Unemployment and the Rate of Change of Money Wage Rates in the United Kingdom, 1862–1957: A Further Analysis," *Economica* 27: 1–31.

Lloyd, W. F. (1834). *A Lecture on the Notion of Value delivered before the University of Oxford in 1833*. Oxford: Oxford University Press.

Lucas, R. E. (1975). "An Equilibrium Model of the Business Cycle," *Journal of Political Economy* 83: 1113–1144.

MacRae, C. Duncan. (1977). "A Political Model of the Business Cycle," *Journal of Political Economy* 85: 239–263.

Malthus, T. R. (1798). *An Essay on the Principle of Population as it Affects the Future Improvement of Society . . .* London: Johnson.

Mankiw, N. Gregory and Romer, David (eds.) (1991). *New Keynesian Economics*. 2 vols. Cambridge MA: MIT Press.

Mayerne-Turquet, L. de. (1611). *La Monarchie Aristodémocratique; ou le Gouvernement compose et meslé des trois formes de légitimes républiques.* Paris: n.p.

Marshall, Alfred. ([1890] 1952). *Principles of Economics*, 8th ed. London: Macmillan.

McCafferty, Stephen. (1990). *Macroeconomic Theory.* New York: Harper & Row.

Meade, J. E. (1951). *The Balance of Payments, Mathematical Supplement.* London: Oxford University Press.

Menger, C. ([1871] 1950). *Principles of Economics* (tr. J. Dingwall and B. F. Hoselitz). Glencoe IL: Free Press.

Mill, John Stuart. ([1848] 1909). *Principles of Political Economy with Some of their Applications to Social Philosophy* (ed. W. J. Ashley). London: Longmans, Green and Co.

———. ([1874] 1969). *Three Essays on Religion*, in *Collected Works of John Stuart Mill* (eds. J. M. Robson, F. E. L. Priestley, D. P. Dryer), Vol. X. Toronto: University of Toronto Press.

Mises, Ludwig von. ([1920] 1935). "Economic Calculation in the Socialist Commonwealth," tr. in Hayek (1935).

———. (1944). *Bureaucracy.* New Haven: Yale University Press.

Montchrétien, A. de. ([1615] 1889). *Traité de l'économie politique* (ed. T. Funck-Brentano). Paris: Plon.

Mundell, R. A. (1961). "The International Disequilibrium System," *Kyklos* 14: 154–172.

Musgrave, R. A. (1938). "The Voluntary Exchange Theory of Public Economy," *Quarterly Journal of Economics* 53: 213–237.

Musgrave, R. A. and Peacock, A. T., eds. (1958). *Classics in the Theory of Public Finance.* New York: St Martin's.

Muth, J. F. (1961). "Rational Expectations and the Theory of Price Movements," *Econometrica* 29: 315–335.

Nelson, Robert A. (2001). *Economics as Religion: From Samuelson to Chicago and Beyond.* University Park, PA: Penn State University Press.

Neumann, J. von ([1938] 1945–46). "A Model of General Economic Equilibrium" (tr. G. Morgenstern), *Review of Economic Studies* 13: 1–9.

Niskanen, W. A. (1971). *Bureaucracy and Representative Government.* Chicago: Aldine-Atherton.

Nordhaus, W. D. (1975). "The Political Business Cycle," *Review of Economic Studies* 42: 169–190.

O'Brien, Connor Cruise. (1993). *The Great Melody.* London: Minerva.

O'Neill, John. (1996). "Who Won the Socialist Calculation Debate?" *History of Political Thought* 17: 431–442.

Pareto, Vilfredo. (1896). *Cours d'Economie Politique.* Geneva: Libraire de l'Université.

———. ([1908] 1971). *Manual of Political Economy* (tr. A. S. Schwier, eds. A. S. Schwier and A. N. Page). New York: Kelley.

Patinkin, D. (1976). "Keynes and Econometrics: On the Interaction between the Macroeconomic Revolution of the Interwar Period," *Econometrica* 44: 1091–1123.

Phelps, E. S. (1967). "Phillips Curves, Expectations of Inflation and Optimal Unemployment over Time," *Economica* 34: 254–281.

——— (ed). (1970). *Microeconomic Foundations of Employment and Inflation Theory.* New York: Norton.

Phillips, A. W. (1958). "The Relation between Unemployment and the Rate of Change of Money Wages in the United Kingdom, 1861–1957," *Economica* 25: 283–299.

Pigou, A. C. (1920). *The Economics of Welfare.* London: Macmillan.

Pontryagin, L. S., Boltyanskii, V. G., Gamkrelidze, R. V., and Mishchenko, E. F. (1962). *The Mathematical Theory of Optimal Processes* (tr. K. N. Tririgoff). New York: Interscience.

Ramaswami, Chitra. (1983). "Equilibrium Unemployment and the Efficient Job-Finding Rate," *Journal of Labor Economics* 1: 171–196.

Ramsay, F. P.(1927). "A Contribution to the Theory of Taxation," *Economic Journal* 37: 47–61.

———. (1928). "A Mathematical Theory of Saving," *Economic Journal* 38: 543–559.

Ricardo, David ([1817] 1911). *The Principles of Political Economy and Taxation.* London: Dent.

Robbins, L. (1932). *An Essay on the Nature and Significance of Economic Science.* London: Macmillan.

Robinson, Joan. (1933). *The Economics of Imperfect Competition.* London: Macmillan.

———. ([1953] 1973). *On Re-reading Marx.* Cambridge: Students' Bookshop, reprinted in Robinson (1973).

———. ([1953–4] 1964a.) "The Production Function and the Theory of Capital," *Review of Economic Studies* 21: 81–106, reprinted in Robinson (1964a).

———. (1964a). *Collected Economic Papers*, Vol. 2. Oxford: Blackwell.

———. (1964b). "Consumer's Sovereignty in a Planned Economy," in *Essays in Honour of Oskar Lange* (1964), reprinted in Robinson (1965).

———. (1965). *Collected Economic Papers*, Vol. 3. Oxford: Blackwell.

———. (1973). *Collected Economic Papers*, Vol. 4. Oxford: Blackwell.

———. (1980). "Introduction" to *Classical and Neoclassical Theories of General Equilibrium: Historical Origins and Mathematical Structure* (ed. Vivian Walsh and Harvey Gram). New York: Oxford University Press.

Ross, S. A. (1973). "The Economic Theory of Agency: The Principals Problems," *American Economic Review* 63: 134–139.

Saint-Paul, Gilles. (2000). "The 'New Political Economy': Recent Books by Allen Drazen and by Torsten Persson and Guido Tabellini," *Journal of Economic Literature* 38: 915–925.

Samuelson, Paul A. ([1946] 1966). "The General Theory," reprinted in *The Collected Scientific Papers of Paul A. Samuelson* (ed. Joseph E. Stiglitz), Vol. 2. Cambridge: MIT Press.

———. (1947). *Foundations of Economic Analysis*. Cambridge: Harvard University Press.

———. (1948). *Economics: An Introductory Analysis*. New York: McGraw Hill.

———. (1950). "Evaluation of Real National Income," *Oxford Economic Papers* 2: 1–29.

———. (1954). "The Pure Theory of Public Expenditures," *Review of Economics and Statistics* 36: 387–389.

———. (1978). "The Canonical Classical Model of Political Economy," *Journal of Economic Literature* 16: 1415–1434.

Samuelson, Paul A. and Solow, R. M. (1953). "Balanced Growth under Constant Returns to Scale," *Econometrica* 21: 412–424, reprinted in Samuelson ([1946] 1966).

Samuelson, Paul A. and Solow, R. M. (1960). "Analytical Aspects of Anti-Inflation Policy," *American Economic Review* 50: 177–194.

Sappington, D. E. M. (1991). "Incentives in Principal-Agent Relationships," *Journal of Economic Perspectives* 5: 45–66.

Sappington, D. E. M. and Stiglitz, J. E. (1987). "Privatization, Information and Incentives," *Journal of Policy Analysis and Management* 6: 567–582.

Sargent, T. J. (1973). "Rational Expectations, the Real Rate of Interest, and the Natural Rate of Unemployment," *Brookings Papers in Economic Activity* 2: 429–472.

Sargent, T. J. and Wallace, N. (1976). "Rational Expectations and the Theory of Economic Policy," *Journal of Monetary Economics* 2: 169–184.

Schumpeter, J. A. ([1943] 1987). *Capitalism, Socialism and Democracy*. London: Unwin.

———. (1954). *History of Economic Analysis*. New York: Oxford University Press.

Scitovsky, T. (1941). "A Note on Welfare Propositions in Economics," *Review of Economic Studies* 9: 77–88.

Sen, A. K. (1967). "Terminal Capital and Optimal Savings," in *Socialism, Capitalism and Economic Growth: Essays Presented to Maurice Dobb* (ed. C. H. Feinstein). Cambridge: Cambridge University Press.

Simon, Herbert A. (1959). "Theories of Decision Making in Economics and Behavioral Science," *American Economic Review* 49: 253–283.

———. (1978). "Rationality as Process and as Product of Thought," *American Economic Review* 68: 1–16.

Skinner, Quentin. (1969). "Meaning and Understanding in the History of Ideas," *History and Theory* 8: 3–53.

Smith, Adam. ([1776] 1976). *An Inquiry into the Nature and Causes of the Wealth of Nations* (eds. Campbell, R. H., Skinner, A. S. and Todd, W. B.), 2 vols. Oxford: Oxford University Press.

Sraffa, Piero. (1926). "The Laws of Return under Competitive Conditions," *Economic Journal* 35: 535–550.

Steuart, J. ([1767] 1966). *An Inquiry into the Principles of Political Œconomy* (ed. A. S. Skinner), 2 vols. Edinburgh: Oliver and Boyd for the Scottish Economic Society.

Stewart, Dugald. ([1794] 1980). *Account of the Life and Writings of Adam Smith, LL.D.*, in Adam Smith, *Essays on Philosophical Subjects* (eds. W. P. D. Wightman, J. C. Bryce, and I. S. Ross). Oxford: Oxford University Press.

Stigler, George. (1961). "The Economics of Information," *Journal of Political Economy* 69: 213–225.

———. (1971). "The Theory of Economic Regulation," *Bell Journal of Economics and Management Science* 2: 3–31.

Stiglitz, Joseph E. (1986). *Economics of the Public Sector.* New York: Norton.

———. (1994). *Whither Socialism?* Cambridge: MIT Press.

Swan, T. W. (1960). "Economic Control in a Dependent Economy," *Economic Record* 36: 51–66.

Sweezy, Paul. (1935). "Economics and the Crisis of Capitalism," *Economic Forum* 3.

Taylor, Fred M. (1929). "The Guidance of Production in the Socialist State," *American Economic Review* 19: 1–8.

Theocharis, Reghinos D. (1961). *Early Developments in Mathematical Economics.* London: MacMillan.

Thünen, Johann Heinrich von (1826). *Der isolierte Staat in Beziehung auf Landwirtschaft und Nationalökonomie.* Hamburg: Perthes.

Tinbergen, Jan. (1935). "Quantitative Fragen der Konjunkturpolitik," *Weltwirtschaftliches Archiv* 42: 316–399.

Trotsky, Leon. (1933). *Soviet Economy in Danger.* New York.

Tullock, G. (1965). *The Politics of Bureaucracy.* Washington: Public Affairs Press.

Turgot, A. R. J. ([1768] 1970). "Observations sur le mémoire de M. de Saint-Péravy en faveur de l'impôt indirect," in A. R. J. Turgot, *Écrits Économiques* (ed. B. Cazes). Paris: Calman-Lévy.

Vaughn, Karen. (1980). "Economic Calculation under Socialism," *Economic Inquiry* 18: 535–554.

———. (1994). *Austrian Economics in America: The Migration of a Tradition.* Cambridge: Cambridge University Press.

Veblen, Thorstein. ([1921] 1965). *The Engineers and the Price System.* New York: Kelley.

Walras, L. ([1874] 1954). *Elements of Pure Economics* (tr. W. Jaffe). London: Allen & Unwin.

Walsh, Vivian and Gram, Harvey. (1980). *Classical and Neoclassical Theories of General Equilibrium: Historical Origins and Mathematical Structure.* New York: Oxford University Press.

Waterman, A. M. C. (1966). "Some Footnotes to the 'Swan Diagram': or, How Dependent is a Dependent Economy?" *Economic Record* 42: 447–464.

———. (1991). *Revolution, Economics and Religion: Christian Political Economy 1798–1833.* Cambridge: Cambridge University Press.

———. (1995). "Peasants, Population and Progress in Malthus and Chalmers," in *The Peasant in Economic Thought* (eds. E. L. Forget and R. A. Lobdell). Aldershot, UK: Elgar.

———. (1996). "Why William Paley was 'the First of the Cambridge Economists'." *Cambridge Journal of Economics* 20: 673–686.

———. (1998a). "Reappraisal of 'Malthus the Economist', 1933–97," *History of Political Economy* 30: 293–334.

———. (1998b). "Malthus, Mathematics and the Mythology of Coherence," *History of Political Economy* 30: 571–599.

———. (2001). "Notes Towards an Un-Canonical, Pre-Classical Model of Political Œconomy," in *Reflections on the Classical Canon in Economics* (eds. E. L. Forget and S. Peart). London: Routledge.

Wicksell, Knut. ([1901] 1935). *Lectures on Political Economy*, 2 vols. (tr. E. Classen, ed. L. Robbins). London: Routledge.

Wicksteed, P. H. (1894). *Essay on the Coordination of the Laws of Distribution.* London: Macmillan.

Wieser, Friedrich von. ([1893] 1971). *Natural Value.* New York: Kelley.

Williamson, Oliver E. (1975). *Markets and Hierarchies: Analysis and Antitrust Implications.* New York: Free Press.

———. (1985). *The Economic Institutions of Capitalism: Firms, Markets, Relational Contracting.* New York: Free Press.

———. (1986). *Economic Organization: Firms, Markets and Policy Control.* New York: New York University Press.

Young, A. A. (1928). "Increasing Returns and Economic Progress," *Economic Journal* 38: 527–542.

PART II

Fiscal Sociology

American Journal of Economics and Sociology, Vol. 61, No. 1 (January, 2002).
© 2002 American Journal of Economics and Sociology, Inc.

Fiscal Sociology

What For?

By Juergen Backhaus[*]

ABSTRACT. In discussing the question, *Fiscal sociology: What for?* we shall first give a short sketch of the history of thought of the field. We will next identify main issues. In discussing the concept of the tax state, we emphasize issues in constitutional public finance. One of the fields in which fiscal sociology has been most important is taxation, and notably income taxation. In citing applications and issues, we identify an entire alphabet of fiscal sociological issues. We conclude by discussing the future of the field in both instruction and research.

I

A Short History of Fiscal Sociology

FISCAL SOCIOLOGY AS A SEPARATE FIELD makes sense only once economics and sociology have parted ways, leaving a void. Originally, when economics started as a separate field of instruction and research, there was no need for a speciality in fiscal sociology. In repeating a perhaps familiar story, economics in an institutional sense started on the European continent when King Frederick William of Prussia, dissatisfied with the state of the instruction of his future civil servants, founded two chairs in cameral sciences at the universities of Halle (Saale) and Frankfurt (Oder) in 1723. Cameral sciences meant, in essence, public finance. Hence, on the Continent, economics as a separate discipline started with public finance as the core subject area, since the purpose of economic thinking and teaching was to develop institutions so as to foster the wealth and happiness (*Wohlstand und Glückseligkeit*) of the states and thereby the people living in the house of the state. Hence, the wealth of a nation was seen as the result of prudent state economic policy. It would take another 99 years before the first chair in political economy was founded in Britain, at Oxford. Here, the ques-

---

* Professor Backhaus holds the Krupp Chair in Public Finance and Fiscal Sociology at the University of Erfurt, Erfurt, Germany.

American Journal of Economics and Sociology, Vol. 61, No. 1 (January, 2002).

tion of the nature and causes of the wealth of nations had been posed rather differently by Adam Smith (1776). He saw the causes as lying in the division of labor as a precondition for extensive trade; the state would be reduced to taxation and upholding the public order, but was not seen as an active participator in economic activity. These two views of economics prevail to this very day, and they can often be seen in the different positions with respect to economic policy under-taken by the European Union.

While on the European continent, ever-larger numbers of students had been trained in economics, instruction in the field was late to come in Britain and the United States. In Britain, the introduction of the tripos by Alfred Marshall brought a very small number of students indeed. In the United States, it was notably the emerging activity of Washington-based agencies in matters of social policy that required a larger number of well-trained economists and statisticians—in other words, a development of the twentieth century. When economics was taught on the European continent from 1723 onwards, it was done in the context of cameral and policy sciences and the law. Cameral sci-ences were essentially economics and public finance embedded in a broad social policy approach with the state and its institutions as the main source of initiative. In addition, the student would be instructed in public administration (*Policeywissenschaften*) and law, with a strong element of technology-related issues covered as well. These might have to do with mining, agriculture, forestry or manufacturing. The entire field of related areas was called *Staatswissenschaften*, and many universities therefore had their own faculties of *Staats-wissenschaften*, binding these fields of what today is law, economics, public administration, political science, sociology and contemporary history and policy together. This organization of instruction and re-search explains why the literature in economics and public finance all through the nineteenth century has a strong multidisciplinary and in-terdisciplinary character, certainly as seen from today's point of view. This is still true for the work of such authors as Werner Sombart, Jo-seph Alois Schumpeter or Max Weber who, although pioneers in soci-ology, did not consider themselves primarily sociologists. They embody the fusion of economics and sociology: in Sombart's case, economic history; in Schumpeter's case, his strong push for economic analysis and econometrics; in Weber's case, the integration of law, his original field of expertise. However, with the pioneering work of Emile Durkheim, Vilfredo Pareto, Georg Simmel and Ferdinand Tönnies, the separate field of sociology emerged.[1]

These separate developments in sociology resulted in the two disciplines, economics on the one hand and sociology on the other, parting ways. With the rapid development of the social sciences in the twentieth century, economics, including public finance, business economics, public administration, sociology, political science and policy science, all came to exist side-by-side with separate research programs, and the links between them on the one hand and law on the other became weaker and weaker.[2]

The differentiation of separate disciplines within what formerly had been *Staatswissenschaften* left lacunae. While methodological eclecticism had reigned within the *Staatswissenschaften* with very few exceptions,[3] now the different disciplines within the social sciences differentiated themselves by the methods used. From a methodological point of view, they became more homogeneous internally, but also became more heterogeneous in terms of distinguishing one from the other. The logical consequence was a formation of clusters linking subjects with the appropriate methods. While some subjects remained amenable to an analysis by different methods, others became neglected. As we compare, for instance, the tables of contents of two Chicago-based journals, the *Journal of Political Economy* and the *American Journal of Sociology,* we notice that many topics recur in both publications, such as issues relating to the family, issues relating to behavior in the workplace or issues relating to the organization of firms and enterprises. Remarkably different are, of course, the questions asked and the methods of analysis used, although both journals emphasize empirical work. On the other hand, the large comprehensive studies leading to ambitious projects of legislation, which characterized the activities of leading social scientists toward the end of the nineteenth and the beginning of the twentieth century became de-emphasized by the end of the twentieth century. The reason is clear. Such large legislative enterprises as the launching of a welfare state, the codification of the civil code or a commercial code, the formation of a system of public law or the construction of a workable comprehensive national system of health care all require carefully combined eclectic methods synchronized with respect to the questions asked, the empirical data generated and used and the policy advice generated so as to be fit for legislation and implementation.

That the differentiation in the social sciences had led to a gap that needed to be filled with a fresh approach became clear toward the end of World War I, when the system of war finance had not only destroyed the state institutions of the allied powers of Germany and Austria to the core; next to the immense human and material losses, the defeated states could not continue their operation after the war in the way they had done before. This was first pointed out by Rudolf Goldscheid, who is also the father of the term fiscal sociology (*Finanzsoziologie*) and therefore one of the first classical authors in the field. His contribution has to be seen next to that of Joseph Schumpeter, since Schumpeter in his classic piece "The Crisis of the Tax State" responded to Goldscheid's analysis and thereby contributed the second classical piece to the field. To this debate, we should now turn.

II

Main Issues

The Debate on the Crisis of the Tax State

The roots of contractarian or constitutional reasoning are to be found in the tradition of liberalism. The doctrines of liberalism, although quite different from the present Leviathan approaches, centered around two related sets of civil rights for which constitutional guarantees were sought as a means of protection against the discretion of the king or sovereign. As far as the absolute ruler was concerned, property and the domain of individual liberties were substitutes; in principle, for each infringement on individual liberties imposed by a ruler to further some of his interests, there was a functional tax equivalent with which these interests could be equally served, and vice versa. This broader view was also taken into account by Goldscheid, who accordingly advanced an evolutionary theory of the state in which, in the beginning, the state as personified by the prince could seek either revenues or services in kind.

Goldscheid's theory systematically relies on this dualism, upon which a second dichotomy is constructed. There are two classes of citizens in the population: the owners of labor and the owners of capital. The state is able to tax the former and, beyond the point of optimal tax extraction, demand services in kind; capital, which is more flexible and powerful in his model, is only borrowed, and the state incurs the public debt. Whereas the first group actually contributes to the state's expenses through taxes or (mostly military) services, the second receives a claim in return, a claim that has to be satisfied later out of the general tax revenue or by services in kind.

These services, in particular the draft, play a crucial role in Goldscheid's politico-economic analysis, which is also designed to explain the extraordinary length of duration of World War I. Both Goldscheid (1919) and Schumpeter (1918, 1942) agreed that some state activities, such as the war, could never have been carried out had the enormous cost immediately and visibly been shifted to an identifiable public through ex-propriative taxes. While Schumpeter, however, argued more technically in terms of the maximum exhaustibility of the tax base, Goldscheid put forward his interest group perspective, postulating that the creditors to the public (capital owners) had no interest to end the war, never expecting to be required to foot the bill, instead receiving reliable promises to be repaid.

In either case, the war debt contributed to *fiscal illusion* in that it covered up the destruction of real resources and property and so helped carry out policies that, had their true costs been obvious to the citizens, would never have been accepted. When honoring the war debt in Goldscheid's model, the labor class would end up with the entire bill, as the creditors to the public demanded their interest and repayment out of the national dividend.

It is here that Goldscheid's peculiar approach to the notion of human capital (*Menschenökonomie*) becomes relevant. Whereas the contributions of the labor class to the expenses of the state represent real goods and services, either taxes that represent part of the national product, services in kind or other infringements on individual liberty, the capital class contributes only credits, which are to be repaid. Thus, even when real capital, human and material, is used up or destroyed, only the owners of material capital continue to present claims. These claims constitute political leverage, which, still according to Goldscheid, the creditors use to have the state governed in their own interest.

Whereas this model was obviously constructed under the impression of politico-economic interaction during World War I in Austria and Germany, Goldscheid's proposal for fiscal reform was based more broadly on his unorthodox interpretation of the fiscal history of the state, from the Middle Ages to his time. This story begins with a strong state, independent and relatively rich, relying on large property holdings. Only after the Thirty Years' War, however, did the rising demands of the budget exercised by war finance and the desolation of the country give rise to a new approach to economic policy: cameralism, in which the state, gradually transforming itself into the tax state, follows policies of economic development in order to strengthen the tax base, notwithstanding engagement in traditional and new forms of public entrepreneurship, both types of policies aiming at long-run revenue maximization. This dual policy is constrained by the two relationships governing fiscal technology as discussed above: first, the cameralist relationship as the interdependence between public spending and the productivity of the tax base; and second, the experience of rising marginal costs of tax extraction, which leads to the definition of a point of optimal extraction (Laffer curve).

The issue of defining a tax constitution has re-emerged on the current political agenda with the European Union beginning to take shape and with elements of an emerging European constitution becoming visible. The tasks that we face today cannot be solved in a technical manner based on simple models. The fiscal constitution of the European Union will have to meet the classical criteria developed in political doctrine; it also has to be in line with the requirements of a modern global economy; and third, it must accommodate member states with very different constitutions and economic and political systems—including different systems of taxation and political decision-making—and also different histories, cultures and sociopolitical visions. In order to meet this challenge, the different disciplines of public finance, law, public administration, political science and sociology will have to join forces as they had in the tradition of *Staatswissenschaften*. In order for such a joint venture to be success-

ful, integrative paradigms such as those of the tax state may very well
be as useful in the future as they have been in the past.

Income Taxation

At a conference of the international Schumpeter Society in Kyoto (Japan),[4] Richard A. Musgrave, a student of Schumpeter's, surprised his
audience by insisting that Schumpeter's contribution to public finance
had been minimal: he had only emphasized, and actually overempha-
sized, the distortions caused by income taxation. In fact, Schumpeter's
name rarely appears in current textbooks on public finance[5] and his
extensive contributions to public finance[6] tend to be collected in his
sociological or political writings.[7]

In this sense, Musgrave is perhaps correct that most of these writings do not fit within his three-winged trinity of public finance dealing
with allocation, distribution and stabilization. Schumpeter stood firmly
in the continental European tradition of public finance, from Puviani
with his emphasis on fiscal illusions, to Wicksell (1896) with his emphasis on taxation and political decision-making and Da Empoli's
(1931) emphasis on the multiple economic and social distortions
caused by all manner of taxation. In this sense, Schumpeter never sev-
ered the ties between public finance and the neighboring disciplines
and can therefore be properly claimed as one of the fathers of fiscal
sociology. Indeed, Musgrave's hint may serve to offer a simple explanation of what fiscal sociology is about.

Applications and Issues

In the simplest of cases, consider a product (bagels) and an excise tax
levy on this product.

The excise tax increases the demand price and decreases the supply price, and the equilibrium quantity decreases from Q_0 to Q_t. The
excess burden is the shaded triangle *bad*, which is equal to the excess burden of the marginal willingness to pay for bagels over the
marginal costs of bagels for those not produced and consumed because of the tax. Here, the textbook treatment ends. Yet the questions
remain: What did the people eat who did not eat those bagels that
have not been produced and consumed? What did the baker do

Figure 1

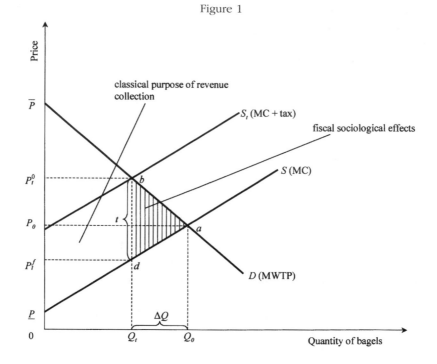

while not producing the bagels? What, in fact, did consumers and bakers hatch as new ideas so as to be able to avoid the tax? Shall we see new products on the market to which the tax does not apply? Can we discern new forms of distribution to which the tax would not apply? Under what circumstances can those forms of tax avoidance arise? Where do they thrive and what further consequences do they entail? All these questions cannot be asked within the traditional concept of tax burden analysis, but all these questions are indeed those we are interested in when thinking about levying, increasing or decreasing a particular tax.

This standard example of excess burden analysis in the partial and static form just presented falls far short of what Schumpeter tried to attempt in the seventh chapter of his "Theory of Economic Development," which is not contained in the English translation nor in the subsequent editions of the German text.[8] Building on the distinction between static and dynamic analysis, partial and total (in the sense of comprehensive) modeling, and introducing entrepreneurial change (defined as new compositions) that affects technology (i.e., the production function) and through this all the other factors involved, Schumpeter tries to describe (verbally) the enormous complexity that would face the economic modeller in the Lausanne tradition. For good reason, he did not try to write such models, but rather tried to use his considerable rhetorical talent to argue a case for a complex analysis in which the argument is always on two levels, a simple and a complex one within the same language structure. Even with today's computer-supported modeling strategies, we have not been able to come up with credible alternatives to Schumpeter's flowering language on various levels, akin to the suspended gardens of Semiramis. Both instruction and research in fiscal sociology will have to take heed from Schumpeter's attempt, both where he succeeded and where he obviously failed. Before addressing such strategies of instruction and research, however, let us turn to a subjective list of issues interesting in the field of fiscal sociology, and let us try to exhaust the Western alphabet.

An Alphabet of Fiscal Sociology

A The existence of *alternatives* or different opportunities to choose from is at the heart of the possibility of doing economics as a science.[9] Only if there are alternatives to choose from can there be any reaction to an action of the government affecting a taxpayer. From the point of view of public policy, the difficulty consists in a central authority's inability to know the full extent of the choices for a citizen who is intent on minimizing the impact of a governmental action on his or her own income or wealth. This knowledge about the alternative ways of avoiding harm, such as the burden of taxation (including both the tax itself and the excess burden), is available only in the decentralized form of knowledge and households, firms and other economic entities. It cannot be systematically collected by any central authority.[10] It is for this reason that knowledge about the excess burden will be systematically underestimated by any conceivable attempt at measurement.

B The *burden* of taxation can be properly identified as the focus of research in fiscal sociology. The difficulty with this subject consists in its elusiveness. As citizens try to minimize the impact of the burden of taxation (and regulation), they invent ever-new forms of legal avoidance. Once this interaction is properly understood, the anticipation of such avoidance behavior can be the cornerstone of public policy itself. By explicitly including loopholes into tax codes and regulations, citizens or firms can be made into agents of public policy.

C For instance, by granting tax *credits* for certain favored investments such as ecologically preferred technologies, a shift in technological development into a desired direction may be accomplished.[11]

D *Depreciations,* in particular accelerated depreciations, can be used to a similar effect. Reginald Hansen[12] has documented extensively how (through the exemptions introduced into the income tax code under Section 7) German authorities were able to rebuild the stock of German housing after World War II, rebuild a commercial fleet and essentially rebuild Eastern Germany after reunification. Instead of enacting all these directly, the government made use of the initiative of private individuals and their desire to reduce the burden of taxation. This approach has two redeeming consequences. First, the financial resources spent on, for instance, rebuilding the historical core of a destroyed city according to municipal zoning guidelines do not have to be raised through taxation; hence there is no excess burden. Second, opportunities for realizing these preferred investments will be found by private entrepreneurs who can use knowledge that would not be available to a government authority either in the quality or to the extent as it is available privately. Although the method looks roundabout, it is more direct than the tax-financed government program that is its alternative.

E The *elasticity* of a particular activity, such as the demand for bagels in the illustration given earlier, determines the extent or size of the excess burden and, by implication, the realm of the fiscal sociological dimensions of a particular policy measure. Only if a particular activity, such as the demand for heating oil, is completely inelastic will there be no excess burden, no opportunity to reduce or avoid the burden of the tax. Such cases of inelastic demand or supply functions are very rare indeed. And this implies, again, that the opportunities for avoiding the burden of taxation (or regulation) are manifold and hard to anticipate by a government agent.

F *Fiscal illusion* is the extent to which the burden of a tax (or regulation) is underestimated by a citizenry or, conversely, the benefits of a particular government program are overestimated. It is in the interest of a government to try to achieve fiscal illusion, and this is as true both for democratic governments that are in need to win re-elections as for non-democratic regimes that likewise need to maintain their grip on power.[13] According to the canons of taxation, fiscal illusion should, of course, be avoided. However, given the incentives on the part of taxing and regulatory authorities, this rule is certainly not self-enforcing. If we do not make a special effort at discovering fiscal illusion, it will remain undetected and uncorrected, with the consequences of inefficiency in the public sector: too many projects that do not fit the demand of the citizenry, and too high a burden of taxation with the concomitant high excess burden, i.e., welfare loss. In this sense, research into fiscal illusion can be welfare-enhancing in uncovering government-caused inefficiencies.

G *Government bonds* can be equivalent to taxation when the strict conditions of the Ricardian equivalence theorem holds. In those cases, the anticipated future burden of taxation needed to service and redeem the bond will be factored into the decisions of current taxpayers who rationally perceive their wealth as being reduced by the future burden of taxation. However, these strict conditions only rarely hold.[14] An admittedly extreme case may illustrate the point. Starting in the 1880s, an extensive net of charitable foundations were set up in Germany, many serving to finance scholarly work, and even entire universities such as the University of Frankfurt (Main). These foundations had to hold their wealth in government bonds. As a consequence, after World War I these foundations lost their wealth; imperial government bonds could no longer be redeemed, including those issued during the war. The hyperinflation resorted to after the *coup d'état* completed the financial destruction of these foundations. In this case, the consequences—the harm done in terms of opportunities foregone for this charitable and scientific work that would otherwise have taken place through these foundations—is extremely difficult to be accurately established. It may not be possible even to attempt a measurement. We thus realize that the limiting conditions of the Ricardian equivalence theorem point to a vast area of research for fiscal sociologists into the burden of government bond issue.[15]

H *Health effects* of taxation can be manifold and surprising. In an effort at harmonizing European excise taxes, Spain departed from its traditional tobacco monopoly, which distributed tobacco products through licensed shops, and introduced an excise tax along with a liberalization of tobacco sales. In particular the international producers of low-tar brands had pushed for this reform, which was also in line with European harmonization efforts. The surprising result, however, was the disappearance of the traditional local tobacco shops (*estancas*) and the appearance of contraband tobacco sales in bars and restaurants. Obviously, this resulted in heavy losses in public revenue; but it also resulted in an increase in the consumption of high-tar tobacco products, which have more adverse health effects than low-tar tobacco products. Without understanding the precise consequences, an established system of taxation (through monopolization) and containment of consumption had been displaced, with the resulting loss in public revenue and an increase in the consumption of the product for which a temperance policy had been envisaged.

I *Income in kind* programs can likewise have surprising consequences. The socialist Allende administration (1970–1973) in Chile had promised to deliver a liter of milk to every child. It started introducing price controls on dairy products, which, along with the heavy inflation that set in shortly after the administration had taken over, first led to a glut in meat, and consequently to a disappearance of dairy products. The administration then bought milk powder in international markets and distributed bags of milk powder to parents of children. Due to the enormous shortage of dairy products, these milk powder bags had a substantial resale value and helped the families suffering under the inflationary devaluation of their wage income to supplement this income through sales in the black market. The outcome, of course, was that the milk did not end up feeding the children targeted by the program. Such a scenario is, perhaps, extreme, but it follows a strict economic logic and is clearly predictable. Whenever aid is granted in kind, one has to look at both the income and substitution effects.[16]

J *Jointness of investment and returns* is an important principle in ensuring that a particular economic activity is seen in its entirety and taxed accordingly. This principle is often violated when income is taxed according to the source principle without consideration of the expenses it affords. Schmoller had insisted that income be measured as that amount that can be consumed without reducing wealth. Hence, if a household consumes €100,000 and its wealth had been €10 million in period 1 and €10 million in period 2, this consumption is the income that has to be taxed. However, if you disjoin consumption and expenditure behavior from income and revenue behavior, interesting effects can occur. The case has been documented of the owner of a landed estate who lived lavishly but never realized any income whatsoever. Hence, he never paid any income tax. In a suggestive way, this can work as follows. Imagine you own a resource that is valued at €10 million. It should increase in value at some rate, and you can therefore increase your borrowing against the asset at the same rate, discounting for interest. If the asset, for instance, is attractive land that benefits from development of bordering tracts of land, the (speculative) increase in value will be much more than the normal market return on bonds, and you can borrow against this asset accordingly. This may again support your lavish lifestyle, while no income is generated, rather further and further debt, when the asset that increases in value serves as collateral. If we insist on defining income in terms of its source instead of what it allows in supporting your lifestyle, that is, if we insist in disjoining assets and returns, we will end up with the paradoxical result that your lavishly maintained lifestyle nevertheless is not subject to income taxation. Only by studying the reality of taxpayer response to particular rules of taxation can we establish a realistic picture of the impact of taxation on people's behavior and the economic effects of these dual causes.

K *Kiddy tax* is a phenomenon that penalizes households having children under the tax code. It can take many forms.[17] To start with, a woman having a child necessarily has to leave the workplace for a while, and it depends on the cultural environment how long this "while" will actually take. It may be three months; it may be three years. There are cultures in which the process takes longer. This means, however, that the mother may lose not only her proficiency in her job, but also the regular salary increments that go along with normal performance. She will thus restart where she stopped, and carry the entire loss forward over the expected duration of her labor experience. From the employer's point of view, this cannot be otherwise, since the wage has to reflect marginal productivity. From the taxation point of view, however, it is quite possible to compensate for this necessary effect. The compensation will have to be higher the more the mother earns—an awkward result when equity in taxation is emphasized in terms of equalizing incomes and wealth. In addition, raising children brings about lots of additional expenses, which, if they are not deductible, in fact weigh in as a "kiddy tax." Some recent programs allow mothers to establish home offices.[18] Instead of granting subsidies to some mothers for such home offices, it would be more effective to grant tax deductions for home offices actually established. That would allow mothers who see an opportunity to combine work with raising their children at home to develop entrepreneurship and establish the proper working environment. It is difficult for a state agency to identify such able, entrepreneurial mothers and to tailor a grant to the needs that actually exist.

L Taxation provides very little in the way of *liability for false returns*. Yet no market can work without the institution of liability in contract and wrongdoing (violating property rights). Tax returns may be used for all manner of ends, not only assessing the tax code, but also different social policy objectives. After all, tax returns are a gold mine of information and this information, if correct, can be effectively used in order to tailor government programs to citizens' needs. However, if rules of taxation are not self-enforcing, the information will be totally misleading and will not be useful for any ulterior government purpose. Since liability for false returns is difficult to be made actionable (without reversing burdens of proof), the self-enforcing mechanism practiced in some Swiss cantons is instructive. Here, the method of self-declaration of income is practiced, but the returns are made public and banks prudently use them for their crediting decisions, lest they be criticized in public themselves. This means that a local entrepreneur cheats on his taxes at the risk of losing his credit line. Banks will deal only with local customers, and the system is closed.

M *Monitoring compliance* is not only important with respect to honesty in taxation. It is particularly difficult for the tax authority when a tax is used as a policy instrument to achieve a particular purpose, such as the use of an ecologically preferred technology, production process or resource. The information required to monitor compliance may be very complex in such cases, and it is important to create a system of self-enforcement. Often, the necessary expertise cannot be assumed to lie within a taxing authority, and certification may thus be required from a different agency. In such cases, the extensive use of tax credits reverses the burden of providing the information from the taxing authority to the taxpayer, who thereby has to prove compliance. This reversal of the burden of proof expedites the tax administration and offers a flexible instrument to achieve many and diverse policy objectives.[19]

N *Nominal gains or losses* (or even fictitious or forfeited incomes) are sometimes used for assessing taxes. In principle, only real entities will affect economic behavior. However, when used for purposes of assessing taxes, fictitious values do indeed become real ones. In this sense, they can affect behavior and by consequence have an influence on real wealth and welfare. Consider the case of the fictitious value of using one's own home. Under the Dutch tax code, for instance, the forfeited benefit of living in one's own home is calculated not on the basis of rents for equivalent leases, but on the basis of the value of the real estate. This figure is then added to the taxable income, adding to the progressive burden of the income tax. In principle, from a social policy point of view, the objective is to have as much home ownership as possible. Home ownership advantages include provisions for old age or other vicissitudes of life, the stability of neighborhoods, health considerations and the general experience that privately-owned housing stock is better and more efficiently maintained than publicly- or institutionally-owned housing. Now consider a family with a modest income that has inherited a valuable house. The fictitious rental value of the house will be added to the income of that family, but the costs of maintaining the house, the opportunity costs of capital contained in the real estate and the opportunity costs of work upon the house are not deducted from this forfeited income. Consequently, the deck is stacked against private home ownership, thereby frustrating attainment of the traditional social policy objective. It is unlikely that this result is based on a conscious decision of parliament.

O *Off-shore activities* are a clear indication of a weak tax administration, as they document opportunities of taxation forgone. The remedy lies in creating a climate in which the business can thrive on-shore and simultaneously serve as a basis for taxation.

P *Public works* intended to overcome chronic unemployment or other forms of economic depression are often funded from tax revenues, thereby adding to the burden of taxation and to the welfare loss of taxation. Even if the measures are effective in creating opportunities for employment, through the method of funding they at the same time decrease similar opportunities in the sector subject to taxation and dampen demand for investment and consumption. For these reasons, self-financing forms of public works are preferable, such as those designed by Wilhelm Lautenbach and implemented between 1932 and 1935. In relying on the Keynesian multiplier and accelerator effects, the funds spent wisely yield a return that constitutes the original fund.[20]

Q *Quality of service* can be tied to taxation through the benefit principle. Wicksell suggested the benefit principle, which has been a core element of the canons of taxation ever since Justi and Adam Smith in a specific institutionalized form. By insisting on consensual taxation (near unanimity rule) and simultaneity of decisions on taxation and expenditure, taxes are tied to the benefits indeed received, and institutional provisions have to be taken to ensure that tax yields decline *in tandem* with benefits and vice versa. This can be accomplished by tying the taxes owed to the receipt and approval of specific services, implying the expression of disapproval by opting out of the bundle of taxes and services.

R The *Ricardian equivalence theorem* holding the equivalence between taxation and bond issue has to be taken as one of the typical theorems of limitation that form the basis of economic analysis. Similar theorems are those by Modigliani-Miller and Coase. In emphasizing the specific conditions under which the theorem holds, our attention is pointed to those cases in which the conditions are not met. Hence, the equivalence theorem cannot be taken at face value. It serves to emphasize the distortions that occur when the future burden of the bond issue is not accurately perceived by the present generation or cannot adequately be compensated for in the present decisions of future taxpayers.[21]

S *Surprises* are the focus of much work in fiscal sociology, as we try to detect and predict the unanticipated consequences of regulation and taxation. For instance, Laband[22] has recently shown that the effects of regulation designed to protect the habitat of endangered species are likely to endanger those very species. For instance, if the habitat of birds that nest in

particular trees is protected and such trees cannot be cut for logging purposes, logging firms will eliminate those trees from their forests before they
attain the required age, thereby eliminating the habitat intended to be protected. If an entire area is targeted for protection, logging firms will relin-
quish their activities in these areas, whereby forestry activity will stop and
land will revert to other uses. In both of these cases, the intended effect of
the regulation is subverted, since the regulation is written *against* the interests of the regulated instead of tying together the interests of the regulated
and of the beneficiary of the regulation.

T *Time* is an important element in determining the intended and unintended effects of taxation and regulation. The bagel diagram shown previously is completely static. In the long run, the effects of regulation and
taxation cumulate and citizens learn to reduce the burden of taxation,
thereby increasing the welfare loss, as the economy moves successively
away from the production possibility frontier and polity and society follow.

U *Utility* is distinguished by Pareto from ophelimity in order to distinguish
between those effects that occur in the economy and those further repercussions that affect society in different ways. In principle, Pareto thought
that utility was in the eye of the beholder, while ophelimity could be measured. Utility can be experienced in terms of oneself or other members of
society, as well as in terms of society's situation and development. About
the latter very little can be done by an individual, and individuals may disagree strongly with each other. Further, an individual's ability to influence
the utility he or she ascribes to the well-being of another is equally constrained. What can be objectively observed is how individuals try to improve their own well-being, and hence ophelimity can in principle be
inferred, at least in an ordinal way. As we move beyond the economic
sphere into the political and social effects of regulation and taxation, we
need to work with both the notion of ophelimity and the different notions
of utility, as Pareto had suggested.

V *Value and votes* are closely connected. For example, in the polity voting is used to determine the outcome of public policy, including the welfare effects of taxation and regulation. While in their individual behavior
voters try to reduce the burden of taxation and regulation, this may not
necessarily be the case in their political behavior, as the benefits from a
particular program may be concentrated on some, while the burden can
be spread over many and in such a way that it is not worth their while to
mount an effort at defeating the burdensome program. Votes are the currency of the political process, and it takes real resources to muster the
political strength as expressed in votes to launch or defeat particular programs.

W *Wealth*, its production, enhancement and preservation, depend critically on very specific aspects of the tax system. This has already been noted in the context of the taxation of fictitious incomes. In fact, in that example the tax structure affects the architectural heritage of the people. Likewise, in assessing wealth, human capital and its formation need to be included along with all manifestations of the cultural heritage, such as libraries, museums, institutions of higher learning, architectural landscapes and the like. All these depend crucially on specific provisions in the tax code, such as education credits, deductions for charitable activities, deductions for maintaining national monuments, encouragement for endowing foundations or chairs at universities and the like. We note that there are countless ramifications and interconnections between the tax structure and all aspects of society that can be ascertained through a wide definition of wealth as we have discussed here, so as to capture all manner of sociological effects of taxation and regulation.

X *X-inefficiency* is the difference between the ability of an organization to perform and its actual performance. As an organization, a firm, a household, a family and the like tries to minimize the burden it has to bear through taxation and regulation, it moves away from its efficient allocation of resources and thereby creates X-inefficiency. Hence, to the extent that we can demonstrate these effects, we can point to strategies of reducing X-inefficiency that do not lie within the organization, but are at the disposal of policymakers as they decide on issues of regulation and taxation that establish the environment in which the organizations have to operate. While organizational theory has emphasized X-inefficiency in the context of intra-organizational strategies of improving performance, a fiscal sociological approach can emphasize extra-organizational strategies to reduce X-inefficiency.

Y The *yield* of taxation tends to be entirely overestimated, as the cost of taxation can never be completely established since taxpayers and agents under regulation have no desire to cheaply provide information about their avoidance behavior. From this point of view, it is advisable to use forms of revenue generation that strictly follow the benefit principle, as the *quid pro quo* between taxes and services tends to leave no excess burden and creates incentives to generate information about the transactions between the government and the private sector.

Z *Zero-based budgeting* has often been suggested as a strategy to make budgets manageable and to contain the growth of government. However, as citizens learn to deal with taxation and regulation just as well as expenditure programs, they are able to decrease distortions over time. When entire programs or tax systems are questioned abruptly, the learning done by individuals and organizations is undone and additional costs of transactions are imposed on economy and society. What is required instead are budgetary procedures that incorporate as much decentralized information as possible. Using the insights from Hayek's piece on the use of knowledge in society, this can be a plea to organize as much governmental activity as possible in a market context so as to make an optimal use of knowledge in society by both public and private market participants.

III

Fiscal Sociology as a Field of Instruction and Research

Instruction

In emphasizing opportunities for research and instruction in fiscal sociology, a good start is Humboldt's principle[23] of a unity of research and teaching at the university level. Although this principle seems to fly in the face of the economic principle of the division of labor, a closer look shows that it actually reinforces this principle. Universities as institutions for basic research and high-level instruction have to maintain, increase and communicate that type of knowledge that is not readily canonized into mass education. It is necessarily the role of a research university to be small in the sense of having many small centers of learning where scholars and students can interact directly. In these terms, teaching and research opportunities can very well overlap.

As a field of teaching, fiscal sociology offers fascinating opportunities at all levels of instruction.

At the bachelor's level, elements of fiscal practice can be integrated into the course of study. Consider the bargaining situation between a regulator and a regulated activity, such as the process of applying for a building permit; alternatively, consider negotiations after filing a tax return. These cases can be realistically simulated in the curriculum and students can be introduced into the climate of adversary negotiations. Through such a method, technical concepts such as the rectangles and the triangles shown in the earlier diagram can be imbued with life and may be readily grasped by students who favor non-technical disciplines and therefore might shy away from taking an economics course.

At the master's level, this experience can be built upon. The expertise would now have to be raised to the professional level; since fiscal sociology includes a study of the unintended impact of taxation as well as regulation, it has implications for almost every activity of government that somehow affects the private sector. In addition to this, there is a wide field of professional activities in both government and the respective governmental counterpart in which a proper understanding of these effects is of great use. Hence, the supply of interesting topics for master theses is inexhaustible.

At the Ph.D. level, it is difficult to encourage students to pursue an academic career, given the current conditions of widespread underfunding of universities and the iron cartel of public universities with few private initiatives that can have a chance under such circumstances. Fiscal sociology, however, is to such an extent an underresearched field that a wealth of research opportunities exists with tangible benefits to both governmental and private agents. And this should, if sufficient effort at convincing sponsors of the use of this work is undertaken, provide for research opportunities that are appealing, even to the most frugal budget administrator.

Research

As we noted previously, before the dissolution of the unity of *Staatswissenschaften*, scholarly activity was able to center on legislative projects, such as the civil code, the welfare state and the like. These concerted efforts can, with difficulty, be accomplished again in the context of focused niche subdisciplines. We have recently seen the emergence of health economics, which is a niche subdiscipline combining every conceivable economic method to analyze health-related issues and institutions. Another such instance is the recent emergence of the subdiscipline of law and economics. Fiscal sociology can be positioned in a similar way. These niche subdisciplines that bridge otherwise separate scholarly pursuits can play a pivotal role in facilitating focused research on major legislative endeavors.[24]

Example 1: With the further integration of the European Union, a repetition of the large legislative project of the civil code will now have to be made. A framework legislation for a common civil code in the European Union, including harmonization and union access, will have to be forthcoming and will have to address issues of taxation and regulation while helping to integrate diverse legal institutions and cultures. Research into unintended side effects of regulation and taxation will be of immense importance for facilitating such a project.

Example 2: The key concept of public finance is Wicksell's principle of just taxation, which entails a simultaneous process of deciding on taxes and expenditures. With the further integration of the European Union, a framework legislation will have to satisfy this principle and also allow for popular decisions to be efficiently and effectively made by acknowledging the different histories, cultures and institutions of the different member states. Frey and Eichenberger's (1999) suggestion of functionally overlapping competing jurisdictions is one such attempt. Research into unintended consequences of such decision making will have to be a necessary companion of launching such initiatives.

Example 3: With further integration of the European Union, some framework legislation for customs and excise taxes will have to be forthcoming that allows for the different member states and their subdivisions to remain sovereign and democratically constituted while at the same time allowing for harmonization and a minimization of the burden of those custom duties and excise taxes. Again, research into the side effects of legislation on excise taxes and customs duties will be necessary in order to help design efficient legislative proposals.

IV

Conclusion

IN CONCLUSION, fiscal sociology offers ample opportunities for research and instruction that can be said to be truly helpful in reducing the adverse effects of government activity and thereby enhancing the welfare and wealth of nations.

Notes

1. The *Deutsche Gesellschaft für Soziologie* was founded in 1909 as an expression of specific research questions and paradigms not generally pursued by economists. For instance, Durkheim and, later, Franz Oppenheimer explored the connections between economic conditions and people's health states;

Durkheim's were the pioneering studies on suicide. Pareto, having completed the *Manual of Political Economy*, saw a need to push beyond economics proper and constructed a generalized social system in his treatise translated as "The Mind and Society" by Livingston. Simmel presented in Schmoller's seminar a socio-philosophical study of money, exploring all those aspects of money that are not economic. See also: Backhaus and Stadermann (2000a) and (2000b). Sombart was interested in the conditions that led to the development of modern capitalism and in his historical studies had to go beyond economic causes, emphasizing social, political and legal preconditions for the development of capitalist institutions. Tönnies emphasized community and society, while Weber left us the gigantic attempt at *Economy and Society.*

2. The last instance of a close cooperation between economists and lawyers may have been the critique of the first draft of the German civil code, mounted by Schmoller and Gierke, which led to the second draft that was signed into law in 1896 and became effective from 1900 to this very day. See also Backhaus (1999a) and (1999b).

3. One may have been the early attempt by Christian Wolff, who tried to put the entire system within his edifice of natural law. See Backhaus (1998a).

4. Shionoya and Perlman (1994).

5. The only exception seems to be Richard E. Wagner's public finance textbook.

6. He taught public finance at the University of Bonn from 1925 to 1932 and contributed fiscal analyses extensively to Wolfgang Stolper's "Der deutsche Volkswirt."

7. Schumpeter, Joseph A. (1928). *Das deutsche Finanzproblem*. Berlin: Der deutsche Volkswirt.

———. (1939). *Business Cycles*. New York: McGraw Hill, 1964.

———. (1943). *Capitalism, Socialism and Democracy*. London: Unwin.

———. (1954a). *A History of Economic Analysis*. New York: Oxford University Press.

———. (1954b). *Dogmenhistorische und biographische Aufsätze*. Tübingen: Mohr Siebeck.

———. (1961). *A Theory of Economic Development*. New York: Oxford University Press.

———. (1965). *Ten Great Economists: From Marx to Keynes*. New York: Oxford University Press.

———. (1967). *Economic Doctrine and Method*. New York: Oxford University Press.

———. (1970). *Das Wesen des Geldes*. Göttingen: Vandenhoek & Ruprecht.

———. (1985). *Aufsätze zur Wirtschaftspolitik*. C. Seidl and W. F. Stolper, eds. Tübingen: Mohr Siebeck.

———. (1992). *Politische Reden*. Tübingen: Mohr Siebeck.

———. (1993). *Aufsätze zur Tagespolitik*. Tübingen: Mohr Siebeck.

———. (2000). *Briefe/Letters*. U. Hetke and R. Swedberg, eds. Tübingen: Mohr Siebeck.

8. Both the original and the translation can be found at our website: www.uni-erfurt.de. Forthcoming in Backhaus (2001).

9. Buchanan (1979).

10. Hayek (1945).

11. Backhaus (1998b).

12. Hansen (1966).

13. Tullock (1987).

14. Backhaus, Holcombe and Zardkoohi (1987).

15. Backhaus (1993).

16. A classical paper is by Bruno S. Frey who showed that increases in development aid may increase weapons imports by the recipient countries. See Frey (1975).

17. Backhaus (1991).

18. Thüringer Ministerium für Wissenschaft, Forschung und Kunst, ThüringerLandeshaushalt, Kapitel 1524 Titelgruppe 84: Förderung von Frauen in Forschung und Lehre, 2000.

19. Backhaus (1998b).

20. Backhaus (1985).

21. On these limitational theorems see Backhaus (1986).

22. See Laband (2000).

23. Incidentally, this forceful reformer of cultural institutions closed the old (1392) University of Erfurt for not being willing to go with the times.

24. The leading journal in economics in the German language area during the time of these large legislative endeavors was notably called *Annals of Legislation, Administration and Economics (Jahrbücher für Gesetzgebung, Verwaltung und Volkswirtschaft)*.

References

Backhaus, Jürgen G. (1985). "An Essay on Keynesianism in Germany," in *Keynes' Economics: Methodological Issues*, T. Lawson and M. H. Pesaran, eds. London: Croom Helm.

———. (1986). "An Impossible Economist," in *No Way: On the Nature of the Impossible*, Phil. J. Davis and David Park, eds. New York: W.R. Freeman.

———, ed. (1991). The Economic Emancipation of Women and the Tax System, *Journal of Economic Studies* 18 (5/6).

———, ed. (1993). "The Economics of Science Policy: An Analysis of the Althoff System," *Journal of Economic Studies* 20 (3/4).

———, ed. (1998a). *Christian Wolff and Law and Economics*. New York: Georg Olms Verlag.

———. (1998b). "When Should the Ecotax Kick In? A Cost and Choice Approach," *Kyklos* 51 (4): 565–575.

————, ed. (1999a). "The German Civil Code of 1896," *European Journal of Law and Economics* 7 (1).

————. (1999b). "Otto von Gierke," in *Elgar Companion to Law and Economics,* Jürgen G. Backhaus, ed. Cheltenham, UK: Edward Elgar.

————. (forthcoming). *Schumpeter (1884–1950): His German Contributions: The European Heritage.* Boston: Kluwer.

Backhaus, Jürgen G., Randall G. Holcombe, and Asghar Zardkoohi. (1987). "Public Investments and Its Effects on the Burden of the Public Debt," *Southern Economic Journal* 54 (1): 145–158.

Backhaus, Jürgen G. and Hans-Joachim Stadermann, eds. (2000). *Georg Simmels Philosophie des Geldes: Einhundert Jahre danach.* Marburg: Metropolis Verlag.

Buchanan, James M. (1979). *Cost and Choice: An Inquiry in Economic Theory.* Chicago: University of Chicago Press.

Da Empoli, Attilio. (1931). *Theory of Economic Equilibrium: A Study of Marginal and Ultramarginal Phenomena.* Chicago: Christiani & Catenacci.

Frey, Bruno S. (1975). "Weapons, Exports and Aid to Developing Countries," *Journal of Conflict Resolution* 1 (2).

Frey, Bruno S. and Reiner Eichenberger. (1999). *The New Democratic Federalism for Europe: Functional, Overlapping and Competing Jurisdictions.* Cheltenham, UK: Edward Elgar.

Goldscheid, Rudolf. (1919a). *Grundfragen des Menschenschicksals: Gesammelte Aufsätze.* Leipzig: E.P. Tal.

————. (1919b). *Sozialisierung der Wirtschaft oder Staatsbankrott: Ein Sanierungsprogramm.* Leipzig: Anzengruber Verlag: Brüder Suschitzky.

Hansen, Reginald. (1996). *Die praktischen Konsequenzen des Methodenstreits.* Berlin: Duncker & Humblot.

Hayek, Friedrich von. (1945). "The Use of Knowledge in Society," *American Economic Review* 35 (4): 519–530.

Laband, David N. (2000). "The Impact of Unfunded Environmental Mandates When Environmental Quality and Timber are Produced Jointly," *European Journal of Law and Economics* 10 (3): 199–216.

Schumpeter, Joseph Alois. ([1918] 1953). *Die Krise des Steuerstaates.* Graz-Leipzig: Leuschner & Lubensky; reprinted as pp. 1–71 of *International Economic Papers,* vol. IV, W. F. Stolper and R. A. Musgrave, trans. London: Macmillan.

————. ([1942] 1976). *Capitalism, Socialism and Democrac.* London: Unwin.

Shionoya, Yuichi and Mark Perlman, eds. (1994). *Schumpeter in the History of Ideas.* Ann Arbor: University of Michigan Press.

Tullock, Gordon. (1987). *Autocracy.* Dordrecht: Kluwer.

Wicksell, Johann Gustav Knut. (1896). *Finanztheoretische Untersuchungen nebst Darstellung und Kritik des Steuerwesens Schwedens.* Jena: Gustav Fischer.

Voters, Parties, and the Endogenous Size of Government

By Jan-Peter Olters[*]

ABSTRACT. Elections, often to a considerable degree, influence the fiscal policies of governments installed on the basis of their results. Yet, economists have tended to view politicians' behaviour either as being determined exogenously or as the result of a social planner's maximisation of a well-defined social-welfare function (subject to some appropriate technology and resource constraints). The latter approach—given (*i*) its inherent abstraction from important politico-economic interactions, (*ii*) the theoretical difficulty in deriving a non-contradictory "collective utility function" (as demonstrated by Arrow), and (*iii*) the inability to estimate a stable relationship that could explain political preferences with economic variables—is viewed as being an unsatisfactory tool for the joint description of a country's economy and polity. On the basis of explicit micro-economic foundations and a democratically coordinated decision-making mechanism over the "optimal" provision of public goods and the corresponding taxes required to finance them, this paper will introduce a simple *economic model of politics* that subjects individuals to a—two-tiered—political decision-making process over party membership and electoral participation, thereby endogenising the evolution of the competing parties' ideologies, households' electoral behaviour, and the key factors explaining the design of fiscal policies. Having the majority party's *median delegate* determine on the "optimal" degree of income redistribution suggests that a country's wealth distribution is a crucial explanatory variable explaining its politico-economic development path.

* Dr. Olters is an Economist with the International Monetary Fund, 700 19th Street NW, Washington, DC 20431; his e-mail address is jolters@imf.org. The paper draws from the author's thesis (*Endogenous Ballot Decisions and "Optimal" Fluctuations—An Economic Model of Politics*, 2000), written at McGill University in Montreal, Canada. Insightful comments and valuable suggestions by Prof. Venkatesh Bala and Prof. Curtis Eberwein have improved the paper considerably and are gratefully acknowledged. The views expressed in the paper are solely those of the author and do not necessarily reflect the position of the IMF. The standard disclaimer applies.

American Journal of Economics and Sociology, Vol. 61, No. 1 (January, 2002).

I

Introduction

THE LATTER HALF OF THE TWENTIETH CENTURY has witnessed a dramatic rise in productivity and wealth, particularly in Western democracies. But rather than being rewarded, their political élites had to counter growing voter indifference and political apathy. In reacting to (*i*) the electorate's increased average prosperity, (*ii*) a trend decline in electoral participation rates, and (*iii*) a waning sense of party loyalty, politicians have been narrowing their parties' differences in *Weltanschauung*. The corresponding ideological conversion, however, did not take place in a symmetric manner. While the large centre-right parties, for the most part, have changed their policies only relatively moderately,[1] their main opponents underwent a remarkable evolution of programmatic reinventions, progressively moderating their programmes and policies.[2] Changes in governments have subsequently become routine events, notwithstanding the smaller and more subtle differences in political priorities.

This paper will show that these three developments—economic growth, de-politicisation, and ideological conversion—have not only occurred concomitantly but are indeed interrelated and self-reinforcing. The results presented in the following imply that the more prosperous a society (and, particularly, the richer the poor), the more equal will be the competing parties' policies, conforming with the observation that both the households' growing reliance on private goods relative to public ones and the centre-left's increasingly more "conservative" policy platforms have made politics increasingly less relevant for the daily lives of many voters. Rather than representing a protest vote, abstentions can be viewed to signify a general acceptance of the politico-economic status quo. Inversely, as has been first argued by Alesina and Rodrik (1992, 1994) and Persson and Tabellini (1994), a high degree of inequality would result in increased pressures on politicians to redistribute income and wealth at the expense of more dynamic growth rates. Hence, the broadening of a country's political "core consensus," following positive saving rates and increased average prosperity, stimulates growth even further as it reduces the political risk in its economic agents' longer-term investment decisions.

Traditional models in political economy—i.e., those that have a *so-*

cial planner maximise a well-defined *social-welfare function* (subject to some appropriate technology and resource constraints)—are, by definition, unable to capture the essential interactions linking a country's polity and economy.[3] The inherent impossibility to derive a theoretical construct that could, in a consistent and non-contradictory manner, order preferences for a society as a whole, as demonstrated by Arrow (1950, 1951),[4] has been accentuated by the large number of economists who have failed to approximate even an "imperfect" social-welfare function (i.e., to find a stable and statistically significant relationship between economic variables and political preferences).[5]

In general, the—undemocratic—social planner, paired with a "representative consumer," can represent politics in a very stylised and internally consistent manner, but the theoretical cost of such an approach includes the abstraction from decision-making processes determining political parties' policy objectives and the resultant politico-economic dynamics caused by the periodic "re-evaluations" of market outcomes.[6]

Using simple tools, this paper aims at modelling the essential dynamics in the relationship among voters, their elected representatives, and the government, which are deemed necessary to understand the mechanisms by which (*i*) parties stick to their promises, (*ii*) individuals express and coordinate their political preferences, and (*iii*) a country's politico-economic development path is determined. Having political parties represent the institutional link between the government and the electorate, and by describing the factors behind the evolution of their respective policy programmes, this paper will argue that Fukuyama's (1989) eulogy on history was premature. In particular, it will be shown that, even in a deterministic system, election results will fluctuate and governments of different political colours succeed one another.

II

Voting on the "Optimal" Size of Government

1. An Economic Model of Politics

In the following, *politics* will be defined as the democratic, interhousehold conflict-resolution mechanism over the provision and corresponding financing of public goods. Beyond their traditional role as *homines oeconomici* (who supply labour and capital to consume goods and services), households are *homines publici* as well. As such, they decide (*i*) whether to participate in a general election, (*ii*) how to vote, and (*iii*) whether to join a political party. In the last case, members are entitled to co-determine that party's pre-election manifesto. While economic actions influence individuals' gross incomes (i.e., their respective wage and capital earnings), individuals' incentives to be politically engaged stem from the knowledge that the collective decision made in the polling booth determines their salaries' net value (as well as their ability to consume the publicly provided good). Clearly, with the added assumption of a balanced budget requirement, the utility effects of a marginal increase in the amount of the publicly provided good depends on a person's income and wealth (the first derivates being negative), thereby injecting political *dynamics* into the model: changes to the households' income and wealth variables influence their political preferences, both in terms of voting and party-membership decisions, which impact the economy, affecting households' earnings, and so on.

Therefore, and in line with Downs' (1957) initial—and, for the purpose of his subsequent analysis, abandoned—characterisation of political parties, these organisations will be represented as entities that are unable to derive utility independently. Owing to the costs of active political participation (membership dues as well as the long hours spent in meetings and discussions), policy platforms are viewed as representing partisan compromises that have been made *within* a political party—in pre-election conventions or through primaries—in order to accommodate members' diverse policy preferences. They subsequently lack the capacity to devise policies that would follow the internal logic of a Downsian vote-maximiser.[7] Clearly, these programmes are not necessarily optimal in maximising the probability of winning an election, but are necessary to hold together the heterogeneous interests of party members and secure partisan cohesion. By representing political parties in this way, it is easier to explain why, for instance, large groups of unpaid volunteers actively support candidates who—even if ultimately successful—are not able to offer any direct benefits in terms of jobs, monetary compensation, or professional promotion.

Figure 1

On the Nature of Politico-Economic Interaction

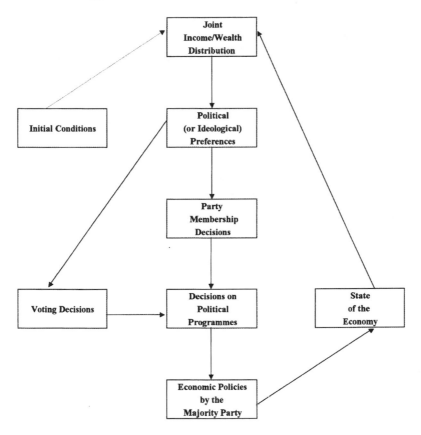

Figure 1 schematically summarises the basic design of the model presented below. Central to its understanding are the particular positions of households[8] within the income/wealth space, which determine the types of policies they would like to see pursued. In turn, the ideological difference in the parties' proposed policies influences the intensity of the households' political interests. If these are particularly strong—i.e., if voters have a lot to gain or lose as a result of a change in policies—households have larger incentives not only to vote but also to join and actively shape the programmes of political parties.

2. The Economy

The underlying economy is described by a "shockless," real-business-cycle-type macro-economic model. Basic economic decisions are made in the three traditional markets of goods, capital, and labour. The following list of additional assumptions will help to focus on the essential elements of the model: (*i*) the economy is closed; (*ii*) the population (the labour force/the electorate) does not grow; (*iii*) prices in all markets are flexible; (*iv*) there is no technological progress; (*v*) government consists of only one (the federal) level; (*vi*) policymakers are obliged to balance their budgets at all times; and (*vii*) there is no inflation.

Firms supply goods and services at market prices, which households consume together with the public good (financed by the government with the revenues from a proportional income tax). The publicly provided good (e.g., health and education), while valued by the voters, neither stimulates nor retards economic growth throughout the course of the current legislative period. A standard Cobb-Douglas production function allocates an income share α (with $\alpha < 1$) to the production factor capital and $(1 - \alpha)$ to labour. A is the economy's productivity parameter. Therefore,

$$Y_t^S = AK_{t-1}^\alpha N^{1-\alpha}, \tag{1}$$

where N represents the labour force and K_{t-1} the stock of capital accumulated until the end of period $t - 1$ for production in period t (that is, K_{t-1} is generally known in t). Consequently, the output level Y_t^S, which is produced by utilising all available production factors at normal levels, is not a function of the economic policies pursued by the government elected for period t. Assuming unfettered competition, all production factors are paid their marginal products. Aggregate capital income, $r_t K_{t-1}$, thus equals αY_t^S. Analogously, aggregate labour (or wage) income, $w_t N$, is equal to $(1 - \alpha)Y_t^S$.

In this closed economy, goods and services will be demanded by the private sector for either consumption, C_t, or investment, I_t, and by the government for the provision of the public good, G_t^j. The superscript j denotes "as being implemented by party j." Therefore,

$$Y_t^D = C_t + I_t + G_t^j. \tag{2}$$

Goods markets are assumed to clear continuously, i.e., $Y_t^S = Y_t^D \equiv Y_t$, $\forall t$. (As the derivation of the "optimal" amount of government spending[9] motivates this paper, G_t^j will be derived in the following.) For reasons of mathematical simplicity, it will furthermore be assumed that the underlying decision-making process leading to the private sector's determination of both consumption and investment remain stable over time and can be represented by linear equations with econometrically determined parameters. Hence,

$$c_{it} = \hat{\beta}_{i0}^c + \hat{\beta}_{iy}^c \left(1 - \tau_t^j\right)\left(w_{it} + r_t k_{it-1}\right), \tag{3}$$

where $\hat{\beta}_{i0}^c$ represents autonomous consumption, $\hat{\beta}_y^c$ the marginal propensity to consume, τ_t^j a proportional income tax, k_{it-1} individual i's non-human capital stock, and w_{it} his or her wage rate. To generate a dispersion in labour incomes, every individual will be represented with a different, exogenously determined degree of labour productivity, denoted φ_i, so that

$$w_{it} = \varphi_i w_t, \text{ with } \varphi_i 0 \, \varepsilon R^+ \text{ and } \frac{1}{N} \sum_{i=1}^N \varphi_i = 1. \tag{4}$$

Defining $\hat{\beta}_0^c = \sum_{i=1}^N \hat{\beta}_{i0}^c$ and $\hat{\beta}_y^c = \frac{1}{N} \sum_{i=1}^N \hat{\beta}_{iy}^c$, equation (3) can be rewritten to yield an expression for aggregate consumption:

$$C_t = \hat{\beta}_0^c + \hat{\beta}_y^c \left(1 - \tau_t^j\right)\left(w_t N + r_t K_{t-1}\right). \tag{5}$$

With the balanced-budget requirement, tax revenues, by definition, are equal to government spending, i.e., $G_t^j = \tau_t^j Y_t$. Rewriting the goods market equilibrium condition in (2)—and substituting (5) and the balanced-budget expression into that equation—yields an expression for aggregate investment (or, equivalently, an expression for the demand for loanable funds):

$$I_t = \sum_{i=1}^{N} S_{it} = -\hat{\beta}_0^c + \left(1 - \hat{\beta}_y^c\right)\left(1 - \tau_t^j\right)Y_t. \tag{6}$$

Consequently, higher government expenditures, requiring higher income-tax rates, reduce aggregate consumption and crowd out private-sector investment as $\partial I_t / \partial \tau_t^j = -(1-\hat{\beta}_y^c)Y_t$. This outcome will affect the next period's—and the next government's—ability to produce goods and services. Every individual inelastically supplies one unit of labour in exchange for a pay check, which is equal to his or her marginal contribution.

3. The Electorate

While the function according to which households derive utility is identical for all individuals, voters are individualised through distinct, exogenously determined degrees of labour productivity and initial wealth endowments. The voters' general satisfaction, denoted u, is defined in terms of present-period consumption of private and public goods, c_{it} and G_t^j:

$$u_{it} = u\left(c_{it}\left(\tau_t^j\right), G_t^j\right), \tag{7}$$

where $\partial u_{it} / \partial \tau_t^j < 0$ and $\partial u_{it} / \partial G_t^j > 0$. The two politically determined variables thus directly affect i's degree of material satisfaction. Therefore, the tradeoff between the marginal disutility caused by an incremental increase in taxes and the marginal utility generated by a corresponding expansion in the provision of the public good ultimately shapes i's political preferences.

Households form expectations in a manner consistent with Simon's (1982) approach—being "boundedly rational," they understand the underlying model as much as the government does, and they possess the ability to form conditional expectations over the one parliamentary term ahead. They are familiar with the relevant econometric techniques needed to make learned forecasts—or, at a minimum, they have costless access to the results of these estimates. Before casting their votes, households calculate the expected income-tax rates and the amount of the public good implicit in the policy programmes presented by the competing parties. On that basis, they compare their expected conditional utility payoffs and decide on their voting intentions:

$$
\left.\begin{array}{l} v_{it}^{(+j)} = 1 \\ v_{it}^{(-j)} = 0 \end{array}\right\} \text{ iff } u_{it}\!\left(c_{it}^{*(+j)}, G_t^{*(+j)}\right) - u_{it}\!\left(c_{it}^{*(-j)}, G_t^{*(-j)}\right) > \xi,
$$

$$
\left.\begin{array}{l} v_{it}^{(+j)} = 0 \\ v_{it}^{(-j)} = 0 \end{array}\right\} \text{ iff } \xi \geq u_{it}\!\left(c_{it}^{*(+j)}, G_t^{*(+j)}\right) - u_{it}\!\left(c_{it}^{*(-j)}, G_t^{*(-j)}\right) \geq -\xi, \qquad (8)
$$

$$
\left.\begin{array}{l} v_{it}^{(+j)} = 0 \\ v_{it}^{(-j)} = 1 \end{array}\right\} \text{ iff } u_{it}\!\left(c_{it}^{*(+j)}, G_t^{*(+j)}\right) - u_{it}\!\left(c_{it}^{*(-j)}, G_t^{*(-j)}\right) < -\xi.
$$

The (exogenous) parameter ξ represents the cost of voting; it is assumed to be zero or small.[10] The superscripts $*(\pm j)$ denote the conditional expectations given the implementation of party $(\pm j)$'s "optimal" policy programme. In cases in which the expected utility differences are smaller than the cost of voting, i is indifferent and therefore abstains. The number of households casting their ballots in the election at time t will be symbolised by N_t^v and those abstaining by N_t^a, where $N_t^v + N_t^a = N$.

4. Political Parties

The two main parties in most Western countries—the centre-right and the centre-left—can trace their historical roots to the political confrontation between *capital* and *labour* in the late nineteenth century. With time, this functional separation of an electorate along production factors has, however, become increasingly meaningless. By contrast, the *economic* aspect of the electorate's socio-economic categorisation still plays an important role in determining the behaviour of an individual inside the voting booth.[11]

Subsequently, political parties are defined as coalitions—or organised interest groups—of households with similar economic characteristics.[12] From that definition, it follows that members seek to gain temporary control over the available fiscal-policy tools in order to improve their overall economic situation. Hence, if elected, party j is expected to fully capitalise on its privilege of incumbency and pursue the policies specified in its pre-election programme.[13] Subsequently, if party j succeeds in securing popular support in excess of 50 per cent

---

BOX 1
Germany's Federal Election in 1998 and the Cost of Voting

Of the 60.8 million Germans entitled to vote in the 1998 federal election,* 46.4 million* chose a party with a realistic chance to clear the threshold of 5 per cent required to be represented in the 656-seat *Bundestag* (Germany's lower house).** A typical constituency thus had a little more than 70,000 voters—implying that every voter's likelihood of having the decisive vote equals about 0.000014.

At the end of 1997, there were 66.2 million* Germans aged 18 and older. During the period 1995–1998, the previous parliamentary term, these Germans earned an (accumulated) average GDP of US$137,430,*** which the central government taxed at an average rate of 31.65 per cent (central government revenue divided by GDP),*** equivalent to US$43,497.

Assuming alternatively proposed (federal) tax rates of 30 and 35 per cent and no change in average income, the implicit tax obligations would equal US$41,229 and US$48,101. If one supposes that the election will result in a political equilibrium, in which the cash value of the public good equals the average tax rate, the "political exposure" of different individuals can be easily calculated:

In US dollars	Individual 1	Individual 2
Income	60,000	300,000
Tax R (30 per cent)	18,000	90,000
Tax L (35 per cent)	21,000	105,000
Difference in "disutility"	3,000	15,000
Public good R	41,229	41,229
Public good L	48,101	48,801
Difference in "utility"	6,872	6,872
Total difference of L over R	+3,872	−8,128

Hence, with unchanged income and a utility function that is linear in private and public consumption, the figures in the above table imply that individuals 1 and 2 would make the "rational decision" to vote for L and R, respectively, if their cost of voting did not exceed 5 and 11 cents.

*Statistisches Bundesamt. (1999). *Statistisches Jahrbuch 1999 für die Bundesrepublik Deutschland*. Stuttgart: Metzler-Poeschel.

**The Social Democrats (SPD), the Christian Democrats (CDU/CSU), the Greens (Bündnis 90/die Grünen), the Liberals (FDP), or the Post-Communists (PDS). In addition to the regular 656 members of parliament, the 14th *Bundestag* has 13 so-called *Überhangmandate*, i.e., seats won in addition to the number a party has gained through proportional representation.

***International Monetary Fund. (2001). *International Financial Statistics—July 2001*. Washington: IMF.

of those households casting ballots, it is democratically legitimised to form the government during period t. Formally, party j, if elected into office, will be denoted J_t :

$$j \rightarrow J_t \text{ iff } V_{jt} = \frac{1}{N_t^v} \sum_{i=1}^{N_t^v} v_{it}^j > \frac{1}{2},$$ (9)

where V_{jt} is the share of votes cast for $j \in \{-j, +j\}$ in t and $V_{(+j)t} + V_{(-j)t} = 1 \ \forall t$.[14] The idea of j caring about the same variables as individuals do is captured by modelling a political objective function, denoted Γ_{jt}, which approximates its members' utility functions:

$$\Gamma_{jt} = \ln\left(N^{-1}\hat{\beta}_0^c + \hat{\beta}_y^c\left(1 - \tau_t^j\right)\left(\Omega_{jt}^w w_t + r_t\Omega_{jt}^k\right)\right) + \frac{\lambda \ln\left(G_t^j\right)}{\left(\Omega_{jt}^w w_t + r_t\Omega_{jt}^k\right)^\vartheta}$$ (10)

where the variable Ω_{jt}^w represents—see (11)—the median amount of human capital (labour productivity) among j's members and Ω_{jt}^k the median non-human capital, thereby reflecting j's "ideological" emphasis on labour and capital income, respectively. The parameter λ captures the exogenously determined cultural differences in the valuation of the public good. Implicit in the definition of party j's objective function is the idea that, for all $\vartheta \neq 0$, its valuation of public goods is inversely related to the median of the party members' gross incomes. The determination of these ideological variables results from j's programmatic pre-election convention, in which all members of j at t, m_{jt}, decide on j's most-favoured ideological positions—Ω_{jt}^w and Ω_{jt}^k.

By assuming that (*i*) the joint distribution of wealth and income is general knowledge, (*ii*) the (opportunity) costs of party membership are relatively high, and (*iii*) the internal balance defining the party's pre-election position is sensitive to shifts in policy positions (leading to defections and, potentially, the breakup of a political party), both pre-election strategising and post-election moral hazard problems become unlikely.[15] And if everyone knows the preferences and the political interests of the party members, voters who are not party members will be able to rationally form expectations over the actual policy programme—even if politicians campaign on policy platforms that are incongruous with the true political agenda. Therefore,

$$\Omega_{jt}^w = \operatorname*{med}_{m_j=1}^{M_{jt}}\left(\varphi_{m_j}\right) \text{ and } \Omega_{jt}^k = \operatorname*{med}_{m_j=1}^{M_{jt}}\left(k_{m_jt-1}\right), \tag{11}$$

where med($\cdot$) represents the median of the M_{jt} party members' income and wealth variables, respectively. If elected, j will pursue fiscal policies as described below.

Prior to the programmatic decision made in (11), i must have determined whether to become a party member (in which case he or she would be privileged to co-determine Ω_{jt}^w and Ω_{jt}^k in the way described above). This decision is a reflection of i's political interest, which is generated by large utility differences implicit in the party programmes proposed during the previous period's election campaign: if the ideological variable has generated excess utility over the alternatively proposed (or implemented) policy programme beyond the constant cost of political participation, denoted Ξ,[16] then i will join j in t, i.e., $i \in j$ iff

$$u_{it-1}\left(c_{it-1}^{*(+j)}, G_{t-1}^{*(+j)}\right) - u_{it-1}\left(c_{it-1}^{*(-j)}, G_{t-1}^{*(-j)}\right) \geq \Xi. \tag{12}$$

Otherwise, the costs of political participation outweigh the benefits and i remains an "armchair democrat."

It is important to note that, while the voting decision is made in a boundedly rational and forward-looking manner, the one regarding party membership is backward-looking. This assumption has been made for two reasons. First, since party-membership decisions precede the determination of the parties' ideologies, as represented by Ω_{jt}^w and Ω_{jt}^k in (11); at that time, individuals are—*per definitionem*—unaware of the eventual programmes (see also Figure 1). The backward-looking manner also reflects the fact that party-membership decisions tend to reflect longer-term commitments, which have been motivated by experiences made in previous periods. Second, the combination of pre-election manifestos (being determined with a one-period lag) and voting decisions (made on the basis of expectations) allows for "corrective actions" and, thus, the generation of electoral fluctuations in a completely deterministic system (see below).

5. "Optimal" Party Platforms and Government Policies

As long as neither r_t nor w_t depend on the present government's policies, the parties' ideology expression can be simplified to read

$$\Omega_{jt} = \Omega_{jt}^w w_t + r_t \Omega_{jt}^k. \tag{13}$$

Once card-carrying members of political parties have established their respective ideology parameters Ω_{jt}^w and Ω_{jt}^k (and, hence, Ω_{jt}), representing the median delegate's gross income, the political parties solve the following constrained maximisation problem:

$$\max_{\{\tau, G\}} \Gamma_{jt} = \ln\left(\frac{\hat{\beta}_0^c}{N} + \hat{\beta}_y^c\left(1 - \tau_t^j\right)\Omega_{jt}\right) + \frac{\lambda}{\Omega_{jt}^\vartheta}\ln\left(G_t^j\right) \tag{14}$$

subject to $\tau_t^j Y_t = G_t$.

The first-order condition, after substituting the constraint into the objective function, is

$$\frac{\partial \Gamma_t}{\partial G_t^j} : \frac{\lambda}{\Omega_{jt}^\vartheta G_t^j} \cdot \frac{\hat{\beta}_y^c \Omega_{jt}}{N^{-1}\hat{\beta}_0^c Y_t + \hat{\beta}_y^c \Omega_{jt}\left(Y_t - G_t^j\right)} \equiv 0. \tag{15}$$

Solving (15) for G_t^j yields the following expression for either party's "optimal" amount of government spending:

$$G_t^{*(\pm j)} = \frac{\left(N^{-1}\hat{\beta}_0^c + \hat{\beta}_y^c \Omega_{jt}\right)\lambda Y_t}{\left(\lambda + \Omega_{jt}^\vartheta\right)\hat{\beta}_y^c \Omega_{jt}}. \tag{16}$$

Given (16), the "optimal" tax rate implicit in $(\pm j)$'s policy programme is $\tau_t^{*(\pm j)} = G_t^{*(\pm j)}/Y_t$. Moreover, the expression demonstrates that (*i*) the "optimal" level of government spending increases with the size of the economy and (*ii*) political parties that represent a clientele with higher streams of labour and capital income will propose a lower level of government spending than do those representing poorer voters, as

$$\frac{\partial G_t^{*(\pm j)}}{\partial \Omega_{jt}} = -\frac{\lambda Y_t\left(N^{-1}\hat{\beta}_0^{\varsigma}\left(\lambda + (\vartheta + 1)\Omega_{jt}^{\vartheta}\right) + \vartheta\hat{\beta}_{\bar{y}}^{\varsigma}\Omega_{jt}^{\vartheta+1}\right)}{\hat{\beta}_{\bar{y}}^{\varsigma}\Omega_{jt}^2\left(\lambda + \Omega_{jt}^{\vartheta}\right)^2} < 0. \qquad (17)$$

Those differences, however, are diminishing with further increases in the policy-platform parameter Ω_{jt} as

$$\frac{\partial^2 G_t^{*(\pm j)}}{\partial \Omega_{jt}^2} = \frac{\lambda Y_t\left(a_1 + a_2\Omega_{jt}^{\vartheta} + a_3\Omega_{jt}^{\vartheta+1} + a_4\Omega_{jt}^{2\vartheta} + a_5\Omega_{jt}^{2\vartheta+1}\right)}{\hat{\beta}_{\bar{y}}^{\varsigma}\Omega_{jt}^3\left(\lambda + \Omega_{jt}^{\vartheta}\right)^3} > 0. \qquad (18)$$

Equation (18) is positive as the terms a_1, a_2, a_4, and a_5 are positive and a_3 non-negative:

$$a_1 = 2N^{-1}\hat{\beta}_0^{\varsigma}\lambda^2 > 0,\, a_2 = (\vartheta + 1)N^{-1}\hat{\beta}_0^{\varsigma}(4 - \vartheta) > 0,$$
$$a_3 = \hat{\beta}_{\bar{y}}^{\varsigma}\vartheta\lambda(1 - \vartheta) \geq 0,\, a_4 = N^{-1}\hat{\beta}_0^{\varsigma}(\vartheta + 1)(\vartheta + 2) > 0, \text{ and}$$
$$a_5 = \hat{\beta}_{\bar{y}}^{\varsigma}\vartheta(\vartheta + 1) > 0.$$

The partial derivatives of $G_t^{*(\pm j)}$ with respect to $\hat{\beta}_{\bar{y}}^{\varsigma}$ also reconfirm economic intuition that, with an increasing marginal propensity to consume (and a balanced-budget requirement), "optimal" government spending decreases.

6. Policy Implications

The economic model of politics (EMP) has sketched the essential elements in the democratic process culminating in the collective decision on the "optimal" size of government as a function of, particularly, total output and the median delegate's income. The proposed approach is broader than most others employed in traditional political-economy models, which—if allowing at all for any explicit element of democratic decision making—have relied on the Downsian median voter or simply the social planner's constrained maximisation of a well-behaved social-welfare function (thus abstracting from any interhousehold *conflicts* that, in the author's view, symbolise the very essence of politics). By representing the social coordination mechanism over the "optimal" provision of public goods as a two-tiered decision-making process regarding votes and party membership, derived on the basis of the households' (explicitly modelled) economic situations, the EMP bases its results on standard micro-economic foundations. Thus, with the median delegate approach, the author believes, the Downsian (1957) median-voter theorem can be extended to add to the comprehension of the political processes and dynamics underlying democratic decisions.

Figure 2 depicts the intuition behind this model's main result. The valuation of public goods by households (and hence the median delegates) is inversely related to their private consumption possibilities. As represented by (17), political parties representing a poorer clientele (L) advocate higher spending, as their supporters greatly benefit from an increased supply of public goods, which are largely financed by voters in higher-income brackets. However, with changing gross incomes, the voters' political preferences change as well; those who see their economic positions improved will become more conservative (and vice versa). This explains why not only voting behaviour, but also party ideologies, change over time. For a country as a whole, this means that, everything else being equal, the result of an (exogenously induced) widening of the income gap will create more dissimilar party programmes and, consequently, larger politically induced fluctuations when a change in government takes place. Hence, the "economic value" of a small degree of inequality in income and wealth can be found in the succession of relatively constant approaches to economic policies—with a correspondingly low amount of politically induced fluctuations and few requirements on the part of firms and households to repeatedly (re)adjust their behaviour, in a substantial manner, to new political environments.

To confirm the intuition behind the EMP, computer simulations have been run, demonstrating the—deterministic—model's ability to generate politico-economic fluctuations and substantiate the aforementioned policy implications.[17] The model's core results are summarized in Figure 3 and represent (*a*) party L's election results (left scale)[18] and overall voter turnout (right scale); (*b*) changes to party-membership and participation rates, including the variation in the median delegates' relative positions; (*c*) the proposed—and actually implemented—income tax rates (left scale) against the background of the development of the country's capital stock (right scale); and (*d*) the households' utility dif-

Figure 2

"Optimal" Amounts of Government Spending

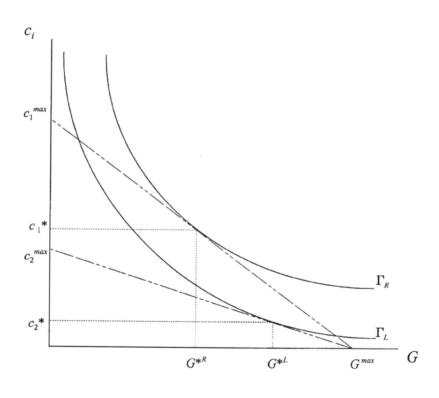

Political preferences: As *homines publici*, individuals determine their preferred composition of consumption goods—i.e., private versus public. In the extreme, if more than half of them decided to pay 100 (0) percent of their income to the government as taxes, every individual's basket of consumption goods would contain only G^{max} (c_i^{max}), with $i \in \{1, 2\}$. In general, however, given the individuals' different levels of income and the two parties' underlying political objective functions, Γ_L and Γ_R, they would—ideally—want to see policies adopted that would allow for a combination $\{c_i^*, G^{*j}\}$, with $j \in \{L, R\}$. With the actual policy determined by the ruling party's *median delegate*—in this case, household 1 (2) for the centre-right (-left) party— one can easily imagine the role that a society's average wealth and its degree of inequality in income and wealth play in determining democratic fiscal policies: a richer economy leads to more conservative left-wing parties, while a more egalitarian society results in milder changes in economic policies following a change in government.

Figure 3

Simulation Results

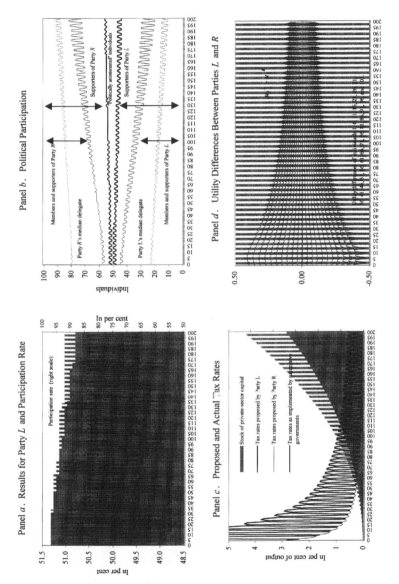

Panel *a*. Results for Party *L* and Participation Rate

Panel *b*. Political Participation

Panel *c*. Proposed and Actual Tax Rates

Panel *d*. Utility Differences Between Parties *L* and *R*

Assumptions: $A = 1.00$, $\alpha = 0.55$, $\beta = 0.45$, $\lambda = 0.045$, $\theta = 1$, $K_{-1} = 630$ (where $k_{101} = 10.0$, $k_{100} = 1.0065 k_{101} - 0.125$, $k_{99} = 1.0065 k_{100} - 0.125$, etc.), $\beta_0 = 0.05$, $\beta_y = 0.75$, $\xi = 0.01$, and $\Xi = 0.05$,

$u = c + \lambda G / (w\Omega_w + r\Omega_r)$.

ferences inherent in the two parties' proposed programmes.[19] In particular, it can be shown that electoral equilibria, if narrowly defined as a given party's unique vote share, do not (necessarily) exist; by contrast, the model shows that democracies move steadily toward an equilibrium "range" within which the key macroeconomic variables oscillate. Furthermore, for the purposes of election forecasts, the centre-left party's *median delegate* appears to be the single most important variable to follow. This result stems from the relatively greater importance of public goods in generating utility for poor households, leading to a larger variability in the pre-election programmes proposed by the party on the left of the political spectrum.

III

Conclusions

THE MEDIAN VOTER DOES NOT VOTE. In fact, he or she is likely not to care about politics at all. Whether one party is in office or another—for the median voter, this will not matter. That, at least, is one of the key results derived in the *economic model of politics* (EMP) discussed above. With politics being defined as the democratic, interhousehold conflict-resolution mechanism over the provision and corresponding financing of public goods, determining the "optimal" redistribution of income and wealth, it is the households further toward the wealth extremes that have the most to gain (or lose) from the political process.

With simple tools, the EMP was able to endogenise essential elements of political behaviour into economic modelling. As such, the EMP extends the median-voter results—so immensely influential in previous political-economy contributions—by having the parties' respective median delegates determine political programmes and policies. In the model, the political process is thus fought both in the centre (deciding elections) and further toward the wealth extremes, where households decide on party membership and policies. As members, they are entitled to co-determine their parties' platforms, with the ultimate programme being "chosen" by the median delegate. Interpreting political parties as coalitions of households with similar economic characteristics, the parties' fiscal policies—if voted into office—would be congruent with the "partisan compromises" found during the party's convention.

Both decisions affect the economy and, by extension, the following period's political preferences, thereby creating fluctuations in the relevant politico-economic variables. Given the two-tiered mechanism of determining the "optimal" provision of public goods, the political process will allow essentially every household, at some point in time, to be represented by a government implementing policies very close to its preferred programme—thereby offering a possible explanation of democracies' longevity.[20]

The EMP simulations highlight a number of interesting insights characterising democratically organised free-market societies. In particular, (*i*) periodic election exercises cause fluctuations in both political and economic variables; (*ii*) "electoral equilibria"—if narrowly defined as a given party's unique vote share—do not (necessarily) exist (the model, however, implies that democracies, when growing, move steadily toward an equilibrium "range," within which the key politico-economic variables oscillate); (*iii*) elections are not necessarily won or lost because a certain number of people has decided to vote differently from the way they used to: crucial variables in the explanation of politico-economic fluctuations are both electoral abstentions and the decisions by households to join or leave a political party; (*iv*) since the relatively larger importance of public relative to private goods for poor households leads to a greater variability in the pre-election programmes proposed by the centre-left party, it follows that the behaviour of its median delegate is, for the purpose of election forecasts, the most important variable to follow; and (*v*) small changes in the households' levels of utility may result in considerable fluctuation in key macro-economic variables. The simulations furthermore imply that, with increased average prosperity, the importance of the government-provided public good decreases—with the result that the parties' programmes become more similar, abstention rates higher, and households' electoral behaviour more fickle. Consequently, richer countries change governments more often, while the changes to their policies become more subtle.

Notes

1. Conservative parties have traditionally favoured low taxes and a limited degree of government intervention; see, e.g., Green (1987), Taitte (1995), and Douglas (1999).

2. This development has culminated in the phenomenon that the centre-left governments that, in the mid to late 1990s, were voted into office in the United States, Canada, and most of Western Europe consistently made fiscal consolidation a key plank of their economic policies. For further details on the programmatic evolution of the main left-of-centre parties in Western Europe, as well as on the meaning and success of "third way" politicians, see, among others, Featherstone (1988), Glyn (1998), Gamble and Wright (1999), and Meyer (1999).

3. This vast and heterogeneous literature has recently been reviewed by Drazen (2000), Persson and Tabellini (2000), and Olters (2001).

4. An insightful survey and in-depth evaluation of the various branches of welfare theoretic approaches to explaining politics can be found in van den Doel and van Velthoven (1993). Several authors, including Bergson (1954), Buchanan (1954), and de Graaff (1962), have argued that the possibility of Arrow-type voting paradoxes might actually be advantageous for the stability of a democracy: societies would thus reduce the likelihood of some minority being exploited permanently.

5. The large literature on vote and popularity functions is based on the seminal contributions by Goodhart and Bhansali (1970), Mueller (1970), Kramer (1971), and Stigler (1973). For recent surveys of its results, see, e.g., Paldam (1981), Nannestad and Paldam (1994), and Marti (1995).

6. The explicit modelling of households' reactions to current and expected future economic policies, in the author's view, represents a key factor explaining the superior economic performances of democracies relative to alternative systems. Alesina and Rodrik (1992) pioneered the—very active—research into the effects of political institutions on growth.

7. The ultimately "non-Downsian" model design proposed here originates largely from the author's conviction that the direct analogy between political optimisation problems (maximising votes) and economic ones (maximising consumption and profits) is misleading, mainly because the relationship between votes and political benefits is a non-monotonous one. Whereas vote-share increases from, say, 48½ to 49½ per cent (or from 50½ to 51½ per cent) would add little or no extra benefits to the party and its politicians, the rise from 49½ to 50½ per cent—marking the difference between opposition and incumbency—would generate (almost) all of the possible utility gains to be won in an election. In fact, too large a majority has, at times, proven to be detrimental to a government's ultimate success, loosening the parliamentary party's internal discipline, and thereby increasing the likelihood of splits. This argument was first brought forward by Frey and Lau (1968) who describe a government as "a conglomeration of subunits" that all "have specific interests of their own but at the same time . . . share a common interest to stay in power. . . . Internal pressures are characterised by the fact that government loses its power not because the voters defeat it in an election, but rather be-

cause it breaks up due to internal inconsistencies" (p. 360). They therefore try to model government behaviour as a function of both *political capital*, representing (re-)election probabilities, and *ideology*, capturing member satisfaction. They, however, fail to derive an explicit mathematical solution.

8. In the following, the terms *households*, *individuals*, and *voters* will be used interchangeably.

9. The quotation marks indicate that the optimality concept employed throughout this paper is unrelated to the Pareto criterion. While every individual acts in his or her own best interest, the collective derivation of the economic policies to be pursued occurs on the basis of democratic rules.

10. Economists have long struggled with the question as to why it is rational for any individual not to abstain from voting as the probability of having the decisive vote approaches zero. Several authors have argued that voters do not only express their preferences for a specific political party but vote for the principle of democracy as well; see, e.g., Downs (1957), Chapter 14. This point has also been discussed in Tullock (1967) and—more formally—in Davis, Hinich, and Ordeshook (1970), Ordeshook (1986), and, more recently, Jones and Hudson (2000). Without a loss in generality, equation (8) can be extended to include the probability of having the decisive vote—which would make ξ "very small." For an intuitive reflection on this point, see also Box 1.

11. See also Przeworski and Sprague (1985).

12. The simulations presented in the following define the party members in period $t = 0$ as a fixed number of the "poorest" and "richest" members of society.

13. This model abstracts from any time-inconsistency problems. This assumption is in line with some recent contributions; see, e.g., Alesina (1988). In his rational, partisan-theoretic model, Alesina provides a framework through which he can demonstrate that rational and forward-looking voters understand that political parties have an incentive to announce convergent platforms in order to increase their electoral chances. As a result, "in a one-shot electoral game the only time-consistent equilibrium is one in which no convergence is possible, the two parties follow their most preferred policies, and the voters rationally expect this outcome" (p. 796).

14. For the purpose of the subsequent computer simulations, it was assumed that if $V_{(+j)\,t} = V_{(-j)\,t} = \frac{1}{2}$, a "grand coalition" of both parties will be formed, with the government's policies representing the average of both parties' programmes.

15. The statement can be made even stronger if one is willing to suppose that party members make that individual the party leader who is—personally—defined through his or her median income and median wealth (relative to all party members). That way, they can ensure the incentive compatibility of the party's compromise platform. That, however, would require the diagonal distribution of labour productivity and wealth endowments.

16. Clearly, party membership costs exceed the costs of voting, i.e., $\Xi > \xi$.

17. For the printout of the computer simulation program and alternative simulation results, see Olters (2000).

18. The corresponding results for R—generated on the basis of 101 households over 200 periods (i.e., 800 years, if a parliamentary term consists of four years)—are simply the inverse.

19. In panel d, periods in which the centre-left (-right) party governs are represented by grey (white) columns. The relative decrease in the proposed (and, consequently, actual) tax rates over the course of the 200 periods (see panel c) stems, to a large extent, from the households' accumulation of non-human capital, resulting in—especially—the centre-left party becoming more moderate in its party platforms. This development is reflected in the decreased political participation (panels a and b) and in the narrowing of the utility differences implicit in the two parties' proposed programmes (see panel d).

20. As such, this model—with its intuitive appeal and realistic results—should serve as a first building block toward a more comprehensive description of the intricate, multi-tiered political processes characterising democracies. This research agenda is aided by the fact that, in contrast to earlier contributions in this area, the EMP does not have to rely on exogenously defined policy functions or the existence of a social-welfare function; the variables defining households' political decisions are those typically considered in consumer theory—with the addition of the *public good*, which has been included in the voters' utility functions. Future research could extend the government's tool variables to include the progressivity of income taxes, specific social-welfare programmes, and budget deficits. It would also be interesting to broaden the underlying economy's structure (e.g., to permit households' income/leisure choices), to introduce the possibility of having a party leadership strategically influence platforms, and/or to use econometrically derived parameter specifications describing specific countries to describe the politico-economic interactions as postulated here and hence to evaluate this model's immanent ability to accurately forecast election outcomes.

References

Alesina, Alberto. (1988). "Macroeconomics and Politics." *NBER Macroeconomics Annual* 188: 13–52.

Alesina, Alberto, and Dani Rodrik. (1992). "Distribution, Political Conflict and Economic Growth: A Simple Theory and Some Empirical Evidence," in *Political Economy, Growth, and Business Cycles*, edited by Alex Cukierman, Zvi Hercowitz, and Leonardo Leiderman. Cambridge: MIT Press.

————. (1994). "Distributive Politics and Economic Growth." *Quarterly Journal of Economics* 40 (2): 1203–1228.

Arrow, Kenneth. (1950). "A Difficulty in the Concept of Social Welfare." *Journal of Political Economy* 58 (4): 328–346.

————. (1963 [1951]). *Social Choice and Individual Values,* 2d ed. New York: John Wiley & Sons.

Bergson, Abram. (1954). "On the Concept of Social Welfare." *Quarterly Journal of Economics* 68 (2): 233–252.

Buchanan, James. (1954). "Social Choice, Democracy, and Free Markets." *Journal of Political Economy* 62 (2): 114–123.

Davis, Otto, Melvin Hinich, and Peter Ordeshook. (1970). "An Expository Development of a Mathematical Model of the Electoral Process." *American Political Science Review* 64 (2): 426–448.

de Graaff, Jan. (1962). "On Making a Recommendation in a Democracy." *Economic Journal* 72 (286): 293–298.

Douglas, Roy. (1999). *Taxation in Britain Since 1660.* New York: St. Martin's Press.

Downs, Anthony. (1957). *An Economic Theory of Democracy.* New York: Harper & Row.

Drazen, A. Michael. (2000). *Political Economy in Macroeconomics.* Princeton: Princeton University Press.

Featherstone, Kevin. (1988). *Socialist Parties and European Integration: A Comparative History.* Manchester: Manchester University Press.

Frey, Bruno, and Lawrence Lau. (1968). "Towards a Mathematical Model of Government Behaviour." *Zeitschrift für Nationalökonomie* 28 (3–4): 355–380.

Fukuyama, Francis. (1989). "The End of History?" *The National Interest* 16 (Summer): 3–8.

Gamble, Andrew, and Tony Wright. (1999). *The New Social Democracy.* Oxford: Blackwell Publishers.

Glyn, Andrew. (1998). "The Assessment: Economic Policy and Social Democracy." *Oxford Review of Economic Policy* 14 (1): 1–18.

Goodhart, C., and R. J. Bhansali. (1970). "Political Economy." *Political Studies* 18: 43–106.

Green, David. (1987). *The New Conservatism: The Counter-Revolution in Political, Economic and Social Thought.* New York: St. Martin's Press.

Jones, Philip, and John Hudson. (2000). "Civic Duty and Expressive Voting: Is Virtue its Own Reward?" *Kyklos* 53 (1): 3–16.

Kramer, Gerald. (1971). "Short-Term Fluctuations in U.S. Voting Behavior, 1896–1964." *American Political Science Review* 65 (1): 131–143.

Marti, Robert. (1995). "Révélation de la fonction de bien-être du politique et instabilité de la fonction de popularité." *Revue Économique* 46 (3): 879–887.

Meyer, Thomas. (1999). "The Third Way at the Crossroads." *Internationale Politik und Gesellschaft* 3/1999: 294–304.

Mueller, John. (1970). "Presidential Popularity From Truman to Johnson." *American Political Science Review* 64 (1): 18–34.

Nannestad, Peter, and Martin Paldam. (1994). "The VP-Function: A Survey of the Literature on Vote and Popularity Functions After 25 Years." *Public Choice* 79 (3–4): 213–245.

Olters, Jan-Peter. (2000). *Endogenous Ballot Decisions and "Optimal" Fluctuations—An Economic Model of Politics.* Ph.D. diss. Montreal: McGill University.

———. (2001). "Modeling Politics with Economic Tools: A Critical Survey of the Literature." *IMF Working Paper* 01/10.

Ordeshook, Peter. (1986). *Game Theory and Political Theory: An Introduction.* Cambridge: Cambridge University Press.

Paldam, Martin. (1981). "A Preliminary Survey of the Theories and Findings on Vote and Popularity Functions." *European Journal of Political Research* 9 (2): 181–199.

Persson, Torsten, and Guido Tabellini. (1994). "Is Inequality Harmful for Growth?" *American Economic Review* 84 (3): 600–621.

———. (2000). *Political Economy: Explaining Economic Policy.* Cambridge: MIT Press.

Przeworski, Adam, and John Sprague. (1985). "Party Strategy, Class Organization, and Individual Voting," in *Capitalism and Social Democracy*, edited by Adam Przeworski. Cambridge: Cambridge University Press.

Stigler, George. (1973). "General Economic Conditions and National Elections." *American Economic Review, Papers and Proceedings* 63 (2): 160–167.

Taitte, Lawson (ed.). (1995). *Liberalism and Conservatism in Their Historical Development.* Austin: University of Texas Press.

Tullock, Gordon. (1967). *Toward a Mathematics of Politics.* Ann Arbor: University of Michigan Press.

van den Doel, Hans, and Ben van Velthoven. (1993). *Democracy and Welfare Economics.* Cambridge: Cambridge University Press.

PART III

Constitutional Economics

American Journal of Economics and Sociology, Vol. 61, No. 1 (January, 2002).
© 2002 American Journal of Economics and Sociology, Inc.

Complexity, Governance and Constitutional Craftsmanship

By RICHARD E. WAGNER[*]

ABSTRACT. Economic policy is commonly treated as a vehicle for selecting among possible allocative outcomes within an economy. An
economy, however, is a complex network of relationships whose patterns can be understood but whose details can be neither predicted
nor controlled. Because of this complexity, allocative outcomes are
not direct objects of choice. They are simply emergent consequences
of human interaction that takes place within some framework of governing rules and conventions. All economic policy can do is modify
some of the rules that govern this interaction. Economic policy is thus
constitutive and not allocative in character, being centrally involved in
shaping the character of the regime that governs our relationships
with each other.

Nearly any introduction to economics will point out, in one way or another, that an economy is a complex pattern of activities that no one
could plan or organize in specific detail. Things work and life proceeds in a generally coordinated fashion, not because someone is in
charge of assuring that this happens, but because no one is in charge.
The complexity of an effort to produce that coordination directly
would overwhelm any attempt to actually do so. The central concern
of economic analysis has been to illuminate the workings of the "invisible hand" processes of economic governance through which economic coordination emerges.

   Despite this emphasis on complexity, spontaneous order, and invis-

   *Richard E. Wagner is Holbert L. Harris Professor of Economics at George Mason Uni-
versity, Fairfax, VA 22030. E-mail: rwagner@gmu.edu. His scholarly writings have covered a broad range of topics on matters of political economy and public policy. His
current research activities fall into three primary categories: catallactical public finance,
coordinationist macroeconomics and constitutional political economy. More information about these activities is posted on his website at http://mason.gmu.edu/frwagner/.
An earlier version of this paper was presented at the University of Pisa and the University of Rome "La Sapienza." I am grateful to the participants in those seminars, and especially to Alberto Vannucci in Pisa and Domenico DaEmpoli in Rome.
American Journal of Economics and Sociology, Vol. 61, No. 1 (January, 2002).

ible hands, the treatment of economic policy has typically proceeded as if the economic process were inherently simple, and as if allocative outcomes were capable of being chosen directly through policy interventions. Recognition of the inherent complexity of the economic process, however, means that economic policy cannot choose allocative outcomes. All that economic policy can do is change some of the rules that govern economic interaction. The resulting allocative outcomes will be generated through the complex interactions among people that are set in motion by the policy, and even by its anticipated enactment. This means that economic policy is necessarily constitutional policy, in that it is principally involved in constituting the rules and conventions that govern economic relationships.

The constitution of governance relationships, moreover, involves both positive and normative elements, as well as an interaction between those elements. Alternative governance relationships entail different patterns and frameworks for human interaction. While there is room for normative appraisal of different possible frameworks, not every imaginable norm is attainable, since reality places limits on what is attainable. Still, normative standards can be reinforced or extinguished to some extent, depending on the particular types of practice that are encouraged or discouraged within a particular framework of governing rules and conventions. This paper first contrasts interventionist and constitutive approaches to economic policy, and then explains how complexity converts all policy into constitutional policy. From there, the paper examines the relation between cognition and valuation as it pertains to governance. It then considers how a process of piecemeal policy drift can generate a transformation in the underlying governance regime, and closes with a consideration of the Germanic tradition of *ordnungspolitik* that has particular relevance for the argument developed here.

I

Allocative Outcomes, Constitutive Rules, and Economic Policy

FOR THE MOST PART, DISCUSSIONS OF ECONOMIC POLICY treat the network of economic relationships that constitute an economy as a relatively simple phenomenon. Economic policy is often treated as a form of mechanics, with policy being much like tinkering with the engine of an automobile. It is thus an intervention into the engine's operation, the purpose of which is to change the performance of the engine in some fashion. Modern legislatures are like large garages with many engines being worked on at the same time. It is common, for instance, to find analyses of economic policy that describe policy as an instrument for selecting among positions along a production frontier.

This presumption of inherent simplicity is revealed again and again in textbook illustrations of the effects of government interventions into particular markets. Rent control, for instance, is portrayed as creating a shortage in the market for rental housing and reducing the return earned by the owners of those units. These effects can be illustrated with reference to Figure 1. Without rent control, the market-clearing price and quantity are P_0 and X_0 respectively. If rents are controlled at P_2, suppliers are willing to supply only X_1 units of rental housing while tenants want X_2 units. Tenants therefore want a greater number of units or a larger amount of space than the owners of rental property are willing to provide. Rent control changes the market outcome (P_0, X_0) to the controlled outcome (P_2, X_2), thus changing resource allocation within a society.

This portrait of rent control as simply changing allocative outcomes seems correct at first glance but turns out upon further consideration to be inadequate, if not wrong. This portrait is one that captures only the direct, immediately visible effects at the point of policy injection. It does not account for all of the subsequent indirect effects that emerge throughout the economy as people respond to the myriad changes in profit opportunities that the policy generates. The very complexity of economic life, moreover, precludes any effort to do so in anything but a formal and highly stylized manner. These changes in profit opportunities all emerge through the intensified competition that rent control sets in motion among tenants. At the market outcome (P_0, X_0), there is no unresolved competition among tenants. This is not to deny that tenants might wish that rents were lower. But rents are what they are by virtue of their having been generated through a process of open competition that has been framed by the rules of private property and freedom of contract. At the market equilibrium, there is no scope for further competition.

Figure 1

Secondary Consequences of Rent Control

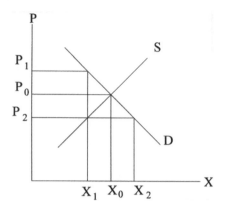

The enactment of rent control generates new opportunities for competition among tenants. At the controlled price of P_2, there are X_2 people competing for X_1 places.[1] A full examination of rent control cannot ignore this competition among tenants. Yet the course of this competition cannot be predicted in exact detail, which means that rent control cannot truly choose allocative outcomes, but can only modify the framework of rules within which outcomes emerge through interaction among market participants.

Setting a rent control at P_2 does not mean that rents actually will be P_2 and not P_1. For one thing, the mere enactment of a law does not mean that it will be effective. There are many drugs whose sale is illegal that nonetheless can be obtained easily. Rents might be controlled at $600 and yet housing might still rent for $800, because people would rather pay $800 than do without. A genuine census of rental contracts might even find instances in which those contracts carried prices of $800 despite the rent control. How frequently this might occur would depend on such things as the penalties for violation of the control and the budget of investigative and enforcement agencies. Far more likely than rental contracts being made above the controlled price is a change in the structure of contracts and contractual relationships that would have much the same effect. There are an indefinitely large number of ways this can be accomplished. The initial impact of rent control is to prevent market participants from making transactions they wish to make. It is easy to understand why those participants would be interested in pursuing other contractual formats to allow them to exploit the gains from trade that rent control otherwise would prevent them from exploiting.

Rent control can change the form that competition among tenants takes, but it cannot eliminate that competition. An open and direct competition will give way to some indirect, more complex, and costlier form of competition. There are an indefinitely large number of particular forms that this more complex competition can take, varying in their degree of complexity and indirectness. One simple illustration is a one-year lease at $600 per month, with that lease requiring also the payment of $2,400 in cash as a condition for securing the lease, therefore bringing the effective monthly rent to $800.[2] Besides an under-the-table payment, there are numerous ways this payment could be given contractual standing. It could be as a deposit against damage, with the owner or his agent serving as the final arbiter of damages. It could also be as a $24,000 deposit that is refundable without interest, provided the interest rate was 10 percent.

It has long been noted that rent controls, or price controls generally, induce tie-in sales to avoid the controlled price. The ability to purchase an item whose price is controlled can be tied to the purchase of an item whose price is not controlled, with the higher price of the latter item being equivalent to the gap between the controlled price and what the market price would have been.[3] In the presence of rent control, price can no longer serve officially as a rationing device. Rent control can restrict and possibly prevent an open competition through price that would otherwise increase price to P_1 in a simple and direct fashion. It cannot, however, keep the full price at P_2. One longstanding example is tying the ability to rent a unit at the controlled price to the lease or purchase of furniture at an above-market price. To be sure, such tied sales are easy to anticipate, and many rent control ordinances try to preclude them. How successful such preclusion might be is a different matter, and in any case we should not assume that a law is followed just because it is enacted, particularly when that law sets in motion the very competition among tenants that generates the incentives to disregard the law.

Furthermore, while some kind of tied sales might be easy to anticipate and perhaps to observe, others will be harder to anticipate and more difficult to observe. As efforts at monitoring and enforcement are increased, we can plausibly anticipate shifts into the use of forms of tie-in that are harder to detect. There are an indefinitely large number of other ways to raise the full price of rental housing once it is recognized that the quality of housing services that are supplied can be varied in numerous ways. For instance, rental housing might have such things as parking and storage that were made freely available without rent control, but that are priced separately after rent control. A pool and sauna that were freely available might be converted into a club with admission charged. The landscaping service that kept the grounds nicely maintained could be dismissed, and the grounds allowed to turn into a weed patch.

Proceeding even further beyond the point of policy injection reveals even more potential for further indirect effects whose precise details cannot be predicted in advance, nor perhaps even accounted for in precise detail after the policy has been in place. These indirect, relatively invisible consequences assert themselves nonetheless through processes of spontaneous ordering. All of these effects take place by consequence of there being X_2 people competing for X_1 units. For instance, the restriction of supply that rent control causes makes standard forms of family living more costly. This surely leads to some increase in alternative living arrangements, lifestyles, cultural patterns, and the like, because people must live somewhere. Among other things, a greater number of people will rent rooms in other people's residences, will have roommates, and so forth. Whatever consequences might emerge out of all these various forms of response set in motion by rent control is anyone's guess, but in any case these consequences are part of the allocative outcomes that can be attributed to rent control. If conventional arrangements and patterns are made more scarce, other arrangements and patterns will spring up.

A society is not an engine and economists are not mechanics. An economy is a complex web of contractual relations and human anticipations. It is a highly evolved organism that no one can apprehend in its substantive details. It is because of this inability to apprehend substantive details that a truly planned economy is impossible. As Paul Craig Roberts (1971) explains, even the so-called planned economies were organized through markets, but those markets were strongly warped and distorted by political power, thus rendered lame in their ability to deliver the goods. What we can apprehend, and all we can apprehend, are the formal, structural properties and principles of operation of an economic regime, which in turn means that economic policy chooses constitutive rules and not allocative outcomes.

II
The Necessarily Constitutive Character of Economic Policy

F. A. HAYEK (1973:35–54) MAKES AN IMPORTANT DISTINCTION between organizations and orders. That distinction is illustrated nicely by comparing troops leaving a parade ground with spectators leaving a stadium. The troops leaving the parade ground comprise an organization. Their detailed movements, i.e., the resulting allocative outcomes, are under someone's explicit control. There is a commander who establishes the order of march as an act of policy. In contrast, spectators leaving a stadium comprise an order. There is no central direction of the movements of the individual fans. The resulting allocative outcomes are not objects of policy choice. Those movements emerge from a self-ordered process that takes place within a framework of general rules and conventions that makes it possible for people to pick rapid paths of exit in a non-directed sea of humanity. Police might erect some barricades and change the timing of some traffic signals. In doing this, however, they are not selecting the outcomes that are represented by the movement of the fans, but are modifying some of the constitutive rules that govern the process of exit. Still, the resulting allocative outcomes emerge through interaction among the fans within the constitutive framework of rules and conventions, and are not chosen directly by someone.

The allocative interpretation of rent control as changing the market outcome (P_0, X_0) in Figure 1 to the controlled outcome (P_2, X_1) is incoherent in many ways, some of which have already been noted. Only in a nation of sheep would (P_2, X_1) even be conceivable. This describes a situation in which the control was announced, and those who could not get housing would be pleased to do without rather than seeking to compete against those who would be able to get that housing. Owners, moreover, would in no way be tempted to accept more lucrative offers from potential tenants or to entertain different forms of contract and transaction that would allow exploitation of the gains from trade that the rent control would prevent.

In a nation of real people, legislation prohibiting people from exploiting gains from trade will not be freely obeyed. The extent of obedience will depend on the size and effectiveness of the policing apparatus that is put in place. Even to mention this, however, is to deny the allocationist story told by Figure 1, because an entirely new activity is injected into the economic process, in addition to the new contractual forms and relationships already noted. Yes, rent control does change allocative outcomes within a society, and does so in a wide variety of ways along an indefinitely large number of margins. The particular character and the details of those outcomes, however, are not the direct choices of policy but are emergent outcomes in response to the constitutive framework erected by policy.

Economic policy cannot be assimilated to such choices of outcomes as choosing an order of march or of fixing an engine. It is more on the order of selecting some of the rules that govern the departure of people from a stadium. All economic policy is constitutional policy in that it is centrally involved in shaping the character of the regime that will govern our relationships with one another. Economic policy does not truly make direct choices among alternative allocative outcomes. It makes choices regarding the framework of rules that govern human relationships. In making policy choices, we constitute the principles by which our relationships with one another are governed.

III

Cognition, Valuation, and Alternative Constitutive Frameworks

STARTING WITH THE FOUNDING SCHOLARSHIP in constitutional economics by James Buchanan and Gordon Tullock (1962), a fundamental analytical distinction has been made between the selection of the rules of a game and the subsequent playing of the game according to the rules previously selected.[4] I do not deny the value of this distinction as an analytical matter. In practice, however, the development of framing constitutive rules and the generation of outcomes within those rules take place simultaneously. In this sense, all economic policy is constitutive in character. Policy can be constitutive in that it maintains a particular regime, or it can be constitutive in that it promotes some transformation in governing regimes. But it is constitutive in character in either case. The transformation of governing regimes may take place through conscious effort, but it can also take place piecemeal, through policy drift.

In *Federalist* No. 1, Alexander Hamilton asks, "whether societies of men are really capable or not of establishing good government from reflection and choice, or whether they are forever destined to depend for their political constitutions on accident and force" (p. 33). Whether reflection and choice can triumph over accident and force is a matter of what might be called "social agriculture." Agriculture attempts to improve upon what Mother Nature offers, by imposing reflection and choice upon what otherwise would be the products of fate. There are both normative and positive elements to social agriculture. Normatively, there must be some standard of what is desirable. Among other things, distinguishing between desirable and undesirable forms of plant life must be possible. Vegetables may be put into the category of desired plant life while weeds are not, though even here the growth of knowledge may reveal useful properties of what were previously thought to be undesirable weeds.

All of the normative wishes in the world are useless, however, without some idea of how to achieve those wishes. People may prefer squash to ragweed, and squash in their stomachs to squash devoured by bugs. Without knowledge of how to restrain the bugs and weeds, the yield of squash for human consumption will be left to fate and chance. It is the same for governance, as Hamilton notes in *Federalist* No. 1. We may recognize that people prefer to go through their lives free from fear of being preyed upon by others, whether in the form of local bandits or thugs or in the form of invasions by foreign hordes. We may likewise recognize that people prefer to see their children grow up in prosperous, free, and peaceful environments, and not be plagued by poverty, enslavement, or war. Mere recognition of these preferences, however, does nothing to satisfy them. Mother Nature may give us islands of peace and periods of prosperity, but to move beyond her offerings and limitations requires more than wishful thinking. It requires the application of intelligence concerning the social equivalents of the principles of soil chemistry and plant genetics so as to allow the flowers and vegetables to flourish while restraining the weeds and bugs.

Norms, moreover, are not independent of practice. They are learned through practice, and they can become extinguished through practice as well. The maintenance of any particular normative regime requires a supporting constitutive framework that reinforces those norms through practice. Otherwise, it is possible for contrary forms of practice eventually to undermine the original norms, thereby producing a shift in the governing regime, not through conscious selection but through the cumulative effects of piecemeal policy.

The ancient Greeks recognized that virtue was a matter of right knowledge reduced to habit through good practice. Conscious choice repeated often becomes habitual and unconscious. Right conduct is cultivated through the ability of right practice to create good habits. Conversely, wrong practice will cultivate bad habits and produce wrong conduct. To be sure, this classical formulation addresses the moral education of individuals. Nonetheless, it has didactic value for thinking about the constitutional framework for economic policy. The characteristics of a system of democratic governance will depend upon the habits of governance that are cultivated through democratic practice. Good habits result from good practice, with the goodness or badness of the practice arising through political, not market, processes. Desirable normative conduct is reduced to unconscious choice if the incentive features contained within a set of institutional arrangements reinforce that conduct. But if institutional arrangements do not reinforce such conduct, the desired normative conduct will diminish. In much the same way, the ancient Greeks recognized that virtue would diminish without its practice. What is necessary, then, is both knowledge about what constitutes good governance and the reduction of that knowledge to habit through good practice, with that practice mediated by an institutional framework that supports good practice over bad.

IV

Policy Drift and Regime Transformation

As a means of characterizing democratic regimes, distinguishing between liberal democracy and social democracy as alternative constitutional frameworks for democratic governance is useful. Liberal democracy reflects the normative orientation that people and their rights are superior to government, with governments existing to secure those rights. It entails the presumption that people can do as they choose without requiring state permission, provided only that people do not abridge the similar rights of other people in the process.

Social democracy represents the normative orientation that government is the source of rights. If liberal democracy is grounded in private property, social democracy is grounded in common or collective property. What people may do individually resides ultimately within the domain of government. There can be no principled limit on the reach of government, because government is the source of rights. Under social democracy, collective judgments trump individual rights. To be sure, people will have spheres of autonomy under social democracy simply because, pragmatically speaking, governments cannot be involved in everything. Those spheres, however, are always subject to change through the political process.

Whether they are made explicitly or left to the fortunes of history, any society inescapably faces a stream of constitutive choices concerning these two different principles by which human relationships are constituted and economic activities governed. These choices can be faced directly with reflection, or they can be faced through accident and force. But they will be faced in either case. One implication of the classical approach to moral education is that law has a didactic element. In this respect, private ordering and public ordering differ in the instruction they present (Wagner 1992). With private ordering, particular allocative outcomes have no normative significance, save to the extent that principles of property and contract are violated within the process through which the allocation emerges. Otherwise, there is toleration over outcomes. For liberal democracy and private ordering, property and contract are the governing institutions for ordering human relationships. In contrast, public ordering trumps the principles of property and contract as a framework for ordering human relationships. Principles of property and contract can be violated freely so long as the violation emanates from the offices of state. With public ordering, the process of collective choice generates some particular expression of preference over outcomes.

Returning to the earlier consideration of rent control, it is easy to appreciate how particular policy measures can contribute to the transformation of regimes. To be sure, one policy measure makes a small transformation. But multiply that by numerous measures across many years, and a quite significant transformation can result. If norms are reinforced or extinguished through practice, particular policy measures can either reinforce or undermine a particular regime. Rent control is a politically sanctioned disregard for the principles of property and contract. With private ordering, one who wants a larger apartment must secure the consent of the owner. With public ordering, however, one can use the legislature to take it. Rent control, along with myriad similar cases, should thus contribute to some erosion in the hold that the rule of law exercises over people's moral imaginations. Rent control is, of course, but one policy measure. But as other measures are enacted and the concrete details of actual practice changes, the framework of governance changes as well.[5]

A widely popular, though nonetheless erroneous, construction holds that we face no dichotomous choice between regimes, but rather have evolved a new form of governance, a *mixed economy*. The problem with this construction is that principles of liberal and social democracy cannot be blended, any more than can water and oil (see, for instance, Ikeda 1997 and Littlechild 1978). Spheres of private and common property may exist simultaneously within a society, but if so, they will be accompanied by continual skirmishes along various boundaries of conflict where the two principles necessarily collide, creating processes of what Robert Young (1988) calls tectonic politics.[6]

The contemporary inhabitants of so-called mixed economies live in the presence of two distinct and incompatible systems of pricing and resource allocation. The incompatibility arises because enterprises that are organized within the political price system of social democracy cannot compete against enterprises that are organized within the openly competitive market price system of liberal democracy. Maffeo Pantaleoni (1911) developed this point nicely in his analysis of the parasitical character of systems of political pricing.[7] The survival of the politically supported enterprises requires continual effort to suppress the forces of open competition and private property; otherwise open competition would overwhelm the political enterprises that are established within the political price system.

The history of urban transportation in the United States is instructive in this regard. Originally, it was mainly organized within a framework of private property and market pricing. One particular market creation was the emergence of jitney service in the first third of the twentieth century (see, for instance, Eckert and Hilton 1972 and Klein 1997). As part of the normal movement of people between home and work, some people who owned cars carried other people at agreeable fares. An orderly pattern of transportation developed, and it was an effective way of dealing with the bi-modal peak demand for transportation in the morning and evening rush periods.

Into this setting, inject the political sponsorship of bus and rail services. These enterprises can be operated either directly by government or indirectly through license. In either case, the political enterprise will not be competitive with private enterprises, and it will need to cover its inefficiency by continually curbing the operation of private property and open competition. One way to do this is through subsidies from taxpayers. Fares thus cover only part of the cost of the enterprise, as people who don't use the service are forced to pay through taxation.

Market-generated competition for political enterprises can also be abridged through regulation. The prohibition of jitney service, for instance, increased the demand for the services of the political enterprise by preventing the forces of open competition from organizing superior enterprises. The licensing of taxicabs is another example, because with truly open competition taxicabs would come quite close to being an alternative form of jitney service. Other examples of how the political enterprise must continually degrade private property in an effort to promote its own survival include such things as quotas on downtown parking and the reservation of highway lanes for car pools. All of these reactions, and many more, illustrate the incongruity between market and political pricing. The survival of enterprises that are sponsored under political pricing will require a concomitant degradation of private property and open competition if they are to survive.

Carolyn Webber and Aaron Wildavsky (1986) argue that budgetary choices involve much more than a choice about how much people will spend at public goods stores relative to private goods stores. They are fundamentally conflict-laden choices among people over how they are to lead their lives. Private property and common property represent the basis for two alternative regimes for ordering human relationships, and these two regimes clash in important respects. Private ordering is based on an affirmation of equality within law, which in turn entails a tolerance across outcomes. Public ordering, by contrast, is based on an ethic of merit and hierarchy, and entails preferences over outcomes.

V

An Inescapable Constitutional Choice

WALTER EUCKEN (1952) ARTICULATED a central distinction between those policy measures that conform to the central operating principles of a market economy and those measures that do not (see also Leipold 1990 and Vanberg 1988). The Germanic tradition of *ordnungspolitik* makes a fundamental constitutional distinction between the choice among principles that will characterize a regime and the particular structure of policy within the framework of that regime. There is a fundamental clash between liberty, private property, spontaneous ordering, and a tolerance over outcomes on the one hand, and servility, relationships based on domination and subordination, collective property, and preferences over outcomes on the other.

Like many such distinctions, this one is surely easier to articulate than it is to implement. To say this, however, is not to dispute the distinction's value as a principle of economic policy. A conformable policy measure is one that is consistent with the principles of property and contract. A non-conformable policy measure is one that clashes with those principles. Eucken's central point is that economic policy is fundamentally a choice about the constitutive principles that govern human relationships within a society. This choice might be confronted directly. Even if not, it will be confronted indirectly and perhaps unwittingly through piecemeal policy. For Eucken the choice was for an economic organization of society in which people related to each other through reciprocity and equality, as provided by a framework of property and contract. One could, of course, opt for a regime governed by principles of domination and supplication and by *noblesse oblige*. This would entail preferences over outcomes, and would require a rejection of principles of liberal democracy, tolerance over outcomes, and the like.

Eucken suggests that economic policy be held to a standard of market conformability. His point can be illustrated by noting that transferable housing vouchers could be market conformable while rent control clearly would not. With housing vouchers, the amounts of housing produced, its prices, the forms of contract, and the like could still be determined through interactions among market participants within the framework provided by property and contract. To be sure, such vouchers might be laden with such efforts at outcome selection as stipulating approved vendors, rendering them non-conformable with liberal ordering principles. Rent control will always violate those principles. Rent control makes ordinary market transactions illegal, but people will nonetheless seek to make those transactions. This involves the use of alternative, more complex forms of contract. It also involves an expansion in police activity and martial attitudes within a society, along with increased tendencies and incentives for citizens to spy and inform on one another. Rent control is inherently venal, in many possible ways. The authority of the state expands, officials are bribed, and citizens are prosecuted.

The distinction between conformable and non-conformable measures, if treated as a constitutional requirement for economic policy, might well serve as a kind of constitutional filter. Starting from a normative affirmation of the central principles of a liberal society, such a filter would declare that a wide range of policy measures are open to the state, subject to the limitation that the particular content of those measures could not violate the principles of property and contract. A state could impose modest tariffs but not quotas. A state could issue transferable rent vouchers, as long as they were administered in a non-discriminatory fashion, but could not control rents. One state could refuse to engage in health care in any manner, while another could mandate that people must participate in some program of health insurance. A state could not, however, regulate insurance programs so as to require some form of community rating, whereby actuarial experience is ignored and contractual principles of open competition violated.

It is easy for piecemeal policy measures to generate incentives that ever more undermine property and contract, in the process replacing liberty and responsibility with servility and dependence. As a source of orientation for the conduct of economic policy for a liberal democracy, there is much merit to a requirement that state policy measures be congruent with the central principles of property and contract, which nurture liberty, autonomy, and responsibility. The opposite, social democratic principle leads to differential ranks of overseers and underlings, to those who dispense *noblesse oblige* and those who are the recipients of that *oblige*.

Augustine, in his *City of God*, tells the story of a pirate who was captured and brought before Alexander the Great. When Alexander castigated the pirate, he responded, "I do my fighting on a tiny ship, and they call me a pirate; you do yours with a large fleet, and they call you commander" (p. 89). Augustine, in noting that the pirate's response to Alexander was wholly accurate, asks, "In the absence of justice, what is sovereignty but organized brigandage?" (p. 88). Justice is possible when reciprocity and exchange govern human relationships. It can never exist when domination and supplication govern them. Augustine is truly a man for the ages, whose themes and wisdom could stand recovery today.

Notes

1. Or, alternatively, people want X_2 of space when only X_1 is available.

2. With a positive rate of interest, it would, of course, take something less than $2,400 to finance the series of $200 monthly payments.

3. For some careful efforts in this vein, see Baird (1980) and Cheung (1975).

4. For further amplification, see, for instance, Buchanan (1975, 1990) and Wagner (1988).

5. For related considerations of private and public ordering, see Epstein (1985), Foldvary (1994), and Streit (1992).

6. Tectonic politics contrasts with the typical representations of politics as being smooth, continuous, and twice differentiable.

7. For a further consideration of Pantaleoni's formulation, see Wagner (1997).

References

Augustine. (1958). *City of God*. New York: Image Books.
Baird, C. W. (1980). *Rent Control: The Perennial Folly*. Washington, DC: Cato Institute.

Buchanan, J. M. (1975). *The Limits of Liberty*. Chicago: University of Chicago Press.

―――. 1990. "The Domain of Constitutional Economics." *Constitutional Political Economy* 1: 1–18.

Buchanan, J. M., and G. Tullock. (1962). *The Calculus of Consent*. Ann Arbor: University of Michigan Press.

Cheung, S. N. S. (1975). "Roofs or Stars? The Stated Intents and Actual Effects of a Rents Ordinance." *Economic Inquiry* 13: 1–21.

Eckert, R. D., and G. W. Hilton. (1972). "The Jitneys." *Journal of Law and Economics* 15: 293–325.

Epstein, R. A. (1985). *Takings: Private Property and the Power of Eminent Domain*. Cambridge: Harvard University Press.

Eucken, W. (1952). *Grundsätze der Wirtschaftspolitik*. Tübingen: J. C. B. Mohr.

Foldvary, F. (1994). *Public Goods and Private Communities*. Hants, UK: Edward Elgar.

Hayek, F. A. (1973). *Rules and Order*, Vol. I of *Law, Legislation, and Liberty*. Chicago: University of Chicago Press.

Ikeda, S. (1997). *Dynamics of the Mixed Economy*. London: Routledge.

Klein, D. B. (1997). *Curb Rights: A Foundation for Free Enterprise in Urban Transit*. Washington, DC: American Enterprise Institute.

Leipold, H. (1990). "Neoliberal *Ordnungstheorie* and Constitutional Economics." *Constitutional Political Economy* 1: 47–65.

Littlechild, S. C. (1978). *The Fallacy of the Mixed Economy*. London: Institute of Economic Affairs.

Pantaleoni, M. (1911). "Considerazioni sulle proprieta di un sistema di prezzi politici." *Giornale degli Economisti* 42: 9–29, 114–133.

Roberts, P. C. (1971). *Alienation and the Soviet Economy*. Albuquerque: University of New Mexico Press.

Rossiter, C. (ed.). (1961). *The Federalist Papers*. New York: New American Library.

Streit, M. (1992). "Economic Order, Private Law, and Public Policy: The Freiberg School of Law and Economics in Perspective." *Journal of Institutional and Theoretical Economics* 148: 675–704.

Vanberg, V. (1988). "*Ordnungstheorie* as Constitutional Economics: The German Conception of a 'Social Market Economy'." *ORDO* 39: 17–31.

Wagner, R. E. (1988). "*The Calculus of Consent*: A Wicksellian Retrospective." *Public Choice*: 56: 153–166.

―――. (1992). "Crafting Social Rules: Common Law vs. Statute Law, Once Again." *Constitutional Political Economy* 3: 381–397.

―――. (1997). "Parasitical Political Pricing, Economic Calculation, and the Size of Government: Variations on a Theme by Maffeo Pantaleoni." *Journal of Public Finance and Public Choice* 15: 135–146.

Webber, C., and A. Wildavsky. (1986). *A History of Taxation and Expenditure in the Western World*. New York: Simon and Schuster.

Young, R. A. (1988). "Tectonic Policies and Political Competition." Pp. 129–
145 in *The Competitive State,* edited by A. Breton, G. Galeotti, P. Salmon,
and R. Wintrobe. Dordrecht: Kluwer Academic Publishers.

Opting-Out: The Constitutional Economics of Exit

By Peter Kurrild-Klitgaard*

Abstract. The central aspect, which makes markets operate differently than governments, is the ability of market actors to "exit" from future interactions. This point is applied to constitutional analysis, with an emphasis on the constitutional possibility of individuals or groups in a society "exiting," wholly or partly, from the political community or from specific institutions within such. Hobbesian and Lockean states-of-nature are sketched using a common framework of some simple games, and the Lockean solution to the danger of tyranny is formalized. This solution is compared to the typical interaction in a market economy, where the possibility of "exit" from future interactions with disagreeable parties introduces severe restrictions on the possible exploitation. This analysis is extended to the political sphere, and it is argued in general terms that a constitutional set-up utilizing a semi-Lockean right to "exit" (e.g., federal structures with rights of secession, voucher systems, etc.) could be an efficient guarantee against sub-optimal solutions and function so as to reduce redistributive conflicts and make welfare-increasing transactions possible.

> It is, indeed, true that the freedom to change what government you serve under will make it easier for you to better your lot. It is also true that this privilege will mean that governments, regardless of their formal structure, will find it necessary to pay considerable attention to the wishes of their citizenry. Gordon Tullock (Tullock 1985: 1080)

Peter Kurrild-Klitgaard is Associate Professor of Political Theory and Comparative Politics at Dept. of Political Science and Public Management, University of Southern Denmark, and Visiting Scholar at Institute for Social and Economic Research and Policy, Columbia University, New York. He was educated at Columbia University and the University of Copenhagen. Earlier versions of the present paper were presented at the Panel on "The Political Economy of Constitutional Design and Evolution" 2000 Annual Meeting of the American Political Science Association, Marriott Wardman Park, Washington DC, 31 August–3 September, 2000, and at 2001 Annual Meeting of the European Public Choice Society, Paris, 17–22 April, 2001. The author is grateful to participants in those meetings as well as Jens Blom-Hansen and Georg Vanberg for constructive suggestions. All the usual reservations apply.

American Journal of Economics and Sociology, Vol. 61, No. 1 (January, 2002).

Introduction

IN THE MODERN STATE the ideal of a political community would very much seem to be that of a geographically circumscribed area within which exists a more or less fixed political hierarchy, which includes all individuals and all political institutions, and whose physical extension is contiguous and non-perforated. The possibility of a citizen, a group of citizens or some unit withdrawing in any way but by physically moving is indeed often viewed as being the cause of weakness, instability and, potentially, chaos. The economist Albert O. Hirschman in his classic *Exit, Voice and Loyalty* (1970) argued that consumers in a market basically can react to declines in product quality either by voicing their dissatisfaction or by "exiting" by not buying it again, but that economists tend to concentrate too much on exit, and that the use of this option not only tends to limit the use of other options but also may be too drastic a tool (Hirschman 1970). More narrowly, a prominent constitutional scholar, Cass Sunstein, has argued that a constitutional right to secede "would increase the risks of ethnic and factional struggle; reduce the prospects for compromise and deliberation in government; raise dramatically the stakes of day-to-day political decisions; introduce irrelevant and illegitimate considerations into these decisions; create dangers of blackmail, strategic behavior, and exploitation; and, most generally, endanger the prospects for long-term self-governance" (Sunstein 1991: 634).

The present paper will argue otherwise, in fact to the contrary. An attempt will be made at demonstrating that a constitutional right to wholly or partly "exit" a political community, or specific institutions within that political community, all else being equal, may be the institutional guarantee against sub-optimal collective decisions. As such it may be what guarantees the strength and peace of a community rather than the opposite. This will be done by, first, presenting the familiar arguments of classical contractarians such as Thomas Hobbes and John Locke and by using some simple game-theoretical forms (Section I). Here it will be shown that the very different constitutional perspectives of Hobbes and Locke may be due to their different conceptualizations of the interaction in the state-of-nature, and that Locke's solution to the dangers of tyranny conceivably could be modeled as a constitutional right to "exit" unattractive arrangements.

Second, an extension of this perspective will be made to the structure of the political community, and the possible constitutional reform thereof, e.g., the relationship between individual citizens and the institutions of the public sector or between units within this (Section II). As such, the analysis supports the by now well-known and widely accepted claim of much rational choice analysis, that a decentralized, federal-like political community would seem to be most able to satisfy popular preferences in a polity with heterogeneous individual preferences (Buchanan & Tullock 1965; Bednar, Eskridge, & Ferejohn 1999). But it also extends this point by arguing that this conclusion might be applicable to a wider set of institutions than often believed.

I

States-of-Nature, Constitutional Set-up and Exit

IT HAS BY NOW BECOME almost standard procedure to utilize game theory to describe the interaction between individuals in a state-of-nature. This is in particular the case when it comes to the character of a Hobbesian state-of-nature and the interaction of the inhabitants therein as something resembling the notoriously famous "Prisoners' Dilemma" and to use this for some form of a contractarian analysis.[1] So far the same has not been done when it comes to the Lockean state-of-nature. This is peculiar in so far as the Lockean constitutional thought figures so prominently in the Western tradition. The present analysis suggests a common framework for analyzing the Hobbesian and the Lockean portrayals of the interaction in a state-of-nature and their quite different conclusions.

Preliminaries

To approach the modeling of the interaction of individuals in a state-of-nature without any centralized enforcing authority, we may begin by outlining the usual form of representing simple situations of interaction between two actors who are facing a simple choice between either cooperating with each other or not. Let us assume that we have a situation with two individuals, players I and II, where player I owns good α, while player II owns good β. To model the situation as a game of potential conflict we may make the initial and important assumption that player I prefers the property of II to his own ($\beta > \alpha$), and that the reverse is true for II ($\alpha > \beta$). We will also make the very general assumption, that the two individuals have a simple choice between two (and only two) options of either exchanging property and thus respecting the other's property rights (called C for cooperating) or violating the other's rights by stealing his property (D for defecting). We will simultaneously make the somewhat restrictive assumption that the players—unless otherwise noted—make their choices simultaneously and independently. We will finally assume that engaging in a violation of the rights of others carries some costs (χ) with it for the violator, at least in the form of time and resources spent stealing, but possibly also in the form of enforced sanctions.

Such a 2 × 2 game gives four possible outcomes, which we may define in terms of the goods α and β and the cost χ, and that we may signify through some simplified payoffs (p, r, s, t).[2] If both players respect each other's property and exchange property rights, then we have the outcome (C, C), where they both receive a payoff in the form of a cooperator's reward (r), i.e., I gives α to II and receives β in return, while II gets α and gives up β [$\beta-\alpha$, $\alpha-\beta$]. If one player chooses C, while another chooses D, i.e., (C, D) or (D, C), the defecting player receives a traitor's payoff (t), while the cooperating player receives a sucker's payoff (s); if, for example, a defecting player I steals β from a cooperative II, he will receive this good but also incur some costs [$\alpha + \beta-\chi$, $-\beta$], while if II steals α from I, he will similarly receive this while incurring costs [$-\alpha$, $\alpha + \beta-\chi$]. If they both steal simultaneously (D, D), they will both receive a payoff of a defector's punishment (p), i.e., where they both have costs and while getting one good also loses another [$\beta-\alpha-\chi$, $\alpha-\beta-\chi$]. This general form of the payoffs of what can be called a State-of-Nature Game is given in Figure 1.

By changing the values of the payoffs this framework allows for a potentially infinite multitude of games portraying various situations. Let us for the present purposes assume that the value of $\alpha = 2$ and $\beta = 3$ for player I, while $\alpha = 3$ and $\beta = 2$ for player II. Given these assumptions we may investigate what happens as a result of changes in

Figure 1

General Payoffs for the State-of-Nature Game

		II	
		C	D
I	C	$\alpha - \beta$ $\beta - \alpha$	$\alpha + \beta - \chi$ $-\alpha$
	D	$-\beta$ $\alpha + \beta - \chi$	$\alpha - \beta - \chi$ $\beta - \alpha - \chi$

the costs; this has been done in Table 1 by computing different values for χ.

The Hobbesian Problem

This framework may be used for the analysis of such situations as those described by the classical contractarians, where a conflict may exist between the rational behavior of individuals and the consequences, which these together produce. Thomas Hobbes (1991) and Hugo Grotius (1901), for example, identified "peace," understood as domestic social order, security of property rights and defense against external aggression, as what today would be termed a "public good." Samuel Pufendorf (1934, 1991) similarly identified the promotion of "sociality," understood as cooperation and mutual respect for rights, as the "fundamental natural law," since that is what enables men to successfully pursue other ends. Finally, John Locke (1988) identified "justice," understood as the lack of violations of the individual's natural right to freely pursue his self-preservation through the use of his property, as a "public good."[3]

But in a state-of-nature, where there is assumed to be nothing to make individuals pursue "peace," "sociality" or "justice" other than their own self-interest, individuals will have a choice not between outcomes but between strategies for how to act. In Hobbes's state-of-nature an individual would, for example, have a simple choice between a strategy of either "peace" or "war." If we for the present purposes assume that "peace," "sociality" or "justice" are synonymous

Table 1.

Payoffs and Preference Orderings*

Values of costs and benefits*				Resulting payoffs				Resulting preference orderings	
α	β	χ	r $(\beta-\alpha)$	s $(-\alpha)$	t $(\alpha+\beta-\chi)$	p $(\beta-\alpha-\chi)$	n (α)	without exit	with exit
2	3	0	1	−2	5	1	2	$t > r \sim p > s$	$t > n > r \sim p > s$
2	3	0.5	1	−2	4.5	0.5	2	$t > r > p > s$	$t > n > r > p > s$
2	3	1	1	−2	4	0	2	$t > r > p > s$	$t > n > r > p > s$
2	3	1.5	1	−2	3.5	−0.5	2	$t > r > p > s$	$t > n > r > p > s$
2	3	2	1	−2	3	−1	2	$t > r > p > s$	$t > n > r > p > s$
2	3	2.5	1	−2	2.5	−1.5	2	$t > r > p > s$	$t > n > r > p > s$
2	3	3	1	−2	2	−2	2	$t > r > s \sim p$	$n \sim t > r > s \sim p$
2	3	3.5	1	−2	1.5	−2.5	2	$t > r > s > p$	$n > t > r > s > p$
2	3	4	1	−2	1	−3	2	$r \sim t > s > p$	$n > r \sim t > s > p$
2	3	4.5	1	−2	0.5	−3.5	2	$r > t > s > p$	$n > r > t > s > p$
2	3	5	1	−2	0	−4	2	$r > t > s > p$	$n > r > t > s > p$
2	3	5.5	1	−2	−0.5	−4.5	2	$r > t > s > p$	$n > r > t > s > p$
2	3	6	1	−2	−1	−5	2	$r > t > s > p$	$n > r > t > s > p$
2	3	6.5	1	−2	−1.5	−5.5	2	$r > t > s > p$	$n > r > t > s > p$
2	3	7	1	−2	−2	−6	2	$r > s \sim t > p$	$n > r > s \sim t > p$
2	3	7.5	1	−2	−2.5	−6.5	2	$r > s > t > p$	$n > r > s > t > p$

* The payoffs given are those for player I. For player II it is assumed that the values of α and β are reverse.

with the general respect of established property rights of others, the possible choice-sets of the individuals can then be subsumed under two general strategies: Respecting or violating property rights, here represented by the individual strategies *C* and *D*.[4]

In a two-person setting each individual will plausibly prefer to have property rights respected in general to having them violated in general; in particular, he will probably prefer having his own property rights respected to having them violated. But he will also *ceteris paribus* (i.e., disregarding costs) prefer to violate the property rights of the other person rather than respect them, and this additional feature is what gives the interdependent situation its particular character. Given these assumptions, and the previous assumptions that the values are $\alpha = 2$ and $\beta = 3$ for player I, while they are $\alpha = 3$ and $\beta = 2$ for player II, we may present the strategic character of the situation as illustrated in the bi-matrix below, which gives the available strategies, the possible outcomes and the relevant payoffs. In that case the all-important factor becomes the size of the costs of stealing. If $\chi < 3$ the dominant strategy of both players will be to steal each other's property (D, D). If, for example, $\chi = 2$ the structure of the payoffs will be $t > r > p > s$, and the interaction will have the character of a Prisoners' Dilemma,[5] as shown in Figure 2.

In this situation each individual prefers a situation where everyone respects property rights (C, C), to one where nobody respects property rights (D, D). But it is simultaneously the case that each individual prefers to have his property rights respected while not respecting

Figure 2

Payoffs for a Prisoners' Dilemma-like State-of-Nature Game

		II			
		C		D	
			1		3
I	C	1		-2	
			-2		-1
	D	3		-1	

those of other individuals, i.e., (D, C) and (C, D) for player I and II, respectively. This structure of the preferences means that any individual who in this situation unilaterally chooses to respect the property rights of others will open himself up to—and be submitted to—predatory actions. It also means that the rational strategy for each individual is to choose not to respect property rights, and to do so no matter what strategy other individuals might choose, and thus that the equilibrium is an outcome where nobody respects property rights. In this case the game thus has the familiar outcome, i.e., the Pareto inferior Nash equilibrium (D, D).

If the interaction between the two individuals is repeated over time, then some mutual recognition of and respect for property rights might evolve as a norm, and the outcome could conceivably be that they would cooperate with each other for mutual benefit (cf., e.g., Axelrod 1984; Milgrom, North, & Weingast 1990). But with symmetric preference orderings, no external sanctions imposed for violations and shortsightedness, the interaction will have the character of a single-play game. In the absence of any enforcement mechanism it will thus be irrational for any individual to perform his part of an agreed-upon action (e.g., a contractual obligation) first.[6]

This situation is in the Hobbesian framework generalized into a "war of all against all," and there are at least two reasons for this. First, the situation is one common to *all* individuals faced with any human interaction in the state-of-nature, since all action necessarily involves the use of scarce resources and hence property rights in some form. It will, in other words, not only characterize the interaction of some particular two individuals, but potentially all the interaction of all individuals. Second, any suggested solution to these forms of interpersonal conflicts will itself constitute a collective action problem, because the protection of rights also is a public good. This is so because while all members of society may agree, that they would all be better off if they respected each others' rights there is a latent conflict between what is individually rational and collectively rational when it comes to actually voluntarily providing the public good of "peace," "sociality" or "justice." If, for example, the securing of the public good is simply seen as the outcome of the individuals voluntarily changing their behavior from violating each others' rights to respecting these, and if there are no changes in the preferences of the individuals, then the choice-set of the separate individual will none-theless still be that of the bi-matrix of the figure.

This is the situation described in the famous passage in Hobbes:

> [It] is manifest, that during the time men live without a common Power to keep them all in awe, they are in that condition which is called Warre; and such a warre, as is of every man, against every man. . . . [The] nature of War, consisteth not in actuall fighting; but in the known disposition thereto, during all the time there is no assurance to the contrary. . . . Whatsoever therefore is consequent to a time of Warre, where every man is Enemy to every man; the same is consequent to the time, wherein men live without other security, than what their own strength, and their own invention shall furnish them withall. In such condition there is no place for Industry; because the fruit thereof is uncertain: and consequently no Culture of the Earth; no Navigation, nor use of the commodities that may be imported by Sea; no commodious Building; no Instruments of moving, and removing such things as require much force; no Knowledge of the face of the Earth; no account of Time; no Arts; no Letters; no Society; and which is worst of all, continuall feare, and danger of violent death; And the life of man, solitary, poore, nasty, brutish and short. (Hobbes 1991, §62: 88–89)

The Hobbesian Solution

Hobbes's well-known solution to the problem of the war of all against all was to argue for the existence of a central authority, which can impose sanctions upon those who seek war rather than peace. Hobbes specifically reasoned that every individual in "the natural condition of mankind" guided by reason will come to realize the "fundamental law of nature," which is, "to seek Peace, and follow it," and accordingly, as the second law, "be willing, when others are so too, as farre-forth as for Peace, and defence of himselfe he shall think it necessary, to lay down this right to all things" (Hobbes 1991, §65: 92). Accordingly, each individual in the state-of-nature must make a covenant with every other individual, in which they mutually promise to give up the right of self-defense by relinquishing that and all other rights to a political authority to be created, either stipulated in each covenant or chosen by a majority. The political authority thus created has full and undivided sovereignty and the obligation to secure internal and external peace and is unconstrained.[7]

The situation created by the Hobbesian political authority corresponds to a revised game, which we may call a Leviathan game, where a third player, the Leviathan, has imposed costs χ such that $\chi >$ 4. This is shown in Figure 3, where $\chi = 5$ and where the resulting preference orderings of the players are $r > t > s > p$.

Here the political authority created by the social contract has succeeded in imposing sanctions upon those who do not respect the property rights of others and thus successfully changed the payoffs of the individuals so as to induce them to cooperate. In this case the game has been turned into a simple coordination game with the one and only Nash equilibrium being (C, C). The costs of violating the rights of others have become so prohibitively high that no single player can do better than to respect the rights of the others.[8]

The Lockean Problem

John Locke in his famous *Two Treatises of Government* (1988) generally shared the Hobbesian point: Political society will be preferable to natural society. But he also pointed toward two important possibilities, which may seriously modify the Hobbesian analysis: That the state-of-nature may not necessarily be a war of all against all, and that political authority itself may be abused and turned into tyranny.

Concerning the first point Locke had a more multi-faceted conception of the state-of-nature than Hobbes: It can be a peaceful, harmonious condition, where human beings live in accordance with the laws of nature, i.e., they do not aggress against other individuals but respect their rights to life, liberty and property. But it can also degenerate into a state-of-war, where people engage in continuous fighting. With an indirect reference to Hobbes, Locke said:

> [Here] we have the plain *difference between the State of Nature, and the State of War*, which however some Men have confounded, are as far distant, as a State of Peace, Good Will, Mutual Assistance, and Preservation, and a State of Enmity, Malice, Violence, and Mutual Destruction are one from another. Men living together according to reason, without a common Superior on Earth, with Authority to judge between them, is properly the State of Nature. But force, or a declared design of force upon the Person of another, where there is no common Superior on Earth to appeal to for relief, *is the State of War*. (Locke 1988, II, §19: 280; italics in orig.)

The reason why this may degenerate into a state-of-war is, according to Locke, that in the absence of any ultimate enforcer of the laws of nature, each individual is permitted to execute the law himself. Hence,

Figure 3

Payoffs for a Leviathan Game

		II	
		C	D
I	C	1 1	0 −2
	D	0 −2	−4 −4

the violation by one individual may result in punishment by and enforced restitution to another, which may turn out to be more than necessary, and which again may result in counter-measures, etc.[9] If this
happens it will be obviously advantageous to join together in a social
contract establishing political authority.[10]

But even this is not necessarily the final outcome: Peace may ensue
if one party acquiesces to the demands of the other: "*the State of War
once begun, continues* . . . until the aggressor offers Peace, and desires
reconciliation on such Terms, as may repair any wrongs he has already done, and secure the innocent for the future" (Locke 1988, II,
§20: 281; italics in orig.). This may or may not be a likely ending, but
Locke does, in other words, suggest that any conflict may be ended
peacefully.

Together these two possibilities suggest, contrary to Hobbes, that it
is not the case that *every* form of political authority *always* is preferable to *any* type of state-of-nature: Political society can result in the
production of public goods not found in the state-of-nature, but it may
also result in tyranny, and the question is thus about the relative value
of the one against the other. Sometimes, although they may be rare,
the state-of-nature may be preferable to a tyrannical state:

> I easily grant, that *Civil Government* is the proper Remedy for the Inconve-
> niences of the State of Nature, which must certainly be Great, . . . But I
> shall desire those who make this Objection, to remember that *Absolute
> Monarchs* are but Men, and if Government is to be the Remedy of those
> Evils, which necessarily follow from Mens being Judges in their own Cases,
> and the State of Nature is therefore not to be endured, I desire to know
> what kind of Government that is, and *how much better it is* than the State
> of Nature, *where one Man commanding a multitude, has the Liberty to be*

Judge in his own Case, and may do to all his Subjects whatever he pleases, without the least liberty to any one to question or controle those who Execute his Pleasure? And in whatsoever he doth, whether led by Reason, Mistake or Passion, must be submitted to? *Much better it is in the State of Nature wherein Men are not bound to submit to the unjust will of another.* And if he that judges, judges amiss in his own, or any other Case, he is answerable for it to the rest of Mankind. (Locke 1988, II, §13: 274; italics partly in orig.)

In this way tyranny, in the form of arbitrary power, is, says Locke, "nothing else, but *the State of War continued, between a lawful Conqueror, and a Captive*" (Locke 1988, II, §23: 284; italics in orig.).[11]

We may model this in the following way by formulating some simple games that utilize the same framework used for the Hobbesian analysis. First, it can be shown that Locke is right in assuming that even if the interests of individuals in a state-of-nature are opposed, they may still settle on an outcome that is not the equivalent of a state-of-war. His suggestion that an aggressor may offer peace and reconciliation on mutually agreeable terms can be read as a suggestion that there is a tradeoff between the costs of fighting and the benefits to be reaped and that occasionally the individual costs of continued fighting between the parties may outweigh the benefits. This is the case (e.g., when there is no enforcement of property rights) when $4 > \chi > 3$; in that case the structure of the payoffs is $t > r > s > p$. If we, for example, assume that $\chi = 3.5$, the game will be as in Figure 4.

This game has two pure-strategy Nash equilibria, (D, C) and (C, D). In this way it is different from the Prisoners' Dilemma and rather fundamentally similar to the well-known Chicken Game. Here the dilemma is that while both players prefer (C, C) to (D, D), it is simultaneously the case that they each most prefer an outcome that is rather unattractive to the other, (D, C) and (C, D), respectively. What the outcome will be depends crucially on what the one player believes the other will do, and hence, e.g., on whether the interaction is with simultaneous or sequential moves. If the player knows that the other will choose C, he will himself choose D, while if he thinks the other will choose D, he will (without much enthusiasm) choose C. The problem is that with simultaneous moves the players may misunderstand each other and both choose D, which result in the worst of

Figure 4

Payoffs for a Chicken-like State-of-Nature Game

		II	
		C	D
I	C	1 1	1.5 −2
	D	−2 1.5	−2.5 −2.5

all outcomes for both. Such a game is in some ways less problematic than that of the Prisoners' Dilemma. If the players are faced with repeated interactions, and if communication is possible, it may be possible to secure positive payoffs through coordination, e.g., by taking turns. On the other hand, the outcome of the game is somewhat indeterminate and with the danger of undesirable outcomes. In this way the analysis adds further to Michael Taylor's suggestion that such public good problems as found in a state-of-nature quite often have a character different from that of the much-used Prisoners' Dilemma, and, e.g., can have the character of a Chicken Game or an Assurance Game.[12] So while the state-of-nature may not necessarily be the best of all worlds, it is not necessarily the worst of all worlds either.[13]

In contrast, the situation of a citizen under the tyranny of a powerful but unconstrained Leviathan is unambiguously unattractive. We may represent this as a game, where the citizen and the Leviathan are interacting, with the choices again being those of either respecting the rights of the other or violating these, but where the payoffs due to the different character and power of the actors become asymmetric. We may specifically assume that the citizen is faced with payoffs such as those between himself and other citizens ($r > t > s > p$), while the Leviathan, constitutionally unconstrained, will only incur few costs from exploiting a citizen and thus is free to act as he chooses, i.e., as an inhabitant of the state-of-nature ($t > r > p > s$). This is done in Figure 5, where we have simply taken the payoffs from the previous games of a Leviathan Game (for the citizen) and the Prisoners' Dilemma-like State-of-Nature Game (for the Leviathan).

Figure 5

Payoffs for a Citizen-Leviathan Game

		Leviathan		
		C		D
Citizen	C	1	1	−2	3
	D	0	−2	−4	−1

In this case the game will have the unique Nash equilibrium (*C*, *D*).[14] The citizen will behave like a good little citizen toward the Leviathan, because the costs of not doing so are considerable, while the Leviathan in contrast will exploit this because his costs of violating the rights of the citizens are negligible. Here we have, in other words, exactly what Locke feared: The decisions of the political authority will have unattractive consequences for the citizens and potentially some that are worse than those found in a Lockean state-of-nature.

The Lockean Solution

There have been many, often conflicting, interpretations of Locke's message, but Locke could be seen as making the argument that if political authority becomes tyrannical, the citizens have the right to withdraw their consent. They have, so speak, a right to "exit" the political obligations they have been under.

In essence Locke argued—as we have seen and as Hobbes argued—that an ultimate political authority is justified as a remedy for an efficient and just enforcement of property rights by the restraining of violence, but also, contrary to Hobbes, that since injustice may also occur under an unconstrained and sovereign political authority, a legitimate government can only be one created by consent and only and solely by giving up those rights (and no more) that are necessary for providing the public good of protecting rights.[15] This is so because a rational individual would never consent to anything but that which makes himself better off, and a group of individuals would thus not agree to a for them Pareto-inferior solution.[16] If, however, those who exercise political authority violate the trust placed in them and act as tyrants, the government is thereby automatically dissolved, i.e., the citizens are released from their political obligations and can decide as they will.[17] "Men," Locke says, "can never be secure from Tyranny, if there be no means to escape it, till they are perfectly under it: And therefore it is, that they have not only a Right to get out of it but to prevent it" (Locke 1988, II, §220: 411).

How are we to make sense of this today? Locke was obviously no political anarchist,[18] i.e., he did not prefer a state-of-nature *per se*. He also did not endorse that everyone should be free to rebel at will and at any given time. One could see the Lockean solution as being a solution attempting to make the constitutional set-up look more like a market: Based on the possibility of a mutually beneficial exchange of property rights and with the possibility of rejecting unfavorable offers. For that purpose it is possible to utilize a relatively simple reformulation of the Prisoners' Dilemma, albeit one with important consequences, which initially was suggested by Gordon Tullock (1985) and later used by others (Vanberg & Congleton 1992). For despite the fact that the use of the Prisoners' Dilemma has become so immensely popular for the description of many social situations, it should, upon reflection, be clear that there are important aspects of the interaction of individuals in the marketplace that makes the game less generally representative there. Even if there are many a traitor's payoff to be reaped in billions of daily interactions all over the world, there would seem to be a rather significant part where people actually do get along, and not just because they are afraid of being detected and prosecuted by a Leviathan.

The important aspect, which makes the Prisoners' Dilemma Game less than perfectly suited for the analysis of market interactions, is that the players lack the possibility of "exit."[19] It is generally not the case that individuals operating on a market only have the choice between making an exchange or stealing; a quite significant possibility is that of simply not doing any business at all, in particular with those who behave in an unattractive way.

In order to incorporate this into the game, we will assume that the players have the further possibility of choosing the strategy of "exit" (*E*), i.e., a player simply refuses to deal with the other player. Specifically we will assume that if one of the players does so, both of them will simply maintain what they already had as their initial endowment, i.e., player I keeps α and player II keeps β. By adding these assumptions to the State-of-Nature Game, we get the revised game shown in Figure 6.

In order to make the game comparable with the 2 × 2 games, we may thus add the payoff "no payoff" (*n*) to those of *p*, *r*, *s* and *t*, as given in Table 1, where the payoffs are recalculated and the preference orderings reordered.[20]

We may now analyze what the consequences may be, if exit is added as an alternative, possible strategy to the games considered. We will do by, first, considering what effect such an assumption may have for an interaction such as that resembling the Prisoners' Dilemma, presumed to be characteristic of the interaction of the individuals in a state-of-nature, and, second, what the consequences may be in a setting with the citizen and the Leviathan interacting.

Considering the interaction in the state-of-nature it is obvious that the outcome, of course, will depend upon the relative values of the payoffs. If the value of the payoffs are $t > r > n > p > s$ (i.e., if $2.5 > \chi > 0$), the basic structure of the game will be that of the Prisoners' Dilemma with the added possibility of Exit, or what will here be called the Prisoners' Dilemma-with-Exit Game. This is shown in Figure 7.[21]

Figure 6

General Payoffs for the State-of-Nature-with-Exit Game

		II		
		C	D	E
I	C	$\alpha - \beta$ $\beta - \alpha$	$\alpha + \beta - \chi$ $-\alpha$	β α
	D	$-\beta$ $\alpha + \beta - \chi$	$\alpha - \beta - \chi$ $\beta - \alpha - \chi$	β α
	E	β α	β α	β α

Figure 7

The Prisoners' Dilemma-with-Exit Game

		II		
		C	D	E
I	C	1 \ 1	3 \ -2	0 \ 0
I	D	-2 \ 3	-1 \ -1	0 \ 0
I	E	0 \ 0	0 \ 0	0 \ 0

The change has significant effects upon the game; the introduction of an exit option in fact fundamentally changes the nature of the game.[22] Instead of having *Defect* as the strictly dominant strategy and the outcome (*D, D*) as the one and only Nash equilibrium, this game has three Nash equilibria (*D, E*), (*E, D*) and (*E, E*), i.e., they all result in the exit option being used by at least one player. If a player feels that defecting is an unattractive choice, he is no longer restricted to choosing to be an unconditional cooperator. Rather, the relative costs and benefits of *Exit* become an important part in the game and hence in what strategies will be viable in the long run, i.e., in repeated games.

It has indeed been shown in a tournament that in repeated games resembling the PDE a strategy of so-called "prudent morality" may do quite well (Vanberg & Congleton 1992:421ff).[23] Such a strategy is one where a player initially always cooperates when he chooses to play the game, but refuses to play with players who have defected in the past.[24] In repeated plays of PDE, a player who is a Prudent Moralist will beat a number of other attractive strategies, including not only a Naive Moralist (who always plays and always cooperates) and an Opportunist (who always plays and always defects), but also the well-known Tit-for-Tat strategy (who always plays and uses the strategy played by the other when they last met) (Vanberg & Congleton 1992:422). In a second tournament it was shown that in repeated PDE games with more than a couple of interactions the Prudent Moralists have the highest total payoff and their presence in the games increases the payoffs of the other players (Vanberg & Congleton 1992: 423ff). It has also been shown, through laboratory experiments, that in situations resembling the PDE game, the players who behave in a way reminiscent of a Prudent Moralist will come out with the highest total payoffs and that this indeed is a widely adopted strategy (Tullock 1999). This suggests that in settings where exit is possible, reputation and trust will be important and indeed result in cooperative behavior by individuals (cf. Klein 1997). It also suggests that a market economy may not generally have the wicked character of a Prisoners' Dilemma.[25]

When it comes to constitutional set-up the analysis suggests, first, that the state-of-nature will not necessarily have the terrible character envisioned by Hobbes and the neo-Hobbesians. If the individuals can refuse to interact, the result may be that life of man is not necessarily nasty, brutish and short—and it might not even be solitary and poor. This again strengthens the Lockean implication that it is not necessarily the case that remaining in the state-of-nature will be less favorable than any political society. And this again implies that rational individuals conceivably would require Leviathan to be constrained through constitutional constraints.

But secondly we may also consider what the consequences would be of a constitutional set-up where a citizen has the right to exit the political society if the conditions prove too unattractive. The games with exit need indeed not have symmetric payoffs (Tullock 1985: 1078), and so we may, and perhaps more importantly, also consider what happens when the citizen and the Leviathan meet and they have the possibility to exit. This is shown in Figure 8, which uses the previous asymmetric payoffs combined with an assumption of $n = 0$.

Figure 8

The Citizen-Leviathan-with-Exit Game

		Leviathan		
		C	D	E
Citizen	C	1 / 1	3 / −2	0 / 0
	D	−2 / 0	−1 / −4	0 / 0
	E	0 / 0	0 / 0	0 / 0

In this case the game has three Nash equilibria, namely again (D, E), (E, D) and (E, E), i.e., which all result in the exit option being used by at least one player. Here it is noteworthy that these three all are Pareto inferior: The Pareto optimal outcome is (C, C), as in, e.g., the standard Prisoners' Dilemma game, i.e., an outcome corresponding to the Leviathan respecting the rights of the citizen and the latter remaining in the political society. At first sight this would then seem to be an unhappy ending.

Nonetheless, the game is different in important aspects. First, all three equilibria are also Pareto superior to the usual PD Nash equilibrium outcome (D, D), and if nothing else the Nash equilibria all have the quality that none of the players are worse off from the game. Second, due to the asymmetric nature of the payoffs, the cooperative strategy is not strictly dominated by both the other strategies: If, for example, the citizen knows that Leviathan will cooperate, he can do no better than cooperate himself. If, for example, the game is played as a sequential game, with the Leviathan moving first and the citizen second, the sub-game perfect equilibrium is one where both cooperate (C, C).[26] Furthermore, if the game is repeated, the risk of a citizen not playing with a Leviathan, who has exploited him in an earlier game, may thus impose a severe restraint on a government. All in all, this suggests that if the players have the possibility of exiting this will, even in an asymmetric game between a powerful government and a single citizen, introduce severe restrictions on what actions the former will take, especially if the interaction is repeated over time.

II

Some Extensions and Implications: Choosing Between Institutions and Communities

THERE ARE UNDOUBTEDLY far fewer tyrants today than in the times of Hobbes and Locke, at least in the Western world. But even in the absence of blatant tyranny, bad government may still occur and even be prevalent. Public organizations do not necessarily supply optimal, welfare-increasing solutions, the representative democracy does not necessarily produce policies agreeable to large parts of society (or even a majority) and even the democratic process itself may be incapable of consistently aggregating the preferences of the citizens (Riker 1982). In such instances citizens run the risk of some form of exploitation by other groups, in the sense of being net-payers to others who are net-beneficiaries.

A way to illustrate this is through one of the classical arguments offered in favor of a decentralized, federal-like system, namely, that it will allow the citizens to group together in units, which will make it easier for heterogeneous preferences to be reflected in the policy outcomes. If we imagine a centralized political community of 100 citizens, where 60 citizens favor policy A while 40 favor policy non-A, the former policy will be adopted, despite the fact that no less than 40 citizens will be dissatisfied. If, on the other hand, we have a decentralized political community, and if policies A and non-A can co-exist in different, but geographically proximate, areas, the end result may very likely be one with less dissatisfied citizens. If, for example, in the first region 50 citizens prefer policy A, while 10 oppose it, and 30 citizens in a second province favor non-A with 10 being in favor of A, the over-all preferences are identical, but the outcomes quite different: Some 60 citizens will get A, while 40 will get non-A, but only 20, rather than 40, citizens will be dissatisfied. If there furthermore is mobility within the political community, citizens will be able to vote with their feet, move between the two provinces and the end result being even more satisfied citizens.[27]

So goes the familiar argument. But the point additionally made here is that if the policies produced by the political community are such that they can be provided without significant externality effects of a "geographical" character, the same advantages may be gained by simply allowing individuals or groups to opt-out from the institutional arrangement, even if they remain in the same place.[28] And even with externalities, we should expect these to be internalized if the costs of exiting are low and the rights to exit and enter are clearly defined.

What is suggested here could be seen as being, in essence, a constitutional extension of the Tiebout Model (1956) and the Coase Theorem (1960, 1988). The former is the argument that if the market for local public goods potentially satisfies the assumptions of neo-classical perfect competition (perfect information, many suppliers and costless mobility), local governments will be constrained, even in the absence of democratic institutions. They must in their policies try to follow the preferences of the citizens, simply in order not to lose these to more attractive competitors.[29] The Coase Theorem would argue, against an objection that a right of exit would create chaos, that if the property rights are properly specified (i.e., if it is clear who are allowed to secede when and how, and what they can and cannot take with them "out"), and if the transaction costs are low, then we should generally expect the overall result to be bargaining between the parties so as to produce long-term improvements for all.

What we are suggesting here is, when taken to its root, what could alternatively be called a non-geographically based federalism. Alternatively one could properly speak of a "polyarchic" constitutional order,[30] but unfortunately the term "polyarchy" has already been expropriated and used for something quite different. Actually, what is proposed here is in principle closest to what has been suggested by the economists Bruno Frey and Reiner Eichenberger in their analysis of what they call FOCJ (Functionally Overlapping Competing Jurisdictions) (Frey & Eichenberger 1999).

It would therefore seem as if a case could be made for why even in Western democracies "opting-out" might seem a constitutional device to consider. We may accordingly rightly ask whether there are any insights from the previous analysis for constitutional design and for an application of what is here called the Lockean solution?[31] The basic insight of the previous would seem to be that the presence of an exit option and the relative costs of using that option is of great importance to the interaction between actors be it in a state-of-nature or inside a political community. The following discussion will, however, only be able to deal with a very few general observations.

Toward an Exit Principle

Could we imagine an institutionalized right of individuals, groups or institutions to "exit" from larger political communities? We might suggest a tentative formulation of a general exit principle to consider: "Individuals in any size group may exit a political unit, when they desire to, and without cost form a new political unit. Once created this unit must provide its own public goods."[32] But this raises a number of questions.

First: This would, however, in many ways seem extremely difficult to implement, at least if we want to remain within what is realistic in a broad sense of the word. It would, for example, be difficult to imagine the idea taken to its furthest logical conclusion, i.e., that of allowing every individual citizen to completely exit a political community at will (cf. Mises 1962:109-110). In addition to being problematic to implement and administer on consequential grounds, it would further-more risk what Locke feared, namely, the degeneration of society into a state-of-war.

Second, in order to avoid very unattractive consequences for many individuals, it would seem necessary to identify and clarify a number of questions, including the necessary and sufficient conditions to be ful-filled in order for exit by some to be permissible. First, who should be allowed to exit? Second, with "what," i.e., what can they exit with, and what actions will they be allowed to take when they have exited?

To begin considering these questions, it is worth recognizing that there would seem to be a vast number of possible, imaginable solu-tions between on the one hand the completely homogenous, central-ized political community and, on the other hand, a literal anarchy. This is in particular the case when it is realized that an exit principle may be applied (or not applied) to several different levels of political organization, and that exit in one "dimension" need not necessarily entail exit in all.

In order to focus the following discussion we may accordingly dis-tinguish between a number of different relations between "levels" of political communities; more could be included, but this would seem sufficient to focus the subsequent discussion:

- Political units vs. political hierarchies (e.g., states vis-à-vis federa-tions, local governments vis-à-vis regions/states, etc.)
- Institutions vs. larger institutions (e.g., an individual public school vis-à-vis a public school system, or a hospital vis-à-vis a public health system, etc.)
- Individuals vs. institutions (e.g., parents of school children vis-à-vis a public school system, patients vis-à-vis a public health system, etc.)

The most obvious way of institutionalization of exit is that of seces-sion, i.e., where one political sub-unit (usually a geographically contiguous and non-perforated entity) exits from a political community, e.g., an individual state from a federal state, and then gains sovereignty. The theoretical and practical arguments for such a federated relationship between political units and for the right of secession have been well established for long.[33]

But secession need strictly speaking not necessarily be in the form of a state vis-à-vis a federal state. It can be one county relative to a state, or a town or another local government relative to a county, or a neighborhood relative to a town, etc., etc. And it can be in the form of either going solo and obtaining separate status, be it in the form of full sovereignty (as in the case of, e.g., Slovenia relative to the Federal Republic of Yugoslavia) or incorporation as a separate entity (as with many towns in the United States).

Many liberal thinkers have championed this idea over the centuries, e.g., the Austrian economist, Ludwig von Mises:

> The right of self-determination in regard to the question of membership in a state thus means: whenever the inhabitants of a particular territory, whether it be a single village, a whole district, or a series of adjacent districts, make it known, by a freely conducted plebiscite, that they no longer wish to remain united to the state to which they belong at the time, but wish either to form an independent state or to attach themselves to some other state, their wishes are to be respected and complied with. This is the only feasible and effective way of preventing revolutions and civil and international wars. (Mises 1962:109),

Mises thus advocated not just national but jurisdictional self-determination, "the right of self-determination of the inhabitants of every territory large enough to form an independent administrative unit" (Mises 1962:109).[34]

John Stuart Mill had prior to Mises, expressed similar ideas. Speaking of the Mormons in the United States and their practice of polygamy, Mill condemned this institution but defended their right to practice it in their own communities as well as the institutional framework:

> [It] is difficult to see on what principles but those of tyranny they can be prevented from living there under what laws they please, provided they commit no aggression on other nations, and allow perfect freedom of departure to those who are dissatisfied with their ways. (Mill 1991:102)

For many, such ideas as suggested by Mill and Mises would seem farfetched and impractical, since it would make it possible for situations to occur, where one state had sovereign "enclaves" within its own borders. Ever since the Peace of Westphalia, and in particular in the post-Napoleonic period, a prominent operating principle regulating the size and shape of states has indeed been that states should be contiguous and non-perforated (Smith 1997). But while prominent this is to a large degree a very simplistic view; there is neither a strict necessity nor a historical basis for insisting that this should apply to all states. Historically, the 1,000 years of the Holy Roman Empire was in fact one long experience in geographically non-contiguous and perforated political communities; here the organizing principle for connection to a political or legal authority was not location relative to an external border, but rather property, allegiance and membership. In terms of states, the most prominent example was that of the Dukes of Burgundy, whose state in the fifteenth century consisted of a dozen parts, some of which were under the suzerainty of the King of France, others under the Holy Roman Emperor, and some which were sovereign, and of which very few were connected.[35]

Even today not all states are geographically contiguous (e.g., the United States) or non-perforated (e.g., Italy and South Africa). The perhaps best illustration may be that of the communities of Baarle-Hertog/Baarle-Nassau on the border between Belgium and the Netherlands.[36] At the Peace of Munster of 1648 the parties could not agree on where exactly to draw a border of some 50 kilometers and hence allowed the citizens of 5,732 parcels to determine their citizenship not after their location but after their nationality, one by one. Still today at least 20 Belgian enclaves exist some five kilometers inside the Netherlands, just as there is a Dutch enclave inside Belgium. Another contemporary examples is the—still non-settled—issue of the Palestinian Authority vis-à-vis that of the state of Israel.[37]

The number of possibilities grow even further when one realizes that it quite often is possible to make only a partial exit, i.e., to exit in one "dimension" while not doing so in another. It is, for example, a well-established idea that political units can choose to band together, either at various levels or policy areas (e.g., NATO, OSCE or the EEC/EU, or some of the various treaties establishing limited cooperation), or local governments and municipalities forming partial cooperation (transportation, hospitals, etc.). But if that is possible, then so is the reverse, i.e., political units exiting in some dimensions; though this is less common that the entry into such alliances, examples exist, e.g., the situation of Greenland relative to the EEC/EU. In 1985 Greenland, which had been given semi-autonomous status within the state of Denmark in 1979, left the EEC following a referendum. Since then Greenland has not been a party to the integration of Denmark into the EU.

What this suggests is that given precisely defined constitutional rights of political entities to exit, we should expect groups to band together and exit and provide their own public goods when the marginal effects of doing so become sufficiently large, due either to a failure to produce sufficient public goods or from an excessive supply of public "bads."

But the exit principle sketched here might, as indicated, conceivably be extended not only to some forms of group secession, but also to the somewhat more modest goal of permitting individual citizens or individuals institutions within a government to opt out of a particular structure within the public sector, while still remaining within the larger political structure.

One could, for example, imagine an exit option applied in the relation of individuals vis-à-vis specific institutions or even taken down to levels of the smallest possible administrative units vis-à-vis higher level units (Mises 1962:109). This is, in essence, what has been taking place in recent decades, where institutional exit from public sector systems has indeed become relatively common in recent decades, e.g., by allowing former government institutions to become independent and operate on market terms. Similarly, individual exit has been encouraged in many previously government dominated areas, e.g., by voucher plans, private pension schemes, etc. One could, for example, imagine giving citizens in a state the right to freely choose between local government institutions and services irrespective of their own physical location.

III

Discussion

In the following an attempt will be made at identifying some of the positive and negative consequences, that could be seen as associated with an exit principle such as described. Since exit has been described in relatively broad and general terms, so will the discussion of the positive and negative consequences.

Positive Consequences

There would seem to be a number of possible benefits to potentially be reaped from the very general set-up described here.

One of the most obvious advantages is that an exit option creates the possibility of peaceful solutions to conflicts. What we have been saying here is basically similar to the suggestion that tyranny is constrained when sub-groups within a political community have the opportunity to "fission," i.e., to exit (Taylor 1982).[38] Instead of both parties investing time and resources in battling over policies, they can separate peacefully. This may, of course, not be what takes place in reality, as evidenced by, e.g., the U.S. Civil War or the war involving Yugoslavia, Bosnia-Herzegovina and Croatia, but if the constitutional framework is in place at the national level, and if the rights are respected, it may be a more peaceful solution than what would otherwise take place and hence diminish the risk of civil war, ethnic cleansing, etc. (Mises 1962:109; Smith 1997).

A second advantage may come out of a different facet of the interaction, i.e., an exit option may be a way to stimulate economic growth. It has been argued that it was exactly the polycentric and decentralized character of medieval Europe, and in particular the hundreds of units making up the Holy Roman Empire, which created the historically unparalleled economic growth of the European miracle (North & Thomas 1973; Rosenberg & Birdzell 1986). One could also make a plausible argument for why it was the extraordinary possibilities of relatively easy exit that played an important role in creating the so far most economically successful state in world history—the United States, in the nineteenth century.

It should also be stressed that a right to exit might even have positive consequences without ever being used. The simple fact that it *could* be used will exert pressure on governments (cf. Buchanan & Faith 1987:1023).

Negative Consequences

There would, however, also seem to be a number of reasonable objections that could be raised against the very general exit principle considered.

One of these is the question of Pareto-violations, i.e., the possibility that while some may be better off due to the possibility of exit, others may be worse off. If the exiting unit is supposed to be able to exit without complete unanimity among the relevant players, the result could be violations of the Pareto-principle when and where the units are made up of individuals with heterogeneous preferences over the options. In that case the choice of exit by, say, a majority would result in the majority being better off, but with a minority being worse off (or reverse). This would suggest the application of a unanimity principle, but that would in turn in most instances raise the decision costs to a prohibitive level (cf. Buchanan & Tullock 1965); this would in turn lower the relative costs of alternatives, such as war. It would, in other words, not necessarily prevent tragedies such as the wars in ex-Yugo-slavia.

A second problem relating to Pareto-violations would be when it comes to those who may not be part of the exiting unit, but who are somehow "left." If the exit is supposed to be decided unilaterally by the exiting unit, this might potentially have significant negative externality effects for the members of the political community to be exited. Bargaining between the parties might solve this, but a fall-back point must exist. If, for example, the members of the political community have a veto right against exits, this may be used for extracting extremely high "exit fees" from the exiting unit.

These issues highlight the necessity for carefully creating the institutional framework that may enable exit. Specifically, such rules would need to precisely point out who are allowed to exit and when, what the decision procedures are to be and what can happen to individuals or groups who may be negatively affected by the exit by others.

IV

Conclusion

AN ATTEMPT HAS BEEN MADE to briefly sketch an argument for why a right of "exit" in the form of, e.g., secession and other forms of institutional exit, should, contrary to Sunstein's assertion, not be seen as being the source of more struggles and of exploitation, but rather for exactly the opposite. The possibility of exit creates a guarantee for the individual player against excessive high external costs, i.e., from decisions made by others. But as such it may also support the promotion of the general good of all players.

The present discussion has been in extremely general and abstract terms and so one should be careful with over-interpretations of the range of implications. An obvious limitation of the theoretical analysis, for example, is that it only draws upon examples from an environment of two-player games. It is quite obvious that the results might be different if the situation was one of n-person interaction. On the other hand, the analysis should perhaps be seen less as the final word than as the tentative beginning of a different way to conceptualize the structure of the public sector and the political community itself.

Notes

1. See, e.g., Buchanan 1975; Axelrod 1984:3–4; Kavka 1986; Hampton 1986; Gauthier 1986; Taylor 1987:125–163; Kraus 1993.

2. The use of such payoffs is quite common, see, e.g., Axelrod 1984; Bates 1988; Vanberg & Congleton 1992. Here small letters have, however, been used for the payoffs in order not to confuse them with strategies, which here are denoted by large letters.

3. On these points, see, e.g., Hobbes 1991, Chs. 13–15:86–111; Pufendorf 1991, I, Ch. 3, §§7–9:35–36; Locke 1988, II, §17:279.

4. Cf., e.g., Pufendorf 1934, VI: Ch. 4; Locke 1988, II: Chs. 2–3.

5. For some of the many similar uses of the Prisoners' Dilemma to illustrate the fundamental character of the public good character of cooperation in states-of-nature, see., e.g., Barry 1990:253–254; Tullock 1974:2, 11–16; Buchanan 1975:26–28, 64–68, 130–146; Gauthier 1986; Hampton 1986:61–63, 75–93, 132–139, 225–232; Kavka 1986:109–113, 124–140, 154–156, 245–246; Schmidtz 1991:57–85. John Rawls also uses the Prisoners' Dilemma in order to illustrate the argument for government provision of public goods (Rawls 1971:269). It is also often used in reviews of contractarian arguments in order to illustrate these (Green 1988; Kraus 1993).

6. See, e.g., Hobbes 1991, §68:96–97. See also Hampton 1986:62–63.

7. See Hobbes 1991, especially Chs. 14–15. Grotius' position was close to Hobbes's, but much less developed (see, e.g., Grotius 1901:63–68). Pufendorf similarly saw the institution of political authority as necessary for preserving and developing the socially beneficial institutions; if "sociality" is not so secured, there is a risk that the seeking of self-preservation by individuals will endanger it. Pufendorf therefore envisioned that individuals in the state-of-nature voluntarily would form a two-stage social contract, whereby it is decided to institute political authority and decide its specific form (cf. especially

Pufendorf 1934, VII: Ch. 2; Pufendorf 1991, I, Ch. 3, §7:35). Of contemporary political contractarians, James Buchanan (1975) has similarly outlined a strictly logical social contractual process also consisting of two stages (or levels), whereby individuals out of consideration of their own utility-maximization are seen as unanimously agreeing on the assignment of property rights and provision of public goods, first and foremost the protection of rights (cf. Buchanan 1975:17–73).

8. For more detailed and elaborate reconstructions and discussions of Hobbes's political theory using game theory, see in particular Hampton 1986; Kavka 1986; Taylor 1987.

9. Cf. "[Where] no such appeal is, as in the State of Nature, for want of positive Laws and Judges with Authority to appeal to, *the State of War once begun, continues*, with a right to the innocent Party, to destroy the other whenever he can. . . . " (Locke 1988, II, §20:281; italics in orig.). On this problem in the state-of-nature, cf. also §§8–13.

10. Cf. "To avoid this State of War (wherein there is no appeal but to Heaven, and wherein every the least difference is apt to end, where there is no Authority to decide between the Contenders) is one great *reason of Mens putting themselves into Society* [i.e. 'political society', the state, *PKK*] and quitting the State of Nature. For where there is an Authority, a Power on Earth, from which relief can be had by *appeal*, there the continuance of the State of War is excluded, and the Controversie is decided by that Power" (Locke 1988, II, §21:282; italics in orig.); "If Man in the State of Nature be so free, as has been said; If he be absolute Lord of his own Person and Possessions, equal to the greatest, and subject to no Body, why will he part with his Freedom? Why will he give up this Empire, and subject himself to the Dominion and Controul of any other Power? To which 'tis obvious to Answer, that though in the state of Nature he hath such a right, yet the Enjoyment of it is very uncertain, and constantly exposed to the Invasion of others. For all being Kings as much as he, every Man his Equal, and the greater part no strict Observers of Equity and Justice, the enjoyment of the property he has in this state is very unsafe, very unsecure. This makes him willing to quit this Condition, which however free, is full of fears and continual dangers: And 'tis not without reason, that he seeks out, and is willing to joyn in Society with others who are already united, or have a mind to unite for the mutual *Preservation* of their Lives, Liberties and Estates, which I call by the general name, *Property*" (Locke 1988, II, §123: 350; italics in orig.).

11. Cf. also: "[Where] an appeal to the Law, and constituted Judges lies open, but the remedy is deny'd by a manifest perverting of Justice, and a barefaced wrestling of the Laws, to protect or indemnifue the violence or injuries of some Men, or Party of Men, *there* it *is* hard to imagine any thing but *a State of War*. For wherever violence is used, and injury done, though by hands appointed to administer Justice, it is still violence and injury, however colour'd

with the Name, Pretences, or Forms of Law, the end whereof being to protect and redress the innocent, by an unbiassed application of it, to all who are under it . . . " (Locke 1988, II, §20:281–282; italics in orig.). John Stuart Mill expressed a similar analysis and fear in *On Liberty* (Mill 1991), cf. pp. 5–6.

12. See Taylor 1987; cf. Schmidtz 1991; Kurrild-Klitgaard 1997.

13. Cf. Taylor 1987. A similar point has recently been made in a formal analysis, which demonstrates that a "predatory" state, where rulers extort taxes for their own ends, can result in less out-put and popular welfare than either organized banditry or pure anarchy, even when the predators also supply public goods (Moselle & Polak 1999).

14. This will also be the sub-game perfect equilibrium in a game with sequential moves if the citizen moves first and the Leviathan last. If the order is the reverse, the sub-game perfect equilibrium will be an outcome where both cooperate (*C, C*).

15. Cf. Locke: The "great and chief end . . . of Mens uniting into Commonwealths, and putting of themselves under Government, is the Preservation of their Property" (Locke 1988, II, §124:350–351); "The *Liberty of Man, in Society*, is to be under no other Legislative Power, but that established, by consent, in the Common-wealth, nor under the Dominion of any Will, or Restraint of any Law, but what the Legislative shall enact, according to the Trust put in it" (Locke 1988, II, §22:283; italics in orig.); "This Freedom from Absolute, Arbitrary Power, is so necessary to, and closely joyned with a Man's Preservation, that he cannot part with it, but by what forfeits his Preservation and Life together. For a Man, not having the Power of his own Life, *cannot*, by Compact, or his own Consent, *enslave himself* to any one, nor put himself under the Absolute, Arbitrary Power of another, to take away his Life, when he pleases" (Locke, 1988, II, §23:284; italics in orig.); "Men being, as has been said, by Nature, all free, equal and independent, no one can be put out of this Estate, and subjected to the Political Power of another, without his own *Consent*. The only way whereby any one devests himself of his Natural Liberty, and *puts on the bonds of Civil Society* is by agreeing with other Men to joyn and unite into a Community, for their comfortable, safe, and peaceable living one amongst another, in a secure Enjoyment of their Properties, and a greater Security against any that are not of it" (Locke 1988, II, §95:330–331; italics in orig.). For other central passages, see Locke 1988, II, §15:278; §99:33.

16. Cf. "But though Men when they enter into Society, give up the Equality, Liberty, and Executive Power they had in the State of Nature, into the hands of the Society, to be so far disposed of by the Legislative, as the good of the Society shall require; yet it being only with an intention in every one the better to preserve his Liberty and Property; (*For no rational Creature can be supposed to change his condition with an intention to be worse*) the Power of the Society, or *Legislative* constituted by them, *can never be suppos'd to extend farther than the common good*; but is obliged to secure every ones Property by pro-

viding against those three defects above-mentioned, that made the State of Nature so unsafe and uneasie" (Locke 1988, II, §131:353; italics partly in orig.).

17. Cf. Locke 1988, II, §§211–243, in particular §§218–232.

18. For a distinction between political anarchism and philosophical anarchism and an excellent discussion of these in relation to the political thought of Locke, see Simmons 1992; Simmons 1993.

19. Albert Hirschman has analyzed the importance and character of "exit" in his classic *Exit, Voice and Loyalty* (Hirschman 1970). For a review of the theoretical and empirical research building on Hirschman, see Dowding et al. 2000.

20. Cf. the payoffs suggested by Tullock (Tullock 1985; Tullock 1999) and Vanberg & Congleton (1992:421).

21. The specific payoffs suggested by Tullock (Tullock 1985; Tullock 1999) and Vanberg and Congleton (1992:422) are as given here, except that $t = 3$, while they have $t = 2$. This does, however, not change the structure of the game.

22. It should be stressed that this is not a claim that the problems entailed by Prisoners' Dilemma-like situations can have an "internal" solution through exit; the latter quite obviously is not an internal solution. The claim is simply that the Prisoners' Dilemma might not be descriptive of a large number of situations, and that when an exit option exists, the consequences will be quite different. It should also be emphasized that many of the points made here depend upon the assumption that the payoffs are $r > n > p$ (Vanberg & Congleton 1992:420).

23. Vanberg and Congleton (1992) conducted a number of "tournaments" by comparing the results produced when using different strategies in a series of tournament games of Prisoners' Dilemma, such as those conducted in the celebrated work by Robert Axelrod (1984).

24. Specifically, the Prudent Morality as a strategy comes in two forms: An intolerant and a tolerant (Vanberg & Congleton 1992:422). With the former a player never plays again with another player who has defected, while with the latter the player gives the defector a second chance after withdrawing for one round. The Tolerant Prudent Morality thus is a solution reminiscent of the strategy called "Even Up" suggested by Robert Ellickson as a solution to collective action dilemmas and as representative of many real-world interactions (Ellickson 1991).

25. Cf. Vanberg and Congleton's conclusion: "[An] implication is that contrary to a common perception, markets are not parasitic on moral attitudes that have to rely, for their nourishment, on other social settings. Instead, the more the essential feature of markets (coordination by voluntary contract) is applicable and secured, the more markets reinforce the virtues of honest behavior that in turn, make them work effectively" (Vanberg & Congleton 1992: 429).

26. If, in contrast, the game is sequential with the citizen moving first, the sub-game perfect equilibrium will be (*E*, *C*) or one of the Nash equilibria (*D*, *E*), (*E*, *D*) and (*E*, *E*).

27. This example is inspired by the work of Charles Tiebout (1956) and Gordon Tullock and is given by Bednar, Eskridge and Ferejohn, 1999.

28. This is what has been termed "internal exit," i.e., "secession by a coalition of people from an existing political unit that will then provide public goods to those who defect from the original unit" (Buchanan & Faith 1987: 1023).

29. For an argument that the Tiebout effect, while important, may not be sufficient to constrain local governments if they can impose property taxes, see Caplan 1997.

30. Such an order might to some seem as being close or similar to what has occasionally been called a "polycentric" legal order, i.e., one in which the legal institutional set-up permits a "multiplicity of ends" and that implies "a multiplicity of independent centres of decision" (Hayek 1982, II:15). A polycentric constitutional order is, however, both broader and narrower in its implications (cf., e.g., Barnett 1998).

31. It might be noted that Locke both recognized that some might not consent to join one political community and might remain outside (or perhaps instead join another), cf. "This [i.e., to agree with other, to join and unite in a political community] any number of Men may do, because it injures not the Freedom of the rest; they are left as they were in the Liberty of the State of Nature" (Locke 1988, II, §95:331). Locke also held that it is not necessarily the case that all living inside the borders of a physical political community or otherwise enjoying the positive external effects of a political community also are citizens therein corresponding with rights and obligations. Cf. Locke 1988, II, §122:349.

32. Cf. the almost identical formulation by Buchanan & Faith 1987:1024.

33. For a lengthy discussion of the pros and cons of a constitutional right to secede, see Buchanan 1991. For a game-theoretical analysis of the interaction between a seceding unit and the other units of a federal state, see Chen & Ordeshook 1994.

34. Mises in fact in principle sympathized with the idea of taking the idea to its ultimate point, but rejected it on consequential grounds: "If it were in any way possible to grant this right of self-determination to every individual person, it would have to be done. This is impractical only because of compelling technical considerations, which make it necessary that a region be governed as a single administrative unit and that the right to self-determination be restricted to the will of the majority of the inhabitants of areas large enough to count as territorial units in the administration of the country" (Mises 1962: 109–110). For a criticism of Mises for being inconsistent on this point, see Baumgarth 1976:92–93.

35. Other interesting examples include the legal system, which often allowed individual entry and exit. It is, for example, a historical fact that in the medieval period numerous legal systems co-existed simultaneously with individuals having the possibility of exiting one and entering another or operating under several at the same time but in different ways (Berman 1983; Benson 1990).

36. I am grateful to Barry Smith and Boudewijn Bouckaert for having drawn my attention to this example and for information about it.

37. There are other interesting examples, although they are rare today. One is that of the Indian Nations in the United States, which are separate political-administrative communities inside or across the borders of the states, most notably the Navajo Nation. The most colorful example is no doubt that of the Sovereign Military Order of Malta, which lost its physical sovereignty more than 200 years ago, but is still recognized as a sovereign entity in international law, and exchanges diplomatic relations with a number of states, despite no longer having any true territory.

38. According to Taylor, fission was common in ancient times, and the creation of states may to a large extent be explained as the result of costly (or the lack of) possibilities of fission within communities (Taylor 1982:135ff). Taylor sees the possibility of fission as constraining tyranny and preserving community and order in society as a whole, because it permits a peaceful solution to what otherwise could result in a bloody conflict.

References

Axelrod, R. (1984). *The evolution of cooperation.* New York: Basic Books.

Barnett, R.E. (1998). *The structure of liberty: Justice and the rule of law.* Oxford: Clarendon Press.

Barry, B. (1990). *Political argument.* Berkeley: University of California Press.

Bates, R.H. (1988). Contra contractarianism: Some reflections on the New Institutionalism, *Politics and Science* 16: 389–401.

Baumgarth, W. (1976). Ludwig von Mises and the justification of the liberal order. In: L.S. Moss (ed.), *The economics of Ludwig von Mises: Toward a critical reappraisal.* Kansas City: Sheed & Ward.

Bednar, J., Eskridge, W.N., & Ferejohn, J.A. (1999). A political theory of federalism, unpublished manuscript.

Benson, B.L. (1990). *The enterprise of law: Justice without the state.* San Francisco: Pacific Research Institute for Public Policy.

Berman, H.J. (1983). *Law and revolution.* Cambridge: Harvard University Press.

Buchanan, A. (1991). *Secession: The morality of political divorce from Fort Sumter to Lithuania and Quebec.* Boulder: Westview Press.

Buchanan, J.M. (1975). *The limits of liberty: Between anarchy and leviathan.* Chicago: University of Chicago Press.

Buchanan, J.M. & Faith, R.L. (1987). Secession and the limits of taxation: Toward a theory of internal exit, *American Economic Review* 77: 1023–1031.

Buchanan, J.M. & Tullock, G. (1965). *The calculus of consent: Logical foundations of constitutional democracy.* Ann Arbor: University of Michigan Press.

Caplan, B. (1997). Standing Tiebout on his head: Tax capitalization and the monopoly power of local governments, unpublished manuscript.

Chen, Y. & Ordeshook, P.C. (1994). Constitutional secession clauses, *Constitutional Political Economy* 5: 45–60.

Coase, R.H. (1960). The problem of social cost, *Journal of Law and Economics* 3: 1–44.

Coase, R.H. (1988). Notes on the problem of social cost. In: Ronald H. Coase (ed.), *The firm, the market and the law.* Chicago: University of Chicago Press.

Dowding, K., John, P., Mergoupis, T., & Vugt, M.V. (2000). Exit, voice and loyalty: Analytic and empirical developments, *European Journal of Political Research* 37: 469–495.

Ellickson, R.C. (1991). *Order without law: How neighbors settle disputes.* Cambridge: Harvard University Press.

Frey, B.S. & Eichenberger, R. (1999). *The new democratic federalism for Europe: Functional, overlapping and competing jurisdictions.* Cheltenham: Edward Elgar.

Gauthier, D. (1986). *Morals by agreement.* Oxford: Oxford University Press.

Green, L. (1988). *The authority of the state.* Oxford: Clarendon Press.

Grotius, H. (1901). *De Jure Belli et Pacis.* Washington: Walter Dunne.

Hampton, J. (1986). *Hobbes and the social contract tradition.* Cambridge: Cambridge University Press.

Hayek, F.A.V. (1982). *Law, legislation and liberty.* London: Routledge & Kegan Paul.

Hirschman, A.O. (1970). *Exit, voice, and loyalty: Responses to decline in firms, organizations, and states.* Cambridge: Harvard University Press.

Hobbes, T. (1991). *Leviathan.* R. Tuck (ed.). Cambridge: Cambridge University Press.

Kavka, G.S. (1986). *Hobbesian moral and political theory.* Princeton: Princeton University Press.

Klein, D. (1997). *Reputation: Studies in the voluntary elicitation of good conduct.* Ann Arbor: University of Michigan Press.

Kraus, J.S. (1993). *The limits of hobbesian contractarianism.* Cambridge: Cambridge University Press.

Kurrild-Klitgaard, P. (1997). *Rational choice, collective action and the paradox of rebellion*. Copenhagen: Institute of Political Science, University of Copenhagen & Copenhagen Political Studies Press.

Locke, J. (1988). *Two treatises of government*. P. Laslett (ed.). Cambridge: Cambridge University Press.

Milgrom, P.R., North, D.C., & Weingast, B.R. (1990). The role of institutions in the revival of trade: The Law Merchant, private judges and the Champagne fairs, *Economics and Politics* 2: 1–23.

Mill, J.S. (1991). *On liberty and other essays*. Oxford: Oxford University Press.

Mises, L.V. (1962). *The free and prosperous commonwealth*. Princeton: Van Nostrand.

Moselle, B. & Polak, B. (1999). A model of a predatory state, unpublished manuscript.

North, D.C. & Thomas, R.P. (1973). *The rise of the western world: A new economic history*. Cambridge: Cambridge University Press.

Pufendorf, S. (1934). *De Jure Naturae et Gentium Libri Octo*. Oxford: Clarendon Press.

Pufendorf, S. (1991). *De Officio Hominis et Civis juxta Legem Naturalem Libri Duo*. J. Tully (ed.). Cambridge: Cambridge University Press.

Rawls, J. (1971). *A theory of justice*. Cambridge: Belknap Press.

Riker, W.H. (1982). *Liberalism against populism: A confrontation between the theory of democracy and the theory of social choice*. San Francisco: W.H. Freeman.

Rosenberg, N. & Birdzell, L.E. (1986). *How the West grew rich: The economic transformation of the industrial world*. London: I.B. Tauris.

Schmidtz, D. (1991). *The limits of government: An essay on the public goods argument*. Boulder: Westview Press.

Simmons, A.J. (1992). *The Lockean theory of rights*. Princeton: Princeton University Press.

Simmons, A.J. (1993). *On the edge of anarchy: Locke, consent, and the limits of society*. Princeton: Princeton University Press.

Smith, B. (1997). The cognitive geometry of war. In: P. Koller & K. Puhl (eds.), *Current issues in political philosophy*. Vienna: Hölder-Pichler-Tempsky.

Sunstein, C.R. (1991). Constitutionalism and secession, *University of Chicago Law Review* 58: 633–670.

Taylor, M. (1982). *Community, anarchy and liberty*. Cambridge: Cambridge University Press.

Taylor, M. (1987). *The possibility of cooperation*. Cambridge: Cambridge University Press.

Tiebout, C. (1956). A pure theory of local expenditures, *Journal of Political Economy* 64: 416–424.

Tullock, G. (1974). *The social dilemma: The economics of war and revolution*. Blacksburg: Center for Study of Public Choice.

Tullock, G. (1985). Adam Smith and the Prisoner's Dilemma, *Quarterly Journal of Economics* 100: 1073–1081.

Tullock, G. (1999). Non-prisoner's dilemma, *Journal of Economic Behavior and Organization* 39: 455–458.

Vanberg, V.J. & Congleton, R.D. (1992). Rationality, morality and exit, *American Political Science Review* 86: 418–431.

PART IV

Austrian School Perspectives

American Journal of Economics and Sociology, Vol. 61, No. 1 (January, 2002).
© 2002 American Journal of Economics and Sociology, Inc.

Post-Classical Political Economy

Polity, Society and Economy in Weber, Mises and Hayek

By Peter J. Boettke and Virgil Henry Storr*

Abstract. This paper explores the relationship of Max Weber's "social economics" to the work of the Austrian School of Economics, and in particular the writings of Ludwig von Mises and F. A. Hayek. We argue that the Austrian school scholars complement and extend the work of Weber. The sophisticated form of methodological individualism found in Weber, Mises and Hayek overcomes the shortcomings of traditional economic and sociological analysis and could provide the analytical structure for a post-classical political economy.

I

Introduction

INCREASINGLY, scholars are becoming dissatisfied with economic theories that fail to consider the social, political, historical and cultural context in which actors find themselves and that fail to endow individuals with customs, values and beliefs. Economic anthropologists, for instance, have been deeply critical of economics' "vain search for generalizations" and have instead stressed the superiority of ethnographic over statistical data and of context-specific analysis over attempts of universal theorizing.[1] Although economic anthropologists have done a great deal of meaningful and important work,[2] this methodological attack, at least as it is often articulated, runs the risk of throwing the epistemological baby (the insights to be gained from economic theorizing) out with the methodological bathwater (the naïve psychology

* The authors are at Department of Economics, George Mason University, Fairfax, Virginia. This paper was previously presented at the SCANCOR workshop on "Crossing Boundaries: Economics, Sociology and Organization Theory" at Stanford University September 30–October 1, 2000. We would like to acknowledge the insightful comments of Mie Augier on an earlier draft. In addition, we acknowledge the financial support of the J. M. Kaplan Fund and SCANCOR. The usual caveat applies.

American Journal of Economics and Sociology, Vol. 61, No. 1 (January, 2002).
© 2002 American Journal of Economics and Sociology, Inc.

of *homoeconomicus* and the fiction of a frictionless, institution-less, culture-less economic environment).[3]

The economic sociologists, on the other hand, have attacked economics not for its attempts at theory making (theorizing is entirely consistent with the sociological perspective) but because it ignores the social and institutional context in which all human activity (including economic activity) takes place. In attacking, they have articulated a compelling alternative to the textbook neoclassical framework. While textbook economics "assumes that actors are not connected to one another," economic sociology "assume[s] that actors are linked with and influenced by others" (Smelser and Swedberg 1994, p. 5).

Economic sociologists, particularly those rooted in the Weberian tradition, have also articulated a far more sophisticated form of methodological individualism than that employed by most neoclassical economists. In standard economics, methodological individualism often degenerates into an atomized conception of the individual. When utilized by economic sociologists, however, it becomes a method of infusing their analysis of the social structures that influence individual activity with "meaning." "Sociology," Weber argues, "is a science concerning itself with the interpretive understanding of social action and thereby with a causal explanation of its course and consequences." To Weber, concrete human action is intelligible to the sociologist because of the subjective meaning that actors themselves place on their behavior. Economic sociologists, following Weber, must understand that "[a]ction is 'social' insofar as its subjective meaning takes account of the behavior of others and is thereby oriented in its course" (Weber 1922, p. 4). Sociological analysis strives not for prediction but understanding, and this understanding is achieved by tracing all social phenomena back to the purposes and plans of the actors whose actions resulted in the phenomena to begin with. Weber, in fact, argues that sociological knowledge, "namely the subjective understanding of the action of component individuals" (1922, p. 15), was privileged in comparison with the natural sciences because we can never truly understand the behavior of cells. We do, however, have access to interpretive understanding in the sciences of human action because we *are* what we study.

Unfortunately, standard economics techniques seem to be unable to aid us in gaining an appreciation of these subjective meaning aspects of social action. And, in spite of economic sociologists' compelling critique of mainstream economic thought and the clear improvements over the rarified neoclassical mode of theorizing that they have articulated, economic sociology's effort to replace standard economics with their alternative framework remains an incomplete project. One reason is that the "new sociology of economic life" (modern economic sociology) has failed to evolve "a sophisticated sociology of money and markets" (Swedberg 1991, p. 270). Another is that many of the insights of Weber's cogent formulation have been lost. A third, and perhaps the most damaging reason, is that economic sociology has failed to find the necessary allies within the disciplinary borders of economics.

Rational choice sociology in the tradition of Gary Becker and James Coleman offers a bridge between economics and sociology, but not one that leads to a correction of either the institutional or behavioral deficiencies that economic sociologists have sought to address in their critique of standard economics. As an alternative to strict rational choice economic sociology, "new institutionalists" economists, following in the tradition of Ronald Coase, Douglass North, Herbert Simon and O. E. Williamson, represent the most likely intellectual accomplices in a shared research program for the study of the sociology of economic life. It is our conjecture, however, that the Austrian economists (Menger, Mises, Hayek, Schutz, Lachmann and Kirzner) are far more natural intellectual fellow-travelers along the road to constructing a sociology of economic life that successfully melds the study of individuals, institutions and the interpretive meaning attributed to both (see Boettke 1998a). While the Austrians construct their economics on a socially embedded foundation from which institutional questions naturally evolve, the "new institutionalists"—often referred to as transaction cost economists for their emphasis that institutions evolve to reduce the cost of doing business in a world of uncertain and unknowable futures—tend to graft a theory of institutions (and institutional evolution) onto the neoclassical frame.

It is worth reviewing, at least briefly, how they pursue this hybridization.[4] As North has asserted, they accomplish it by retaining and building on "the fundamental assumption of scarcity and hence competition" while abandoning "instrumental rationality—the assumption of neoclassical economics that has made it an institution-free theory" (1995, p. 17). In a world of instrumental rationality, North continues, "institutions are unnecessary; ideas and ideologies don't matter; and efficient markets—both economic and political—characterize economies." The "new institutionalists," however, recognize that the "information [available to actors] is incomplete and [that individuals posses a] limited mental capacity by which to process [that incomplete] information. . . . Human beings, in consequence, [must and do] impose constraints on human interaction" (ibid.). Although a considerable improvement over the friction-less and, so, institution-less world employed in economics textbooks, the "new institutionalists" still present what some have characterized as a "thin" account of how norms and values affect human (particularly economic) action and, thus, of how society and polity affect the economy.[5]

Although the "new institutionalists" are indeed allies in the intellectual battle against the rarified economics of the textbook and the isolated, disembodied *homoeconomicus* in work, economic sociology is not entirely compatible with the "new institutionalist" approach to sociological matters. In Williamson's description of the research agenda of new institutionalism, he argues that literature on social embeddedness lacks theoretical specification and thus the identification and explication of the mechanism through which institutional change occurs at this level of analysis. Furthermore, since in the Williamson classification scheme these questions deal with institutions that change very slowly (on the order of centuries or millennia), it is valid for most social scientists to treat these institutions as part of the *given* background to the analysis (Williamson 2000, p. 596). But to treat as a given that which must be explained in social action artificially truncates the progress that can be made.

It is our contention that in the Austrian school of economics and with Mises and Hayek, the recognized heads of that school, in particular, economic sociologists will not only find a scholarly tradition that shares many of the same intellectual forebears but that is a more comfortable bedfellow than the new institutional economics. It is our further contention that the Austrians have retained much of value from Weber's *Sozialökonomik* that modern economic sociology ("the new sociology of economic life") has lost and that forging a closer alliance, that is, encouraging a closer reading of Austrian texts by economic sociologists and vice versa would therefore be a useful effort,[6] particularly since the Austrians also have much of value to say about methodology, markets and money—areas where in Swedberg's (1991) opinion a "sophisticated sociology" has yet to evolve. Before defending our claims, however, it is essential that we locate (carve out a space for) the Weber-Austrian approach in the modern discourse on the intersections between economy, polity and society. We, therefore, begin with a consideration of Granovetter's (1985) pivotal article.

II

The Problem of "Single" Embeddedness

SWEDBERG HAS IDENTIFIED Mark Granovetter's "Economic Action and Social Structure: The Problem of Embeddedness" as a key article in the "new sociology of economic life." This article, according to Swedberg, was a "recognized . . . trendsetter" that "contained a sophisticated and elegant argument for the use of networks in the analysis of the economy" and that "strengthened the confidence that sociologists could solve a number of problems that by tradition only economists had done work on" (1991, p. 268).

By embedding the individual in a context of "ongoing social relations," Granovetter calls attention to the organizational and institutional context in which individuals act, while overcoming the problems of the *under-* and *oversocialized* view of the individual that is evident in standard economics and standard sociology. As Granovetter argues (1985, p. 483), the standard economics starts with an atomized individual with purely pecuniary motives and places him or her in a problem situation where the problems of society and polity, "of social structure and social relations," on economic activities (that is, on production, distribution and consumption) are assumed away. More often than not, economists discuss actors as if they have no families, are citizens of no countries, are members of no communities and are believers in nothing at all except the pursuit of "hedonistic" utility. Individuals, in the hands of economists, are typically *undersocialized*, isolated creatures, unaffected by society or polity. Deviations from this position introduce problems in the analysis that often are taken as evidence of economic inefficiencies. In the presence of interdependencies, for example, voluntary choice alone cannot be trusted to produce efficient outcomes.[7]

When economists do take social influences seriously, Granovetter argues, they end up at the other extreme, as do many sociologists: with an *oversocialized* conception of individuals. They assume "that people follow customs, habits or norms automatically and unconditionally" (ibid.). According to Granovetter, "nearly all economists' treatment of 'norms' has this flavor and [their] discussions of 'conventions' also run the risk of sliding into an oversocialized treatment" (ibid.).[8] It is noteworthy that Granovetter's criticism of both these misconceptions of human action (the *under-* and *oversocialized* views) echo sentiments found in Weber and amongst the Austrians; Granovetter, however, fails to connect his criticisms to either of these traditions.[9] It is also noteworthy, that like Weber and the Austrians, Granovetter overcomes the pitfalls of positing either an *over-* or *undersocialized* view of the individual by maintaining that his or her behavior is *affected* by, *influenced* by, even *directed* by social structures and relations but not *determined* by them: "Actors do not behave or decide to behave as atoms outside a social context, nor do they adhere slavishly to a script written for them by the particular intersection of social categories that they happen to occupy" (ibid., p. 487).

Although he stresses that action is embedded in social relations (and, by implication, that economic activity takes place within society), Granovetter does recognize, albeit superficially, that the arrow of influence also runs in the opposite direction, that is, from the individual to the social context and from the economy to the society. "That business relations spill over into sociability and vice versa, especially among business elites," he argues, "is one of the best-documented facts in the sociological study of business" (ibid., p. 495). And, in a more recent presentation of his theory of embeddedness, he states that "economic institutions do not emerge automatically in response to economic needs. Rather, they are *constructed by individuals* whose action is both facilitated and constrained by the structure and resources available in social networks in which they are embedded" (1992, p. 7; emphasis added).

It is our contention, however, that these statements by Granovetter do not go far enough in recognizing the multiple levels of embeddedness. Noting that "business relations spill over into sociability," for instance, is a weak acknowledgment of that fact that some social relations are *economically conditioned*. And, although Granovetter's work emphasizes that economic institutions are "constructed by individuals," he insists on placing that construction in an ever-expanding, all- encompassing web of social networks. How these social networks come to be established and what meaning individuals attach to them are questions that are not considered. This silence results not because economic sociology is incapable of dealing with these issues, but instead because the "new sociology of economic life" is inadequately rooted in Weberian traditions.[10]

III

Weber's *Sozialökonomik*: Toward a Richer Conception of Embeddedness

WEBER HAS DESCRIBED "social economics" as the study of (a) economic phenomena, (b) economically relevant phenomena and (c) economically conditioned phenomena.[11] "The first of these categories covers economic phenomena in a strict sense, such as economic events and economic institutions; and Weber has little to say about this category except that it includes phenomena 'the economic aspects of which constitute their primary cultural significance for us'" (Swedberg 1998, p. 19). *Economically relevant phenomena* describes events and institutions that are not economic in the strict sense but that do have economic consequences. Protestantism, to the extent that it impacts the work ethnic of its adherents, would be an *economically relevant phenomena* according to this schema.[12] As would, to the extent that they shape economic motives, many of the sociological categorizations employed by the social sciences, such as family, community and society. Granovetter's work on embeddedness similarly falls into this category of Weber's *Sozialökonomik*.

The third of Weber's categories, *economically conditioned phenomena*, is what distinguishes his notion of embeddedness from what we have hitherto referred to as "single embeddedness" (the conception of embeddedness articulated by Granovetter and the "new economic sociologists"). By *economically conditioned phenomena*, Weber means to describe "behavior in non-'economic' affairs [that] is partly influenced by economic phenomena"[13] ("Objectivity," cited in Swedberg

1998, p. 193). The public choice arguments articulated by the Virginia school of political economy (e.g., the work of Buchanan and Tullock) would fall into this category, in which politicians and public servants motivated by a desire for power and votes engage in pork-barrel spending, log-rolling and rent-seeking activities. And, although Weber would reject the tenor of Marx's historical materialism, particularly since it leaves no room for anything but *economically conditioned phenomena*, Marxist arguments, albeit less sweeping, would also fall into Weber's schema. Additionally, when the "new institutionalists" describe the development of institutions such as property rights, contracts, contract law and even norms and values as being a response to economic incentives, they are characterizing them as what Weber has called *economically conditioned phenomena*. Recognizing that these sorts of phenomena exist alongside the *economically relevant phenomena* considered in the embeddedness arguments is merely a first step, however, in moving us beyond the concept of "single embeddedness" that we have criticized above.

To see this, imagine three circles of potentially different sizes representing the society, the polity and the economy, respectively. If we were to arrange these circles in a configuration that would reflect Granovetter's embeddedness argument, we would have to conceive of the circle representing the society as the largest, the polity as the second largest and the economy as the smallest, located within the larger two (see Figure 1). Economic life, in this configuration, is always located within "concrete ongoing social relations"; it is always society that influences and constrains economic behavior. Note, however, that there is nothing that is logically inconsistent with imagining an entirely opposite configuration. We could, for instance, place the society within the economy. Indeed, this is precisely the configuration that Marx, when he conceived of the base, profound and pervasive effect it has on the superstructure (society within economy), had in mind.

To a lesser degree, this is also how the "new institutionalists" conceive of the relationship between society and economy. Economic motives are extrasocial. Institutions are constructed, organizations are established and relationships are developed in an endogenous manner so that economic life can be more efficient. Society is shaped by economic considerations. Consider, for instance, how the "new institutionalists" understand the evolution of property rights, as seen

Figure 1

Single Embeddedness

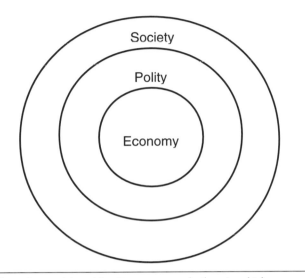

The configuration envisioned by Granovetter and others in which economic life is always located within "concrete ongoing social relations"; it is always society that influences and constrains economic behavior.

in North's statement that "[c]hanges in relative prices or relative scarcities of any kind lead to the creation of property rights when it becomes worthwhile to incur the cost of devising such rights" (North 1990, p. 51).[14]

Rather than privileging one or the other of these configurations, however, Weber's analysis suggests a third way of conceiving the relationship between the society, the economy and the polity. Whereas the embeddedness argument suggests that we place the economy within the society and Marx's materialist arguments suggest the opposite, Weber's insistence that we consider both *economically relevant* and *economically conditioned phenomena* suggests that we view the economy, the society and the polity as three overlapping circles (see Figure 2). The society, the polity and the economy are elevated, if you will, to the same level of prominence, and dual and treble notions of embeddedness are conceived of and utilized. As such, discussing the economy becomes nearly impossible without discussing social mores and political and legal institutions. Similarly, discussing the society becomes nearly impossible without discussing the economy and the polity and discussing the polity is nearly impossible without discussing the other two.[15] This is nowhere more evident than when Weber discusses "the spirit of capitalism," protestantism, bureaucratization, the legal system, "capitalism and rural society in Germany" and the caste system in India.[16] This is what we meant when we conjectured that Weber had a richer conception of embeddedness than is found in Granovetter and in the "new economic sociology." Why is Weber able to arrive at this richer conception of embeddedness when others are not? It is our conjecture that Weber avoids articulating a "single embeddedness" argument by embracing a sophisticated form of methodological individualism.

IV

Versteben: The Weberian Concept of "Understanding"

WEBER HOPED TO CONSTRUCT an interpretive sociology, that is, a sociology that was oriented toward the reality as understood by the actors that dwell within it. Weberian sociology is a sociological research program that aims at understanding the meaning that an individual attaches to his or her actions (Käsler 1979, p. 176; see also Lachmann 1971). It is important to remember, however, that "meaning" is intended in Weber's schema as a determining factor in human action. "[T]his [is] the central premise of every interpretive approach . . . the actor attaches a 'meaning' to his or her action and this 'meaning' acts at the very least as a contributory determinant to the action" (ibid.). Social phenomena, social structures, social relationships and social actions are unintelligible without considering how actors subjectively perceive them. And so our analysis must necessarily begin with the individual because it is only at the level of the individual that we can attribute meaning to purposeful action. Advocating an atomistic individualism of the sort championed by many economists would be as dissatisfying as the "structural-functional" explanations offered by Durkheim and others that stand in opposition to Weber's interpretive sociology.

Just like the embeddedness arguments, a sophisticated methodological individualism situates the actor within a *context of ongoing social meanings* (Aggasi 1960, 1975; Boettke 1989, 1990a, 1990b; Prychitko 1989/90). In addition to being influenced and affected by the *context of meanings* in which he or she is located, however, the Weberian actor is also conceived of as the producer of, the creator of, that *context*. As such, a Weberian individualism neither proceeds with disembodied actors, unaffected by the social institutions within which their actions are embedded, nor with social structures and relations dissociated from the *web of meanings* that give them life. Society, polity and economy, as such, become difficult to isolate in Weber's analysis. That is to say, what distinguishes social from political and economic phenomena is only the meaning that actors attach to them, and the context within which actions are attributed this meaning.

Consider, for instance, how Weber defines *economically oriented action* and the economy. He states: "Action *will* be said to be 'economically oriented' so far as, according to its subjective meaning, it is concerned with the satisfaction of a desire for 'utilities' (*Nutleistungen*)" (Weber 1947, p. 158). And "an 'economy' (*Wirtschaft*) is autocephalous economic action." He continues, "the definition of economic action must be as general as possible and must bring out the fact that all 'economic' processes and objects are characterized as such entirely by the meaning they have for human action in such roles as ends, means, obstacles, and by-products" (ibid.).

Earlier we noted that social actions are actions that take "account of the behaviour of others and is thereby oriented in its course" (ibid., p. 88). Weber, therefore, sees the study of institutions (social structures) as critical to understanding this orientation process. The Weberian (and Austrian) economist Ludwig Lachmann describes the role that institutions play in shaping human action and in Weber's analysis as "there . . . are certain superindividual schemes of thought, namely, *institutions*, to which the schemes of thought of the first order, the plans [that individuals make], must be oriented, and which serve therefore, to some extent, the coordination of individual plans. They constitute, we may say, 'interpersonal orientation tables,' schemes of thought of the second order" (Lachmann 1977, p. 62). Earlier, Lachmann had written: "Institutions are at the same time instruments of, *and* constraints upon, human action" (1971, p. 141). But institutions should not only be viewed as signposts ("interpersonal orientation tables") to be considered when attempting to understand human behavior, that is, as merely the *context of meaning* in which the Weberian actor is embedded. Indeed, institutions only become understandable because the Weberian actor is placed in a complex problem situation; it is as impossible to predict the behavior of others with certainty in Weberian *Sozialökonomik,* because of the sophisticated method individualism he employs, as it is in the real world.[17] For example, it is precisely because, absent a legal framework, parties would be unable to negotiate and conclude contracts that legal rules have evolved.

As noted earlier, the *quest for meaning* was always at the forefront of Weber's analysis. The "structural-functional" brand of social theory misses this fundamental aspect of Weber's approach, and even some of his strongest *advocates* miss the critical role that Weber's institutional individualism played in his analysis.[18] Weber's methodological individualism cannot simply be regarded as the curious and, for that matter, indirect method by which he arrived at his social theory. Indeed, it is our contention that it is precisely because Weber strictly adheres to the method of *Verstehen* rather than because it occupies some minor place in his social theory as some have suggested (see Smelser and Swedberg 1994, p. 5) that Weber was able to construct a social theory that could conceive of the meaning that individuals attach to their actions and to social phenomena while avoiding atomism and naïve holism.[19] Additionally, we contend, it is precisely because of his strict adherence to the method of *Verstehen* that Weber was able to develop a concept of embeddedness that is substantially richer than the "simple" conception traditionally expressed. Weber's *Sozialökonomik* and his adherence to the method of *Verstehen* should, therefore, be seen as a corrective to many of the theoretical shortcomings of the "new sociology of economic life."

Having provided some textual evidence in support of the first of our conjectures, that the "new economic sociology" could be enriched by a direct engagement with Weber, we are now in a position to argue for another claim we made but have not yet explored: that the Austrians, particularly Carl Menger, Ludwig von Mises and Fredrich von Hayek, are the intellectual *heir apparents* of Max Weber and thus represent economic sociology's natural allies within the disciplinary borders of economics.[20] Indeed, not only do the Austrians avoid many of the pitfalls of their economic brethren (atomism, determinism, ahistoricism, reductionism, etc.), like Weber, they avoid some of the problems that plague the "new economic sociology" (particularly the problem of a "single-level" versus a "multiple-levels" conception of embeddedness) while delivering a sophisticated analysis of money and markets.[21]

V

The Weberian Approach of Mises and Hayek[22]

WEBER AND THE AUSTRIANS have a deep and symbiotic relationship; they share many of the same intellectual forebears and a commitment to the same methodological approach. Not surprisingly, Weber was deeply influenced by the Austrian school of economics. Weber had read and appreciated Carl Menger's and Eugen Böhm-Bawerk's contributions to economic theory and methodology. He invited both Friedrich von Wieser and Joseph Schumpeter to contribute volumes to his encyclopedic project in social theory.[23] And, in his magnum opus, *Economy and Society*, Weber, at key junctures in the development of his own arguments concerning monetary calculation and economic calculation (1922, pp. 78, 93, 107), favorably references Ludwig von Mises's *Theory of Money and Credit* (1912) and Mises's (1920) essay on the problem of economic calculation under socialism. Mises, in turn, devoted considerable attention to the systematic, critical study of Weber, which is reflected in his *Epistemological Problems of Economics* (1933) and *Human Action* (1949). As Ludwig Lachmann stated in his review of Mises's *Human Action*, "In reading this book we must never forget that it is the work of Max Weber that is being carried on here" (1977, p. 94).

Weber's connection to the Austrians was quite close, though this is not really appreciated by traditional sociologists.[24] In Swedberg's (1990) interviews with the leading scholars at the edge of both disciplines, Weber is referenced 34 times, but Hayek is referenced only once and Mises not at all. Schumpeter is referred to 16 times, but Menger is referred to only twice, neither reference being substantive, and Lachmann (who wrote a book on the Weberian legacy in economics) is not referenced at all. Etzoni's *The Moral Dimension* (1988) cites neither Mises nor Hayek, though Machlup is cited a few times with respect to methodological points. Hayek's *Law, Legislation and Liberty*, on the other hand, makes the bibliography and warrants a few references to the concept of spontaneous order in James Coleman's *Foundations of Social Theory* (1990). But Hayek's work does not play a prominent role in Coleman's theory construction, nor does Coleman deal with the intellectual history issue of Weber's connection to the Austrians. In the index to *The Handbook of Economic Sociology* (Smelser and Swedberg, 1994), Hayek is referenced six times and Mises twice, while there are 36 references to Weber and 17 to Schumpeter. Even George Stigler is referenced more often than Mises and Hayek combined, namely 11 times. The Austrian economists have failed to make an impression on scholars working in the field of economic sociology.

The relationship between the Austrians and Weber, however, was a mutually beneficial one in which each learned from the other and influenced the development of their respective work. This connection is apparent when we consider how economy, society and polity enter into their respective social theories and when we review the mode of analysis they employed. As argued above, Weber's commitment to methodological individualism results in an approach to the study of social phenomena that considers the meaning individuals attach to their activities and that evolves a "rich" conception of embeddedness. The Austrians share Weber's commitment to the method of *Verstehen* and his conceptualizations of economy, society and polity and the relationship between them.

As noted earlier, many of the criticisms leveled against standard economics by the economic sociologists simply do not apply to the Austrians. The brush with which Granovetter condemns methodological individualism as necessarily atomistic, for instance, is entirely too broad. Like Weber, Mises, because of his commitment to *Verstehen,* rather than becoming atomistic, threads a similar path between the *under-* and *oversocialized* views that Granovetter attempts:

> Inheritance and environment direct a man's actions. They suggest to him both the ends and the means. He lives not simply as man *in abstracto*; he

lives as a son of his family, his people, and his age; as a citizen of his country; as a member of a definite social group; as a practitioner of a certain vocation; as a follower of definite religious, metaphysical, philosophical, and political ideas; as a partisan in many feuds and controversies. He does not himself create his ideas and standards of value; he borrows them from other people. His ideology is what his environment enjoins upon him. (Mises 1949, p. 46)[25]

Individual actions are embedded in a context of "ongoing social relations." Atomistic individualism is vehemently rejected. Notice, however, that "inheritance and environment" direct "a man's actions" but do not determine it; man is not *oversocialized* either. Mises continues, "[M]an does *choose*. He *chooses* to adopt traditional patterns or patterns adopted by other people because he is convinced that this procedure is best fitted to achieve his own welfare. And he is *ready to change* his ideology and consequently his mode of action whenever he becomes convinced that this would better serve his own interests" (ibid.; emphasis added).

Mises's individualism was able to thread a path between the *under-* and *oversocialized* conceptions of individual action similar to Weber's because their understanding of the implications of *Verstehen* were identical.[26] Compare Mises's expression of methodological individualism to Weber's. Mises writes:

> It is meaning which the acting individuals and all those who are touched by their action attribute to an action, that determines its character. It is the meaning that marks one action as the action of an individual and another action as the action of the state or of the municipality. The hangman, not the state, executes the criminal. It is the meaning of those concerned that discerns in the hangman's action an action of the state. (1949, p. 42)

And from Weber:

> . . . for the subjective interpretation of action in sociological work . . . collectivities must be treated as *solely* the resultants and modes of organization of the particular acts of individual persons, since these alone can be treated as agents in a course of *subjectively understandable action.* (1947, p. 101; emphasis added)

The effect that this shared commitment to *Verstehen* had on the sorts of social theory they applied is profound. Thus, understanding the implications of a sophisticated methodological individualism on social theory is critical if we are to really appreciate the differences between the interpretive sociology and economics of Weber, Mises and Hayek and the structural-functional theories of the received sociology and the atomistic, deterministic theories of the received economics.

Commenting on the implications of the Weber-Austrian commitment to methodological individualism, Holton and Turner have pointed out,

> Weber and the Austrian School are not obliged to deny the reality of institutions or the idea that actors may act under institutional constraints, or that this constraint may be experienced as an external compulsive force or imperative. Nor need they hold to a social contract or design theory of institutions. Only two propositions are excluded. The first is that social life can be explained without reference to the causal consequences of the meaning individuals give to their actions. The second is that institutions act as organic, causally effective entities through the structural imposition of rules or constraints on unwilling actors, and irrespective of the actions of such actors. (1989, pp. 42–43)

Individuals, in the Weber-Austrian approach, are not assumed to maximize within an institutionless vacuum, nor are they assumed to be merely puppets of structural forces beyond their control. Reasonableness substitutes for hyper-rationality, and spontaneous ordering processes substitute for equilibrium end-states.

As stated earlier, this commitment to methodological individualism, methodological subjectivism and spontaneous ordering analysis found in the Weber-Austrian approach also results in a richer conception of embeddedness than is commonly articulated. That is, it results in a conception of embeddedness in which the economy and the polity do not merely form concentric circles located within the society but where the relationship between economy, polity and society is constantly reconsidered and recast.[27]

VI

Examples of Austrian Analytical Narratives Grounded in Embeddedness

A COGENT EXAMPLE OF THIS APPROACH to the social sciences, in which the complex relationship between polity, society and economy is recog-

Figure 2

The Weberian Conception of Embeddedness

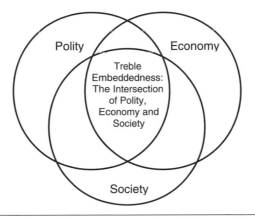

The society, the polity and the economy are elevated, if you will, to the same level of prominence, and dual and treble notions of embeddedness are conceived of and utilized.

nized and embraced and a "rich" conception of embeddedness informs the analysis, is Chamlee-Wright's (1997, 2000a, 2000b) studies of market women in Zimbabwe and Ghana. Consider, for example, her discussion of the social, cultural, political and economic barriers female entrepreneurs must overcome in order to succeed in Harare. As she informs, in Zimbabwe among the Shona people she studied, it is still quite common for male suitors to offer their intended's family a *labola*, that is, to pay a bride price:

> . . . the prospective husband is expected to make significant sacrifices to his wife's natal family. Traditionally, a Shona marriage is a process that takes place over a long period of time, requiring the husband to give the bride's family small gifts, indicating his intentions, followed by several substantial payments in the form of cattle in order to gain sexual rights and eventually the rights to the bride's labor as she moves to the husband's home. (2000a)

This social convention, common in patrilineal societies throughout sub-Saharan Africa, has evolved, as Chamlee-Wright argues, because of the economic implications of marriage for the woman's family. Unlike matrilineal societies, where after marriage it is still quite likely that a woman will continue to make economic contributions to her natal family, among the Shona the bonds between the bride and her family become secondary after the wedding. The *labola* sought and paid in Shona societies can, therefore, be viewed as compensation to the woman's natal family for the material loss they suffer after she is married.[28]

The social and political implications of this *economically conditioned phenomena* are profound. The woman's political and economic autonomy, her capacity to respond to abuse or neglect by her husband and her control over her resources and her children all diminish once the *labola* is paid and the marriage performed. The *labola* also acts, Chamlee-Wright informs us, as an impediment to the development of a dynamic class of female entrepreneurs.

Because Chamlee-Wright has embraced a "rich" conception of embeddedness, she is able to notice and identify both *economically relevant* and *economically conditioned phenomena* in her economic analysis. That is, she is able to conceive of the economic roots of a social convention such as the *labola* and of the economic consequences of a social configuration such as the relationship between a woman and her natal family after marriage in a patrilineal society.

Another example of how the economy, polity and society are embedded in each other can be found in an examination of entrepreneurship and privatization in the former Soviet Union.[29] Market exchange and entrepreneurship existed in the general sense throughout the Soviet period, and continue to exist in the post-Soviet period. The poor economic performance of either the Soviet system or the post-Soviet transition is not due to a lack of entrepreneurial spirit. Instead, we must recognize that the form that entrepreneurial activity takes depends on the social-cultural and political-legal nexus as well as the array of economic opportunities within which it takes place. To use a blunt example, both the market for milk and the market for cocaine are driven by an entrepreneurial spirit, but the manner in which individuals act entrepreneurially changes drastically depending on the context of their choice. The drug dealer and the milkman exercise their entrepreneurial skill to buy low and sell high. The point to stress is that the diverse character of these two markets is not a function of the particular commodity being traded, but the social (informal) and legal (formal) context within which that commodity is traded—change the context, and you change the nature of the behavior of the actors within that market. Behavior, in turn, rebounds to shape the polity and society, which governs in an explicit and implicit manner the actions of individuals. We speak nervously of the drug culture in our inner cities today, and yearn for a yesteryear when milk was delivered at our back door fresh every other day. What meaning are we to attribute to these impressions? During Prohibition in the United States, the speakeasy and gangs who trafficked in alcohol produced the same unease as our contemporary drug culture—we don't experience that unease in our local grocery store today when we shop for beer or wine. Same commodity, different cultural context; and the social ties and networks, as well as the sort of entrepreneurial activities that dominate, are transformed.

A helpful metaphor in the context of Russia is a three-legged bar stool with each leg representing the society, the polity and the economy (see Boettke 2001). Unless all three legs are strong and reinforce one another, the bar stool will be weak and teeter when any weight is applied. Russia's problems in the post-Soviet period have little to do with a lack of entrepreneurial spirit or the absence of the economic institutions of advanced capitalism. Russia's problems are instead a consequence of social/cultural and political/legal contexts that direct economic activity away from realizing opportunities for mutual advantage and toward zero-sum transactions.[30] This is a legacy of the Soviet period, when the sociology of economic life was one of a shortage economy and when there was little to no alternative supply network. In such an environment, the everyday experience with markets would be an unpleasant one, enabling one to obtain the goods desired, but at terms dictated almost exclusively by the seller. It is this experience that helped form the "tacit presuppositions" of everyman within the political economy of the Soviet-type system (see Buchanan 1997, pp. 93–107). The implications of this argument are that absent a certain specified institutional setting (both formal rules and informal norms), the transactions that transpire (while being mutually beneficial to the parties involved) may generate destructive consequences for social cooperation for the broader community. Transitional political economy cannot be content with policies designed at getting the prices right, nor with wise council about getting the institutions right. It must somehow tap into and shift the culture of everyday life in a way that reinforces the institutional changes required for a market economy to operate effectively in order to guide resource use and spur the discovery of new and better ways to utilize resources to satisfy the demands of others within the economy.

Finally, the point about the cultural shaping of entrepreneurship can be found in Storr's (2000a) discussion of the lingering effect of the Bahamian "pirate" culture and the potential impediment this represents to generalized economic development. Development is largely a consequence of adopting institutions of governance that ward off both private and public predation, increasing the level of trust found in a community and giving entrepreneurs an incentive to engage in long-term projects. In the Bahamas, however, there exists an institutional/cultural matrix that rewards and encourages piracy rather than more productive practices. As Storr argues, many of the stories Bahamians tell, histories Bahamians study, museums Bahamians visit and rituals Bahamians practice glorify and celebrate the Bahamas' "pirate" past. Buccaneers such as Blackbeard and Ann Bonney loom large in Bahamian folklore, and industries such as gun-smuggling and rum-running are held up as sources of tremendous wealth and are touted as the reason why the Bahamas has enjoyed what little prosperity it has. Indeed, virtually all models of success to be found in the Bahamas' economic past have to be characterized as *piratical* in nature: piracy and privateering in the early 1700s, *shipwrecking* in the eighteenth and nineteenth centuries, blockade running (gun-smuggling) during the American Civil War, rum smuggling during Prohibition, drug smuggling in the 1980s and offshore banking (and the attendant money laundering) in the 1990s.

As Storr argues, the success of these "pirate" industries and the celebration of the Bahamas' "pirate" past in ritual and folklore has profoundly affected the kinds of enterprises Bahamians pursue and has "created" an entrepreneur who is acutely "alert" to opportunities for profiteering. Rather than investing in good will, promoting customer service, attempting to innovate and compete or expanding their enterprises, for instance, Bahamian businessmen tend to offer poor service, to *price gouge*, and to pursue "rents" rather than profits. As Storr's effort demonstrates, development economics cannot be satisfied with approaches that refuse to locate the entrepreneur at the heart of the development process and fail to consider how actors are affected by and affect their cultural, historical and social contexts.

VII

Conclusion

THE CROSS-FERTILIZATION OF Weberian sociology and Austrian economics promises a way back from scientistic models of irrelevance in the social sciences and a return to the "life-world" of human existence. Similarly, reexamining the way that the society, the economy and the polity enter into their analysis not only moves us beyond the conceptions of embeddedness found in economic sociology, but puts an emphasis on the "meaning" that actors attach to their actions and to social phenomena. Individuals are neither disembodied from the institutions that shape and influence individual choice nor are institutions dissociated from the *web of meanings* that give them life. The excesses of both economism and historicism can be avoided, while the benefits of analytical structure and narrative detail can be exploited to render social phenomena intelligible.

Embracing the form of methodological individualism advocated here reveals the theoretical shortcomings of both standard economics and sociology. While sociology asks the interesting questions, it remains hobbled by a lack of analytical structure. And while economics possesses an analytical structure, it remains hobbled by an undue restriction of the questions it can ask. Both Weberian sociology and Austrian economics, however, overcome these deficiencies. Using criticisms of neoclassical conceptions of man, for instance, to dismiss Mises's and Hayek's understanding of the progressive influence of markets in social development simply does not engage the issue. Nor do critiques of naïve holism "stick" to Weber's sociological conceptions.

The obstacles that prevent engaging the issues in the current dialogue over the economics and the sociology of the Weber-Austrian approach must simply be overcome. So, too, the obstacles that hinder the (re)infusing of Weberian and Austrian themes into the "new economic sociology." Indeed, the Weber-Austrian connection promises to avoid many of the pitfalls that plague their economic brethren and the "new sociology of economic life" and may represent what has appeared so elusive in the twentieth century: a social theory that is at once logically coherent, empirically useful, humanistic in its method and humanitarian in its concerns.

Notes

1. See Hill (1986), Halperin (1994) and Wilk (1996) for excellent reviews of economic anthropology's critique of economics.

2. See especially Malinowski ([1922] 1961), Geertz (1963), Gudeman (1986), Bird-David (1992).

3. Recent efforts in economic anthropology have shown encouraging movement away from the *a priori* rejection of universal theorizing.

4. For a survey of new and neo-institutionalist contributions see Eggertsson (1990). Eggertsson makes a distinction between new and neo-institutionalism on the basis of the behavioral foundations of the respective approaches. New institutionalism utilizes the bounded rationality approach, while neo-institutionalism employs the maximizing approach. Furubotn and Richter (1998) present a survey of the literature in which the maximizing paradigm and the *imperfect rationality* of agents are not contrasted, but instead blended together in the basic framework of institutional analysis. New institutionalism is envisioned in this presentation as a broad framework that incorporates the developments in economic thought on imperfect information, transaction costs, opportunism, property rights, moral hazard, corporate culture, contract theory and modern political economy. Kasper and Streit (1998) provide a more textbook treatment of the new institutionalism, which attempts a hybrid of Austrian and German ordo-liberalism with recent developments in institutional analysis.

5. See especially Granovetter (1985, p. 505). Granovetter argues that "the main thrust of 'new institutional economist' is to deflect the analysis of institutions from sociological, historical, and legal argumentation and show instead that they arise as the efficient solution to economic problems. This mission and the pervasive functionalism it implies discourage the detailed analysis of social structure that I argue here is the key to understanding how existing institutions arrived at their present state."

6. Although this presentation will focus primarily on the benefits of reclaiming Weberian insights and of infusing economic sociology with Austrian themes, we believe that an alliance would not be one-sided but mutually ben-

eficial. For one, Austrian economics would benefit a great deal from economic sociology's healthy attitude toward "thick" empirical work. On the potential importance of the *analytical narrative* approach for social theory see Boettke (forthcoming).

7. George Stigler states the point clearly: "Economic relationships are never perfectly competitive if they involve any personal relationships between economic units" (1946, p. 24). "Traditional equilibrium theory," Frank Hahn points out, " does best when the individual is of no importance—he is of measure zero. My theory does best when all the given theoretical problems arising from the individual's mattering do not have to be taken into account" (1973, p. 33).

8. It is important to stress that since 1985 the topic of norms and conventions has become an important area of research for scholars working within a rational choice framework. This research has been aided by the use of game theory as well as by the invisible hand methodology of classical political economy.

9. This is not entirely true. In a more recent statement of his embeddedness argument, Granovetter recognizes, although briefly, that his approach and the approaches of his contemporaries is consistent with Weberian insights. "The more recent generation of economic sociologists, who constitute what I call the 'New Economic Sociology', have looked much more at core economic institutions, and are closer to such intellectual forebears as Emile Durkheim and Max Weber—who regarded economic action as a subordinate and special case of social action—than to the accommodationist stance of mid-century sociologists" (1992, p. 4). Still, no effort is made to crystallize those connections or to cite and expound on Weber's contributions to our understanding of embeddedness. Granovetter's exegesis of the theoretical agenda of economic sociology, however, is quite encouraging. In it, he (2001) draws substantially from the Austrian literature on entrepreneurship, particularly Kirzner and Schumpeter, and repeatedly references Weber's contributions to our understanding of the sociology of economic life.

10. An alternate thesis is that Granovetter fails to consider the origins of social networks and the meanings individuals attach to them because he thinks of analyzing them as a necessarily subordinate step. For example, he states, "I should add that the level of casual analysis adopted in the embeddedness argument is a rather proximate one. I have had little to say about what broad historical or macrostructural circumstances have led systems to display the social-structural characteristics they have, so I make no claims for this analysis to answer large-scale questions about the nature of modern society or the sources of economic and political change. But the focus on proximate causes is intentional, for these broader questions cannot be satisfactorily addressed without more detailed understanding of the mechanisms by which sweeping change has its effects. My claim is that one of the most important and least analyzed of such mechanisms is the impact of such change on the social relations in which economic life is embedded. If this is so, no adequate link

between macro- and micro-level theories can be established without a much fuller understanding of these relations" (1985, p. 506). But insisting that how institutions come to be established and modified and the meaning that individuals attach to these institutions can somehow be practically separated from how those institutions affect individual choice is, we believe, an unconvincing argument. Even if we were to accept his arguments, however, we are still left with a vacuum to fill after proximate analyses are carried out. Rather than a corrective, Weber and the Austrians become a necessary complement to the "new economic sociology" and their consideration remains vital.

11. See Weber's "Objectivity," cited in Swedberg 1998, p. 193. See also Swedberg 1999.

12. Remember Weber's argument in *The Protestant Ethic and the Spirit of Capitalism* ([1930] 1998): "The emphasis on the ascetic importance of a fixed calling provided an ethical justification of the modern specialized division of labour. In a similar way the providential interpretation of profit-making justified the activities of the business man. The superior indulgence of the *seigneur* and the parvenu ostentation of the *nouveau riche* are equally detestable to asceticism. But, on the other hand, it has the highest ethical appreciation of the sober, middle-class, self-made man" (p.163).

13. Note that over time Weber broadened his conception of what constituted *economically conditioned phenomena* beyond the narrow conception expressed here. Swedberg states, "[I]n his later work it means roughly noneconomic phenomena that are directly influenced by economic phenomena" (1998, p. 193).

14. Although North has revised this formulation to include the impact that special interests have had on property rights, the view presented here still serves as the foundation of his theory of institutional evolution.

15. We use the term "nearly" to reflect our recognition that for certain purposes one can treat the other two as part of the "given" background to the analysis of the economy, society and polity. In this sense the circles intersect rather than completely overlap.

16. To take one example, consider Weber's explanation for "Why No Capitalism in China?" It is not the monocausal theory often characterized, but instead one that blends the social, the political/legal and the economic. As explained in his *General Economic History*, the move from arbitrary taxation to a fixed tax system is just as vital to the explanation as is the spirit of enterprise—in fact, they are interconnected. See Boettke, "The Political Infrastructure of Economic Development" in Boettke (2001) and the references therein.

17. The Austrians further *problematize* the context in which they embed their actor by allowing time to pass. See O'Driscoll and Rizzo (1985), *The Economics of Time and Ignorance*, for a cogent expansion of the consequences of allowing time to pass and individuals to hold imperfect information: "To say that Austrian economics is the economics of time and ignorance is to say

that it is the economics of *coping* with the problems posed by real time and radical ignorance. Although individuals are not paralyzed by these problems, they do not automatically or completely overcome them. The behavior generated by this predicament in which human beings find themselves is a source of market phenomena and institutions. It is also the source of prudential limits to our institutions, both markets and governmental" (p. xiv).

18. Lachmann writes: "Weber was concerned with the meaning the actor attributes to his action. Most social-system theories ignore this aspect of action . . . [M]ost of the theories mentioned, by contrast, aim at establishing their 'systems' in terms of recurrent patterns of action *without* reference to the meaning such action has to the individuals acting. We believe we are making legitimate usufruct of Weber's legacy. It follows that we can hardly hope to draw benefit from social-system theories of the type characterized" (1971, p. 74). The contrast between a Weberian approach grounded in subjective and intersubjective meanings and the structural-functionalist approach was nowhere more evident than in the debate over Weber's intellectual legacy in sociological analysis involving Alfred Schutz and Talcott Parsons. See Grathoff (1978) for the correspondence between Schutz and Parsons.

19. The problem with standard economics is not methodological individualism but that standard economics only superficially embraces it. A sophisticated methodological individualism ends up with a truly radical subjectivity and extends that subjectivity to the institutional context in which individuals choose.

20. Alfred Schutz is a major figure in the Weber/Austrian connection. First, Schutz was a student of Mises and his first work in the methodology of the social sciences was an attempt to reconstruct Weber's argument in a manner that defended it against the criticisms made by Mises of Weber's ideal type methodology *for general economic and* sociological *theory*. Schutz in this and other works developed the argument for the different levels of understanding and the method of typification. One of the puzzles he saw himself addressing was how social cooperation could emerge with anonymous types. In addressing this issue the role of knowledge (its discovery and its use) becomes prominent. Schutz also grounded his understanding of the individual in the "life-world"—the social setting within which we are all born. Thus, while anonymous types are employed in theory construction, they are not disembodied actors but social actors. A special issue of *The Review of Austrian Economics*, which was being edited by Boettke and Koppl, appeared as Vol. 14, no. 2–3 (2001).

21. Recall Swedberg's charge that the "new sociology of economic life" is hobbled by economic sociologists' failure to develop a sophisticated sociology of money and markets. It is in describing markets and the role of money that the Austrian economists first illustrated the strength of their unique approach to studying economic and social institutions (see Menger 1883). From the Austrians we learn, for instance, that "we must look at the price system as

such a mechanism for communicating information if we want to understand its real function—a function which, of course, it fulfils less perfectly as prices grow more rigid. The most significant fact about this system is the economy of knowledge with which it operates, or how little the individual participants need to know in order to be able to take the right action. In abbreviated form, by a kind of symbol, only the most essential information is passed on and passed on only to those concerned. It is more than a metaphor to describe the price system as a kind of machinery for registering change, or a system of tele-communications which enables individual producers to watch merely the movement of a few pointers, as engineers might watch the hands of a few di-als, in order to adjust their activities to changes of which they may never know more than is reflected in the price mechanism" (Hayek 1948, p. 86).

22. That Mises and Hayek are two sides of the same coin is a view that is sometimes controversial but it is nonetheless the view we assume here. For a defense of that view see Boettke (1990c, 1998b).

23. Schumpeter was trained in the Austrian tradition under Bohm-Bawerk and Wieser, but in his technical economics he pursued the "functionalist" approach as developed in the work of Walras, instead of the "genetic-causal" approach first laid out by Menger. Schumpeter's theoretical endorsement of equilibrium economics, as opposed to the process theory of the Austrians, and his methodological stance, led him (and the other Austrian economists) to distance themselves from one another. However, whenever Schumpeter stepped beyond the bounds of technical economics to the realm of social theory the imprint of his Austrian training is evident. On the differences between functionalist and genetic-causal approaches to economics see Cowan and Rizzo (1994).

24. Although see the discussion in Holton and Turner (1989, pp. 30–67) and Swedberg's (1998) summary of Weber's economic sociology.

25. For a similar statement from Hayek see *Individualism and Economic Order* (1948). "What, then, are the essential characteristics of true individualism? The first thing that should be said is that it is primarily a *theory* of society, an attempt to understand the forces which determine the social life of man, and only in the second instance a set of political maxims derived from this view of society. This fact should by itself be sufficient to refute the silliest of the common misunderstandings: the belief that individualism postulates (or bases its arguments on the assumption of) the existence of isolated or self-contained individuals, instead of starting from men whose whole nature and character is determined by their existence in society" (p. 6).

26. Sciabarra (1995) has argued that Hayek and Mises, by implication, were able to avoid articulating an atomistic individualism not because they embraced a sophisticated individualism as we have argued here, but because Hayek's social theory was *fundamentally dialectical:* "It is a distortion to view Hayek's approach as *either* individualistic *or* holistic. Hayek's method is *fundamentally dialectical*, encompassing elements of individualism *and* holism,

while repudiating all forms of reductionism, atomism, ahistoricism, and strict organicity. This claim is at once disorienting and provocative. Indeed, Hayek's disciples on the free market right and his critics on the socialist left might view the very notion of 'Hayekian dialectics' as an oxymoron . . . yet, a more detailed examination of Hayek's mode of inquiry suggests that the distinguished neoliberal social philosopher was highly dialectical in many significant ways" (p. 17).

27. An Austrian analysis of commuting, for instance, would have to view it simultaneously as social, political and economic. To the extent that commuting occurs because economies of scale are to be had by locating workers in the same geographic location, it is an economic phenomena. To the extent that zoning laws, for instance, have resulted in geographic configurations where businesses and homes are located in separate parts of town, commuting should at least in part be considered a politically conditioned phenomenon. An Austrian discussion of commuting would insist on referring to both the economics and politics of the phenomena. See Boettke (1993, 2001), Chamlee-Wright (1997, 2000a, 2000b) and Storr (2000a, 2000b) for Austrian analysis that combines considerations of economic, political and social factors in an empirical examination of phenomena. Also see Boettke's essay, "Putting the Political Back into Political Economy" (Boettke 2000) and the implications of the status quo and the compensation principle for political economy once embeddedness is taken into account.

28. Although the *labola* does vary with the earning potential of the woman (the families of college graduates receive a higher *labola*), the tradition should not be viewed as the purchasing of a bride as it does not establish outright ownership of the woman. It has, however, been used as a justification of male control.

29. Entrepreneurship can be understood at a theoretical level as an aspect of all human action. In this limited sense, entrepreneurship is simply the act of being alert to opportunities to better one's situation. Treating entrepreneurial action in this manner serves an important theoretical purpose in providing a theory of the path toward equilibrium in a hypothetical market economy (see Kirzner 1973). But this conceptualization of the entrepreneurial act is predicated by the textbook model of the economic system that it is trying to improve upon. Entrepreneurship is arbitrage and within the model is able to fill in a theoretical lacunae that the model of perfect competition possesses—namely, how in a world of price takers do prices ever change to clear the market? Beyond that purpose and this version of entrepreneurship must be viewed as "empty." If entrepreneurship is a universal aspect of all of human action, then how can it aid us in forming an explanation of the extent and form that entrepreneurship takes in the real world? It cannot, as Lavoie (1991) has argued, unless complemented by a theory of cultural influence. A rich understanding of entrepreneurship must recognize the cultural context that shapes the individual's perceptions of what opportunities for betterment exist.

Culture, in other words, influences the "window" through which actors see the world and their place within it.

30. On the general theme of how human progress follows from transitioning from zero-sum to positive-sum games of life see Robert Wright (2000).

References

Agassi, Joseph. (1960). "Methodological Individualism," *British Journal of Sociology* 11 (September): 244–270.

———. (1975). "Institutional Individualism," *British Journal of Sociology* 26 (June): 144–155.

Berger, Brigitte. (1991). *The Culture of Entrepreneurship.* San Francisco: ICS Press.

Bird-David, Nurit. (1992a). "Beyond 'The Affluent Society': A Culturalist Reformation, and Discussion," *Current Anthropology* 33: 25–34.

———. (1992b). "Beyond 'The Hunting and Gathering Mode of Subsistence': Culture-Sensitive Observations on the Nayaka and Other Modern Hunter-Gatherers," *Man* 27: 19–44.

Boettke, Peter J. (1989). "Evolution and Economics: Austrians as Institutionalists," *Research in the History of Economic Thought and Methodology* 6: 73–89.

———. (1990a). "Institutions and Individuals," *Critical Review* 4 (1–2): 10–26.

———. (1990b). "The Theory of Spontaneous Order and Cultural Evolution in the Social Theory of F. A. Hayek," *Cultural Dynamics* 3 (1): 61–83.

———. (1990c). "Interpretive Reasoning and the Study of Social Life," *Methodus: Bulletin of the International Network for Economic Method* 2 (December): 35–45.

———. (1993). *Why Perestroika Failed: The Politics and Economics of Socialist Transformation.* New York: Routledge.

———, ed. (1994). *The Elgar Companion to Austrian Economics.* Cheltenham, UK: Edward Elgar.

———. (1998a). "Rational Choice and Human Agency in Economics and Sociology," in *Merits and Limits of Markets,* H. Giersch, ed. Berlin: Springer-Verlag.

———. (1998b). "Economic Calculation: The Austrian Contribution to Political Economy," *Advances in Austrian Economics* 5: 131–158.

———. (2000). "Putting the Political Back into Political Economy," Department of Economics, George Mason University, Working Paper.

———. (2001). *Calculation and Coordination: Essays on Socialism and Transitional Political Economy.* London: Routledge.

———. (forthcoming). "Review of Robert Bates, et. al., *Analytical Narrative*," *Constitutional Political Economy.*

Boettke, Peter J., and Roger Koppl, eds. (2001). *Review of Austrian Economics: Special Issue on the Contributions of Alfred Schutz* 14 (2–3).

Buchanan, James. (1997). *Post-Socialist Political Economy*. Cheltenham, UK: Edward Elgar.

Chamlee, Emily. (1993). "Indigenous African Institutions," *Cato Journal* 13: 79–99.

Chamlee-Wright, Emily. (1997). *The Cultural Foundations of Economic Development: Urban Female Entrepreneurship in Ghana*. New York: Routledge.

———. (2000a). "Economic Strategies of Urban Market Women in Harare, Zimbabawe." Working Paper.

———. (2000b). "Entrepreneurial Response to 'Bottom-Up' Development Strategies in Zimbabwe." Working Paper.

Coleman, James. (1990). *Foundations of Social Theory*.

Cowan, Robin, and Mario Rizzo. (1996). "The Genetic-Causal Tradition and Modern Economic Theory," *Kyklos* 49 (3): 273–316.

Eggertsson, T. (1990). *Economic Behavior and Institutions*. New York: Cambridge University Press.

Etzioni, Amitai. (1988). *The Moral Dimensions*.

Furubotn, Eirik G., and Rudolf Richter. (1998). *Institutions and Economic Theory: The Contribution of the New Institutional Economics*. Ann Arbor: University of Michigan Press.

Geertz, Clifford. (1963). *Peddlers and Princes: Social Development and Economic Change*. Chicago: University of Chicago Press.

Gerth, H. H., and C. Wright Mills. (1946). *From Max Weber: Essays in Sociology*. New York: Oxford University Press.

Granovetter, Mark. (1985). "Economic Action and Social Structure: The Problem of Embeddedness," *American Journal of Sociology* 91: 481–510.

———. (1992). "Economic Institutions as Social Constructions: A Framework for Analysis," *Acta Sociologica* 35: 3–11.

———. (2001). "A Theoretical Agenda for Economic Sociology," in *Economic Sociology at the Millennium*, Guillen Collins, ed. New York: Russell Sage.

Grathoff, R., ed. (1978). *The Theory of Social Action: The Correspondence of Alfred Schutz and Talcott Parsons*. Bloomington: Indiana University Press.

Gudeman, Stephen. (1986). *Economics as Culture: Models and Metaphors of Livelihood*. London: Routledge.

Hahn, Frank. (1973). *On the Notion of Equilibrium in Economics*. Cambridge: Cambridge University Press.

Halperin, Rhonda H. (1994). *Cultural Economics: Past and Present*. Austin: University of Texas Press.

Hayek, F. A. (1948). *Individualism and Economic Order*. Chicago: University of Chicago Press.

———. (1960). *The Constitution of Liberty*. Chicago: University of Chicago Press.

———. (1973). *Law, Legislation and Liberty: Volume I Rules and Order*. Chicago: University of Chicago Press.

————. (1988). *The Fatal Conceit: The Errors of Socialism*. Chicago: University of Chicago Press.

Hill, Polly. (1986). *Development Economics on Trial: The Anthropological Case for a Prosecution*. New York: Cambridge University Press.

Holton, Robert J., and Bryan S. Turner. (1989). *Max Weber on Economy and Society*. New York: Routledge.

Käsler, Dirk. ([1979] 1988). *Max Weber: An Introduction to His Life and Work*. Chicago: University of Chicago Press.

Kasper, Wolfgang, and Manfred Streit. (1998). *Institutional Economics: Social Order and Public Policy*. Cheltenham, UK: Edward Elgar.

Kirzner, Israel M. (1973). *Competition and Entrepreneurship*. Chicago: University of Chicago Press.

Lachmann, Ludwig M. (1971). *The Legacy of Max Weber*. Berkeley, CA: Glendessary Press.

————. (1977). *Capital, Expectations, and the Market Process: Essays on the Theory of the Market Economy*. Menlo Park, CA: Institute for Humane Studies.

————. (1994). *Expectations and the Meaning of Institutions: Essays in Economics*. New York: Routledge.

Lavoie, Don. (1990). "Hermeneutics, Subjectivity, and the Lester/ Machlup Debate: Toward a More Anthropological Approach to Empirical Economics," in *Economics as Discourse: An Analysis of the Language of Economics*, W. Samuels, ed. Boston, MA: Kluwer Academic Publishing.

————. (1991). "The Discovery and Interpretation of Profit Opportunities: Culture and the Kirznerian Entrepreneur," in *The Culture of Entrepreneurship*, B. Berger, ed. San Francisco: ICS Press.

Lavoie, Don, and Emily Chamlee-Wright. (2000). *Culture and Enterprise: The Development, Representation, and Morality of Business*. New York: Routledge.

Malinowski, Bronislaw. ([1922] 1961). *Argonauts of the Western Pacific*. New York: Dutton.

Menger, Carl. ([1883] 1994). *Principles of Economics*. Grove City, PA: Libertarian Press.

Mises, Ludwig von. (1933). *Epistemological Problems of Economics*.

————. (1949). *Human Action: A Treatise on Economics*. San Francisco: Fox & Wilkes.

Mommsen, Wolfgang J. (1998). *The Political and Social Theory of Max Weber*. Chicago: University of Chicago Press.

North, Douglass C. (1990). *Institutions, Institutional Change and Economic Performance*. New York: Cambridge University Press.

————. (1991). "Institutions," *Journal of Economic Perspectives* 5: 97–112.

————. (1995). "The New Institutional Economics and Third World Development," in *The New Institutional Economics and Third World Development* J. Harriss, J. Hunter, and C. Lewis, eds. New York: Routledge.

O' Driscoll, Gerald P., and Mario Rizzo. (1985). *The Economics of Time and Ignorance.* New York: Routledge.

Prychitko, David. (1989/90). "Methodological Individualism and the Austrian School," *Journal des Economistes et des Etudes Humaines* 1 (1): 171–179.

Ringer, Fritz. (1997). *Max Weber's Methodology: The Unification of the Cultural and Social Sciences.* Cambridge: Harvard University Press.

Sciabarra, Chris Matthew. (1995). *Marx, Hayek and Utopia.* Albany: State University of New York.

Schutz, Alfred. ([1932] 1967). *The Phenomenology of the Social World.* Evanston, IL: Northwestern University Press.

Smelser, Neil J., and Richard Swedberg, eds. (1994). *The Handbook of Economic Sociology.* Princeton, NJ: Princeton University Press.

Stigler, George. (1946). *The Theory of Price.* Chicago: Rand-McNally.

Storr, Virgil. (2000a). "Expulsis Piratis? The Enduring Culture of Bahamian Entrepreneurs." Working Paper.

———. (2000b). "All We've Learnt: Colonial Teachings and Caribbean Underdevelopment." Working Paper.

Swedberg, Richard. (1990). *Economics and Sociology.* Princeton, NJ: Princeton University Press.

———. (1991). "Major Traditions of Economic Sociology," *Annual Review of Sociology* 17: 251–276.

———. (1998). *Max Weber and the Idea of Economic Sociology.* Princeton, NJ: Princeton University Press.

Weber, Max. ([1922] 1978). *Economy and Society.* Berkeley: University of California Press.

———. ([1930] 1992). *The Protestant Ethic and the Spirit of Capitalism.* London: Routledge.

———. ([1930] 1998). *The Protestant Ethic and the Spirit of Capitalism.* Los Angeles: Roxbury Publishing.

———. (1947). *The Theory of Social and Economic Organization.* New York: Free Press.

———. (1999). *Essays in Economic Sociology.* Princeton, NJ: Princeton University Press.

Wilk, Richard R. (1996). *Economies and Cultures: Foundations of Economic Anthropology.* Boulder, CO: Westview Press.

Williamson, Oliver. (2000). "New Institutional Economics: Taking Stock, Looking Ahead," *Journal of Economic Literature* 38 (3): 595–613.

Wright, Robert. (2000). *Non-Zero: The Logic of Human Destiny.* New York: Pantheon Books.

New Political Economy, Scientism and Knowledge

A Critique from a Hayekian Perspective, and a Proposal for an Extension of the Research Agenda

By Jan Schnellenbach[*]

ABSTRACT. New Political Economy has something very important in common with welfare economics: its focus on static, technical efficiency criteria to judge the rationality of a social, political or economic order. This often leads theorists to perceive their objects of research as well-defined problems to which clear-cut solutions can be found and prescribed as policy proposals, addressed at the policymaker or the democratic sovereign. This perspective frequently excludes important empirical phenomena from the research agenda. Although, for example, certain well-defined informational asymmetries are frequently modeled, fundamental knowledge problems such as ignorance of the true model of the economy are usually ignored. In the present paper, this approach is criticized from a Hayekian point of view, with an emphasis on the problems of "scientism" (i.e., the inappropriate transfer of methods from the natural to the social sciences) and irremediably imperfect knowledge, troubling both the agents in the theoretical model and the theorist. Furthermore, it is argued and illustrated with two examples that an extension of Public Choice's research agenda along Hayekian lines may be fruitful, because it leads to a fresh perception even of such problems that already have been extensively researched within the traditional framework.

*The author is research associate at the Swiss Institute of International Economics and Applied Economic Research (SIAW) at the University of St. Gallen, Switzerland, where he also teaches. His research interests include traditional areas of Public Choice and Public Finance, such as the theory of fiscal federalism, but also the theory of economic policy making under uncertainty, the history of economic thought and the methodology of economic science.

American Journal of Economics and Sociology, Vol. 61, No. 1 (January, 2002).

I

Introduction

THE PRESENT PAPER IS an attempt to have a close look at the extraordinarily successful research program of New Political Economy (or Public Choice) from a distinctly Hayekian perspective. This involves two important points that have been central to the economic thought of Friedrich August von Hayek. One is the problem of scientism, a term coined to signify the inappropriate transfer of methods from the natural sciences, especially physics, to the social sciences, where the complexity of the object under research is usually much higher. The other point is the knowledge problem. Hayek was a pioneer in making the necessarily incomplete and dispersed knowledge of economic agents *the* departing point of his economic research. From his point of view, it was never primarily the problem of economic theory to determine the mathematical conditions of general equilibrium, but rather to explain how the voluntary coordination of individual plans is in fact achieved, i.e., how the price system allows to make efficient use of knowledge that is dispersed throughout the economy.

The argument will proceed as follows: In Sections II and III, the emphasis will be on the problem of scientism. In Section II, we will refute a claim that often at least implicitly shines through in normative Public Choice, namely that Political Economy can be a tool to find an ideal institutional framework for a rational society. This point will be reinforced in Section III, where the knowledge problem is introduced. Furthermore, Hayek's argument concerning the distinction between an evolution of rules and pretentious constructivism aiming at the implementation of an ideal social order is reconstructed with regard to public law, on which, after all, the main focus of Public Choice rests. Section IV will give two examples of how a change of perspective from traditional Public Choice to knowledge-oriented Public Choice may look like. To make this as illustrative as possible, two examples that have already been quite extensively researched from the traditional point of view are chosen: democratic competition for office and the competition between jurisdictions for mobile resources. Finally, Section V draws some conclusions.

II

New Political Economy and the Search for an Ideal
Institutional Framework

HANS ALBERT, arguably one of the most influential proponents of a criticist social philosophy, has repeatedly challenged neoclassical welfare economics on grounds of its pursuit of an ideal (i.e., perfectly efficient) production and its complete disregard for value judgments that can be made about the mode of production itself.[1] For example, where do the socialist, who prefers massive government intervention and is willing to surrender some efficiency, or the classical liberal, who would rather preserve his personal liberty than have each and every externality corrected by the government, fit into normative welfare economics? Welfare economics is technocratic in the sense that it makes statements about production and exchange efficiency, but disregards the possible quarrels that arise from differing preferences concerning, for instance, the legitimate scope of government in society.

There is no ideal production if the mode of production is itself subject to value judgments, which of course will differ between individuals in an open society. Normative Public Choice theory appears to own a similarity to welfare economics in the sense that the underlying question of many theoretical Public Choice approaches is: "How can we achieve rational collective decision making?" instead of "How can we achieve rational production of commodities?" Both questions are of the same nature because both ask for the necessary conditions for social rationality from the perspective of an omniscient observer, but the meaning of rationality is not as clear in Public Choice as it is in welfare economics: In some contributions, a political process is considered to be rational if its outcome coincides with the median voter's preferences, while others equate rationality with the transitivity of the social preference ordering, and still other contributions continue to use the yardstick of Pareto-efficiency to evaluate the results of the political process and thereby judge its rationality.

In the half-century since Kenneth J. Arrow established his theorem, more and more imperfections of political decision-making processes have found the interest of Public Choice scholars and, usually, those valuable positive insights have been followed up by attempts to find remedies. To name but a few examples: Arrow's impossibility theorem sparked an enormous Social Choice literature devoted to finding conditions of avoiding cycles under different majority requirements.[2] When William A. Niskanen hinted toward the fact that bureaucrats pursue their own interest[3] and that this may not coincide with the interest of the median voter, proposals for the optimal control of bureaucrats soon followed. When the steady growth of governments during the post-war decades was difficult to explain as the will of the democratic sovereign, normative Constitutional Political Economy took the stage to develop means of controlling Leviathan.[4] And today, in times of "globalization," demands for policy coordination between governments arise, because it is feared that the competition for mobile resources between democratic governments will lead to a Pareto-inferior outcome.[5]

In these examples, we find at least two targets for critical remarks. First, it becomes obvious that New Political Economy, if understood as an analytical tool to produce value-free statements about the preferability of alternative social orders, is bound to fail. Even if we leave the Hayekian, knowledge-related objections that will be outlined in the next section out of consideration for the moment, this follows from the fact that New Political Economy is interested in (at least) three often contradictory criteria of collective rationality: the realization of the median voter's preferences, the implementation of a voting mechanism that leads to transitive results and the attainment of a Pareto-optimum. But what happens if the median voter is the above-mentioned socialist or the classical liberal and wants to surrender some efficiency for political ideals? Or how does New Political Economy respond to an autocrat who wants to maximize GDP growth but has no interest in the will of his or her people?

New Political Economy, it seems, is not a handy tool to craft normative statements about an ideal configuration of society, or to put it differently: it is not and cannot be a substitute for political philosophy and for critical reasoning about the adequate order of society. Consider, for instance, the classical liberal argument that a policy needs majority approval to be legitimate, but that not every policy approved by a majority is to be considered a legitimate policy.[6] New Political

Economy cannot offer a scientific foundation to define the set of legitimate policies—whether a person is, for example, willing to sacrifice political ideals for increased efficiency of production is essentially a subjective value judgment, sometimes based on philosophical considerations. Nevertheless, political economy can play an important role in enabling individuals to come to informed value judgments. It can inform individuals, for instance, that the choice of a given set of political institutions is associated with certain kinds of efficiency losses, with political instability due to cycling majorities or with a lack of control in the principal-agent relationship between voters and government.[7] Obviously, from this perspective one would attribute far greater importance to positive than to normative political economy.

The second target of our critique is that, with the habit of routinely responding with normative policy proposals to the imperfections of the political decision-making process discovered by positive Public Choice, it may be that our interpretation of the criteria of social rationality changes. This point is probably best illustrated by the example of the criterion of Pareto-optimality, which has a relevance as an analytical tool within theoretical models: it allows us to state whether we can expect that, under certain conditions, individual decisions lead to an outcome in which production and exchange efficiency prevails. But if we look at the welfare economic literature today, we see quite often that even the most remotely policy-relevant problem is approached in two steps: (i) by showing that some deficiency, e.g., an externality or a coordination failure, leads to a sub-optimal result *in the model* and (ii) by then proposing a policy instrument that, it is promised, leads to a Pareto-improvement *in the real world*. All of a sudden, the methodological status of the Pareto-optimum is changed from an analytical tool in a highly simplified model to an attainable state of the real world.[8]

This procedure of recklessly inferring policy recommendations from economic models has been extensively criticized by Friedrich A. von Hayek when he speaks of a *"pretence of knowledge"* by economists.[9] This pretence is composed of a number of implicit assumptions that are made when a policy recommendation is derived from a theoretical model: (a) the model is assumed to be the correct model, (b) it is assumed to be complete in the sense that it takes account of all relevant interdependencies, (c) it is assumed that the model describes a relationship between the independent and the dependent variables that is stable in historical time and (d) it is assumed that all the relevant parameter values can be reliably ascertained and are also stable. According to Hayek, we cannot expect these assumptions to be true when we are dealing with the extraordinarily complex system of a market economy. Discretionary government intervention into the spontaneous order that emerges from individual decisions on the market may sometimes, by chance, lead to an improvement—but often the unexpected distorting effects that were not accounted for in the simplified model will lead to a decline in efficiency.[10] The relevant question in our context, however, is whether this knowledge-related argument against the possibility of successful social engineering that Hayek developed with regard to market interventions has any relevance for Public Choice theory, which is, after all, interested in non-market decisions.

III

The Neglect of the Knowledge Problem in Modern Public Choice Theory

IN HIS WORK ON *Law, Legislation and Liberty*, Hayek makes a distinction between two types of rules: *nomos* and *thesis*.[11] *Nomos* denotes a rule that forbids a clearly defined number of actions of the infinitely many possible actions from which an individual may choose, while *thesis* denotes a rule that exactly instructs a person how to act under certain clearly defined circumstances. Decisions under a regime of the first type of rules will lead to spontaneous order, of which the market is a familiar example. Spontaneous orders are characterized by a high degree of complexity—usually, these are too complex to be governed by rules of the second type, which are associated with organizations, of which government is an example.

As far as rules of the *nomos* category are concerned, Hayek is convinced that they are almost exclusively the result of an invisible-hand evolutionary process, or, to use a familiar phrase, they are the result of human action, but not of human design.[12] On the other hand, rules of the *thesis* category are assumed to be the result of purposeful, conscious design. Hayek's notion of *nomos*, inspired by the Anglo-Saxon common law tradition, comprehends most, if not all, of civil law; he assumes the rules that govern the voluntary coordination of individuals to be merely found and formalized, but not designed, by judges or legislatures. The realm of *thesis*, on the other hand, is confined to consciously designed organizations of relatively low complexity, which also comprehends public law[13]—and in the emergence of *thesis*, conscious design is assumed to play a more prominent role.

Taking these remarks about conceptions of different types of rules into consideration, one may conclude that it is perfectly in line with a Hayekian approach to ponder the *design* of efficient rules of political decision making—and, in fact, this is exactly what Hayek himself did when he proposed a model constitution with the aim of limiting the leeway of purposeful governmental intervention into spontaneous orders. This procedure, however, is subject to the same critical remarks that have been made above: Any model constitution involves value judgments—in Hayek's case, the value judgments of a classical liberal. And independent from how much we individually sympathize with this value judgment, we still have to accept that there may be other individuals who, for instance, are willing to sacrifice some of the advantages of the spontaneous order if in turn their ideal of an egalitarian society is realized. In Hayek's contributions, as well as in Public Choice, political economy is still not able to provide us with a formula for an ideal set of rules governing political decision making based purely on scientific considerations. But (Hayekian) political economy is able to provide us with invaluable information about the opportunity cost of an intervention into the spontaneous order, and thus plays an important role in the critical discussion of the adequacy of a proposed social order.[14]

A second objection is that even when we are dealing with the problem of designing rules governing the political process, we may be confronted with serious knowledge problems. In some sense, the division between *nomos* and *thesis* is highly artificial, because eventually, public law does not only govern the organization of government, but it also affects the decisions that government can make with respect to intervening into the spontaneous order: *thesis* is a source of repercussions into the spontaneous order, albeit these effects are more indirect than in the case of *nomos*. The complexity does not simply disappear when we turn from *nomos* to *thesis*; therefore, the problem of finding public law that fits our purposes, i.e., that is suitable to effectuate a libertarian society, a socialist society, some sort of third way or whatever kind of societal order we consider adequate, will still be a problem to be solved by trial and error and not by rational construction on a social engineer's drawing board. This rationalist procedure would, when it comes to *thesis*, be no more practicable than when we are dealing with *nomos*.

What divides *nomos* and *thesis* is a gradual difference, not a difference in principle. *Nomos* is the result of an evolutionary process with a very long time-horizon. Hayek is skeptical of purposive interventions into this process, because whoever intervenes pretends to utilize knowledge that is superior to all the knowledge that was used and accumulated in the long-run evolutionary process. *Thesis* is also the result of an evolutionary process, but one in which purposive intervention has a role to play. In fact, purposive intervention is the driving force without which this evolutionary process would not occur. Purposive changes of public law create a diversity of social orders from which we can learn for future, similarly purposive changes of public law. The important point is that this, although involving purposive interventions, is still an evolutionary process of learning from institutional experiments.

The implications for political economy are, at this point, twofold. The first implication is to practice a bit more modesty. Policy proposals concerning the change of the institutions of public law ought to be just that: *fallible proposals*, acknowledged to be more or less well founded by theoretical models and, ideally, some empirical evidence. At least in the welfare economic literature, it happens too often that policy instruments, constructed on the basis of simplified models, are being advertised as scientific solutions of well-defined problems, comparable to solutions of well-defined problems in, for instance, physics or engineering. Public Choice certainly should not follow that lead. The second implication is that political economy may foster the learning process about the effects of institutional frameworks by maintaining a strong empirical (and therefore positive) branch dedicated to the comparative analysis of actual institutions. And, probably, a considerable part of this empirical research will have to be non-econometric, because quantitative analysis necessarily has to represent actual institutions by the few variables for which quantitative data are available, amended maybe with some dummy variables representing very few qualitative characteristics. In some cases, this may be simply too much simplification where a precise glance at the details would be more promising.

IV

Expanding Hayek's Knowledge-Oriented Research Program to Political Economy

A. Some Preliminary Remarks

In the above remarks on the neglect of the knowledge problem in Public Choice, we focused mainly on methodological issues. The aim was to shed some light on the limitations placed on political economy by the complexity of its subject and the associated knowledge problem. In Hayek's work, this knowledge problem has, however, a significant second meaning, because he also takes it as a point of departure for his research program concerned with the positive analysis of the use of dispersed knowledge in society.[15] He asserts that general equilibrium analysis, when it makes the assumption of perfect knowledge held by all acting individuals, is no more than a tautology: the solution of the system of equations is completely determined by the assumptions. The problem economic research should rather concern itself with is, according to Hayek, the question of finding mechanisms that lead to a convergence of the individuals' subjective conjectures toward objectively true data. This leads to his interpretation of the price system as a mechanism of aggregating and transmitting dispersed knowledge[16] and culminates in the well-known interpretation of competition as a discovery procedure, i.e., a mechanism offering incentives to discover new, previously completely unknown knowledge.[17]

The problem we face, though, is that Hayek's theory of knowledge accumulation is very much tailored to analyze learning in the market economy. Informed individual decisions on the market are possible because of the information transmitted by the price system, and individuals are guided to act efficiently by the forces of competition. And market competition involves also incentives to enlarge one's own stock of knowledge, because the uncertainty about the innovative activities of competitors gives an agent a reason to search for superior problem-solving routines him- or herself. When we turn our attention to Public Choice, we see that the environment of non-market decision making is quite different, lacking market prices, market-like competition and a lot of the entrepreneurial uncertainty of the market process. The ensuing question then is whether an economic approach can contribute anything to a theory of learning mechanisms regarding non-market decisions.

In the traditional Public Choice literature, we usually examine political competition as a possible means of leading the political process to a result that is in compliance with the preferences of the median voter. To do so, we assume either perfect knowledge of all agents in the model or we introduce some rather narrowly defined information problems, leading to various kinds of principal-agent problems. Taking this line of research as a point of departure, it will be useful to make a clarifying distinction between problems of *information* and of *knowledge*.

The neoclassical literature on incomplete information understands information as a commodity that is exogenously supplied and simply waits to be discovered, although often at significant cost.[18] Without any doubt, there are problems for which this approach makes perfect sense, for instance, when an incompletely informed consumer's search for a satisfying price offer is to be modeled. Hayek's objection toward general equilibrium analysis was that the dispersed information about relative prices can never be centralized, but this does not rule out that from the perspective of an individual agent at a given place and time, the particular prices that interest him or her appear as objectively-given data of which he or she can inform him- or herself at some cost. In fact, the Hayekian notion of knowledge does not contradict the neoclassical notion of information, but encompasses and enlarges it. In Hayek (1937) it is argued that the term "equilibrium" makes sense, not for society as a whole, but only for an individual whose subjective plans are confirmed by experience. A subjective plan contains knowledge of certain particular data, the information of neoclassical theory. But to be complete, it also has to comprise theoretical conjectures about the functioning of the economy. The individual has to form a subjective expectation about the future state of the economy and about the impact of his or her own factual and potential actions on this future state in order to come to a rational decision regarding which action he or she wants to pursue.[19]

This is certainly true for economic policy makers. They need to have some cognitive model of the economy and the causal relationships governing it when they decide on which policy they want to execute. The theoretical problem at this stage is not the coordination of subjective plans, as it is in a market context, but is the question of how rational (in the sense of how close to the true model of the economy) we can expect these subjective conjectures to be. Obviously, not even an economist, at least if he or she was brought up in the epistemological spirit of critical rationalism, can be sure to know the correct model of the economy, so there is a certain lack of a reliable benchmark to judge the rationality of a given, particular policy.[20] Nevertheless, it should be possible to come to general statements about the learning mechanisms that individuals are subject to under different institutional settings. For example, the goal has to be to predict patterns of knowledge accumulation under different institutional settings, rather than to predict the direction and judge the rationality of a particular learning process. One relevant part of this institutional puzzle may be democratic competition.

B. Example I: Political Competition in Democracy

Despite acknowledging the considerable differences between market processes and the political process, one may understand democracy as a discovery procedure, similar to Hayek's attribution of market competition.[21] In such a framework, professional politicians and interest groups play the role of political entrepreneurs who force new problems onto the agenda or offer new explanations and new solutions to given problems. The public discourse on policy serves the individuals as a facility to form opinions, i.e., to find theories about what is possible and preferences about which objectives ought to be pursued. As Wohlgemuth (1999) demonstrates, it can convincingly be shown on these grounds that democracy is far superior to autocratic political systems.[22]

But on the other hand, one democratic institutional framework that we observe in practice is usually quite different from the other. One is a direct democracy, the other purely representative; one has term limits, the other has none; one is a multi-chamber system, the other has only one parliament, and so on. This means that, for a political economist interested in understanding political learning mechanisms by comparative institutional analysis, plenty of work still waits to be done. In other words, the work is not completed by comparing democracy and autocracy, but comparative institutional analysis ought to proceed toward a comparative analysis of knowledge accumulation under differing democratic frameworks.

There are also some problems remaining to be covered by a deeper theoretical analysis. First of all, how can we explain the occurrence of the political entrepreneur? One may expect that political entrepreneurship is a rather risky business for a politician in office. *Ex ante*, he or she may be personally confident that a new policy measure leads, for instance, to higher rates of GDP growth, but as long as his or her conjecture is not confirmed by experience, he or she bears the risk of failure and of being punished by the electorate for a potentially costly, failed policy experiment. Would it not be much more rational for him or her to adhere to familiar policy routines, so that there is an undersupply of policy experiments? If, on the other hand, the entrepreneur is in the opposition, then he or she has not the means of putting his or her proposed new routine to the practical test. He or she can represent his or her conjectures in the political discourse—but why should any of the other individuals, who may have invested considerable costs into building their present set of coherent conjectures, be willing to give up this present set of conjectures for a new one that is not even backed by experience? To explain the emergence of new policy routines, it is certainly not satisfactory to rely only upon a Schumpeterian explanation of entrepreneurship, which rests solely on personal characteristics of the entrepreneur. Such an explanation is given, among others, by Kuran (1995), who refers to the expressive needs of the political entrepreneur. Unfortunately, such an explanation avoids the problem of finding institutional prerequisites for entrepreneurial activity in the political sphere.

In this context, consider also the familiar statement of the traditional theory that in a two-party system, and under certain conditions also in a multi-party system, the political parties will converge toward the interests of the median voter in order to maximize their respective chances of winning an election. If this is the case, then we will certainly also have to expect a tendency of parties to move toward the median voter's conjectures in order to theoretically substantiate their position in the political discourse. Consider then the assumption that the members of the respective parties have policy-oriented preferences, i.e., they want to maintain a position that is defined by a certain political philosophy and there is no tendency toward the median position. In this case, the representatives of these parties would have an incentive to adhere to the traditional policy routines of their parties, but certainly not to act as political entrepreneurs.

Given these second thoughts, the idea of party competition in democracy being a discovery procedure looks not as overwhelmingly convincing as it may have appeared on first sight. Nevertheless, every now and then we do indeed observe political entrepreneurship in the sense that completely new routines of problem solving are introduced and therefore, by means of a policy experiment, new knowledge about the effects of different rules of the *thesis* kind is produced. What is missing so far is a sound theoretical identification of the conditions under which we observe it. One element of this puzzle may be learning from the experience of others, in a setting of decentralized policy making.

C. Example II: The Political Economy of Tax Competition

In recent years, tax competition between autonomous jurisdictions, be it on the level of municipalities, sub-federal states or competing nations, has become an increasingly popular topic of research within the public finance literature. The problem that jurisdiction A, by setting taxes without coordinating its activities with jurisdiction B, may attract mobile tax bases from B or repel its own mobile tax bases to B, can be scrutinized from a number of different perspectives, of which two have already been extensively taken. The traditional public finance perspective is the one of the omniscient observer who wishes to maximize total welfare of A and B. For him or her, uncoordinated tax policy will usually lead to inefficiently low tax rates and an undersupply of public goods, because the decentralized decision maker in A does not account for the positive externality that his or her supply of public goods may mean for B and he or she also ignores that if a higher tax rate is set, the mobile tax base will not disappear from the economy as a whole, but only migrate to B, which also is a positive externality. From this perspective, there is a strong case for centralizing the authority of policy making.

The perspective of the Public Choice theorist toward the same problem is quite different. He or she has in mind the deficiencies of the political process, in particular the imperfect capability of the citizens to control their representatives. From this point of view, the exit option of tax bases is a welcome remedy for the inherent tendency of government to usurp a larger share of resources from the private sector than the legitimate share preferred by the median voter. This argument is not only put forward with regard to the size of the budget, but also regarding the quality of public goods: tax bases will migrate to that jurisdiction that supplies the desired bundle of public goods for a tax price considered appropriate. In equilibrium, every citizen lives in the jurisdiction whose supply is the closest to his or her preferences. The overall efficiency of the public sector is improved compared to a situation in which only one government can act as an uncontested monopolist.

From a knowledge-oriented perspective, the matter would again present itself in a different light. First of all, the problem calls for an explanation of the diversity of tax and expenditure policies that we can observe throughout the world, which seemingly leads us into a dilemma: if the observed policies are rational, in the sense that they are optimal solutions under the specific conditions of the respective jurisdictions, then there is no need for further learning and evolution—what is, is efficient; if, on the other hand, the observed policies are not rational, then there may be no need to further advocate diversity, but it may instead be indicated to centrally implement optimal solutions. As so often, the truth probably lies somewhere in the middle: It is not entirely unrealistic to assume that we do not know an optimal tax and expenditure policy for a given, real jurisdiction. Obviously, we do know a lot about optimal tax and expenditure policies for model economies, but so far, this knowledge has been proven to be impossible to implement into real economies. The reasons are that we lack secure knowledge about particular data, such as the precise values of certain elasticities of supply and demand, and also that real jurisdictions are characterized by restrictions—from specific market imperfections to political and sociological peculiarities—that simply have (as yet) no place in the optimal taxation literature.

Optimal taxation theory may offer some guidance, but it cannot serve as a blueprint. The task is to gradually improve given tax and expenditure policies, but not to enforce complete schemes that have proven themselves only theoretically and only under extremely simplifying assumptions. The actual tax and expenditure policies we observe are diverse, because they are the result of differing, path-dependent politico-economic processes in the respective jurisdictions, and they are probably not optimal solutions, because there is no reason to assume that the path-dependent processes generating them are directed toward the optimality criteria of normative welfare economics. Therefore, there is presumably a lot to be discovered, for instance, about efficiency reserves that may be made accessible with better tax and expenditure policies—but the term "to be discovered" has to be taken literally, because no omniscient observer has complete knowledge about which policy package serves best the specific conditions of any given jurisdiction.

These general remarks can be illustrated by means of a very simple (and therefore unrealistic, but useful) example, which is depicted in Figure 1. Suppose that it is the task of a benevolent government in period t-1 to find s^*, the tax rate that allows a supply of productive public goods that maximizes GDP growth in period t. This is indeed a very trivial task if the shape of the curve is known to the decision maker. If, on the other hand, the shape is not known, then we can think of infinitely many possible shapes, each backed by more or less plausible theoretical arguments. We may expect the maximum to be more to the left or to the right, we may assume the curve to be monotonously upward- or downward-sloping or we might expect the attainable growth rate to be lower. There are many subjective conjectures that the agents in our model could reasonably develop.

Above, we alluded to the proposition that we expect the learning

Figure 1

Searching for the Optimal Tax Rate

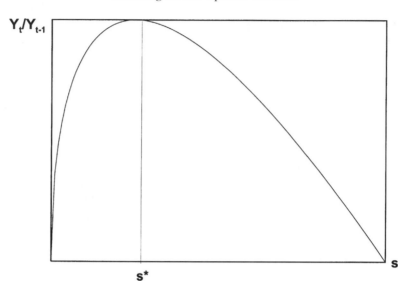

processes within the jurisdictions to be path-dependent. Assume that our benevolent government, for want of a better clue, accepts and follows the conjecture that the majority of its citizens believe in. The probability that an individual citizen accepts a certain conjecture is assumed to depend positively on the number of fellow individuals who already hold this belief. This can reflect, for instance, the frequency with which a given conjecture appears in the media, which certainly has an effect on its credibility. Assuming sequential decision making, i.e., one individual deciding after the other, it can be shown that such a process converges toward a stable distribution of beliefs within the respective societies, but that the distribution toward which the process converges is itself determined by chance (i.e., by the incidental sequence of individuals deciding).[23] With such a process running simultaneously within different jurisdictions, we have a mechanism that endogenously produces variety in the chosen tax rate s, even among otherwise completely similar jurisdictions.

And for the purpose of accumulating knowledge, it is important that otherwise relatively similar jurisdictions experiment with different approaches to tax and expenditure policy. The reason lies in the above-mentioned reluctance of individuals to void their given set of conjectures, into which they may have invested considerable costs. Usually, individuals will follow a strategy to defend and immunize their given knowledge,[24] especially if their knowledge is intertwined with vested interests. But this strategy will be easier to follow the less similar are the more-successful jurisdictions to the own jurisdiction. This means that from a Hayekian point of view, the argument for decentralized tax and expenditure policies is not only valid when regions differ from each other, e.g., in their citizens' preferences for public goods, but also in the case in which regions are completely similar, because here a comparatively frictionless diffusion of knowledge from policy experiments can be expected.

Looking at a decentralized setting of policy making, we can find the source of variety in economic policy that was missing in the centralized setting. It is not entirely clear, however, how this variety responds to inter-jurisdictional competition for mobile tax bases. Besley and Case (1995) have provided evidence that yardstick competition plays an important role in decentralized policy making: decisionmakers tend to mimic the decisions of neighboring jurisdictions, which may in the end lead to a harmonization of policies *ex post*, although no explicit policy coordination has taken place. On the other hand, one can think of restrictions that make it impossible for the decisionmaker in A to mimic his or her colleague in B. Returning to our earlier optimizing example, consider the case that in A, the tax rate s_A is relatively high because the voters have preferences for a high level of redistribution. At the same time, B, with a lower s_B, enjoys a higher rate of GDP growth, but has a low supply of social security.

The decision maker in A then has an incentive to look for means of raising GDP growth, because the results of his or her policy are assessed in comparison with those of the policy in B; however, simply mimicking B's policy is not feasible, because a reduction of s_A and the corresponding level of social security would be against the voters' preferences and reduces the chances of reelection. The policymaker in A will then have to look elsewhere to enhance growth. For instance, to attract mobile capital from B, he or she may try to find more efficient means of regulating industries, or may try to re-structure the tax system in a more efficient way that induces a smaller dead-weight-loss on capital. There are a lot of possible reactions that preserve or even enlarge the variety of policies and therefore the conditions for the further accumulation of knowledge about efficient means of problem solving in economic policy. Somewhat surprisingly, they seem to be positively correlated with the degree of specific jurisdictional inflexibilities in policy making, which prevent perfect mimicking and instead make the search for new problem-solving routines necessary.

V

Conclusions

IN THIS PAPER, we have made two distinctly Hayekian points with respect to the current state and possible future development of New Political Economy, or Public Choice. One is the criticism of scientism, i.e., the uncritical application of the methodology of the natural sciences to economic problems. Economic problems are not as well defined as the problems of the natural sciences because (i) we have no undisputed normative criterion, i.e., the scientist cannot know for certain what the citizen wants him or her to maximize, (ii) even if we had such a criterion, the problem of our ignorance of particular data would remain and (iii) even if we knew all the particular data, we could still never be sure that our simplified models take into account all relevant interdependencies and causal relationships of the real world. What follows is that we have to understand policy proposals from economic theory, not as clear-cut solutions to well-defined problems, but rather as fallible proposals of problem-solving routines that, if applied, are likely to be replaced by better routines at some time in the future.

If we subscribe to this view, we will probably have to put a greater weight on the issue of how knowledge about problem-solving routines concerning not only economic policy, but also the entire realm of public law, is generated and accumulated. Political entrepreneurship has to be explained and, on a larger scale, the emergence and maintenance of a variety of observable solutions. Similarly, a lot remains to be understood about the process of diffusion of knowledge from one decisionmaker to the other. What seems to be necessary, therefore, is an extension of Public Choice's research agenda to include these knowledge-related issues. This would be, however, not only an extension of the agenda of Public Choice, but also an extension of Hayek's knowledge-related research program, which is very much focused on knowledge generation and diffusion on the marketplace, rather than the evolution of knowledge concerning public law and policy. Section IV of this paper has offered some hints toward the problems that are to be tackled, although these pictures have been painted with a rather broad brush and wait to be transferred into more stringent and formal research.

Notes

1. See Albert (1953) and, more recently, Albert (1998).

2. See Arrow (1951) for the spark and Enelow (1997) for an excellent survey of the subsequent literature.

3. See Niskanen (1971). However, previously Mises (1944) had shown that problems arise from the fact that bureaucracy is not subject to the control of the market.

4. See Brennan and Buchanan (1980).

5. See Inman and Rubinfeld (1996) for an overview.

6. For a convincing summary of this constitutionalist argument, see Chapter 12 of Hayek (1960).

7. See also Albert (1985), especially Chapters 2–4 and 7, for an introduction to the criticist approach to the problem of finding an adequate social order.

8. Considering the theory of the second best, this is often even inconsistent within the framework of welfare economics, since it may be possible that two inefficiencies offset each other. Therefore, if we follow a policy proposal from a model that is designed to consider only one inefficiency and if we eliminate only one of the offsetting inefficiencies, we may end up in a situation that is actually more inefficient than the starting point. As long as we do not know of all the possibly offsetting real-world deviations from first best utopia, any theoretically efficiency-enhancing intervention bears the risk of actually making things worse.

9. See his Nobel Lecture, Hayek (1974), and, for a more detailed account of the methodological problems posed by complexity, Hayek (1964).

10. Note that here we confine ourselves to the welfare economic notion of static efficiency. If we would understand efficiency as dynamic efficiency, i.e., the capability of an economy to smoothly adjust to unforeseen changes of

variables, then the prospects of finding an efficient intervention would be even more bleak.

11. See Hayek (1973), Chapters 5 and 6.

12. For our purposes, it is not necessary to go into detail about the functioning of the evolutionary mechanism as Hayek sees it. For critical summaries of this evolutionary theory of the development of rules, see Vanberg (1986) as well as Schmidtchen (2000). The most concise treatment of the problem by Hayek himself is probably to be found in his late work, Hayek (1988).

13. Note that this conclusion from the type of rules to their origin is merely an approximative rule of thumb, because it may well happen that we find a general, but deliberately designed, rule or a command that is the result of an evolutionary process without a definitive purpose. The defining characteristic of the two types of rules is whether they are general rules or exact commands.

14. Obviously, such an account of the costs of interventionism cannot be expressed in exact monetary terms or in units of utility, but it can give us an idea about which mechanisms a society dedicated to interventionism or egalitarianism ceases to employ. See, in particular, Hayek (1968).

15. The seeds of this research program have been planted rather early, in Hayek (1937).

16. See Hayek (1945).

17. See Hayek (1968).

18. See Stigler (1961) for the original contribution that sparked this stream of literature.

19. See, in particular, Hayek (1952) for this point.

20. Note, however, the contribution by Wood (1997), which gives its reader the uneasy feeling that even the most well-founded and (within the economics profession) widely accepted economic theories have little impact on the conventional wisdom held by the general public and economic policy makers.

21. See Wohlgemuth (1999) for such an approach.

22. See also Chapter VII of Hayek (1960) for an argument in a similar vein.

23. See, in particular, the work of W. Brian Arthur in Arthur (1994).

24. See Dopfer (1991) for this point.

References

Albert, Hans. (1953). "Der Trugschluss in der Lehre vom Gütermaximum," *Zeitschrift für Nationalökonomie* 14: 90–103.

———. (1985). *Treatise on Critical Reason*. Princeton: Princeton University Press.

———. (1998). *Bemerkungen zur Wertproblematik. Von der Bewertung des Sozialprodukts zur Analyse der sozialen Ordnung.* Lectiones Jenenses 15. Jena: Max-Planck-Institute for Research into Economic Systems.

Arrow, Kenneth J. (1951). *Social Choice and Individual Values*. New York: Wiley.

Arthur, W. Brian. (1994). *Increasing Returns and Path-Dependence in the Economy*. Ann Arbor: University of Michigan Press.

Besley, Timothy, and Anne Case. (1995). "Incumbent Behavior: Vote-Seeking, Tax-Setting and Yardstick Competition," *American Economic Review* 85: 25–45.

Brennan, Geoffrey, and James M. Buchanan. (1980). *The Power to Tax: Analytical Foundations of a Fiscal Constitution*. Cambridge: Cambridge University Press.

Dopfer, Kurt. (1991). "Toward a Theory of Economic Institutions: Synergy and Path Dependency," *Journal of Economic Issues* 25: 535–550.

Enelow, James M. (1997). "Cycling and Majority Rule," in Dennis C. Mueller (ed.), *Public Choice: A Handbook*. Cambridge: Cambridge University Press.

Hayek, Friedrich A. von. (1937). "Economics and Knowledge," *Economica* 4: 33–54.

———. (1945). "The Use of Knowledge in Society," *American Economic Review* 35: 519–530.

———. (1952). *The Counter Revolution of Science: Studies in the Abuse of Reason*. Glencoe, IL: Free Press.

———. (1960). *The Constitution of Liberty*. Chicago: University of Chicago Press.

———. (1964). "The Theory of Complex Phenomena," in Mario A. Bunge (ed.), *The Critical Approach to Science and Philosophy. Essays in Honor of K. R. Popper*. New York: Free Press of Glencoe.

———. (1968). "Competition as a Discovery Procedure," reprinted in Friedrich A. von Hayek (1978). *New Studies in Philosophy, Politics and Economics*. Chicago: University of Chicago Press.

———. (1973). *Rules and Order: A New Statement of the Liberal Principles of Justice and Political Economy*, Vol. 1 of *Law, Legislation and Liberty*. London: Routledge & Kegan Paul.

———. (1974). "The Pretence of Knowledge," reprinted in Friedrich A. von Hayek (1978). *New Studies in Philosophy, Politics and Economics*. Chicago: University of Chicago Press.

———. (1988). *The Fatal Conceit: The Errors of Socialism*. London: Routledge & Kegan Paul.

Inman, Robert P., and Daniel L. Rubinfeld. (1996). "Designing Tax Policy in Federalist Economies: An Overview," *Journal of Public Economics* 60: 307–334.

Kuran, Timur. (1995). *Private Truths, Public Lies: The Social Consequences of Preference Falsification*. Cambridge: Harvard University Press.

Mises, Ludwig von. (1944). *Bureaucracy*. New Haven: Yale University Press.

Niskanen, William A. (1971). *Bureaucracy and Representative Government.* Chicago: Aldine-Atherton.

Schmidtchen, Dieter. (2000). "Rules and Order," in Boudewijn Bouckaert and Annette Godart-van der Kroon (eds.), *Hayek Revisited.* Cheltenham, UK: Elgar.

Stigler, George J. (1961). "The Economics of Information," *Journal of Political Economy* 69: 213–225.

Wohlgemuth, Michael. (1999). *Democracy as a Discovery Procedure. Toward an Austrian Economics of the Political Process.* Discussion Paper 17-99. Jena: Max-Planck-Institute for Research into Economic Systems.

Wood, Geoffrey. (1997). *Economic Fallacies Exposed.* Institute of Economic Affairs Occasional Papers 102. London: Institute of Economic Affairs.

Vanberg, Viktor. (1986). "Spontaneous Market Order and Social Rules: A Critical Examination of F. A. Hayek's Theory of Cultural Evolution," *Economics and Philosophy* 2: 75–100.

PART V

New Perspectives on Transition Economies: Europe

American Journal of Economics and Sociology, Vol. 61, No. 1 (January, 2002).

The "New" Political Economies

(A View from Russia)

By VLADIMIR KOLLONTAI[*]

ABSTRACT. This paper analyses some of the problems created by a rapidly changing interaction between the political and the economic spheres in society. In periods of condensed social change this interaction is profoundly different from customary evolutionary developments. In Russia various political economic concepts during the last century have led to profound shifts in economic mechanisms and structures (first toward a planned economy, later toward a market one). A knowledge of this experience (and the new problems that surface) might be useful if globalisation, environmental issues and the transition to a post-industrial society should lead to periods of condensed socioeconomic change in the West.

I

POLITICAL ECONOMY, though it often purports to discover (formulate) universal, eternal truths, is in real life a constantly changing set of concepts and theories, reflecting transformations in the economy and polity (and this interaction), in historic contexts and country specifics, in perceptions and ideologies.[1] Accordingly, there is always something new and something old in any political economy. In this sense we can speak of many different political economies.

* Valdimir Kollontai is senior research fellow at the Institute of World Economics and International Affairs (IMEMO) of the Russian Academy of Sciences (23 Profsojuznaja str, Moscow 117859, Russian Federation. E-mail: <v.kollontai@mtu-net.ru>). He worked for eight years at the United Nations (UNCTAD and UNEP) and later was visiting professor at universities in Paris (the Sorbonne), Edinburgh, Sydney, Vienna, Barcelona and Grenoble and at the European University Institute in Florence, Italy. His interests include development and environment issues and the interaction between socioeconomic and cultural change. The author of many books and articles (mainly in Russian) on development theory and social transformations, he is now writing a book in English on socioeconomic transformations in Russia.

American Journal of Economics and Sociology, Vol. 61, No. 1 (January, 2002).
© 2002 American Journal of Economics and Sociology, Inc.

Political economies attempt to understand the functioning of an economy in a broader societal context. This is a task of growing complexity, given the constantly increasing division of labour, interdependencies, changing technologies, regulatory mechanisms, and evolving economic, organisational, management and other structures. As distinct from pure economics—which concentrates on the internal logic of economic systems—political economies in varying degrees acknowledge the impact on economic developments of political and (to a lesser extent) ideological, cultural and other societal factors and make it a part of their analysis.

In economically forerunner countries, the interrelationship between economics and politics evolved gradually. Economic development created many prerequisites of modern democratic politics. The policies pursued were indispensable in shaping existing market structures and mechanisms (granting a predominant place to free market and free competition thinking). A special effort was made to channel the interaction between economic development and politics into a preconceived, stable pattern, aiming *inter alia* at a certain independence of one from the other.

In late-comer, peripheral countries of the world economy (developing and ex-socialist countries), which are trying to modernise and catch up, by definition the role of politics (and ideology) in economic development is much greater. Decisions have to be taken as to what goals should be set and in what priority, what elements of modern societies could be transplanted, in what sequence and timeframe, and so forth. This inevitably leads to periods of condensed social change with extreme political, ideological and economic shifts and confrontations. Moreover, modernisation presupposes profound societal transformations, which give rise to serious problems of legitimacy. In these circumstances economic considerations of efficiency are constantly tempered by considerations of expanding the social base of the modernising regime, by attempts to gain internal and external political support and stability, etc. Such a preeminence of political considerations is especially evident in the early stages of condensed social change, before a new pattern of society begins to crystallise. All this leads to a myriad of various political economies with abundant protectionist features.

In contemporary Western societies, globalisation, environmental issues and the transition to post-industrial, knowledge-based societies are also raising the prospect of condensed social changes and its numerous related questions. To what extent are existing property rights, economic structures and mechanisms, political institutions and so on going to change and what are the likely social consequences of these changes? To what extent will new trends and processes modify our previous perceptions of the interaction between politics and economics? Hence the endless references to a "new" political economy.

In debating these issues it might be useful to take a look at the Russian experience of socioeconomic transformations. During the twentieth century Russia has gone through two fundamental transformations, both instigated to a large degree by perceived knowledge (alleged understanding) of societal processes, by vested interests and by related ideologies.

II

Some Russian Specifics

SOCIETAL TRANSFORMATIONS INEVITABLY must overcome various forms of social inertia that often constitute a major cause of gross deviations of results from intents. It is therefore necessary to dwell briefly on some of the major specifics of Russian socioeconomic development that have accumulated through the ages and that profoundly influence political economies in Russia.

1. Russia is a vast country with a very harsh climate. As a result there are major additional costs (transport, heating and so on) for practically all economic activities. Competitiveness can often be achieved only through disproportionally large inputs and/or lowering labour costs and standards of living. An often-implicit understanding of this has resulted in a widespread distrust of market economy and economic liberalism, leading to a yearning for alternative approaches.[2]

2. Historically, central governments have had a rather limited impact on vast areas outside of a few major centres. This has created a situation in which even very important laws often have been laxly enforced; traditions of being law-abiding have been extremely weak. Most issues have been decided by local authorities acting on their own under little restraint from the central power. Hence, widespread corruption and local tyranny has prevailed. Most people have tended to evade the formal judicial system, re-

solving conflicts outside of the courts on the basis of customs, traditions, local perceptions of justice and equality. All this was only partially modified under the Soviet regime.[3]

3. Historically and geographically, Russia has been under much less pressure than smaller nations to move toward more intensive production patterns or to adopt more conciliatory (based on compromises) social concepts and institutions. For a very long time there existed in Russia the option of escaping to unsettled territories and thus putting off the need to solve problems. As a result there is little heritage of compromise politics. In an extremely socially polarised society, the prevailing attitude has most often been one of the winner taking all and defining the course of future developments. This is a source of serious macro-instability in Russian society.[4]

4. Vast territories (and poor communication) have hindered the development of grassroots movements and the involvement of the majority of the population in central, and even local, politics. Accordingly, politics (except for spontaneous uprisings) remained the preserve of a rather restricted elite. The existing political administrations (be it under the Tsar or under the Communist regime) leaned heavily on a rapidly expanding bureaucracy, whose powers constantly grew. Moreover, there developed a deep rift between the ruling circles and the intelligenscia. The latter (distrusted by the powers that be and by the broad masses of the population) most often have adopted a highly critical stance toward existing situations, fomenting discontent and demands for change.

5. The Russian mentality (as is not uncommon in less modernised societies) always has had trouble with specialised social sciences, with the artificial separation of closely interrelated phenomena and processes and with the unrealistic assumptions and abstractions that formed the foundation of pure economics. Hence a marked preference for political economy over pure economics.[5]

III

The Soviet Experiment

THE OCTOBER (1917) REVOLUTION IN RUSSIA was ideologically motivated by the desire to free humanity, or at least the Russian people, from the negative features of previous capitalist development. This was an extremist ideology, envisaging the total abolition of private property and all vestiges of market economy. In this it had the active support of the vast majority of the population and, accordingly, those who came to

power at first had no serious legitimacy problems. However, the profound changes initiated and the coercive methods employed soon created a situation analogous to the one that recently resulted from shock
therapy (a term not known at the time). Existing socioeconomic structures and networks were brutally disrupted; legal perceptions and
rules were overturned. Production (already undermined by the years
of World War I) decreased further, accentuating deficits in many areas
and making life even more difficult. Legitimacy and support for the
new regime started to wane under the stress of growing economic
problems.

Very soon the government realised that the initiated transformations
had to give way to the imperatives of retaining political power. Persuasion was increasingly supplanted by coercion. Proclaimed socioeconomic transformations were postponed and a new economic
policy (NEP) was inaugurated, reintroducing many elements of market
relations and small-scale capitalist entrepreneurship. Only toward the
end of the 1920s, after a certain degree of political stability had been
attained, did economic development become a political priority in its
own right.

The main socioeconomic objective of the Soviet regime was defined
as the creation of a modern economy, free from the negative features
of capitalism and guaranteeing a minimum of social security to working people. During the 70 years of Soviet rule the concrete details of
this program changed many times, but the proclaimed objectives remained essentially the same.[6]

Industrialisation was considered to be the main method of achieving this goal. This implied large-scale transplantation of technologies
and production structures from abroad. But the use of private property and market mechanisms was precluded by prevailing ideologies
and political commitments. Accordingly, a totally new system of organising and managing the economy—at the macro as well as the micro levels—had to be conceived and made to function. The
trial-and-error establishment of centralised planning and its problems
gave rise to what later became known as socialist political economy
(Atlas 1962; Roumjantsev 1970; Kouzmin 1975). Its central tenets were
a totally new relationship between economics and politics, a preeminence of state property, and control over all major economic activities

through central planning (concentrated in Gosplan). This inevitably presupposed a profound shift not only in economic structures but also in regulatory mechanisms, as well as in mentalities, motivations, value systems, priorities, *ad infinitum.*

At first the biggest problems were deemed to be the purely economic ones. The problem of incentives at all levels was not seen as unsurmountably difficult: a mixture of material and moral incentives combined with a constant fear of repression in cases of failure was rather rapidly installed. Economic efficiency was considered to be a function of rational planning, of well-conceived structures, of eliminating costly intermediation. Mobilising and allocating resources was also not viewed as excessively difficult. The State in Russia had always played a leading role in economic accumulation, and this role was strengthened by the introduction of various new financial, budgetary and accountancy innovations.[7]

The major difficulties in central planning were considered to be the long-term (five to ten years) assessment of future economic structures and the day-to-day functional interconnection of mutually dependent but separate (discrete) enterprises. Central planning in Russia continually had to ensure current interconnections between enterprises with major long-term shifts in economic structures (Ljubunj 1977). This focused attention on backward and forward linkages (rigid in the short term and more flexible in the medium and long term). Many ingenious new approaches, concepts and methodologies were worked out to solve such problems; for example, elaborate enterprise and industry balance sheets of inputs and outputs were constantly compiled. V. Leontieff (in his earlier years a staff member of Gosplan) later elaborated these into his well-known input-output tables and analyses.

By mobilising large resources and concentrating them in a few priority areas, central planning opened up new possibilities, not just of transplanting existing structures and industrialisation patterns, but of elaborating more innovative approaches to industrialisation strategies (e.g., changing sequences, leap-frogging, emphasis on machine building, etc.).[8]

Industrialisation and modernisation strategies always had a tangible political component. An emphasis on large-scale plants stemmed not only from prevailing concepts of economies of scale, but also from the fact that large plants were more amenable to central control and planning.[9] The Soviet industrialisation pattern envisaged the creation of thousands of one-plant towns, which would be inevitably highly dependent on existing inter-industry networks (in defence industries, heightened secrecy was also an important consideration). Large-scale, specialised, interdependent enterprises, integrated into a complex inter-industry network, was viewed by many as a serious integrative factor inside the Soviet Union.

As the economy grew and became more complex, the existing centralisation of decision making and the cumbersome bureaucratic procedures involved in planning transformed central planning from an instrument of economic development into a serious impediment. The flow of hundreds of thousands of different product groups and the inputs and outputs of hundreds of thousands of enterprises could not be centrally traced, let alone centrally coordinated and approved. Moreover, each year hundreds of new products had to be introduced into this process. The task was becoming impossible, even using computer technologies. Decentralisation of decision making became imperative. But numerous attempts at economic reform in this direction (e.g., the Kosygin reform) were shattered at the political level by apprehensions of loss of control and power.

In the Breznev era the political imperatives of consolidating a weakening but rigid elitist power structure came into increasing conflict with the economic imperatives of an increasingly complex, interdependent economy. A feeling of imminent social change pervaded society, most elements of which were ready for Perestrojka (Kollontai 1999).

IV

Contemporary Reforms in Russia

THE RUSSIAN TRANSFORMATIONS THAT BEGAN in the middle of the 1980s are far from completed. Moreover, their outcome is by no means evident. Processes (and forces) have been unleashed whose final results are in many ways unpredictable. What is clear is that these transformations are radically different from those undertaken after the October Revolution.

To begin with, the present transformations in Russia had a very limited social base and degree of legitimacy. Although change was desired, what type of society should take the place of the old was (and in a narrower sense still is) a point of serious controversy. During Perestrojka the emphasis was on reforming socialism, but this reform movement soon got out of control (Afanasjev 1988). In the late 1980s and early 1990s a broad propaganda offensive was undertaken, instilling the idea that there is no alternative to a Western-type market economy and democratic society. For some time the main question seemed to be what model of market-cum-democratic-society would be desirable and could be feasible in Russia: a social democracy (along the lines of Sweden, Austria, etc.) or a free market democracy (along the lines of the United States). These questions were discussed at an abstract level in intellectual and political circles and (in even more general terms) in the mass media. But many of the most important issues were never seriously raised or debated. Both the leadership and the man in the street had vague ideas of both the market and Western-style democracy, to say nothing of the problems involved in such a transition (Zaslavskaja 1996).

Perestrojka had escalated pressures for change and undermined the organisational and managerial foundations (one-party rule, the law enforcement apparatus) of the old system; toward 1990–1991 this precipitated a deep political and economic crisis. The breakup of the Soviet Union created a brand-new situation and brought to a head many latent problems. Future developments unrolled in a highly ideologically-polarised society in which shock therapy and liberal approaches prevailed (Gaidar 1997, 2000; Mau 1996; Uljukaev 1996). Ideological commitments and animosities, personal ambition and the struggle for power were too often the main driving force of most strategic decisions taken by the executive powers, who ignored dissenting opinions. A simplistic but far-reaching program of free market liberal reform was *de facto* being realized in a situation in which the general public could not yet grasp the full significance of what was happening, let alone influence events to any extent.[10]

Recent years have imparted a very high level of dynamism into Russian society and brought about profound change (for better and for worse).

The previous centres of power (the Communist party, the KGB) have been reorganized, placed into a completely new setting and stripped of much of their previous authority and strength. But the lack of a social base has forced the powers that be to relax their hold in several areas in an attempt to gain legitimacy and support in society. As a result, new centres of power have surfaced. Strong oligarchic groups have crystallised that exert serious pressure on societal processes through their hold on the economy. Regions were given new rights and privileges; this has led to a protracted draining of power and resources from the centre to the regions (Goskomstat 1998; Jivalov 2000, chs. 3–5). By the end of the 1990s a new kind of societal disintegration was beginning to take shape. Putin's first measures as president were aimed at curbing these tendencies.

In the political sphere the need for a division of power has been broadly acknowledged and many of the relevant institutions have been established.[11] Though many of them are modelled according to existing Western patterns, their functioning is still largely distorted by the enduring societal environment and the inertia of old mentalities, values and priorities. Through lack of competence (i.e., insufficient knowledge by lawmakers of the concrete functioning of markets and democratic institutions) and later through pressure by various vested interests, most of the laws passed by parliament (especially in the first years of its work) created a highly unsatisfactory judicial system, full of loopholes, conflicting rules and inconsistencies. This in turn hampers and distorts the functioning of law enforcement agencies and the courts.

In the cultural sphere, tremendous shifts have taken place in the motivations, value systems and priorities of various social groupings (Shalin 1996; Artemov 1999; Zaslavskaja 1999, 2000). Large segments of society are becoming increasingly alienated and disinterested (disenchanted) with politics, elections and other aspects of democracy after a spurt of interest in social affairs and expectations of changes for the better.[12] Individualism is increasingly replacing collectivist approaches. With various misgivings, a growing number of people are subordinating their activities to pecuniary interests and profit motives. Many individuals are becoming split personalities in their motivations and assessments. An ever-more-important role in forming individual and group identities is played by the mass media. People previously unaccustomed to advertising and image-making public relations take much of what they see and hear at face value and act accordingly in everyday life (i.e., lifestyles), at elections and so forth.

In the economic sphere, the last decade and a half has been a period of endless clashes between divergent politico-economic approaches, at first in very broad conceptual terms and later in more practical, specific areas. During Perestrojka (1985–1991), the debates were predominantly confined to criticisms of the prevailing political economy of socialism (its autarchic orientation, its neglect of micro-efficiency and so on) and to attempts to inject some market elements into the prevailing thinking.

With the breakup of the Soviet Union, Yeltsin's coming to power, and the resultant suspension of the Communist party, disbanding of the previous administrative apparatus, and legal system, free market approaches became the basis of economic policy (Aslund and Layard 1993; Aslund 1995; Layard and Parker 1996; Leitzel 1995). This shift was actively criticised by the vast majority of intellectuals, academics and many representatives in the legislature (the branch of political power most closely connected with the population at large).[13]

A confrontation developed between the executive branch and the legislature that led to a stalemate in most legislation related to market formation. Presidential decrees, not parliamentary-adopted laws, became the main basis of market-forming activities in many vital areas. The absence of a substantive legal base distorted most aspects of market formation in Russia for nearly a decade, directing them into highly unregulated channels.[14]

The disintegration of the Soviet Union split up a highly interdependent economic complex and was a major cause of a rapid fall in production. Given the enormous gap between relative prices inside Russia and those in the world economy, price liberalisation and deregulation of foreign trade inevitably made some economic sectors extremely profitable and others unjustifiably inefficient. Enormous shifts in resource allocation ensued, accompanied by a rapid fall in overall production and rampant hyper-inflation; the latter quickly devoured accumulated savings, investment funds and current transaction resources. This in turn diminished purchasing power and caused enormous shifts in production and consumption patterns (especially in the first three years of reform).[15]

The effect of the three years of shock therapy have reverberated throughout the economy. For four years, 1994–1998, the country was in a state of deep depression, resulting in contracted production, consumption and financial flows due to extreme monetarist policies. Insufficient monetary flows forced large segments of the economy into barter transactions and even semi-subsistence. This in turn led to a dangerous shrinking of budgetary revenues and expenditures. At the same time, far-reaching structural shifts were taking place—contraction of arms production, imports replacing local production, large-scale nonpayment of debt inside the country and rapidly growing foreign indebtedness—culminating in the default of August 1998. Once more the situation changed drastically: imports became less profitable, new possibilities for local production opened up and many economic parameters stabilised. However, the upturn of the last three years (Goskomstat 2001) cannot quickly alleviate the dismal state of the Russian economy.[16]

In the meantime, privatisation opened up the prospect of very large parts of global production facilities and assets coming up for grabs. This inaugurated a period of feverish primary accumulation, in which political ties, accumulated financial resources and speculative prowess gave a winning advantage to the more unscrupulous and reckless. Growing budget deficits, endless legal loopholes and a dearth of comprehensive socially-oriented legislature transformed privatisation into a battle without restraints. The entrepreneurs emerging as winners in these battles most often have very little in common with the entrepreneurs described in present political economy theories. Unravelling these problems will take a very long time (Choubais 2000; Kouzenkov 2000; Komaritzkij 2000).

One of the main reasons of the far-from-satisfactory results of economic reform in Russia was the commitment by a majority of the ruling politicians to an ideology of unregulated free market instead of a pragmatic approach to unprecedented economic problems. On politico-ideological grounds, they would not and could not embrace a mixed economy approach to the transformation process. Moreover, there was a dearth of knowledgeable people capable of finding pragmatic solutions, unbiased by ideology and/or by political economy dogmas. The period after the 1998 default saw an attempt at one such solution (BEA 2000), but it was short-lived, unacceptable to the powers in charge. At present there is an attempt to curb disintegrating forces, create a more comprehensive judicial system and establish conditions for Russia's entry on an equal footing into the world community. Studies are being prepared, suggesting alternative strategies of socioeconomic development, stressing the social component of development, envisaging large-scale reallocation of resources, etc. (Abalkin 1999; Lvov 2000; Korolev 2000; Belousov 2001). But even though the role of the state in economic development has been somewhat reaffirmed, the political and ideological battle around the degree of market freedom and predominance is far from over.

In such a situation it is evidently too early to try to formulate a theoretical (as opposed to a descriptive) political economy of contemporary Russia.

V

Conclusion

POLITICAL ECONOMIES HAVE different levels of generalisation and abstractions. At their most general, they purport to give insights into the major interactions within the economic sphere and between the economy and other aspects of society; most of these conclusions are valid for more-or-less stable, slowly changing situations. They constitute a comprehensive (often normative) framework for thinking about how the socioeconomic sphere functions and evolves.

Nowadays, however, all societies have to cope with accelerating developments—globalisation, environmental issues, the transition to knowledge-based societies (in peripheral societies, these problems are aggravated by the imperatives of modernisation). Accordingly, all societies, albeit in different degrees and forms, are being pushed into situations of condensed social change, often with multidimensional vectors. In these circumstances it is extremely difficult (if even possible) to create a comprehensive overall political economy. The number of economic and non-economic factors defining a society's development pattern is increasing exponentially and their constellations are becoming infinite. A binding, steadfast political economy might easily lead to rigid approaches toward rapidly changing problems.

At best what can be achieved in periods of condensed social change are various insights into the possible impact of this or that factor or policy and an accumulation of knowledge about different outcomes in discrete situations. This is not a new general political economy, but it has a tremendous value of its own. In situations of condensed social change no hard and fast rules can prompt satisfactory solutions; they have to be tailor-made according to concrete circumstances, and worked out on the basis of previous experience and open-minded improvisations. For this it is most important to have a good knowledge of available experiences and an unbiased, ideologically unprejudiced approach. The earlier that emerging problems are faced and discussed, the more chances there will be of finding widely acceptable, workable solutions in time.

Notes

1. There is also a problem of scope and degree of generality. At one extreme, political economy purports to give generally applicable knowledge about the functioning of any and all economies (and the best mechanisms thereto); at the other extreme, political economies dwell on the policy mixes to achieve this or that result, analysing very concrete situations.

2. The whole industrialisation process in Russia had a very large element of state subsidies (especially in the energy and transport sectors) built into it. The resulting structural imbalances and territorial dislocations (accumulated over time) constantly raise various problems for the present market reform process in Russia.

3. The purges of the 1930s not only instilled fear in the population, but also strengthened the mindset that the legal system is not geared toward effectively defending rights, except those of the state and the ruling elite.

4. This *inter alia* has hindered in many ways the development of entrepreneurship.

5. Since society in Russia was not (until recently) very group conscious, many social scientists adhered to a holistic approach toward societal issues, focusing attention on society as a whole rather than on its subsystems. Political economy as an area combining two major fields of societal life was more or less widely understood and accepted, though usually with substantial injections of moral and ethical considerations, demands of equity and justice, etc.

Economics as such was first introduced to students in the 1960s, and its future development was seriously tempered by the needs and context of central planning.

6. This elicited enthusiasm in a large part of the population and served as a major driving force in society, regardless of growing problems and inconsistencies between words and deeds.

7. Distrust of monetary and price indicators fostered a general shift toward physical criteria. Results of economic activities—both at the micro and macro levels—were assessed primarily in physical volume terms (so many tons of steel or grain). Financial and price criteria were relegated to a derivative, secondary role; prices themselves increasingly became derivatives (instruments) (corollary) of planning procedures and at best instruments of plan implementation. Moreover a strict distinction was made between cash payments of wages, pensions and other incomes to the population (which were central to labour and consumer goods flows) and non-cash inter-industry payments that were transacted through special state financial institutions (to facilitate resource mobilisation and control over plan fulfillment).

8. An emphasis on machine building (e.g., for the textile industry) accelerated the development of downstream industries and brought about large savings of foreign exchange when acquiring needed equipment. At the same time, machine building was seen as imperative for the defence industries.

9. Even now, three-quarters of Russian industrial production comes from plants with 1,000 or more workers each. The share of small-scale enterprises in the GDP is in Russia five to six times smaller than in other major countries.

10. Most elections were fought, not so much on issues of positive change, as on questions of eliminating a return to the past.

11. The responsibilities and functions of the new political units are still being delineated, though a disproportionately high concentration of power in the executive branch persists.

12. Many manifestations of free speech and human rights have become commonplace and are no longer considered achievements. On the other hand, people are less politically active; increasingly, a turnout of 25 percent is declared sufficient for elections to be considered valid.

13. Most specialists in the Russian economy were against rapid reform and shock therapy, stressing the dangers of structural imbalances, social disruption and backlash (see Abalkin 1999; Jaremenko; Nekipelov 1996; Jakovetz, etc., and, more generally, the journals *Problems of Forecasting, Economic Questions,* and *Russian Journal of Economic Science*). But their opinion was discarded as too conservative.

14. This decade, however, contributed substantially to the understanding of contemporary market formation and functioning. At first a simplistic view prevailed that price liberalisation, privatisation and a deregulation of economic activity would semi-automatically lead to the establishment of market econo-

mies. Subsequently, the need to create a broad network of indispensable intermediaries (banking, insurance, stock and commodity exchanges, etc.) became evident. With time the importance of cultural and historical factors manifested itself in many different ways. At present the role of the legal (including law enforcement) framework for the market is receiving special attention, as are the problems of integration into the global market (Korolev 2000).

15. Overall, during 1992–1994 these shifts led to a 40 percent fall in production and a 16 percent fall in household consumption (*Problemi Prognozirovanija* 2001, N2:5).

16. According to a recent comprehensive study, during 1991–1999 material production fell in Russia by nearly 50 percent and household consumption fell by 27 percent. The difference is made up by increased imports and by a drastic reduction in investments (fivefold) and in defence spending. Net capital outflows have increased, from 4 to 5 percent of GDP in 1996–1997 to 18 to 19 percent in 1999. Available internal resources have shrunk to 10 to 11 percent of GDP (Belousov 2001:27–34).

References

Abalkin, L. (ed). (1999). *Rossia—2015. Optimistitcheskij scenarij.* Moscow: MMVB.

Abalkin, L. et. al. (1997). *Na pouti k Tzivilizovannomu rinotchnomu choziajstvu.* Moscow: Aviaisdat.

Afanasjev, Y. (ed). (1988). *Inogo ne dano: Soudbi perestrojki.* Moscow: Progress.

Artemov, V. et al. (1999). *Socialnaja traektorija reformiroujemoj Rossii.* Novosibirsk: Nauka.

Aslund, A. (1995). *How Russia became a market economy.* Washington, DC: Brookings Institution.

Aslund, A., and R. Layard. (1993). *Changing the economic system in Russia.* New York: St. Martins Press.

Atlas, M. et al. (eds.) (1962). *Politicheskaja ekonomija socialisma.* Moscow: Ekonomika.

BEA.(2000). *Obzor ekonomitcheskoj politiki v Rossii v 1999.* Moscow: TEIC.

Belousov, A. (2001). Effektivnij ekonomitcheskij rost v 2001–2010 gg.: ouslovija i ogranichenija. *Problemi prognozirovanija* N-1: 27–46.

Choubais, A. (ed.) (2000). *Privatizatsija po-rousski.* Moscow: Vagrius.

Gaidar, E. (2000.) *Rossijskaja ekonomika: tendentsii i perspektivi.* Moscow: IEPP.

———. (1997). *Ekonomitcheskije reformi i ierarchitcheskije stroukturi.* Moscow: Evrasia.

Glasjev, S. (1996). *Za krititcheskoi chertoi.* Moscow: NIR.

Goskomstat Rossii. (2001). Osnovnije socialno-ekonomitcheskije pokazateli po rissijskoj federatsii za 1996–2001 gg. *Voprosi Statistiki* N-8: 31–42.

232   *American Journal of Economics and Sociology*

————. (1998). *Rossijskij statistitcheskij ejegodnik.* Moscow: Goskomstat.
Jivalov, V. (2000). *Finansovije potoki v rossijskoi ekonomike.* Moscow: Ekonomika.
Kollontai, V. (1999). Social transformations in Russia. *International Social Science Journal* (UNESCO) N-159: 105–121.
Korolev, I. (ed.) (2000). *Konkourentosposobnostj Rossii v 90-e godi. (Mezstranovoj makroekonomitcheskij analis)* Moscow: IMEMO.
Komaritzkij, S. (2000). *Privatizazija: pravovije problemi.* Moscow: Statout.
Kouzenkov, A. (2000). Perspektivi privatizazii v Rossii. *Problemi prognozirovanija* N-2: 74–84.
Kouzmin, I., and S. Rogatcheva. (1975). *Politicheskaja ekonomija socialisma.* Moscow: Mislj.
Layard, R., and J. Parker. (1996). *The coming Russian boom.* New York: Free Press.
Leitzel, J. (1995). *Russian economic reform.* New York: Routledge.
Ljubunj, V. (1977). *Problema planomernogo, proportzionalnogo razvitija narodnogo choziajstva v ssovetskoj ekonomitcheskoj literature.* Moscow: INHP.
Lvov, D. (2000) Boudouchee Rousskoj ekonomiki. *Ekonomist* (Moscow) N-12: 3–18.
Martinov, V. (ed). (1999). *Nekotorije aspekti teorii perechodnoj ekonomiki.* Moscow: IMEMO.
Mau, V. (1996). *Ekonomika i vlastj: Polititcheskaja istorija ekonomitcheskich reform v Rossii 1985–1994.* Moscow: Delo.
Menshikov, S. (1996). *Ekonomika Rossii: Praktitcheskije i teoretitcheskije voprosi perechoda k pinku.* Moscow: Mezdounarodnije otnoshenija.
Nekipelov, A. (1996). *Otcherki po ekonomike postkommounizma.* Moscow: IMEPI.
Roumjantsev, A. (1970). *Politicheskaja ekonomija socialisma.* Moscow: Ekonomika.
Shalin, D. N. (1996). *Russian culture at the crossroads.* Boulder, CO: Westview Press.
Uljukaev, A. (1996). *Rossija na pouti reform.* Moscow: Evrasia.
Yaremenko, Y. (2000). *Prioriteti strouktournoj politiki i opit reform.* Moscow: Nauka.
Zaslavskaja, T. (ed.) (1996). *Kouda idet Rossia? . . . Socialnie transformatzii postsovjetskogo prostranstva.* Moscow: Aspekt-press.
————. (ed). (1999). *Kouda idet Rossia? . . . Krizis institoutzionalnich sistem.* Moscow: Lotos.
————. (ed). (2000). *Kouda idet Rossia?. . . Vlastj, obschestvo, litchnostj.* Moscow: MVSSPN.

Toward Capitalism or Away from Russia?

Early Stage of Post-Soviet Economic Reforms in Belarus and the Baltics

By Andrew Savchenko[*]

ABSTRACT. While at the start of systemic economic transformations in Eastern Europe, both indigenous reformers and Western observers tended to interpret the events as a rationally conceived and executed replacement of an economic system of inferior performance by another one whose superiority was proven, the developments that followed the disintegration of the Soviet polity did not support this view. Shortly after the former Soviet republics gained independence, they exhibited marked variations in speed and sometimes direction of market transformation that could not be satisfactorily explained within the framework of economic theories used by promoters of reforms. In this paper I compare the early stages of economic transformation in Belarus, where reforms were eventually abandoned, with the three Baltic states (Latvia, Lithuania, Estonia), which are the most successful emerging market economies among the former Soviet republics. In this comparison I will attempt to highlight non-economic factors that might have contributed to this difference.

I.

THE COLLAPSE OF THE SOVIET SYSTEM revealed not only the inadequacy of its socioeconomic and political structures but also the lack of suitable explanatory frameworks. This applies both to the developments preceding the collapse and to the post-Soviet transformations. As the reforms were conducted in the dire circumstances of the unravelling Communist economies, it was only natural that many outside observers were eager to combine theoretical explanation with practical advice. However, these combinations often founded strong practical

* The author is a visiting scholar at the Watson Institute for International Studies at Brown University. He teaches sociology at the University of Rhode Island and international relations at the College of the Holy Cross. The author is grateful to Professor Laurence S. Moss for his suggestions and helpful comments.

American Journal of Economics and Sociology, Vol. 61, No. 1 (January, 2002).

recommendations on theories that had not been tested in conditions approaching those of post-Communist economies and societies.

One of the theories developed without a specific reference to the post-Communist transition process and not intended as a foundation of policy decision making, but nonetheless used as a tool for policy formulation, was the property rights approach to economic efficiency. The authors of the original property rights theory never regarded the system of property rights as something easily changeable by policy decisions. However, as we shall see in the discussion that follows, their theory was interpreted in a way that made it a foundation for economic reform policies.

Studies of post-Soviet economic transformations, as well as recommendations for policy decisions, tend to concentrate almost exclusively on rapid government-conducted changes of the property system. The goal of the government is seen as dismantling the old Socialist system of property rights and replacing it with the economy based on private property. Only then, after a period of forceful government action, is the state supposed to assume a purely *laissez-faire* position in economic matters. The view of the government-originated system of private property rights as the main vehicle toward a market economy borrows its theoretical premises from the property rights approach to economic efficiency.

On a more abstract level, relations between power and efficiency within complex organizations were discussed by Armen Alchian (1950). Later, studies in economic history by Douglass North (1971, 1981) and comparative economics by Svetozar Pejovich (1969) introduced the main elements of property rights theory. These authors, each choosing his own approach to the problem and method of its investigation, convincingly argued that there is a correlation between institutional arrangements and economic efficiency.

At the start of the post-Communist economic transformations, the property rights perspective was the only theoretical paradigm that could directly address the problems of systemic transition. The other major paradigm applied to post-Communist developments, namely neoclassical economics, defined the desirable state of affairs (the free market) but did not provide specific suggestions as to how it could be achieved. At the same time, in the context of post-Communist reforms these two paradigms became compatible and mutually complementing as two parts of a single transition design.

Since in the neoliberal economic paradigm the pure and free market is regarded as the most efficient of all economic systems, a suboptimal efficiency is ascribed to non-economic forces interfering with the workings of the spontaneous market mechanism. The latter point is elaborated in property rights theory. Alchian maintains that there is a direct link between economic efficiency and political arrangements. In his view, if an economic system operates below its optimal level of efficiency, this is due to political constraints blocking rearrangements of the existing property rights structure (Alchian 1950). North establishes historical relations between the political power of the state and the property rights system. According to him, the power of the state influences the system of property rights in the following ways. First, states specify fundamental rules of the property rights structure. Second, states provide a set of goods and services designed to lower transaction costs (thus indirectly strengthening the existing property rights system) (North 1981). Pejovich, in his recent work, provides a detailed account of the mechanism whereby the property rights system, supported by political power arrangements, influences the performance of various economic systems (Pejovich 1995). In the works of the reform-oriented East European economists (e.g., Winiecki 1990, 1995) as well as Western observers (e.g., Cooter 1991; Newbery 1992), the correlation between property rights and economic efficiency, as well as the role the state plays in maintaining a system of property rights already in existence, was taken to imply that changing the existing property rights by governmental decree would immediately expose enterprises to market forces, which in turn would facilitate the overall efficiency of the whole economic system. An example of such optimistic predictions based on the property rights approach can be found in the work of Jan Winiecki (1990). He maintained that there would be no opposition to privatization among the industrial blue-collar workers because the privatized enterprises would immediately increase their efficiency and this increase would have a speedy and tangible positive impact on the workers' living conditions.

The above view was based on what Winiecki called "the methodological directive" that, in accordance with theoretical postulates developed by Alchian and North, pointed to political constraints as the main obstacle to the efficiency-increasing change (Winiecki 1990:10). In this view political changes are necessary and sufficient for rapid market change of the former state enterprises, which in turn would lead to a capitalist market economy. Winiecki discounted the emergence of small private enterprises as a viable path toward the capitalist market. He maintained that without prior mass privatization of large state-owned enterprises the emerging private business will be "contaminated" by the dominant property rights structure, and its expansion will not bring tangible benefits for the process of economic transformation (*ibid.,* p. 12). The implicit corollary is that this contamination could be avoided by rapid state actions directed not only toward creation of a new structure of property rights, but also toward forcible conversion of the hitherto state-owned economic entities into private enterprises. In this he is echoed by David Newbery, who asserts that "the rapid, unambiguous creation and defense of private property" is a viable task for the state apparatus (Newbery 1992:217). Interestingly enough, he does not distinguish between such different tasks as defense and creation of private property. Thus, even though the basic premises of the property rights approach were adopted by proponents of rapid privatization, the approach was substantially modified. From a descriptive theory based on verifiable information pertaining to long-term socioeconomic development, the property rights approach became an analytical tool for activist economic policy of relatively short-term reforms conducted by centralized government bureaucracies.

Proponents of the property rights approach to post-Communist economic transformation interpreted the inefficiency of state-owned enterprises as a manifestation of a purely technical problem rooted primarily in the asymmetry of information available to various economic actors. Institutional economics sees the cause of this problem in the "principal-agent" relationship. This relationship exists where one party (the agent) is supposed to act in the interests of another party (the principal). The problem arises under the following two conditions: first, the agent's objectives differ from those of the principal, and second, the former possesses more information about actual performance of the economic unit entrusted to him or her than is available

to the latter. In Soviet-type economies, where the state was the principal and enterprise managers, agents, the above conditions did exist.
They were recognized as a major cause of low economic performance
of centrally planned economic structures. However, some researchers
cautioned against the tendency to ascribe a purely informational nature to the "principal-agent" problem in Soviet type economies (STEs)
(Kornai 1992:371). Others pointed out that this problem exists for
large, privately-owned enterprises with dispersed ownership and not
only for publicly-owned economic units (George 1991:170; Milor
1994:6–7). However, the problem was particularly acute in STEs, and
rapid privatization of large state-owned enterprises was considered a
solution whereby the agent receives more incentives for efficient performance than under the state ownership.

Despite the predominance of the above approach to post-Communist economic reforms in academic discourse and its support and acceptance as a foundation for economic policies by international
economic agencies, it was by no means universally shared.

Mancur Olson pointed out that the term "privatization" as applied to
post-Soviet societies is ambiguous and "does not have the clear meaning that it has in the mature democracies of the West" (Olson 1992:
71). Kazimierz Poznanski, while accepting the main postulates of the
property rights theory, expressed serious doubts about the effectiveness of economic reforms based on this approach (Poznanski 1992).
Peter Murrell is among the most vocal critics of the activist interpretations of the property rights theory. As early as 1992 he warned that
privatizing state-owned enterprises is bound to be a long and costly
process and that reformers' energy would be more effectively applied
to facilitating the growth of the new private sector (Murrell 1992:52).

From the start of economic reforms in Eastern Europe, the idea of
rapid government-led privatization of large state-controlled enterprises was distinctly more popular among the reformers and their advisors than was a more cautious and less activist approach based on
gradual development of private property generated by small,
newly-emerged private enterprises. Now, more than 10 years after the
first laws on privatization were passed in post-Soviet countries, it is
possible to make some comparative assessments of these two forms of
economic restructuring. In order to do so, I will examine contrasting

experiences of the early stages of economic reforms in Belarus and
the three Baltic states: Lithuania, Latvia, and Estonia.

II.

BELARUS, LITHUANIA, LATVIA, AND ESTONIA shared the same network of institutions of the Soviet-type economy and therefore were roughly
equally distant from the developed capitalist market economy as late
as 1989–1990. By 1994 it had become apparent that market development in the three Baltic states had gained momentum and become irreversible. However, market transformations in Belarus were going
slowly, and in the summer of 1994 the policy of market reforms had
been abandoned by the new Byelorussian government. According to
the European Bank for Reconstruction and Development, in 1994 55
percent of Estonia's GNP was produced in the private sector; the figure was the same for Latvia and slightly lower for Lithuania (50 percent). At the same time, in Belarus only 15 percent of GNP was
produced in the private sector (EBRD 1994). Thus, while by 1994 the
three Baltic states had approached a "critical mass" of irreversible market transformations, which since have proven to be immune to the va-
garies of post-Soviet political life, the situation in Belarus permitted
keeping its economy on the old Soviet track. More recent reports indicate that these two divergent trends continue. According to the EBRD
Transition Report, Lithuania, Latvia, and Estonia are currently experiencing economic growth driven primarily by private enterprises, while
Belarus has taken steps backward from already low level of reforms
(EBRD 1997). Even allowing for the short time involved, the differences in market transformation between Belarus and the three Baltic
states are so profound that they cannot be regarded merely as matters
of degree. Clearly, different outcomes of the first years of reforms
were due to equally significant differences in reform policies.

While means and ends of economic reforms vary from country to
country, economic reforms themselves have an important aspect in
common: all are political actions. While their intended outcome might
be a new economic system, reforms are based on distribution of
power among various social groups. Whatever the original intentions
of reformers, political considerations are introduced in market reform
design from the outset and often prevail over economic rationality.

The predominance of political motives manifests itself in many ways and at every stage of privatization, from the initial valuation of assets to managing privatized enterprises.

In most countries the state-owned assets singled out for privatization are evaluated by government agencies, with little regard for possible market demand (or in close cooperation with large investment funds closely related to the state apparatus). A significant number of shares are typically given to the workers and managers of privatized enterprises. In some countries (for example, Russia), privatization amounts to a transfer of controlling stakes of shares to insiders as well as to other enterprises, banks, and investment funds directly or indirectly controlled by the state (Nellis 1994). Ira Lieberman (1995:15) observes that, as a result of mass privatization programs, state institutions (such as state property funds and committees) invariably end up being the largest single shareholders in the country due to the accumulation of unsold shares. This is true for almost all former Soviet-type economies, regardless of the government's commitment to introduce market reforms.

By 1994 in Lithuania, more than half of the former state enterprises had been privatized, amounting to 46 percent of the total number of enterprises in industry, 39 percent in transportation, 55 percent in trade and commerce, and 77 percent in services. The initial goal of the reformers was to achieve greater economic efficiency through the rapid privatization of all state-owned assets. This aim was reflected in its first version of the mass privatization program, according to which two-thirds of the state-owned property was to be privatized within two to three years; an autonomous structure of privatization bodies was to be created to assure their independence from political pressures; and employees of state-owned enterprises being privatized were allowed to buy up to 10 percent of the shares of the enterprise on favorable terms without any additional privileges (Simenas 1995:108).

The Latvian mass privatization program, despite ambitious plans to privatize around 700 medium- and large-scale enterprises by the end of 1993, came to an almost complete halt, with only 85 enterprises privatized by April 1994. However, the privatization of small enterprises proceeded at a much faster pace. By April 1994 two-thirds of such enterprises had been sold to private owners (IMF 1994b).

A similar situation emerged in Estonia, where more than 90 percent of small enterprises in retail trade and 80 percent in services had been privatized by the end of 1993. At the same time, privatization of medium- and large-scale enterprises was not as successful, with only 50 companies having been sold. It is important to note that the Estonian reformers, not unlike their Polish counterparts, have tried to conduct their privatization program by using open tenders in which all potential investors (both foreign and domestic) can take part. Later, a public sale of shares was increasingly used as a method of privatization, although without much success (IMF 1994a).

On the surface, both the program and progress of the mass privatization in Belarus did not seem to differ from that in Lithuania or Latvia. The legal framework created by 1993 allowed both large- and small-scale enterprises to be privatized. The main privatization agency—the Ministry of State Property and Privatization—was in a position to make decisions and determine privatization policies independently of other ministries. Judging by the sheer numbers of the privatized enterprises, privatization in Belarus has been moderately successful compared, for example, to Poland or Latvia. Privatization started in 1991 and by the end of 1992 more than 270 enterprises were leased to private entities. In 1993, after the Law on Privatization of State Property and the Law on Privatization Vouchers had been approved, the privatization process entered a new phase. According to the Ministry of Management of State Property and Privatization of the Republic of Belarus, mass privatization of state-owned enterprises began in June 1993 and by the end of that year 140 enterprises had been privatized. By May 1994 another 73 enterprises were privatized, largely through the conversion of state-owned enterprises into joint-stock companies. As in other countries, few enterprises were sold through auctions and tenders (18 in 1993, and only four in the first half of 1994).

The results of privatization seem to indicate that by 1994 in Belarus some progress had been made in changing forms of property and that the country had made not insignificant strides toward a market economy. In fact, if we consider progress of privatization as an important criterion of the success of market-oriented reforms, Belarus in 1994 could be seen as being in a better position than Latvia, where mass privatization then had not yet started in earnest. However, these numbers are misleading.

If judged by their respective shares of GNP produced by the private sector, Belarus with 15 percent was in its market transition far behind the three Baltic states, where this share was in each case in excess of 50 percent. This comparison clearly puts in doubt the assumed correlation between a success of mass privatization and progress toward a market economy. As indicated above, all three Baltic states, particularly Estonia, while experiencing political constraints on rapid privatization of large enterprises, by 1994 had managed to privatize up to 90 percent of small state-owned enterprises, thus creating necessary conditions for the emergence of a competitive market. What are the major conceptual differences between privatization of large and small enterprises?

One outcome of government-led privatization of large industrial enterprises is that workers (or workers and the government) actually exercise property rights, whereas other investors either do not exist or are small and dispersed and thus unable to effectively influence decision making. Thus, the "principal-agent" problem in its classical form remains even after the property rights system has been modified.

Since the workers (together with management and the government) are the ones who exercise property rights, their interests are likely to be predominant in the restructuring of privatized enterprises. Personnel of any organization are interested in two things: collectively, in the organization's survival, and individually, in receiving the highest possible rewards. Survival of industrial enterprises is tacitly guaranteed by the state, which remains a major stockholder and is very reluctant to implement the existing bankruptcy laws. Stable (if not very high) income is guaranteed by the monopolistic position of virtually every enterprise in an environment characterized by high demand and low supply of even the most basic goods and services.

Janusz Lewandowski, one of the principal architects of Polish economic reforms and the former Polish privatization minister once said that mass privatization is a device to "sell enterprises that nobody owns and nobody wants to people who cannot pay" (quoted in Stark 1994). Clearly, it was not this situation he and his colleagues in Poland and other post-Communist countries hoped for when they were creating blueprints for economic reforms. However, extra-economic realities forced them to choose a less than economically optimal method of privatization.

Privatization of small-scale enterprises is conceptually different from large-scale privatization, particularly in relation to the "principal-agent" problem. In the former Soviet Union, even the small enterprises in services and retail trade had been owned and controlled by the state. In many post-Soviet countries, privatization of small economic units had started earlier and has been much more successful than more ambitious plans to privatize large- and medium-scale enterprises. This was the case in the Baltics, although much less so in Belarus. Usually this process is conducted separately from large-scale mass privatization programs. What makes small-scale privatization different?

A small enterprise is easier to privatize than a large one. A small number of investors means that a clear-cut property title can be established, usually without a residual number of shares retained by the state. Even if the initial owners are the employees, their small number does not allow the separation of ownership and control, thus preventing the emergence of the "principal-agent" problem. Besides, unlike employees of a large enterprise, employees/owners of a small enterprise are less likely to rely upon profit reserves and asset-stripping for the immediate improvement of their living conditions. Profit reserves are likely to be small or nonexistent; and asset-stripping—given that small enterprises have very little slack—will result in the disappearance of the enterprise. Therefore, owners of a small enterprise have to increase its efficiency in order to ensure its survival and their own well-being.

The most important difference between privatization of large and small enterprises is that the latter does not entail major political considerations. While large enterprises are politically important because of their sheer size and are therefore in a position to demand continuing support from the state, small enterprises do not have the same political clout. The state can easily withdraw its direct support once these enterprises have been privatized.

Not only are small enterprises easier to privatize (due to the absence of political constraints), but they also contribute to the development of a market economy to a larger extent than do large enterprises. Because the "principal-agent" problem is nonexistent for small enterprises, their incentives for efficient performance are not constrained by this controversy. Not surprisingly, most experienced and successful reformers listed the development of the private sector through privatization of small assets as among the top priorities of transitional policies (Balcerowicz and Gelb 1994). In fact, privatization of small enterprises can be regarded as the emergence of new small private firms via the acquisition of the previously state-owned assets by individual owners.

Performance levels of small-scale private enterprises cannot be measured in detail due to the lack of reliable data (the old statistical system tends to underestimate the performance of small private economic entities), but aggregate indicators suggest they are quite impressive. In Latvia, where by 1994 the large-scale privatization had barely started and, consequently, most large and medium enterprises still were controlled by the state, the private sector accounted for more than half of GNP in 1994. By 1995, the Polish private sector accounted for one third of industrial output, even though its fixed assets were only one sixth of the total (Poznanski 1996:280). In Lithuania, small private companies have higher efficiency and better overall performance than both remaining state-owned and the privatized large and medium firms (Semeta 1995:117). In Latvia, small private enterprises had absorbed a 44 percent increase in the state sector unemployment between 1990 and 1993 (IMF 1994b:27). In transitional economies with stagnating enterprises still under government control and with successfully privatized firms undergoing painful restructuring (often with workforce reduction), small enterprises have become a major source of new jobs, thus alleviating rapid increases in unemployment.

Those countries where small enterprises were successfully privatized are making significant progress toward market economy. Whether this progress will lead to a modern capitalist economy similar to that of the developed capitalist countries remains to be seen. However, its contribution to the emerging market is already recognizable. In Poland, where small-scale privatization conducted by local governments had included more than 20,000 enterprises, private firms grew faster, hired a larger number of new employees, and invested more than state-owned enterprises (UN 1996:69). In all three Baltic states the situation was essentially the same. In Lithuania, Latvia, and Estonia, privatization of small enterprises had been completed by 1994 and the private sector in all these countries accounted for 50 (Latvia) to 55 (Lithuania and Estonia) percent of GNP. At the same time, in Belarus, where privatization of small enterprises was much slower, the market is almost nonexistent and the economy continues to decline (World Bank 1997:xviii).

In Belarus, progress in small-scale privatization up to 1994 had been actually worse than progress in mass large-scale privatization (although the latter had been bad enough). While in other countries of the region the privatized small enterprises (mostly in retail trade and services) were counted by the thousand, in Belarus they were still counted by single units. According to Belarus's Ministry of State Property and Privatization, in 1993 only two state-owned firms (one in retail trade and one in services) had been privatized by the small-scale privatization program. In the first half of 1994 this number was only six firms (one in retail trade, five in services). As of 1996, only 10 percent of small enterprises had been privatized (World Bank 1997:xviii). In fact, even the modest progress of large-scale privatization in Belarus, for all its artificial nature and inefficient outcomes, looks impressive if compared to the small-scale privatization. Not surprisingly, when in 1994 the new administration in Belarus decided to reverse the course of economic reforms, there were too few people whose livelihood depended on private enterprise and who consequently had a stake in protecting market institutions.

III.

THE ABOVE DISCUSSION OF large-scale versus small-scale privatization illustrates limits of government involvement in transformation of the structure of property rights. Government involvement in what amounts to the active creation not only of a new system of property rights, but also, in the case of large-scale privatization, of private economic entities, is bound to be met with negative political pressure that impedes privatization of large enterprises or makes it artificial. Small-scale privatization and facilitation of the emergence of new private enterprises that contribute to the foundation of a new, more efficient property rights system and do not require continuous government support have proved a more viable method of market transition. However, the process of political pressure from the existing distributional coalitions continues as long as alongside the newly emerged private market there exist a number of essentially Soviet-type enterprises, controlled jointly by workers, management, and government and relying on state-supported monopoly position for their existence. The new private economy demands institutionalized competition, a healthy monetary system, a limited fiscal burden, and stable currency. These elements, necessary for growth and development of private enterprise, come in conflict with continuous requests by the existing state-controlled economic entities that continue to demand state-enforced barriers for competition and government subsidies for financially unviable enterprises. As distributional coalitions based on Soviet-type industrial structures are well organized and possess substantial political clout, the reforming government has to find a way to effectively neutralize their influence on economic policy formulation. This is an essentially political action based on the existing patterns of legitimation. As we shall see in the discussion that follows, the exclusion of a distributive coalition from discussions of economic policy may be based on the particular ethnic composition and geopolitical situation of the reforming society.

At the beginning of the reform process, governments of the newly independent states had to address immediate and basic economic problems—first and foremost, how to ensure an uninterrupted supply of basic goods and services. Of course, monetary adjustments were necessary, but they were considered only as long as they had a direct positive effect on the procurement and distribution of basic goods.

In the three Baltic states, the problem was approached as a short-term economic stabilization by means of trade liberalization. The logic of the first stage of the reforms was based on the recognition of one fact: the old enterprises that worked within the division of labor in the former USSR were unable to ensure a continuous supply of necessary commodities, and their immediate restructuring was impossible. Therefore, the state should reduce entry barriers for new economic agents, whose private activities would keep the economy alive. The emergence of viable economic entities on domestic markets would take time. Meanwhile, the foreign trade policy should be liberalized. Since foreign trade with the former Soviet republics was unlikely to produce positive results, efforts should be made to reorient foreign trade away from the former USSR. The key prerequisite to this move was the introduction of a stable domestic currency.

To facilitate the emergence of private economic agents, the necessary laws on rights of private ownership were passed in all three Baltic states between 1990 and 1992. However, by 1992 the private sector was still in *statu nascendi*, its development hampered by chaos in the banking and monetary system, as well as by the continuing domination of large industrial monopolies in the economy. The laws that liberalized foreign trade had been passed shortly after independence. At the same time, the Baltic states started to negotiate bilateral trade agreements with Western economies, seeking mutual preferential trade status and the removal of covert barriers to free exchanges. However, the results of these actions were delayed by the financial instability of the Baltic economies caused by their lack of control over their monetary systems.

Thus, the problem of monetary stability had a direct bearing upon the success of economic liberalization. Foreign trade with countries outside the former Soviet Union could not be conducted in non-cash Russian rubles, the only kind of currency the Baltic states could issue. Exit from the ruble zone and introduction of their own currency had become an urgent task. These actions would also benefit the incipient domestic private firms by easing access to credit and reducing uncertainty.

By 1992, Estonia, Latvia, and Lithuania had exited the ruble zone and started to introduce their own currencies. Lithuania introduced its provisional Talonas in May of 1992 and made it the sole legal tender by September of the same year, when all Russian rubles had been withdrawn from circulation. The Latvian Rublis (also provisional) was introduced in May 1992 and became the sole legal tender two months later. The Estonian Kroon had been the sole legal tender since its introduction in June 1992.

Both Latvia and Lithuania followed a two-step process in the introduction of their respective currencies. During the first stage, the goal was simply to introduce the national currency and establish control over monetary circulation. This stage did not include stabilization of the currency and its convertibility vis-à-vis the main Western currencies. Permanent, stable, and convertible currencies were introduced in Lithuania and Latvia in 1993. Estonia introduced its Kroon as a permanent currency from the outset and ensured its stability and convertibilty by pegging its value to the German Mark and providing full backing by the country's gold and foreign currency reserves.

The introduction of national currencies, indeed, the creation of monetary systems from scratch, was a process of high technical complexity. The local experts, who had little or no knowledge of the modern monetary system, could not provide adequate expertise. Thus, technical assistance was actively sought in the West. For all three countries, assistance was provided by the World Bank, the International Monetary Fund, and the European Bank for Reconstruction and Development. In addition, Estonia received technical help from Finland and Sweden. This was facilitated by geographical proximity, historical and cultural ties and, in the case of Finland, the absence of the language barrier. Close cooperation of Estonian financial authorities and experts with their counterparts in Finland and Sweden (in fact a Swedish economist became Deputy Chairman of the Estonian National Bank) partly accounts for Estonia's success in the introduction of its currency.

While Western technical assistance to the Baltic states was indispensable for the establishment of adequate monetary and banking systems, it also contributed to a significant paradigm shift among the local economic experts and decision makers. Nationalist politicians, who came to power in the Baltics, had national independence as their first priority, while paying little attention to particulars of economic transition. Now they were easily persuaded by their Western advisors to adopt the radical "shock therapy" version of market reforms.

Several factors contributed to this paradigm shift. First, the Western experts possessed vital knowledge necessary to make viable economic decisions regarding highly complex technical issues. This gave credibility to their overall vision of economic transformation. Second, as Marie Lavigne (1995:120) points out, the "shock therapy" model was the only approach to the problems of market reforms that was sufficiently detailed to provide a foundation for economic policy.

The introduction of new currencies in the Baltic states and their exit from the ruble zone had almost immediate positive effects. Inflation in all three countries was brought under control in 1993 and did not exceed 10 percent a month. Foreign trade was rapidly oriented away from the former USSR and toward the West. A dramatic increase in foreign trade with countries outside the former Soviet Union coincided with the exit from the ruble zone. For Lithuania, the share of former Soviet republics in total volume of exports fell from 95 percent in 1991 to 68 percent in 1993. In 1991 only 13 percent of Latvia's imports came from outside the former Soviet Union, while in 1993 this figure was 31 percent. In Estonia, the share of non-Soviet countries in the total volume of imports increased even more dramatically, from 15 percent in 1991 to 76 percent in 1993 (Shen 1994).

The first stage of the economic reforms provided the Baltic states with the necessary conditions for market development. They established stable monetary and banking systems, reduced the uncertainty inherent in hyper-inflation, and opened the incipient market to competition (both domestic and foreign). Most importantly, the economic collapse that seemed inevitable in the first year of independence was successfully avoided.

In the long run, the re-orientation of foreign trade should allow the Baltic states to drastically reduce, or even completely eliminate, their dependence on Russian oil supplies. The first steps toward this goal were made in 1992 and 1993, when each of the Baltic states started to build oil terminals that in future will be used to import oil by sea (Zidovicz 1994:73).

By comparison with the Baltics, Byelorussian foreign trade in the first years of independence was still concentrated on the continuing exchange with the former Soviet republics. The volume of trade with countries outside the former Soviet Union dropped precipitously, almost by 40 percent, in 1991 and 1992 (IMF 1994a). In relative terms, in 1993 countries outside the former Soviet Union accounted for 1.77 percent of the Byelorussian imports and 2.72 percent of exports (IMF 1994a). In fact, the official Byelorussian statistical documents did not include the trade with the former Soviet republics in the category of foreign trade, suggesting the unwillingness of the Byelorussian authorities to part with the Soviet-style division of labor.

Belarus had chosen to remain in the ruble zone. It was confronted with the same problem as its Baltic neighbors: the chaotic and unpredictable nature of cash injections from other republics into the domestic economy. When it became clear that Russia would not coordinate its supply of rubles to Belarus with Byelorussian needs, haphazard steps toward the introduction of a Byelorussian currency were finally taken. In May 1992, the Byelorussian ruble was introduced into circulation. However, unlike the case of its Baltic counterparts, it was not intended as a permanent currency or even as a step toward its eventual introduction. Officially defined as a "payment coupon," it was intended to supplement the Russian ruble during the temporary shortages of the latter on the Byelorussian territory (IMF 1994a). The new Byelorussian ruble was to be used only in cash transactions, with all non-cash operations still conducted in Russian rubles. As late as in the summer of 1994, the Byelorussian ruble had not yet become the sole legal tender in Belarus.

Price liberalization in Belarus started in 1991 and continued along lines similar to the measures of the Polish communist government in the early 1980s. Prices were divided into three categories: "controlled," "limited," and "free." Prices in the first category were subsidized by the state. Both wholesale prices of oil and other energy sources delivered to enterprises and retail prices of heat and electricity used by households belonged to this category. "Limited" prices included those on products of the enterprises considered to occupy a monopolist position. These enterprises were allowed to raise prices up to a certain limit established by the authorities. Since most enterprises were monopolies in their respective fields, this measure amounted to the Soviet-style price control and was just as inefficient. The last category included all goods and services delivered to the non-state sector, as well as goods and services produced by it. This last feature of the Byelorussian price system discriminated against the few nascent non-state enterprises. Unable to compete with the subsidized state industries, private entrepreneurs were forced to concentrate on retail trade, where the cost of inputs did not present a major disadvantage.

Inter-enterprise arrears, which reached 126 billion rubles by July 1992, were annulled by the Byelorussian prime minister, thus effectively adding this sum to the budget deficit (which translated itself into increased inflation). Negative-interest loans were routinely issued to the state industrial and agricultural enterprises. The Byelorussian authorities did not express any intention of bringing interest rates closer to the rate of inflation. In fact, such attempts by the chairman of the Byelorussian National Bank were expressly prohibited by the government.

In this crisis, similar in its nature and magnitude to those experienced by the Baltic states, the strategy of the Byelorussian leaders was the opposite of the one adopted by their Baltic counterparts. Instead of monetary stabilization and economic liberalization, the Byelorussians opted for continuing subsidies and protection of state enterprises. Their hope for revitalizing the economy lay in close relations with Russia. To explain the differences between the economic strategies of the Baltic and Byelorussian leaders, we should examine the interests of crucial social groups and the cognitive models of the ruling elites.

It would be incongruous to ask what social groups in post-Soviet countries benefitted the most from hyper-inflation and other elements of the economic collapse. In a situation of total economic chaos, only a small number of profiteers have something to gain. The vast majority of the population loses, both in material and emotional terms. However, the losses are not evenly distributed among all social groups. Some stand to lose more than others, depending on their position in the political and economic system.

In the post-Soviet societies, the workers and managers of large industrial enterprises were positioned better than any other social group to use inflationary processes for protection from imminent economic dislocation. Politically, their strong organization and the potentially dangerous consequences of unemployment gave them a strong bargaining position and allowed them to successfully demand expansion of cheap credit. Economically, most enterprises were monopolist producers, which allowed them to raise prices. Thus, the situation had all the elements necessary for the classical cost inflation model as presented by Don Patinkin: strong labor combined with the state's declared policy of maintaining an absolutely continuous state of full employment (Patinkin 1989:310).

For the managers and employees of the state-controlled, mostly large industrial enterprises, measures for economic stabilization and liberalization were detrimental, at least in the short run, exposing these enterprises to the competition of foreign and then domestic producers. They would eliminate the soft budget constraints in their modified form of the negative interest rate credit and toleration of insolvency. This would effectively terminate the state policy of full employment and protection of all enterprise from bankruptcy. Of course, it would take some time actually to enforce the existing laws on bankruptcy, and a modicum of protection would be extended to the enterprises by any government willing to avoid an explosive growth in unemployment and related social problems. Still, even the relatively gradual encroachment of market forces on the comfortable monopolist positions of the state-controlled enterprises was not welcomed by their employees and managers.

In the Baltics, the industrial management well understood the full long-term implications of the introduction of the new currencies and the steps toward their convertibility against Western currencies (but not against the Russian ruble). Anatol Lieven quotes a Russian manager of an Estonian factory on the issue of the convertible Kroon: "If the Kroon really does become a hard currency, it could kill off most of the Estonian production, because the quality of Western production is so much higher than ours. At present, 90 percent of our trade is with the former Soviet Union. If we introduce the Kroon without full agreement on how to carry on payments, this will lead to practical blockade" (Lieven 1993:356). The resistance of the managers of the state-controlled enterprises in the Baltics to the introduction of national currencies is also pointed out by Shen (1994).

Industrial workers and managers in the Baltics, as well as in Belarus, constituted a formidable force, highly mobilized and capable of concerted and sustained actions. In the last years of the Soviet rule, as well as after the collapse of the Soviet Union, these groups successfully used their organization in the struggle for continuing government subsidies. For example, in the spring of 1992, the threat of industrial actions by workers' organizations in Eastern Estonia caused the government to provide subsidies, thus straining the financial system at the crucial time of the introduction of the Kroon. Similar demands were put forward during strikes in Latvia and Lithuania.

However, for the managers and employees of industrial enterprises in the Baltics, the ability to force concessions from the government did not translate into active participation in policy decision making. This was due not to lack of power, but rather to the specific pattern of mobilization and the image of workers' movements in the eyes of the new nationalist elites. In the last years of Soviet rule in the Baltics, industrial workers were mobilized around the Soviet imperial idea. Then, as an opposition to the fledgling nationalist movements, Moscow authorities, together with local hard-line Communists, initiated the creation of mass anti-independence, pro-Soviet, and pro-Communist movements. In Estonia, it was "The International Movement of Workers in the Estonian SSR"; in Latvia the similar movement was called the "International Front"; in Lithuania it was known as "Unity."

These movements were centered around large industrial enterprises and quickly acquired a truly mass character. Their organizers capitalized on the ethnic composition of the industrial workforce. In Latvia, where the share of non-indigenous population in industrial employment was the largest of the three Baltic states, Russian-speaking workers constituted 59.4 percent of the total number of industrial workers (Karklins 1994:133). This figure was similar in Estonia, where the Russian-speaking population was concentrated in industrial centers in the east. Fears of the non-indigenous population, whose future status in the independent Baltic states was unclear and who often distrusted the nationalist leaders, proved fertile ground for the cultivation of Soviet loyalism, especially when combined with economic considerations. All these movements proclaimed their loyalty to the Soviet Union and opposed any action of the nationalist movements by staging mass demonstrations and industrial actions. Two examples may serve to illustrate the agenda of these "international workers' movements." In 1989, they organized a wave of mass demonstrations and strikes in Lithuania, Latvia, and Estonia to protest against measures to make indigenous languages official (Nahaylo and Swoboda 1990:319). In August 1989, the Estonian International Movement organized a general strike to stop attempts by Estonian authorities to remove enterprises from the control of Moscow (Lieven 1993:193). Both these actions involved tens of thousands of participants.

The workers' movements in the Baltics actively participated in the

1990 elections in local legislative bodies. They supported candidates who shared their agenda (often, but not necessarily, also supported by the official Communist establishment) and who, when elected, formed parliamentary factions that were not only pro-worker, but also pro-Soviet. After these movements' active support of the Soviet military actions in Lithuania and Latvia in the winter of 1991, as well as the August 1991 coup, deputies belonging to these factions had their mandates annulled. Thus, when the crucial first steps of economic reforms were taken, industrial workers and management did not have political representation.

The actions of the workers' movements prior to independence, as well as the openly pro-Soviet stance of the parliamentary factions supported by these movements, contributed to the image of large industrial enterprises as a potential pro-Russian "fifth column." Thus, they were regarded by the decisionmakers not as legitimate participants in the reform process but as an alien force to be reckoned with, but not cooperated with. The fact that in 1992 in all three Baltic states positions crucial for the formulation of reform policies (prime ministers, their deputies, and chairpersons of national banks) were held by staunch nationalists served further to reinforce this attitude. The exclusion of the industrial workers and managers from political discourse regarding specific elements of the reforms made it easier for the reformers in the Baltics to introduce stabilization measures in compliance with the requirements of the World Bank and the IMF. Many industrial managers well understood the long-term consequences of such policies. However, the highly complex technical nature of the issues involved made it difficult to mobilize workers against them.

In Belarus, large industrial enterprises had support not only in legislation, where more than 30 percent of deputies were managers of state-controlled firms, but also in the executive branch of government. In my interviews with five high-ranking members of the Byelorussian government apparatus (three directors of departments in the Ministry of Economics, the Deputy Finance Minister, and the Chair of the State Anti-Monopoly Committee), all five interviewees pointed to very close connections between directors of industrial enterprises and the actual decisionmakers in the government. The latter, confined mostly to the prime minister and his deputies, would make their decisions on economic policies only after consultations with the former. Thus, unlike their Baltic counterparts, Byelorussian industrial managers were actively participating in detailed analyses and in the formulation of economic policy decisions. Their control of the legislature ensured that only those laws that satisfied them would pass.

The above comparison of the influence of industrial managers and workers on the reform process in Belarus and the Baltics might seem to fall into Olson's model of "distributional coalitions" and their role in the economic progress of societies (Olson 1982). Indeed, in his later work (1993) he attributed both the Soviet economic collapse and post-Soviet stagnation to the negative influence of such coalitions. In our case, the first stage of economic reforms succeeded in the Baltics because "distributional coalitions" were excluded from decision making, while in Belarus reforms faltered because these coalitions retained their influence. However, if we consider the causes of the different influence of large industrial enterprises in Belarus as compared to the Baltics, the applicability of Olson's model becomes less obvious. The power of industrial enterprises in the Baltics was equal to or even greater than that of their counterparts in Belarus. The main reason for their exclusion from decision making was the value-pattern of the nationalist ruling elites. In Belarus, on the other hand, the ruling elite's attitude toward industrial enterprises was universally positive. Thus, the exclusion of "distributional coalitions" in the Baltics and their participation in decision making in Belarus were due to factors that are beyond the frame of reference adopted by Olson and rational action theory in general.

The first stage of economic reforms in the Baltics had been much more successful than in Belarus. This difference was to a large extent due to the value-system of the ruling elites, particularly their attitudes toward Russia, as well as to the place of the existing industrial structure in the legitimation pattern.

References

Alchian, A. (1950). "Uncertainty, Evolution and Economic Theory," *Journal of Political Economy* 58(3): 211–221.

Balcerowicz, L., and A. Gelb. (1994). "How to Stabilize—Policy Lessons from Early Reformers," *Transition* 5(May–June): 4.

Bronshtein, M. (1993). "Comment," in *Economic Consequences of Soviet Disin-*

tegration, edited by J. Williamson. Washington, DC: Institute for International Economics.

Byelorussian State Committee for Anti-Monopoly Policy. (1994). *Kompleksnaya Programma Demonopolizatsii Narodnogo Khoziaistva Respubliki Belarus (A Complex Program of Demonopolization of the National Economy of the Republic of Belarus).* Minsk: Byelorussian State Committee for Anti-Monopoly Policy.

Cooter, R. (1991). "Organizational Property and Privatization in Russia," in *Law and Democracy in the New Russia,* edited by B. L. Smith and G. M. Danilenko. Washington, DC: Brookings Institute.

European Bank for Reconstruction and Development (EBRD). (1994). *Report on Economic Transition in Eastern Europe and the Former Soviet Union in 1994.* London: European Bank for Reconstruction and Development.

———. (1997). *Transition Report 1997.* London: European Bank for Reconstruction and Development.

George, K. (1991). "Public Ownership versus Privatization," in *Competition in Europe: Essays in Honor of Henk de Jong,* edited by P. de Wolf. Dordrecht: Kluwer Academic Publishers.

Habermas, J. (1975). *Legitimation Crisis.* Boston, MA: Beacon Press.

———. (1990). "What Does Socialism Mean Today? The Rectifying Revolution and the Need for New Thinking on the Left," *New Left Review* 183(September–October): 3–22.

Ickes, B., and R. Ryterman. (1992). "The Interenterprise Arrears Crisis in Russia," *Post-Soviet Affairs* 8(4): 331–361.

International Monetary Fund (IMF). (1994a). *Economic Review: Belarus.* Washington, DC: International Monetary Fund.

———. (1994b). *Economic Review: Estonia.* Washington, DC: International Monetary Fund.

———. (1994c). *Economic Review: Latvia.* Washington, DC: International Monetary Fund.

———. (1994d). *Economic Review: Lithuania.* Washington, DC: International Monetary Fund.

Karklins, R. (1994). *Ethnopolitics and Transition to Democracy: The Collapse of the USSR and Latvia.* Washington, DC: Woodrow Wilson Center Press.

Keerna, A. (1988). "Khozraschiot Regional'nyi" ("Regional Self-financing"), *Voprosy Ekonomiki* 8: 65–76.

Kehris, O. (1989). "Ob Ekonomicheskoi Modeli Latvii" ("On the Latvian Economic Model"), *Atmoda* 27 March.

Keynes, J. M. (1923 [1963]). "Social Consequences of Changes in the Value of Money," in J. M. Keynes, *Essays in Persuasion.* New York: W.W. Norton.

Kornai, J. (1990). *The Road to a Free Economy. Shifting from a Socialist System: The Example of Hungary.* New York: W.W. Norton.

———. (1992). *The Socialist System: The Political Economy of Communism.* Princeton, NJ: Princeton University Press.

Lavigne, M. (1995). *The Economics of Transition*. New York: St. Martin's Press.

Lieberman, I. (1995). "Mass Privatization in Central and Eastern Europe and the Former Soviet Union: A Comparative Analysis," in *Mass Privatization: An Initial Assessment*. Paris: Organization for Economic Cooperation and Development.

Lieven, A. (1993). *The Baltic Revolution*. New Haven: Yale University Press.

Milor, V. (1994). "Changing Political Economies: An Introduction," in *Changing Political Economies: Privatization in Post-Communist and Reforming Communist States*, edited by V. Milor. London: Lynn Rienner Publishers.

Murrell, P. (1992). "Evolution in Economics and the Economic Reform of the Centrally Planned Economies," in *The Emergence of Market Economies in Eastern Europe*, edited by C. Clague and G. C. Rausser. New York: Blackwell.

Nahaylo, B., and V. Swoboda. (1990). *Soviet Disunion*. New York: Free Press.

Nellis, J. (1994). "Successful Privatization in Estonia: Unusual Features," *Transition* 5(July–August): 5.

Newbery, D. (1992). "The Safety Net During Transformation: Hungary," in *The Emergence of Market Economies in Eastern Europe*, edited by C. Clague and G. C. Rausser. New York: Blackwell.

North, D. (1971). "Institutional Change and Economic Growth," *Journal of Economic History* 31: 118–125.

———. (1981). *Structure and Change in Economic History*. New York: Norton.

———. (1990). *Institutions, Institutional Change and Economic Performance*. Cambridge: Cambridge University Press.

Olson, M. (1982). *The Rise and Decline of Nations: Economic Growth, Stagflation, and Social Rigidities*. New Haven: Yale University Press.

———. (1993). "The Hidden Path to a Successful Economy," in *The Emergence of Market Economies in Eastern Europe*, edited by C. Clague and G. C. Rausser. New York: Blackwell.

Patinkin, D. (1989). *Money, Interest, and Prices*. Cambridge, MA: MIT Press.

Pejovich, S. (1969). "The Firm, Monetary Policy and Property Rights," *Western Economic Journal* 7: 193–200.

———. (1995). *Economic Analysis of Institutions and Systems*. Dordrecht: Kluwer Academic Publishers.

Poznanski, K. (1992). "Property Rights Perspective on Evolution of Communist-Type Economies," in *Constructing Capitalism: The Reemergence of Civil Society and Liberal Economy in the Post-Communist World*, edited by K. Poznanski. Boulder, CO: Westview Press.

———. (1996). *Poland's Protracted Transition: Institutional Change and Economic Growth 1970–1994*. Cambridge: Cambridge University Press.

Semeta, A. (1995). "Post-Privatization Secondary Markets in Lithuania," in

Mass Privatization: An Initial Assessment. Paris: Organization for Economic Cooperation and Development.

Shen, R. (1994). *Restructuring the Baltic Economies.* Westport, CT: Praeger.

Simenas, A. (1995). "Privatization in Lithuania," in *Mass Privatization: An Initial Assessment.* Paris: Organization for Economic Cooperation and Development.

Stark, D. (1994). "Path Dependence and Privatization Strategy in East-Central Europe," in *Changing Political Economics,* edited by V. Milor. London: Lynne Rienner Publishers.

Steinbuka, I. (1993). "The Baltics," in *Economic Consequences of Soviet Disintegration,* edited by J. Williamson. Washington, DC: Institute for International Economics.

Sutela, P. (1991). *Economic Thought and Economic Reform in the Soviet Union.* Cambridge: Cambridge University Press.

United Nations (UN). (1996). *Economic Survey of Europe in 1995–1996.* Geneva: United Nations.

Williamson, J. (1993). "Trade and Payments After Soviet Disintegration," in *Economic Consequences of Soviet Disintegration,* edited by J. Williamson. Washington, DC: Institute for International Economics.

Winiecki, J. (1990). *Resistance to Change in the Soviet Economic System.* New York: Routledge.

———. (1995). "Polish Mass Privatization Program: The Unloved Child in a Suspect Family," in *Mass Privatization: An Initial Assessment.* Paris: Organization for Economic Cooperation and Development.

World Bank. (1997). *Belarus: Prices, Markets, and Enterprise Reform.* Washington, DC: World Bank.

Židovicz, K. (1994). "Fatalne Uzaleznie—Miećc Albo Nie Miećc" ("Fatal Dependency: To Have or Not To Have"), *Eurazja* 3/4: 40–47.

A Political Economy Approach to the Neoclassical Model of Transition

By John Marangos[*]

ABSTRACT. The neoclassical model of transition from a centrally-administered socialist economic system to a market-based economic system was implemented in Russia and Eastern Europe. The neoclassical process took the form of either shock therapy or gradualism. However, each approach actually involved a combination of shock therapy and gradualist policies, making the distinction between the two approaches unfounded. In addition, both approaches suffered by the innate inadequacies of neoclassical economic analysis as being politically/institutionally naked. Both shock therapy supporters and gradualist neoclassical economists did not provide a specific process of institutional development, favouring a gradual market-driven institutional outcome. With regard to the political structure, democracy was inconsistent with shock therapy, while active state intervention during transition was inconsistent with the ultimate goal of the gradualist neoclassical economists of competitive capitalism.

I

Introduction

THE DOMINANCE OF NEOCLASSICAL ECONOMICS in the economic literature and of economic policies in market economies was the only decisive factor in determining the transition strategy of Russia and Eastern Europe. The neoclassical model of transition from a centrally-administered socialist economy to a capitalist market economy provided a set of liberalisation, stabilisation, and privatisation policies based on the

* John Marangos teaches economics at the School of Business, University of Ballarat, Victoria, Australia. He is also a Ph.D. student at LaTrobe University, Melbourne, Australia under the supervision of John King. His Ph.D. thesis is titled "Alternative Models of Transition for the Russian and Eastern European Economies." His research interests are transition economics and teaching of economics. The author would like to thank John King and Alicia Glenane for their useful comments. Email: *J.Marangos@ballarat. edu.au*.

American Journal of Economics and Sociology, Vol. 61, No. 1 (January, 2002).

neoclassical body of economic analysis. The neoclassical model of transition was also adopted as the only solution to the transition problem by the international financial institutions—International Monetary Fund (IMF) and the World Bank—that provided financial aid upon the implementation of policies recommended by the neoclassical model. Consequently, the debate on transition had nothing to do with the goal, method, or ideology underpinning the transition process. These elements had already been decided and imposed upon transition economies. The goal had to be competitive capitalism, the methodology neoclassical economics, and the ideological foundation of the reform had to be self-interest. Nor were the initial conditions of each country a concern. As a result, the debate on transition was restricted to the speed of the reforms. The only concern was whether transition economies should immediately liberalise, stabilise, and privatise, the shock therapy approach, or implement the neoclassical policies at a slow pace, the gradualist approach.

The aim of this paper is to demonstrate that the debate between shock therapy supporters and the gradualist neoclassical economists[1] was immaterial. Both transition approaches adopted a combination of shock therapy and gradualist strategies. A careful investigation of the reforms recommended and implemented with regard to price liberalisation and stabilisation, privatisation, monetary and fiscal policies, and international trade policies reveals contradictions and inconsistencies in each approach to the point that the distinction is, in fact, invalid. Meanwhile, it is important to recognise that the transition process also depended on developments in the institutional and political structure. Incorporating the institutional and political structure into the transition analysis, which is consistent with a political economy approach, further highlights the contradictions of shock therapy and gradualism, reinforcing the inadequacies of neoclassical economic analysis as being politically/institutionally naked.

II

Economic Reforms in Transition Economies

THE SHOCK THERAPY MODEL derived its name from Poland's stabilisation and liberalisation program, initiated on January 1, 1990. The countries that followed this approach are Czechoslovakia (starting on January 1, 1991), Bulgaria (February 1, 1991), Russia (February 2, 1992), Albania (July 1992), Estonia (September 1992), and Latvia (June 5, 1993). Jeffrey Sachs was an advisor to the Polish government and both he and Anders Aslund advised the Russian government and guided its shock therapy reform process in 1992 to 1993 (Schlack 1996:617). Aslund was, in fact, an economic advisor to the Russian government from November 1991 to January 1994 (Aslund 1995:xi). Sachs and Aslund "shared the belief that the economy [in Russia] was in such a terrible mess that a radical, comprehensive, liberal program would be needed to introduce any kind of rational order" (*ibid.*, p.16).

The shock therapy model highlights the interdependent, mutually supportive, and interactive character of economic relationships, implying that reforms should be introduced simultaneously. Fragmented changes are ineffective. "The idea that there is choice between doing one radical measure or another is simply wrong. There is no trade-off but, on the contrary, complementarity" (Aslund 1997b:187). Thus macroeconomic and microeconomic reforms must be concurrent (Sachs 1990:21). This was why the reform program needed to be sweeping and expedient. Jeffrey Sachs stated, "Poland's goal is to establish the economic, legal and institutional basis for a private-sector market economy in just one year" (1990:19). The program has been described as a "leap to a market economy" (Sachs and Lipton 1990:48) and a "jump to a market economy" (Sachs 1993).

The fundamental basis of the gradualist neoclassical approach to transition was the need to establish economic, institutional, political, and ideological structures before any attempt to liberalise. Without this minimum foundation, radical reforms would have inhibited the transition to a competitive market capitalist system. Moreover, the implementation of the reform program required minimum standards of living; otherwise the social fabric of the whole society would have been at risk. The aim of the gradual neoclassical transition process was to initiate a profound and unique change, a "transformational recession" (Kornai 1993a:182, 189; 1994:41), and to overcome the "shortageflation" syndrome (Kolodko 1993:21) by initiating "preventive therapy" (Kornai 1997:183). This was only possible by taking "the longest road" (Abel and Bonin 1993:230), or by "rebuilding the boat in the open sea" (Elster, Offe, and Preuss 1997). The gradualist neoclassical transition process was implemented in Romania (Poirot 1996), Hungary, which has a tradition of a gradual transformation starting in 1968 with the New Economic Mechanism (Kornai 1993a; Samonis and Hunyadi 1993; Szekely and Newbery 1993; Wolf 1991; Hare 1991), and Slovenia (Kornai 1997).

A. Price Liberalisation and Stabilisation

Price liberalisation and stabilisation were preconditions for a successful reform process (Blanchard and Layard 1993). The shock therapy economists were in favour of an adjustment approach, which involved an immediate jump in the price level. It was better to face a single increase in prices than high and persistent inflation, since there was nothing beneficial associated with high inflation and its resulting corruption (Aslund 1995), and so that investment decisions would not be distorted by transitional prices. In contrast, for the gradualist neoclassical economists, the adjustment to the new price levels needed to be gradual (Kornai 1994). Stable domestic price levels permitted greater domestic financial deepening and higher real deposit rates, reducing risks and greatly simplifying the liberalisation and stabilisation of the real exchange rate (McKinnon 1993). The price controls were not a fruitless exercise; they facilitated the transition and reduced the associated costs to society.

An efficiently functioning labour market was a principal prerequisite to a successful transition process (Frydman, Rapaczynski, and Turkewitz 1997). Strangely enough, while the objective of both approaches was market-determined wages, both approaches argued that it was in the interest of society in the transition phase to maintain some control over wages and to avoid the wage-price spiral. Whereas this is consistent with gradualism, it is inconsistent with shock therapy. Sachs and Lipton (1990) recommended a tax-based wage policy to encourage wage increases below the increases in inflation. For example, the Polish government initiated penalties on wage increases, the so-called *popiwek* (Balcerowicz, Blaszcyzk, and Dabrowski 1997). Enterprises conceding wage increases above the norm were heavily taxed (Sachs and Lipton 1990). The gradual process of reaching equilibrium wages recommended by the shock therapy supporters through a tax-based wage policy was in agreement with gradualist neoclassical economists (Kornai 1996; Fischer and Gelb 1991; Nuti 1991). Progressive taxation above the predetermined norm would act as a disincentive to excessive wage increases (Fisher and Frenkel 1992; Kolodko 1999a), while partial indexation of wages, not automatic indexation, would maintain industrial peace and reduce inflation (Bim 1992; Kornai 1996; Fischer and Gelb 1991).

B. Privatisation

Privatisation and financial restructuring manifested the greatest intellectual and political complexities of the entire transition program (Sachs 1991a; Aslund 1992). This was because privatisation was driven by conflicting objectives (fairness, compensation, restitution, enterprise efficiency, budgetary revenues, and employment) and based on previously unknown methods (vouchers, management acquisitions, and workers buyouts) (Sachs 1996a). It was also fraught with administrative complexity as thousands of small, medium, and large enterprises operated within incomplete markets and a legal vacuum, making corruption highly probable (*ibid.*). For the shock therapy supporters the privatisation process had to be initiated concurrently for all enterprises, using across-the-board mechanisms. Therefore, privatisation should take place through a combination of different methods but, preferably, privatisation of industry should be through free distribution of vouchers (Sachs 1991b).

The concerns and reservations that shock therapy economists had about the privatisation process were unfounded. The aim of the shock therapy process was to develop an economy based on market relations without the presence of discretionary power. Whether the privatisation process gave ownership of state enterprises to the workers, management, or general members of society, these owners would only be able to retain their ownership rights if they used their property productively by satisfying market demand at minimum cost. Hence, in a competitive market, which is the ultimate goal of shock therapy supporters, only efficient owners and efficient behaviour would be able to survive, irregardless of how the initial distribution of ownership took place. Consequently, the development of a free market process would derive an efficient ownership structure in due time, making the method of privatisation unimportant. The distribution of private property to the efficient owners through the impersonal market process could only take place after some considerable time.

Kornai (1990) argued that the transformation of state property into private property could only take place by auctioning state enterprises and selling them to the highest bidder. The Hungarian government agreed that privatisation had to result in "real owners" or "strong owners" rather than artificial recipients of state assets (Frydman, Rapaczynski, and Turkewitz 1997; Samonis and Hunyadi 1993; Mihalyi 1993). Ironically, large state enterprises had to be renationalised before they could be privatised, and, even then, the gradual neoclassical approach was not gradual (Stark 1990). Instead of a gradual process of privatisation, enterprises were put up for auction. Hence, the gradualist neoclassical privatisation process was more of a "deferred shock therapy privatisation" process. The only difference between the gradualists and shock therapy supporters was the timing of privatisation, not its speed.

C. Monetary and Fiscal Policies

Shock therapy supporters believed that the independent central bank had to establish credit targets to hold overall money growth to levels consistent with a rapid elimination of inflation (Sachs 1993), implying the elimination of the soft budget constraint. This is because inflation is a monetary phenomenon (Aslund 1993; Rostowski 1993). By establishing an independent central bank with the monetary rule written in its constitution, inflation and the soft budget constraint would be eliminated. But laying the institutional foundations to ensure an independent central bank was a lengthy process.

The gradualist neoclassical economists argued that the imposition of hard budget constraint on enterprises, in the context of macroeconomic stabilisation, was the driving force of adjustment. The soft budget constraint resulted in inefficiency, breakdown of consumer sovereignty, and distorted investment decisions. Thus, reform of the financial system had to be a high priority (Calvo and Frenkel 1991). Meanwhile, the elimination of the soft budget constraint could only evolve gradually, as for example in Hungary (Kornai 1997, 1993b; Csaba 1995). Consequently, an independent central bank was inconsistent with the gradual elimination of the soft budget constraint.

The reduction of large budget deficits was required in order to eliminate hyper-inflation. As the budget deficit was the main source of money creation, and hence inflationary, the reduction of the budget deficit topped the agenda of any economic reform plan (Fedorov 1992). Sachs (1994) argued that while reducing the budget deficit could reduce inflation, altering the way in which the deficit was financed could also reduce inflation. In as much as the budget deficit was financed by foreign financial resources (such as foreign borrowing, grants, and aid) or by domestic borrowing (by the creation of a Treasury bill market), inflation would not result. Consequently, it was possible to have low inflation with a budget deficit. In fact, the shock therapy supporters recognised that the goal of a balanced budget could not be achieved immediately. Sachs (*ibid.*) was critical of the IMF's insistent focus on budget cuts rather than deficit financing and effectively retaining a budget deficit. In actual fact, IMF aid was conditional on reducing the budget deficit (Martinez-Vazquez, Rioja, Skogstad, and Valen 2001).

Balancing the budget was a long-term concern for the gradualist neoclassical economists (Csaba 1995). However, in order to avoid further inflationary explosions, "effective fiscal reforms must come much earlier in their transitions" (McKinnon 1995a:96). While every effort had to be made to reduce the budget deficit—or ideally to produce a surplus (Roe 1991)—a reduction was seen as unlikely in the first years of transition (Kornai 1992a; Csaba 1995). Reducing the deficit too drastically or too quickly would be dangerous. Rapid and drastic cuts in government expenditure would suddenly reduce aggregate demand and cause deeper recession. As a result, the urgency for growth did not require an immediate reduction in the budget deficit (Kornai 1995a). Instead, privatisation of the state enterprises through auctions increased state revenue, funding the budget deficit (Kornai 1992b; Hare 1991; Roe 1991).

Thus, both approaches were in favour of maintaining the budget deficit and achieving a balanced budget gradually. The disagreement lay in the financing of the deficit. Of course, this was directly linked to the method of privatisation. The shock therapist supporters opted for mainly free distribution of vouchers, which did not provide any revenue; thus, the budget deficit had to be financed by borrowing or grants. The gradualist neoclassical economists supported auctioning of state enterprises, thus giving rise to the necessary revenue to finance the budget deficit.

D. International Trade Policies

The liberalisation of international trade and the establishment of a convertible exchange rate were among the most important prerequisites for successful capitalism (Aslund 1995). Essentially, "convertibility and external liberalisation are natural bedfellows" (Sutela 1992:89). Sachs (1996b, 1997), Aslund (1995), and Sutela (1992) were in favour of a pegged exchange rate at the start of the stabilisation program, changing to a more flexible rate after one or two years. This was because the pegged exchange rate had some advantages in times of high inflation. In the transition economies, the early peggers—Czechoslovakia, Estonia, Hungary, Poland, and Slovakia—performed much better than the floaters, both in terms of the rate and cost of disinflation. The peggers achieved inflation below 100 percent per year by 1994 (Sachs 1996b:149). Meanwhile, the successful short-term implementation of the pegged exchange rate can be interpreted as an argument in favour of a fixed exchange rate system and gradualism.

The gradualist neoclassical economists argued that it was in the interest of transition economies to have coordinated price liberalisation, budgetary, and credit reforms. Williamson (1991, 1992), Van Brabant (1991), Kregel, Matzner, and Grabher (1992), Fischer and Frenkel (1992), and Dornbusch (1993) were all in favour of the establishment of a "payments union" between transition economies. An organisation similar to the European Payments Union (EPU), which operated from mid 1950 to 1958, was suggested (Eichengreen, Grilli, and Fischer 1993), because the convertibility of the exchange rate would not otherwise be sustainable due to the inelasticity of import and export demand. Through the payments union, transition economies would have been able to establish current account convertibility more rapidly between the member states and with the rest of the world and avoid large depreciation of the exchange rate (Williamson 1992). The union would have achieved currency convertibility, intraregional economic collaboration, exploitation of comparative advantage, structural adjustment, reduction in the social cost of transition, and development of rational trade and prices, and would have prepared transition economies for participation in international trade. However, the idea was rejected (Williamson 1991).

III

Institutional Reforms in Transition Economies

THE AIM OF THE TRANSITION PROCESS was not only to eliminate the unreasonable distortions of the central allocation of resources, but also to establish the appropriate institutions in organising the new market mechanism for allocating resources. A proper institutional structure was "the Achilles heel" (Svejnar 1991:134) of transition, because "institutions matter" (Bardhan 2000:245). Private property and the building of institutions are fundamental to a free market (Kolodko 2000, 1999b; Wagener 2000).

The shock therapy process utilised market incentives to internalise the developmental process of institutions instead of relying on the government, an external actor to the whole process: institutional change was a derivative. Consequently, a radical reform process would not inhibit the development of the institutional structure. In contrast, the mere fact of the existence of private enterprises and market relations created the need for an appropriate institutional environment. "The evidence suggests that institutional development is stimulated by early and radical reform" (Aslund, Boone, and Johnson 1996:249).

Hence the shock therapy advocates, while prescribing an immediate transition to a market economy, argued that the market could only deliver operative institutions. Effectively and paradoxically, the shock therapy approach recommended a gradual development of market institutions. The imperative of not using government intervention in the market resulted in a contradiction in the shock therapy model. In theory, shock therapists required the immediate destruction of the institutions of central administration, which implied the establishment of market institutions by the government, thus minimising the time necessary to create institutions. In reality, the shock therapy economists were willing to sacrifice speed in this context so as to avoid government intervention, which they regarded as completely undesirable.

The gradualist neoclassical economists used the evolutionary paradigm of institutional development to justify their approach to reform (Smyth 1998; Kolodko 1999b). Gradualist economists argued that the transition to a market economy needed to be facilitated by an institutional structure, the development of which had to be gradual, natural, organic, and voluntary, as opposed to the constructivist, state-directed establishment of institutions (Kolodko 2000; Kornai 1992b, 1995b, 1997; Csaba 1995; Gustafson 1999; Murrell 1992). A gradual process allowed time to clarify the institutional principles and to test institutional adjustment. Institutional development was a complex evolutionary process, causing the ineffective institutions to wither away and facilitating the survival of those institutions that truly were fit for the task (Kornai 1992b, 1995b; Nelson 1995).

In summary, the development of the institutional structure of the shock therapy and the gradualist neoclassical processes appeared to be quite similar. However, while both approaches argued that market institutions can only result from market forces, gradualist neoclassical economists allowed institutions to develop concurrently with market relations. For shock therapy supporters, the goal was first the development of market relations, with the assumption that the institutions will follow in due time. The gradualist neoclassical argument suffered from the same flaws as shock therapy. Gradualist neoclassical writings failed to offer a concrete process of institutional development, simply leaving the end-state to be determined by the market, and assuming that the most efficient institutions would emerge. The gradualist neoclassical break with shock therapy was far less complete than it appeared to be.

IV

Political Reforms in Transition Economies

SHOCK THERAPY SUPPORTERS FAVOURED a democratic process of decision making (Aslund 1995, 1994, 1997a). Thus, "the market revolution has gone hand in hand with a democratic revolution" (Sachs 1995:50). However, was democracy consistent with the shock therapy process? Actually, a democratic political process was inconsistent with the shock therapy process of transition because democracy requires the continuous responsiveness of the government to the preferences of the members of society. Policy making reflects the variety of preferences and interests of society.

But the shock therapy supporters argued that there had to be no political interference. The shock therapy process had to be implemented independently of the political process and consistently, in spite of criticism. It could not favour anyone; everybody had to follow the basic rules. This could only take place by stripping the government of its discretionary power and assigning it the responsibility of maintaining the rules written in the constitution in the tradition of Hayek (1944) and Friedman (1980). Consequently, the shock therapy model was only consistent with a non-elected government that did not exercise discretionary power, rather than a government that was democratic but intervened in the market, distorting and thus withholding the attainment of a free market. When Intriligator stated that "democracy is neither necessary nor sufficient for good economic performance" (Intriligator 1998:241), this was an implicit agreement with Walters's reference to the transition economies that "we should not claim democracy as either sufficient or even necessary for a liberal society with a market economy" (1992:101).

The implementation of the shock therapy model was short-lived. Despite the substantial initial support for governments initiating the process in transition economies, considerable undesirable outcomes resulted, such as unemployment and inflation. This led to the governments' unpopularity. High inflation and unemployment caused social and political instability, threatening the fragile democratic governments. Intrinsically, these governments did not have the power to pursue the policies required by the shock therapy platform. In a democratic environment, the substantial reduction in output and employment associated with the shock therapy process of transition resulted in the ultimate downfall of these governments through the electoral process. The shift to gradualism took place in Poland on September 19, 1993; in Russia on December 12, 1993; in Bulgaria on December 18, 1994; in Estonia on March 5, 1995; in the Czech Republic on June 1, 1996; and in Latvia on July 25, 1997. In all cases, these shifts occurred after unfavourable election results for the shock therapy governments (Marangos forthcoming).

The goal of the gradualist neoclassical process of transition was a democratic political structure combined with a market economy. In contrast to the shock therapist approach, the policies of the gradualist neoclassical approach had to be approved by the democratic political process in order to facilitate the transition. However, the policy prescriptions presented an unfortunate policy dilemma for the gradualist neoclassical economists. In order to secure macroeconomic stabilisation in the short run, important pricing, enterprise, banking, and international trade policies had to move counter to the ultimate goal of long-term liberalisation. Transition governments were encouraged by the gradualist neoclassical economists to seize financial assets of enterprises, command outputs through state orders, reinstitute price controls, restructure enterprises, and coordinate international trade policies. Consequently, the recommendation was for reregulation of the financial system and reregulation of international trade, together with the reregulation of state enterprises (Kolodko 1999b; McKinnon 1995b, 1995a; Stark 1990). The gradualist neoclassical economists implied that, once the transition was completed, state intervention in the economy would be unnecessary. As markets developed and the pace of reforms gained momentum, the role of the state would be reduced and with it any remaining discretionary power.

As competitive capitalism was the ultimate goal of gradualist neoclassical economists, there was an apparent contradiction with the transition strategy recommended. A competitive capitalist system required a government with no discretion. However, reregulation and renationalisation occurred during the transition period: the government's discretionary power was thus increased in the name of gaining control of economic affairs to guide the gradual process of transition. There was a direct link between increased government power and the interests of the bureaucracy and lobby groups. The crucial question was how could an economy, from a system of increasing government power during the transition period, be transformed into a free market system with no government discretion? The gradualist neoclassical economists failed to reveal how this would be achieved. Strangely enough, the state was expected to "wither away" and function as a "minimum state"—implementing only the rules—consistent with the tradition of Hayek and Friedman (Csaba 1995; Abel and Bonin 1993). Notwithstanding, Stalin advanced a similar argument during the 1930s. For the state to wither away, its power first had to be maximised (Nove 1989). However, the state would never wither away because it was linked with the interests and privileges of the bureaucracy, lobby groups, and sectoral interests. These groups would have resisted their own dissolution and state power and intervention would have continued. Gradualist neoclassical economists advanced a similar argument to explain the lack of reform in the Stalinist system. The same argument finds validity in the gradualist neoclassical process of transition.

V

Conclusion

A POLITICAL ECONOMY EXAMINATION of the neoclassical model of transition in either the shock therapy or gradualist approach reveals the internal inconsistencies of each. The shock therapy approach recommended a gradualist process of implementation of the neoclassical policies with regard to wages (wage-tax policy), privatisation (efficient ownership structure as only market-determined), monetary policy (establishment of an independent central bank), fiscal policy (maintaining the budget deficit), and the foreign exchange (pegged exchange rate). The gradualist neoclassical process, while advocating gradualism in transition, opted for a shock therapy privatisation process by auctioning off state enterprises. Both approaches favoured gradual market-driven institutional development. However, an institutional structure as a result of the market process was a very time-consuming method, resulting in corruption and illegal activities. A democratic political structure was inconsistent with shock therapy, while active state intervention during transition was inconsistent with the ultimate goal of the gradualist neoclassical economists of competitive capitalism.

The implementation of the neoclassical model of transition in Russia and Eastern Europe in either form, shock therapy or gradualism, had to varying degrees common outcomes. These were inflation, reduced output, unemployment, external imbalances, the destruction of the welfare system, and corruption. The neoclassical economists presented these outcomes as "short-term necessary adjustments." Actually, these outcomes were the result of the innate inadequacies of neoclassical economics associated not only with inconsistent policy prescriptions but also with the effective exclusion of the institutional and political elements of the transition.

Note

1. A gradualist transition model could also take the form of a post-Keynesian transition process or a market socialist approach, such as in China. The analysis in this paper is restricted to the neoclassical model.

References

Abel, I., and J. P. Bonin. (1993). "State Desertion and Convertibility: The Case of Hungary," in *Hungary: An Economy in Transition*, edited by I. P. Szekely and D. M. G. Newberry. Cambridge: Cambridge University Press.

Aslund, A. (1992). *Post-Communist Economic Revolutions. How Big a Bang?* Washington, DC: Center for Strategic and International Studies.

———. (1993). "Comment on 'Gradual versus Rapid Liberalisation in Socialist Economies' by McKinnon," *Proceedings of the World Bank Annual Conference on Development Economies.* Washington, DC: World Bank.

———. (1994). "The Case for Radical Reform," *Journal of Democracy* 5 (4): 63–74.

———. (1995). *How Russia Became a Market Economy.* Washington, DC: Brookings Institution.

———. (1997a). *Russia's Economic Transformation in the 1990s.* London: Pinter.

———. (1997b). "Epilogue," in *Russia's Economic Transformation in the 1990's,* edited by A. Ashlund. London: Pinter.

Aslund, A., P. P. Boone, and S. Johnson. (1996). "How to Stabilise; Lessons from Post-Communist Countries," *Brooking Papers on Economic Activity* 1: 217–291.

Balcerowicz, L., B. Blaszczyk, and M. Dabrowski. (1997). "The Polish Way to the Market Economy 1989–1995," in *Economies in Transition: Comparing Asia and Europe,* edited by W. T. Woo, S. Parker, and J. D. Sachs. Cambridge: MIT Press.

Bardhan, P. (2000). "The Nature of Institutional Impediments to Economic Development," in *A Not-So-Dismal Science: A Broader View of Economics and Societies,* edited by M. Olson and S. Kahkonen. New York: Oxford University Press.

Bim, A. (1992). "The Role of the State in Transitional Postcommunist Economies," in *The Post-Soviet Economy: Soviet and Western Perspectives,* edited by A. Aslund. New York: St. Martin's Press.

Blanchard, O., and R. Layard. (1993). "Overview," in *Post-Communist Reform: Pain and Progress,* edited by O. Blanchard, M. Boycko, R. Dabrowski, R. Dornbusch, R. Layard, and A. Shleifer. Cambridge: MIT Press.

Calvo, G. A., and J. A. Frenkel. (1991). "Credit Markets, Credibility and Economic Transformation," *Journal of Economic Perspectives* 5(4): 139–148.

Csaba, L. (1995). *The Capitalist Revolution in Eastern Europe: A Contribution to the Economic Theory of Systemic Change.* Cheltnam, UK: Edward Elgar.

Dornbusch, R. (1993). "Payments Arrangements Among the Republics" in *Post-Communist Reform: Pain and Progress,* edited by O. Blanchard, M. Boycko, R. Dabrowski, R. Dornbusch, R. Layard, and A. Shleifer. Cambridge: MIT Press.

Eichengreen, B., V. Grilli, and S. Fischer. (1993). "A Payments Mechanism for the Former Soviet Union: Is the EPU a Relevant Precedent?: Discussion," *Economic Policy* 17(October): 309–353.

Elster, I., C. Offe, and K. Preuss. (1997). *Institutional Design in Post-Communist Societies: Rebuilding the Ship at Sea.* Cambridge: Cambridge University Press.

Fedorov, B. (1992). "Monetary, Financial and Foreign Exchange Policy," in *The Post-Soviet Economy: Soviet and Western Perspectives,* edited by A. Aslund. New York: St. Martin's Press.

Fischer, S., and J. Frenkel. (1992). "Macroeconomic Issues of Soviet Reform," *American Economic Review Papers and Proceedings* 82(2): 37–42.

Fischer, S., and A. Gelb. (1991). "The Process of Socialist Economic Transformation," *Journal of Economic Perspectives* 5(4): 91–105.

Friedman, M. (1980). *Free to Choose.* Melbourne: Macmillan.

Frydman, R., A. Rapaczynski, and J. Turkewitz. (1997). "Transition to a Private Property Regime in the Czech Republic and Hungary," in *Economies in Transition: Comparing Asia and Europe,* edited by W. T. Woo, S. Parker, and J. D. Sachs. Cambridge: MIT Press.

Gustafson, T. (1999). *Capitalism Russian-Style.* Cambridge: Cambridge University Press.

Hare, P. G. (1991). "Hungary: In Transition to a Market Economy," *Journal of Economic Perspectives* 5(4): 195–201.

Hayek, F. A. (1986 [1944]). *The Road to Serfdom.* London: Ark Edition.

Intriligator, M. D. (1998). "Democracy in Reforming Collapsed Communist Economies: Blessing Or Curse?," *Contemporary Economic Policy* 16(2): 241–246.

Kolodko, G. W. (1993). "Stabilization, Recession, and Growth in a Post-Socialist Economy," *MOCT-MOST: Economic Journal on Eastern Europe and the Former Soviet Union* 1(January): 3–38.

———. (1999a). "Incomes Policy, Equity Issues, and Poverty Reduction in Transition Economies," *Finance and Development* September: 32–34.

———. (1999b). "Transition to a Market Economy and Sustained Growth. Implications for the Post-Washington Consensus," *Communist and Post-Communist Studies* 32(3): 233–261.

———. (2000). "Transition to a Market and Entrepreneurship: The Systemic Factors and Policy Options," *Communist and Post-Communist Studies* 33(3): 271–293.

Kornai, J. (1990). *The Road to a Free Economy.* New York: W.W. Norton.

———. (1992a). *The Socialist System: The Political Economy of Communism.* Oxford: Clarendon Press.

———. (1992b). "The Principles of Privatisation in Eastern Europe," *De Economist* 140(2): 153–176.

———. (1993a). "Transformational Recession: A General Phenomenon Examined through the Example of Hungary's Development," *In Economic Appliquee* 46(2): 181–227.

———. (1993b). "The Evolution of Financial Discipline under the Postsocialist System," *Kyklos* 46: 315–336.

———. (1994). "Transformational Recession: The Main Causes," *Journal of Comparative Economics* 19(1): 39–63.

———. (1995a). "Lasting Growth as the Top Priority: Macroeconomic Tensions and Government Economic Policy in Hungary," *Acta Oeconomica* 47(1–2): 1–38.

———. (1995b). *Highway and Byways: Studies on Reform and Post-Communist Transition.* Cambridge: MIT Press.

———. (1996). "Growth and Macroeconomic Disequilibria in Hungary," *Academia Economic Papers.* 24(1): 1–44.

———. (1997). *Struggle and Hope: Essays on Stabilization and Reform in a Post-Socialist Economy.* Cheltnam, UK: Edward Elgar.

Kregel, J., E. Matzner, and G. Grabher. (1992). *The Market Shock.* Vienna: AGENDA Group.

McKinnon, R. I. (1993). *The Order of Economic Liberalization: Financial Control in the Transition to a Market Economy.* Baltimore, MD: John Hopkins University Press.

———. (1995a). "Financial Growth and Macroeconomic Stability in the People's Republic of China 1978–1992: Implications for Russia and Eastern Europe," in *From Centrally Planned to Market Economies: The Asian Approach,* edited by P. B. Rana and N. Hamid. New York: Oxford University Press.

———. (1995b). "Taxation, Money, and Credit in the Transition from Central Planning," in *From Centrally Planned to Market Economies: The Asian*

Approach, edited by P. B. Rana and N. Hamid. New York: Oxford University Press.

Marangos, J. (forthcoming). "The Political Economy of Shock Therapy," *Journal of Economic Surveys.*

Martinez-Vazquez, J., F. Rioja, S. Skogstad, and N. Valen. (2001). "IMF Conditionality and Objections. The Russian Case," *American Journal of Economics and Sociology* 60(2): 501–517.

Mihalyi, P. (1993). "Hungary: A Unique Approach to Privatisation—Past, Present and Future," in *Hungary: An Economy in Transition,* edited by I. P. Szekely and D. M. G. Newbery. Cambridge: Cambridge University Press.

Murrell, P. (1992). "Evolutionary and Radical Approaches to Economic Reform," *Economics of Planning* 25: 79–95.

Nelson, R. R. (1995). "Recent Evolutionary Theorizing About Economic Change," *Journal of Economic Literature* 33(March): 48–90.

Nove, A. (1989). *Stalinism and After: The Road to Gorbachev.* London: Unwin Hyman.

Nuti, D. M. (1991). "Stabilization and Sequencing in the Reform of Socialist Economies," in *Managing Inflation in Socialist Economies in Transition,* edited by S. Commander. Washington, DC: World Bank.

Poirot, C. (1996). "Macroeconomic Policy in a Transitional Environment: Romania 1989–1994," *Journal of Economic Issues* 30(4): 1057–1075.

Roe, A. (1991). "Managing Inflation in Socialist Economies," in *Managing Inflation in Socialist Economies in Transition,* edited by S. Commander. Washington, DC: World Bank.

Rostowski, J. (1993). "Comment on 'Gradual versus Rapid Liberalisation in Socialist Economies' by McKinnon," *Proceedings of the World Bank Annual Conference on Development Economies.* Washington DC: World Bank.

Sachs J. (1990). "What is to be Done?," *Economist* January 13: 19–24.

———. (1991a). "Crossing the Valley of Tears in East European Reform," *Challenge* 34(5): 26–32.

———. (1991b). "Sachs on Poland," *Economist* January 19: 67.

———. (1993). *Poland's Jump to the Market Economy.* Cambridge: MIT Press.

———. (1994). "Toward Glasnost in the IMF," *Challenge* 37(3): 4–11.

———. (1995). "Consolidating Capitalism," *Foreign Policy* 98(Spring): 50–64.

———. (1996a). "The Transition in the Mid Decade," *American Economic Review Papers and Proceedings* 86(2): 128–133.

———. (1996b). "Economic Transition and the Exchange-Rate Regime," *American Economic Review Papers and Proceedings* 86(2): 147–152.

———. (1997). "An Overview of Stabilisation Issues Facing Economies in Transition," in *Economies in Transition: Comparing Asia and Europe,* edited by W. T. Woo, S. Parker, and J. D. Sachs. Cambridge: MIT Press.

Sachs, J., and D. Lipton. (1990). "Poland's Economic Reform," *Foreign Affairs* 69(3): 47–66.

Samonis, V., and C. Hunyadi. (1993). *Big Bang and Acceleration: Models for the Postcommunist Economic Transformation.* New York: Nova Science.

Schlack, R. F. (1996). "Economics of Transition: Hypotheses Toward a Reasonable Economics," *Journal of Economic Issues* 30(2): 617–627.

Smyth, R. (1998). "New Institutional Economics in the Post-Socialist Transformation Debate," *Journal of Economic Surveys* 12(4): 361–398.

Stark, D. (1990). "Privatization in Hungary: From Plan to Market or from Plan to Clan?," *East European Politics and Societies* 4(3): 351–392.

Sutela, P. (1992) "The Role of the External Sector during the Transition," in *The Post-Soviet Economy: Soviet and Western Perspectives,* edited by A. Aslund. New York: St. Martin's Press.

Svejnar, J. (1991). "Microeconomic Issues in the Transition to a Market Economy," *Journal of Economic Perspectives* 5(4): 123–138.

Szekely, I. P., and D. M. G. Newbery. (1993). "Introduction," in *Hungary: An Economy in Transition,* edited by I. P. Szekely and D. M. G. Newbery. Cambridge: Cambridge University Press.

Van Brabant, J. M. (1991). "Convertibility in Eastern Europe Through a Payments Union," in *Currency Convertability in Eastern Europe,* edited by J. Williamson. Washington, DC: Institute for International Economics.

Wagener, H. J. (2000). "Has Russia Missed the Boat?," *Journal of Institutional and Theoretical Economics* 156(1): 125–130.

Walters, A. (1992). "The Transition to a Market Economy," in *The Emergence of Market Economies in Eastern Europe,* edited by C. Clauge and G. Rausser. Cambridge, MA: Blackwell.

Williamson, J. (1991). "The Case for a Payments Union," *International Economic Insights* September/October: 11–14.

———. (1992). *Trade and Payments After Soviet Disintegration.* Washington, DC: Institute of International Economics.

Wolf, T. A. (1991). "The Lessons of Limited Market-Oriented Reform," *Journal of Economic Perspectives* 5(4): 45–58.

PART VI

New Perspectives on Transition Economies: Asia

American Journal of Economics and Sociology, Vol. 61, No. 1 (January, 2002).

Privilege and Corruption

The Problems of China's Socialist Market Economy

By SHUNTIAN YAO

ABSTRACT. It is well known that China's corruption problem has become more and more serious during the period of economic reform. This paper examines China's corruption problem with the help of several simple economic models. The author proposes the concepts of implicit corruption and explicit corruption. We explain how the granting of privileges has directly created implicit corruption in China's socialist market economy. We argue that the long-term existence of the same privileged group in Chinese society has led to widespread collusion among its members, and as a result, these privileged group members, by utilizing their monopoly power, are able to seize almost all the wealth created by the ordinary Chinese people. This seizure is accomplished by means of a two-part tariff in pricing their administrative service, which is the essence of the explicit corruption. Finally, we point out that, because both implicit corruption and explicit corruption are generated by China's political system, which grants and protects privileges, unless a political reform is initiated and privileges are eliminated, China's problem of corruption will never be solved.

I

Introduction

SEVERAL YEARS AGO, when I discussed China's problem of corruption with a simple game theoretical model (Yao 1997), I predicted that, as the GNP grew, the level of corruption and the emphasis on anti-corruption by the Chinese Communist Party (CCP) leaders would in-

*Shuntian Yao, Associate Professor at Division of Applied Economics, Nanyang Business School, Nanyang Technological University, Singapore, has interests in Game Theory, Mathematical Economics and the Chinese Economic Reform. He has publications in *Journal of Economic Theory, Journal of Mathematical Economics*, and *Games and Economic Behavior*. A joint paper with Professor Young Sik Kim on a money search model is forthcoming in *The Economic Journal*. The particulars of Shuntian Yao are: Tel: 65 790 5559; E-mail: *astyao@ntu.edu.sg*.

American Journal of Economics and Sociology, Vol. 61, No. 1 (January, 2002).

crease simultaneously. In the last several years, my prediction has been proved completely accurate, although this does not give me any satisfaction. Recently, Ms He Qinglian, a well-known Chinese political economic expert, has some good publications (He 1997, 1998) on China's political and economic problems during the economic reform. In particular she has correctly pointed out that the widespread corruption problem is generated by China's political and economic system. The general arguments and the analysis I will present in this paper will provide support to He's assessment.

In the game theoretical model in Yao (1997), my main focus was on the political relationships between three groups of individuals in the Chinese population. In this paper, however, I will analyze the corruption problem by concentrating on the basic economic mechanism of China's socialist market economy. Through the analysis of some simple economic models, we point out that the fundamental cause of corruption is privilege, which is granted and protected by the ruling class—the CCP.

The rest of the paper is divided into six sections. In Section II we provide some arguments as to what is the root of corruption. Some different views concerning this question are quoted, together with our comments on them. We then present our general arguments, pointing out that the presence of privilege in China's political system is the fundamental cause of implicit corruption in the short run and of explicit corruption in the long run. To make our general arguments convincing, we examine some formal economic models. A basic general equilibrium model is constructed in Section III. Then in the subsequent sections we compare the Walrasian equilibria that result in different political and economic environments. The readers will see that all the results derived from our mathematical models do support our general arguments. We conclude our discussion in Section VII.

II

The Root of China's Corruption

Since Deng Xiaoping launched China's economic reform in the late 1970s, the Chinese economy has been growing at an exceedingly high rate, but corruption crimes have become more and more widespread and the average social wealth loss in each corruption case has become more and more substantial. Today, no one, including the Chinese Communist Party leaders, would deny that corruption has become a fatal problem of China's economy and a cancer of the Chinese society. However, with respect to the fundamental cause of the corruption problems, there exist many diversified views.

The so-called New Leftists, with Dr. Cui Zhiyuan as one of their representatives, accuse that corruption is caused by the capitalist market mechanism introduced by China's open-door policy. These leftists spare no effort to criticize the Reform. They argue that China's rapid economic development in the past 20 years actually benefitted from the solid economic foundation laid in Mao's era. On the other hand, all the bad things, such as inflation, unemployment and corruption, according to their arguments, are direct consequence of the Reform because capitalism has been introduced and people have become completely money-oriented. (Refer to, for example, the article by Xin Mao in Issue zs9809a of the online magazine "China and the World.") They advocate that China should restore Mao's socialist political and economic system, arguing that this is the only way to save China from all kinds of social troubles. (See the article by Zheng Yanshi, "On the Merits of Mao Zedong and Mao Zedong Thought—In Memory of Mao Zedong on his 105 Birthday," Issues zs9709a–zs9801a of "China and the World.")

The New Leftist scholars have not been able to find many supporters except a small number of former CCP officials (and their children and relatives) who have lost their powers or privilege during the Reform. The majority of the Chinese people, including many of the unemployed workers, have never forgotten their sufferings in Mao's era during the economic and political movements such as the Great Leap Forward and the Great Cultural Revolution. While they hate corruption and are not satisfied with the current economic situation, they have no good memory of the Mao era. After all, as can be seen from our analysis that follows, Mao cannot escape responsibility for the offense that it was he who created a political system granting and protecting privilege, which is the very root of China's corruption problems.

Some people hold the view that China's corruption problems have their root deep in the Chinese culture. They argue that the Chinese people, as well as most of their counterparts in Asian countries, have a long tradition of placing personal connections above the law, and that this is the real source of corruption. They conclude that, no matter what political system China chooses, the corruption problem can never be avoided. Many CCP officials and business bigwigs agree with this view, although they do not admit it in public. I have had discussions with several friends who are either CCP officials or very successful businessmen; all of them privately supported this view. They even argued that corruption was not too bad, and that if you could take advantage of it, it could work for you very efficiently, and that, after all, you had to accept it if you wanted to survive in China.

The culture-root view fails to realize that, while culture might affect people's social behavior, a political system together with a legal system of society could introduce a new social norm, changing people's way of thinking and their behavior, and changing culture itself gradually. In China's history, such as during the early Han Dynasty and the early Tang Dynasty, there were actually periods of rule of law, and no serious corruption crimes were recorded. On the other hand, the darkest periods in China's history are all related to a corrupt political system and to the illegal behaviors of a tiny group of bigwigs or aristocrats who were protected by a fatuous and self-indulgent ruler.

Most Chinese economists and scholars, however, correctly observe that the cause of China's current corruption problems is the lack of separation between business and government brought about by efforts to open up the Chinese economy. Dr. Xu Cheng Gang, a lecturer at the London School of Economics, argues that, with China in the midst of economic upheaval, the government continues to allocate resources, placing officials at the center of the market and enabling them to channel profits into their own pockets. (Refer to BBC News, September 13, 2000.) The observation of Dr. Xu is of course correct. However, like most other Chinese scholars, he does not go the further step, and expose the root of corruption in China's political and economic system.

Since the CCP came into power, in order to secure their hold, their top leaders have been paying great attention to the problem of selection of "successors." A tiny percentage of their former subordinates and many children of the top CCP leaders—the princelings—have been chosen as candidates. The princelings, beginning from a young age, have enjoyed various kinds of privileges, from attending the top universities to choosing the best occupations. After a period of training and practice, many of the princelings have been promoted to heads of CCP organizations or to heads of important government departments. Today, the leading members in the CCP central committee, the top-level central government officials, the highest-ranked military officials, the heads of the provincial governments and the heads of the major state-owned enterprises, except for a very tiny percentage, are all members of this privileged class.

Although a privileged group member may be incompetent and may have low IQ, his position nevertheless makes him an important figure in political and economic affairs. To the paramount CCP leaders, he is their reliable representative in a state department or in a local region of the country, monitoring the public for them; to the ordinary people working in his department or living in his region, he is the law. Usually what he himself has to do is no more than drawing circles on documents and then signing his name on them, or passing on the instructions of the paramount leaders to their subordinates and reporting to his boss the main events or trends in his region. All these duties are of primary importance, according to the CCP tradition. The state grants him many special benefits in exchange for his loyalty, providing him and his family with cars and drivers, nurses and housekeepers, and even paying most of his expenses, although his salary is much higher than any ordinary employee. While these high-ranked officials firmly control the power of making decisions, many of the real administration duties are actually done by their secretaries and their subordinates. Thus what they exploit from society by far exceeds what they actually contribute to it. We will refer to this as *implicit corruption*. We call this "corruption" because it leads to social unfairness and destroys economic efficiency. We use the adjective "implicit" because the utility received by a privileged group member to some extent reflects his important role in decision making, given a CCP political and economic environment. The total utility he receives could be regarded as an equilibrium price for his service in a Walrasian market subject to some environment constraints. To put it another way, although a privileged group member receives many more benefits than he ought to according to the criterion of a *free market*, these benefits are "legally" entitled to him by the CCP political and economic system. He obtains these benefits without doing anything against the law.

Implicit corruption continued to be the dominant form of corruption in China until Mao's death. We suggest two reasons for it. First, Mao had always maintained his superior position over all his comrades in the CCP central committee. While he admitted the existence of the privileged class, he wanted to control the privileges of its members within some dimensions. He never allowed them to collude with each other to make higher political or economic benefits than were allowed. He regarded any kind of collusion among the privileged group members as a potential threat against his control over them and over all important national affairs. Second, before the Reform, there did not exist any significant private sector or private business in China's economy; almost all the economic activities were under the control of the state. As a result, the privileged group members did not have the chance to fully utilize their power to exploit any substantial economic benefits.

After Mao's death, Deng became the top leader of the CCP, but he did not have a superior position over the other paramount CCP officials, and thus was not able to prevent the aristocratic households from consolidating their connections among each other and expanding their privilege. This led to a widespread *explicit corruption* in the early 1980s. The naïve form of explicit corruption is "doing business through the back doors," which has two meanings. Between the high-ranked officials themselves, it refers to their bribing each other with the state-owned resources they control. The head of a state-owned TV production company, say, could present color TVs as gifts to the head of a human resource department in exchange for decent official positions for his family members. Between these high-ranked officials and the majority of the people, it refers to the fact that the latter must bribe the former in order to do business with them. Otherwise, any request could be denied by these officials even if the request is within their duty. Complaining is useless because all these officials have formed collusion, thus no one would take notice.

In this aspect my experience could serve as a good example. After I completed my Ph.D. degree in the United States I returned to Guangzhou in early 1989, upon request by the Chinese government, to serve in Guangzhou University. However, it took eight months for me to restore my residence permit in Guangzhou, and when it finally came through I had spent quite a substantial amount of money for bribes. We call extortion of bribes "explicit" corruption of the privileged class members, because obtaining personal benefits in such a way is not legally allowed by the political system, although this kind of behavior is tolerated by the CCP leaders in most cases.

As China's economy grows in the Reform, explicit corruption also evolves. Many of the privileged group members have learned how to utilize their monopoly power in the markets. They became price searchers, demanding higher and higher bribes for doing business with ordinary people. The bribes could be a very substantial amount of money and privately are referred to as "commissions," although this is not an adequate term. The "commission" incomes of these privileged group members are never recorded in any account, and could be thousands of times higher than their normal wages. (See Yao 1997.) Just as we will describe in a formal economic model, these privileged group members have learned the two-part tariff strategy of a monopolist. The commission fees they charge are very much the same as the entrance fee charged by the monopolist in order to exploit all the consumer surplus of his customers. It is in this sense that the New Leftists accuse that China's corruption is caused by the introduction of capitalism. Yet there are fundamental differences between a monopolist and a Chinese privileged group member. A monopolist works for himself, uses his private-owned capital, and pays tax against his profit, whereas a Chinese privileged group member works for the state in name, uses state-owned resources, and pays no tax against the unrecorded "commission" income. Thus explicit corruption has its specifically Chinese characteristics.

We have told a sufficiently long story concerning China's corruption. Our main point is that the presence of privilege is the root of China's corruption problem. In the next several sections, we will justify our assertions with the analysis of several formal economic models.

III

Description of a Formal Model

CHINA HAS ONE OF the largest economies in the world. It is very difficult to establish any quantitatively precise general equilibrium model for it. Fortunately, to analyze the problem of privilege and corruption, we can deal with the basic economic principles and basic economic structures. As a result, it is possible to examine this problem with a very simple theoretical model without going into precise quantitative details.

Consider an economy E with two consumer goods, say good 1 and good 2. Assume that there are a continuum of individuals with a measure of 1, which may be represented by all the points in the closed real number interval of [0, 1]. Assume that all the individuals are *ex ante* identical, and that each individual is endowed with 1 unit of labor per period and each has the following utility function:

$$u = z_1 z_2 \tag{1}$$

where z_1 and z_2, respectively, are the amounts of good 1 and good 2 each individual consumes.

Further assume that to produce consumer goods, while labor is always a necessary input, an intermediate good, good 3, is also required. In our model, good 3 may be referred to as high-level administrative service, or the service of providing permits for setting up business and providing major financial assistance, etc. To be specific, let us assume that each individual has the same Cobb-Douglas production function for the production of good 1 and good 2:

$$q_j = \max\left\{0, \left(l_j - a\right)s_j^\alpha\right\}, \, j = 1,2 \tag{2}$$

where q_j is the quantity of good j produced, l_j and s_j are the labor input and the service input, respectively, a is a positive constant and α is a positive constant less than 1. From (2) we can see that the production function of any consumer good is weakly convex in the labor input, and is strictly concave in the input of administration service.

On the other hand, let us assume that each individual has the same production function for good 3:

$$s = \max \{0, c(l - b)\} \tag{3}$$

where s is the quantity of good 3 produced, l is the labor input and b and c are two positive constants. The constants a and b in the production functions can be interpreted as fixed production costs or learning costs. We assume that $0 < a < 1$ and $0 < b < 1$. According to China's situation, we may also assume that

$$a + b \geq 1 \tag{4}$$

The implication of (4) is that any individual who chooses the occupation of high-level administrative service (or high-ranked bureaucrat) will completely specialize in his profession.

We assume that the transaction efficiency coefficient for any consumer good is k with $0 < k \leq 1$, meaning that if any individual purchases an amount y of any consumer good, then the amount that individual finally receives and consumes is ky. We assume that the transaction efficiency coefficient for the administration service is 1.

IV

A Free Market Economy

WE FIRST CONSIDER an ideal society in which every individual is allowed to choose her occupation freely. As a result, a decision plan of individual i is $d^i = (l^i_1, l^i_2, l^i_3; x^i_1, x^i_2, x^i_3, y^i_1, y^i_2, y^i_3)$, where l^i_j is the amount of labor she allocates for good j's production, x^i_j is the amount of good j she sells and y^i_j is the amount of good j she buys. The following constraints must be satisfied:

$$l^i_1 \geq 0, l^i_1 + l^i_2 + l^i_3 \leq 1; \; 0 \leq x^i_j \leq q^i_j, \; j = 1,2;$$
$$y^i_j \geq 0, \; p_1 y^i_1 + p_2 y^i_2 + p_3 y^i_3 \leq p_1 x^i_1 + p_2 x^i_2 + p_3 x^i_3 \tag{*}$$

where q^i_j (q^i_3 now represents the amount of the administrative service produced) are as defined in equations (2) and (3) with all the variables having a superscript i. Obviously when we use the notation in equation (2) for q^i_1 and q^i_2, the above-mentioned constraints imply that $s^i_1 + 1s^i_2 \leq \max\{0, c(l^i_3 - b)\} - x^i_3 + y^i_3$. The final consumption of i

can be computed by $z^i_j = \max\{0,(l_j - a)\, s^i_{ja}\} - x^i_j + k y^i_j, j = 1,2$. Thus i achieves a utility of $u(z^i_1 z^i_2) = z^i_1 z^i_2$.

A *Walrasian equilibrium* of such an economy is defined as a price vector $p = (p_1, p_2, p_3)$ and a decision plan d^i for every individual i in the population, such that (a) given p, d^i maximizes the utility of i when she is allowed to choose among all feasible decision plans $(l^i_1, l^i_2, l^i_3; x^i_1, x^i_2, x^i_3, y^i_1, y^i_2, y^i_3)$ satisfying (*), and (b) the excess demand of every good is less than or equal to zero: $\int_{[0,1]} y^i_j \leq \int_{[0,1]} x^i_j, j = 1,2,3$.

It is not difficult to establish the following:

Proposition 1. In our model with *ex ante* identical individuals and freedom of choice of professions, every individual must achieve the same equilibrium utility. Moreover, when the transaction efficiency is sufficiently close to 1 in any Walrasian equilibrium of the economy, the equilibrium utility is $U^* = k^{1+\alpha}(1 - a)^2 c^{2\alpha}(1 - b)^{2\alpha}\alpha^{2\alpha}(1 - \alpha)^{2-2\alpha}/4$. In particular, when $a = 0.2, b = 0.5, c = 10, \alpha = 0.1$, we have $U^* = 0.115226 k^{1.1}$.

The proof of this proposition is given in the Appendix.

V

A Market Economy with the Presence of Privilege

IN THE LATE 1980s, the head of a large joint venture company in Shenzhen who was a princeling and former high-ranked Communist Party official of Guangdong Province, told me that in doing business he could take advantage of both of China's socialist political system and the capitalist market mechanism. I totally agreed with him. It was China's socialist political system that granted him the privilege of choosing his occupation as head of a joint venture company in the SEZ, and it was the capitalist market mechanism that enabled him to earn a huge amount of money through domestic and foreign business.

As is well known, in China it is not the case that every citizen is able to freely choose his or her occupation. Whether or not one is qualified for a desirable job does not generally depend on one's intelligence or capability. In particular, the occupation of high-level administrator is the privilege granted by CCP to a tiny group of people who are either high-ranked Chinese Communist Party cadres or the princelings. According to the Chinese leaders, an economy with the power to make high-level decisions firmly controlled by a tiny group of high-ranked CCP officials is referred to as a *socialist market economy*.

To model such an economy, let us assume that a small portion ρ of individuals are chosen by the CCP leaders to be permitted to work as high-level administrators. Of course they are also allowed to choose other professions if they wish, and as a result, each one of them has the same set of feasible decision plans as described in the last section. However, as we can see below, if ρ is sufficiently small, every one of them will be happy to enjoy his or her privilege and will choose the profession of high-level administrative service. On the other hand, all the other individuals are only allowed to produce consumer goods. Hence in their decision plans $(l^i_1, l^i_2, l^i_3; x^i_1, x^i_2, x^i_3, y^i_1, y^i_2, y^i_3)$ an additional constraint is added, namely $l^i_3 = 0$. The definition of a Walrasian equilibrium is thus revised accordingly. With this change, even at equilibrium we can no longer guarantee utility equalization across the whole population. Because any individual not allowed to choose the profession of an administrator is subject to one more constraints, his or her equilibrium utility must be always less than or at most equal to that of those having the privilege.

Proposition 2. If only a subset of individuals in the population are allowed to choose any profession freely, then any member in this subset will always achieve a utility level larger or equal to those not in the subset. In particular, if only a very tiny percentage of individuals are allowed to choose the profession of high-level administrative service, at the Walrasian equilibrium, each member of this privileged group could achieve a much higher utility than any individual lacking this privilege.

Remark

That ρ is far less than the percentage of high-level administrators required by a free market is in accordance with China's situation. One reason is that the CCP restricts the selection to those high-ranked party cadres or their successors, and a second reason is that the CCP wants to have a firm control over the high-level economic decision making.

The proof of Proposition 2 can be found in the Appendix.

To give a numerical comparison of these results with what we obtained in the previous section, let us assume that $a = 0.2$, $b = 0.5$, $c = 10$, $\alpha = 0.1$ and that $k = 0.9$, $(1 - \rho)/\rho = 20$.[1] We then have

$$p = 0.3134, \quad U^* = 0.10262, \quad U' = 0.49724, \quad U'(B) = 0.086116 \qquad (5)$$

where U^* is the equilibrium utility in a free market economy, as was obtained in the last section, U' is the equilibrium utility of every privileged group member and $U'(B)$ is the equilibrium utility for every ordinary individual. We thus see in our numerical example that with the presence of privilege, the utility of ordinary people declines by 20 percent, while the utility of any privileged group member increases 390 percent. This unfairness in wealth distribution among *ex ante* identical individuals is directly created by the political system that grants and protects privileges. As mentioned in Section II, we refer to it as an *implicit corruption* problem of the socialist market economy.

We can also compare the consumption of any individual in the free market economy as described in Section III with that in the socialist market economy as described in this section. From the Appendix, it is easy to verify that in the free market economy as described in the previous section, any consumer good producer consumes 0.33767 units of his or her production and 0.30390 units of the other consumer good, and any administrator consumes 0.32034 units of each of the two consumer goods. In the socialist market economy as described in this section, we can also compute that any consumer good producer consumes 0.30933 units of his or her production and 0.27840 units of the other consumer good, and any individual in the privileged group consumes 0.70515 unit of each of the two consumer goods.

VI

Connection, Collusion, Two-Part Tariff and Explicit Corruption

WE NOW CONTINUE the discussion of our story of China's socialist market economy. Although such an economy is usually not efficient and leads to an unfair wealth distribution, it would not have been too bad if every individual in the privileged group acted independently as a price taker in a Walrasian market. As in our analysis in Section V, the price of the administrative service could be not too high because of the competition among the privileged group members themselves. Unfortunately, the real situation in China is much worse. These privileged group members in Chinese society, because of their similar political backgrounds, have steadily built up political and economic connections between themselves since the CCP came into power, especially after Mao's death and after the open-door policy had been introduced by Deng. As a result, when playing any political or economic games, they can actually collude with each other. If their nationwide collusion is not solid enough, at least the collusion of any small group in their regional area is nearly complete. Thus, in the socialist market economy, these individuals are no longer price takers; instead they act more like monopolists.

To revise our model accordingly, we may imagine that there is an agent who acts for the interests of all the administrators, and who will utilize his monopoly power by introducing two-part tariffs to sell their administrative service. Every individual outside the privileged group is required to pay an entrance fee (for bribery) to the privileged group in order to set up a business relationship with them. Let us assume that the entrance fee F can be paid by credit in terms of the producer's produce. Then the new decision problem of any good j producer is to choose a pair of (s,y) to solve

$$\max u = k\big[(1 - a)s^a - F - ps - y\big]y \tag{6}$$

The following constraint must be satisfied:

$$y \geq 0, \ (1 - a)s^a - F - ps - y \geq 0 \tag{7}$$

It is easy to verify that the utility in (6) is maximized when $y = [(1 - a) s^a - F - ps]/2$ and $s = [\alpha(1 - a)/p]^{1/(1-\alpha)}$. Thus we can see that the price for administrative service is the same as that determined in Section V. On the other hand, the entrance fee F depends on the reservation utility of this consumer good producer. In an extreme case, the reservation utility for a consumer good producer could be as low as what could be derived from her "unemployment benefit," which she could receive from the government if she had failed to set up her business. If u is the reservation utility for every ordinary individual not in the privileged group, then after computing p and s as mentioned above, the entrance fee F is determined by

$$\frac{k\left[(1-a)s^a - F - ps\right]^2}{4} = u \tag{8}$$

On the other hand, it is easy to verify that, under two-part tariff pricing, each member in the privileged group will achieve a utility of

$$U'' = 0.25k^2\left\{a(1-a)c^a(1-b)^a[(1-\rho)/(5\rho)]^{1-a} + 0.5F\right\}^2 \tag{9}$$

Obviously, if u were quite small, then F could be quite large, and U'' could be much larger then U'. This leads to the following.

Proposition 3. With connection and collusion, each member of the privileged group, through levying an entrance fee on every consumer good producer who requires his administrative service, could consume much larger amounts of consumer goods than he could consume in a Walrasian market and achieve a much higher utility.

To interpret this idea, we return to the numerical example previously discussed. Assume that the reservation utility for any ordinary person is $u = 0.04k = 0.036$, which is achieved when her final consumption amount of her production is 0.2 and her final consumption amount of the other consumer good is $0.2k = 0.18$. Comparing this with our results in Section V, we see that from each consumer good producer, the agent of the privileged group can charge an entrance fee equal to $2(0.30933 - 0.2) = 0.21866$ units of her produce. Therefore, each member in the privileged group can consume $0.70515 + [0.5(1 - \rho)/\rho](0.21866k) = 2.67309$ units of each of the two consumer goods, ending up with a utility of 7.14541. Thus, by levying entrance fees, any privileged group member consumes more than 10 times as much as any ordinary individual. Of course our numerical results are only good for illustration, and actually the uneven wealth distribution in today's Chinese society is even much more serious. According to some China experts, "The phenomenon of an increasing gap between rich and poor also applies to China where by now the richest 1.3% of the families control 31.5% of the assets and the poorest 44% of the families control 3%." (See *Le Monde Diplomatique*, January 1999, pp. 16–17.)

While levying entrance fees has become extremely widespread in Chinese society today and is usually tolerated by the CCP leaders, bribery is still regarded as illegal by the law, at least theoretically. Thus as mentioned in Section II, we refer to this kind of corruption as *explicit corruption*.

VII

Concluding Remarks

IN THE ABOVE DISCUSSION we have seen that, while implicit corruption makes an economy inefficient, explicit corruption could produce an extremely uneven wealth distribution in a society, creating instability and turmoil. As we have pointed out, implicit corruption is directly generated by privilege. On the other hand, if the existence of the same privileged group lasts for a sufficiently long period, the connection and collusion among its members will be inevitable. Therefore, explicit corruption can be regarded as a long-term product of privilege. We thus see that all of China's corruption problems actually are rooted in its political system that grants and protects privileges. To some extent, our argument explains why corruption can exist in Chinese society in the Economic Reform Period, and why it has become more and more serious during the last 10 years, at the same time as the CCP leaders frequently pledge to raise a war against it.

In fact, as pointed out by Yao (1997), unless a political reform is initiated and all kinds of privileges are eliminated, China's corruption problem will never be thoroughly solved.

Appendix

Proof of Proposition 1. We first prove that all individuals must have the same equilibrium utility. Assume the contrary, that at a Walrasian equilibrium an individual i has an equilibrium utility lower than another individual i'. Then i could make an improvement by switching to the configuration chosen by i' and making the same decision as i', which implies that the original decision of i is not a utility maximization decision! Thus the first part of the theorem is proved.

We now compute a Walrasian equilibrium of the above-mentioned economy E, which is a relatively more difficult task. Because of the symmetry in good 1 and good 2, we expect an equilibrium price vector being $(1,1,p)$, where p is the equilibrium price of the administrative service. According to the generalized Wen Theorem (refer to Wen 1998 and Yao 2000), with increasing returns to scale production techniques, any Walrasian equilibrium can be achieved in such a way that every individual sells at most one good, and that every individual will not simultaneously produce and buy the same good. We therefore divide the consumer good producers into two groups, each characterized by the good its members sell. At equilibrium we can expect that the measure of the group of good 1 sellers, say μ, should be the same as that of the group of good 2 sellers, and that the measure of the group of professional administrators is $1 - 2v$ $(0 < \mu < 1)$. Here the value of μ is to be determined.

To examine the decision of a seller of good 1, we first observe that there are three types of basic decision plans available to her: (O) autarky—not trading at all, (A) buying good 3 with credit, producing both of the consumer goods, selling good 1, and (B) buying good 3 with credit, producing good 1, selling good 1, buying good 2. We will refer to each of these decision plans as a configuration. Because the administrative service is a necessary input in any production process, this good 1 seller can only achieve utility of 0 in the autarky structure (O). We now consider configuration (A). Assume that this individual buys s units of administrative service, then uses s_j units of it for the production of consumer good j. Assume that she allocates $l_j \cdot a$ units of labor for good j's production. Then she will produce $q_j = (l_j - a)s_j$ units of good j. Let x be the amount of good 1 she sells in the market; for her budget to balance it must hold that $x = ps$. Note that we must have $s_2 = s - s_1$ and $l_2 = 1 - 2a - l_1$. As a result her final consumption is given by $z_1 = [(l_1-a)s_1{}^\alpha -ps]$ and $z_2 = (1-l_1 - a)(1 + s - s_1)\alpha$. Therefore if this individual wants to choose configuration (A), her decision plan is to find a (l_1,s,s_1) to maximize

$$u = [(l_1 - a)s_1^\alpha - ps](1 - l_1 - a)(1 + s - s_1)\alpha \tag{A1}$$

The following constraints must be satisfied:

$$a \le l_1 \le l - a, (l_1 - a)s_1^a - ps \le 0, 0 \le s_1 \le s \qquad (A2)$$

Note that (A2) defines a compact set in (l_1, s, s_1)-space and that u defined in (A1) is continuous on this compact set. As a result, u must attain its maximal value somewhere in the set. We will denote this maximal value of u by $U(A)$.

We now consider configuration (B). In this case this individual will devote all her labor and all the administrative services she buys for the production of good 1. Let y be the amount of good 2 she will purchase. In addition to the amount of ps of good 1 she has to sell in exchange for the administrative service, she now has to sell y units more in exchange for good 2 in order to achieve budget balance. As a result, her final consumption is given by

$$z_1 = [(1 - a)s^a - ps - y], z_2 = ky \qquad (A3)$$

Therefore, her decision problem is to choose a (s, y) to maximize

$$u = [k(1 - a)s^a - ps - y]y \qquad (A4)$$

The following constraint must be satisfied:

$$y \ge 0, (1 - a)s^a - ps - y \ge 0 \qquad (A5)$$

Please note that (A5) also defines a compact set in the (s, y)-plane. Thus the maximal value of u defined in (A4) is achieved somewhere in this set. We will denoted it by $U(B)$.

Although to compute the maximum of (A1) is not so easy, we can establish a useful result concerning $U(A)$ and $U(B)$.

Lemma 1. When the transaction efficiency k is sufficiently close to 1, we have $U(B) > U(A)$. As a result, every good 1 producer specializes in good 1's production.

Proof. Assume that the maximum of (A1) is (l_1^*, s^*, s_1^*). In (A4) we choose $s = s^*$, and $y^* = [(1 - a)s^* {}^{\alpha} - ps^*]/2$. Obviously we have

$$U(B) \ge u(s^*, y^*) = k[(1 - s)s^{*a} - ps^*]^2 / 4 \qquad (A6)$$

What we need to show is that $u(s^*, y^*) > U(A)$ when k is sufficiently close to 1. In fact, by the relationship of the geometric mean and the arithmetic mean of two non-negative real numbers, we have

$$U(A) = [(l_1^* - a)s_1^{*a} - ps^*](1 - l_1^* - a)(1 + s^* - s_1^*)^\alpha < [(l_1^* -$$
$$a)s^{*a} - ps^*](1 - l_1^* - a)s^{*a} \cdot [(l_1^* - a)s^* - ps^* + (1 - l_1^* - \qquad \text{(A7)}$$
$$a)s^{*a}]^2 / 4 = [(1 - 2a)s^{*a} - ps^*]^2 / 4 < [(1 - a)s^{*a} - ps]^2 / 4$$

Now comparing (A6) with (A7), it is obvious that $U(A) < U(B)$ when k is sufficiently close to 1. Lemma 1 is thus proved.

We can now continue the proof of Proposition 1. To compute $U(B)$ by the relationship of the geometric mean and the arithmetic mean again, we see that

$$k[(1 - a)s^\alpha - ps - y]y \leq k[(1 - a)s^\alpha - ps]^2 / 4 \qquad \text{(A8)}$$

And (A8) becomes an equality if and only if

$$y = [(1 - a)s^\alpha - ps] / 2 \qquad \text{(A9)}$$

Furthermore, the right-hand side of (A8) is maximized at

$$s = [\alpha(1 - a) / p]^{1/(1-\alpha)} \qquad \text{(A10)}$$

We thus have

$$U(B) = k(1 - a)^{2/(1-\alpha)}\alpha^{2\alpha/(1-\alpha)}(1 - \alpha)^2 / [4p^{2\alpha/(1-\alpha)}] \qquad \text{(A11)}$$

By symmetry, any good 2 seller must have the same maximal equilibrium utility.

Now consider the decision of any administrative service producer. The maximal amount of service he can produce is $c(1 - b)$. By symmetry he will spend half of it in exchange for good 1, and half for good 2, consuming an amount

$$z = pkc(1 - b) / 2 \qquad \text{(A12)}$$

of each consumer good. As a result his equilibrium utility is

$$U = k^2p^2c^2(1 - b)^2 / 4 \qquad \text{(A13)}$$

To continue the equilibrium computation, according to Proposition 1, at equilibrium we must have

$$k^2 p^2 c^2 (1 - b)^2 / 4 = k(1 - a)^{2/(1-a)} a^{2a/(1-a)} (1 - a)^2 / [4 p^{2a/(1-a)}] \text{ (A14)}$$

from which we can solve

$$p = \frac{(1 - a) a^a (1 - a)^{1-a}}{k^{(1-a)/2} c^{1-a} (1 - b)^{1-a}} \qquad \text{(A15)}$$

Substituting (A15) into (A13) we get

$$U = U(B) = U^* = k^{1+a} (1 - a)^2 c^{2a} (1 - b)^{2a} a^{2a} (1 - a)^{2-2a} / 4 \qquad \text{(A16)}$$

which is the equilibrium utility for every individual in E. Substituting (A15) into (A10), we get

$$s = k^{1/2} a c (1 - b) / (1 - a) \qquad \text{(A17)}$$

For the market to be cleared, we must have

$$2\mu [k^{1/2} a c (1 - b) / (1 - a)] = (1 - 2\mu) c (1 - b) \qquad \text{(A18)}$$

from which one solves

$$\mu = (1 - a) / [2(1 - a) + 2a k^{1/2}], \ 1 - 2\mu = a k^{1/2} / [(1 - a) + a k^{1/2}] \qquad \text{(A19)}$$

Finally, let us assume that $a = 0.2$, $b = 0.5$, $c = 10$, $\alpha = 0.1$. Substituting them into the above formulas we get

$$U^* = 0.115226 k^{11}, \ p = 0.13578 k^{-0.45}, \ \mu = 9 / (18 + 2k^{1/2}),$$
$$1 - 2\mu = k^{1/2} / (9 + k^{1/2}), \ s = 0.55555 k^{0.5}, \ z_1 = y = 0.33944 k^{0.05},$$
$$z_2 = 0.33944 k^{1.05}, \ z = 0.33945 k^{0.55} \qquad \text{(A20)}$$

The proof of Proposition 1 is thus complete.

Proof of Proposition 2. We need only do some calculations. Let us assume that all the individuals having the privilege take advantage of it and choose the profession of high-level administrative service. Then, while equations (A10), (A11), (A12), and (A13) are still valid, equation (A14) must be replaced by the market-clearing condition for administrative service:

$$(1 - \rho)[\alpha(1 - a) / p]^{1/(1-\alpha)} = \rho c(1 - b) \qquad (A14')$$

From (A14') one solves

$$\rho = \alpha(1 - a)[(1 - \rho) / (5\rho c(1 - b))]^{1-\alpha} \qquad (A21)$$

Substituting into (A13) one can obtain the equilibrium utility for the administrative service professionals:

$$U' = 0.25k^2\alpha^2(1 - a)^2 c^{2\alpha}(1 - b)^{2\alpha}[(1 - \rho) / (5\rho)]^{2-2\alpha} \qquad (A22)$$

On the other hand, it is easy to compute the equilibrium utility for any consumer good producer:

$$U'(B) = 0.25k^2(1 - a)^2(1 - \alpha)^2 c^{2\alpha}(1 - b)^{2\alpha}[5\rho / (1 - \rho)]^{1/5} \qquad (A23)$$

Obviously, if ρ is sufficiently small, U' can be much larger than $U'(B)$. We therefore have proved Proposition 2.

Note

1. It is easy to verify that with $k = 0.9$, every consumer good producer should choose completely specialization.

References

He, Qinglian. (1997). *The Primary Capital Accumulation in Contemporary China*. Hong Kong: Mirror Book.

———. (1998). *The Pitfalls of China's Modernization*. Hong Kong: Mirror Book.

Hong Kong Christian Industrial Committee—Change. (1999). "Difficulties in the Chinese Economy," May. Hong Kong Christian Industrial Committee

Hua, S., X. Zhang, and X. Lo. (1998). "Ten Years in China's Reform: Looking Back, Reflection, and Prospect," *Economic Research* 9, 11, 12.

Lawrence, Susan V. (1998). "Excising the Cancer," *Far Eastern Economic Review*, August 20.

Lin, J. Y. (1998). "The Current State of China's Economic Reforms," in *China in the New Millennium: Market Reforms and Social Development*, James Dorn, ed. Washington, DC: CATO Institutes.

Ramonet, I. (1999). "Towards a New Century," *Le Monde Diplomatique* January 16–17.

Sachs, J., W. T. Woo, and X. Yang. (2000). "Economic Reform and Constitutional Transition," Monash University, Economics Department Discussion Paper.

Wen H. (1998). "An Analytical Framework of the Consumer-Producers, Economies of Specialization and Transaction Costs," in *Increasing Returns and Economic Analysis*, K. Arrow, Y-K. Ng, and X. Yang, eds. London: MacMillan.

Xin, M. (1998). "Superior or Inferior to the Right-Left Wing's Theory," *China and the World* 2598099a.

Xu, C. G. (2000). Interview with BBC News. September 13.

Yao, Shuntian. (1993). "Market Mechanism for the State-Owned Enterprises, and Government Taxation: A Game Theoretical Analysis of the Situation in China," *Mathematical Social Science* 25.

———. (1997). "Corruption and the Anti-corruption Movement: The Modelling and Analysis of the Situation in China" *Australian Economic Papers*.

———. ( ) "Walrasian Equilibrium Computation, Network Formation and the Wen Theorem," submitted to *Review of Development Economics*, 2000.

Zeng, Y. (1997, 1998). "On the Merits of Mao Zedong and Mao Zudong Thought—In Memory of Mao Zedong on his 105 Birthday," *China and the World* 259701a–9812c.

Political Culture, Economic Structure and Policy

The Laffont-Tirole Model Extended to Modern Japan

By Warren Young and Joris Meijaard*

ABSTRACT. This paper deals with two issues. By linking culture and political systems, we develop alternatives to the "Developmental State" approach and propose, among other types, the "Bureaucratic State" for explaining the case of Japan. We extend the Laffont-Tirole (L-T) model of regulatory capture and propose a "bureaucratic capture" model. Variations of capture are shown to apply, *given* particular cultural predispositions. The case of atomic energy in Japan and the United States is then studied to assess the predictive efficacy of the extended L-T model. We conclude that cultural predispositions and the corresponding state types affect the degree to which capture takes place.

I

Introduction

IN THIS PAPER we discuss the interaction between economic policy and political culture and identify an intriguing correlation between the economic policy system and national culture. A measure of culture (Hofstede 1980, 1991) can be coupled to the typical nature of the state

*Warren Young, Ph.D. (Cantab.) is Associate Professor, Dept. of Economics, Bar Ilan University, Ramat Gan, Israel. His recent publications include: *Atomic Energy Costing* (Kluwer Press, 1998); "Atomic Energy and Early Models of Technological Change, 1946–54," *History of Political Economy* (Supplement) 33: 2000; and "The Early History of Rational and Implicit Expectations," *History of Political Economy*, 34:2001 (with William Darity, Jr.). Email: *youngw@mail.biu.ac.il.* Joris Meijaard, Ph.D. (Tinbergen Institute, Rotterdam) is Assistant Professor at the Rotterdam School of Management, Erasmus University, Rotterdam, specializing in decision-making across cultures and economics of innovation. He would like to thank the Roosevelt Foundation, Fulbright Foundation and SEOB for financial support. His recent publications include: "Dutch innovation policy and the construction sector" in A. Manseau (ed.), *Innovation Systems in Construction* (Edward Elgar, 2000) and *Decision-making in research and development: a comparative study of multinational companies in the Netherlands and the United States"* (Thesis publishers, Amsterdam, 1998). Email: *jmeijaard@fac.fbk.eur.nl.*

American Journal of Economics and Sociology, Vol. 61, No. 1 (January, 2002).

and its political manifestation (Olson 1965; Stigler 1971; Wade 1990; Laffont and Tirole 1991, 1993). The imperative task in our paper emanates from two sources. The first is the recent search for alternatives to the "Developmental State" explanation regarding economic structure and policy making in general and in the Japanese case in particular (e.g., Fine 1999; Chan et al. 1998). In this regard, we propose a number of alternate models, including the "Bureaucratic State," to explain the Japanese case. The second is the lack of explanation beyond the regulatory capture model, and here we propose alternate forms of capture, including "bureaucratic capture."

We show that variations of the capture or interest group theory apply, *given* the particular cultural predispositions of people in countries. We present an extension of the static Laffont-Tirole (L-T) model (1991, 1993) covering four types of capture in economic policy making. The case study of atomic energy in Japan and the United States is then used to evaluate the predictive efficacy of the extended L-T model. The extended model is evaluated in terms of stability, resulting in the conclusion that only the regulatory capture is truly incentive-compatible if one assumes that government agents are self-maximizing. The use of the term "rents" in this paper, therefore, refers to rent-seeking behavior of bureaucrats and politicians; that is, the replacement of market decisions by government control or another type of collective decision making that benefits a small group of bureaucrats and politicians or individual bureaucrat or politician accordingly.

II

Culture and its Dimensions

SOCIAL SCIENCES differ in the degree to which they attach importance to the consequences of culture. Anthropologists, sociologists and political scientists largely agree on a dominant influence of culture, as do most psychologists, but economists often still deny the relevance of culture as a direct determinant of economic behavior, despite the work of Wildavsky and others (e.g., Wildavsky 1994; Wildavsky et al. 1990; Trentmann 1998; Inglehart 1998; Abrams and Lewis 1995; Grief 1994). Moreover, the economics mainstream and many economists have forgotten that in his works, Veblen looked upon human behavior and economic activity as cultural behavior (e.g., Veblen 1898, 1904, 1906).

Since culture has several meanings, a definition is needed here. The first meaning of culture is *"the training or refining of the mind."* The second meaning may be captured as *"the collective programming of the mind"* (Hofstcde 1991). This definition of culture distinguishes individual members of a group from individuals who are not members of the group. It corresponds to the use of the term in anthropology, and is the meaning that we will use throughout this paper.

Several crucial features of culture should be stressed. First, culture is always a collective phenomenon. It is the *collective* meaning that is attached to values, symbols and norms. Culture is always learned. It is not inherited, but rather derives from extensive interaction with one's context. Culture is not human nature and it is not individual personality. It is in between. Culture may be traced back to one's nationality, one's residence, one's social class, one's generation or onc's employment. We focus on the first root of culture: the nation state. It should be stressed that features of national culture probably take ages to develop. They are largely history-dependent, and only major catastrophes seem to change cultural predispositions in the short run.

Geert Hofstede (1980, 1991) has derived five main dimensions of national culture. Hofstede labeled these dimensions as *power distance* (attitude toward hierarchy and communication), *uncertainty avoidance* (attitude toward rules and risks), *individualism* (attitude toward oneself and others), *masculinity* (attitude toward rivalry and consensus), and *long-term orientation* (attitude toward status and social order).

Power distance and individualism are rather strongly correlated with the level of per capita GDP. A large per capita GDP generally means small power distance and strong individualism. A small per capita GDP generally means large power distance and strong collectivism. This seems to relate to education and personal freedom as well, but for the sake of argument here, it does not really matter which causes what. Only countries that are characterized by a strong long-term orientation (Confucianism) seem able to balance relatively large power distances and collectivism with relatively high levels of GDP per capita.

Figure 1

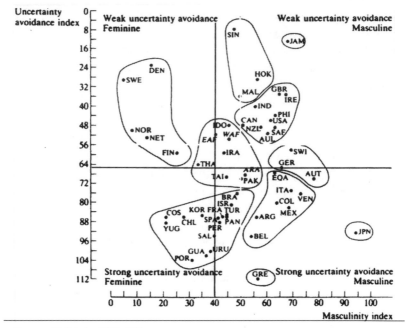

Source: Hofstede (1991:123).

In the Hofstede dimensions, the Western world differs most significantly on the scale labeled masculinity (M). Northern Europeans are typically more consensus-minded, less competitive and more focused on solidarity ("feminine") than other Western countries. The United States and most Commonwealth countries are characterized by more assertive and decisive behavior, combined with a larger eagerness to "fight out" conflicts ("masculine"). These latter characteristics are shared with the Latin and German-speaking countries. This M-dimension may be equated to *performance-driven*, *rent-seeking* behavior.

The dimension labeled uncertainty avoidance (UA) creates another substantial separation within the Western world, but now primarily between the southern European countries and the rest. The southern European (Latin) countries are most uncertainty avoidant, followed by the German-speaking countries, the Anglo-Saxon countries and the northern European countries. The UA-dimension relates very closely to mutual trust and mutual openness between agents (i.e., not withholding information).

III

Political Culture

WE WOULD LIKE to emphasize correspondence between the cultural variation across countries and the variation in political systems. It seems that cultural predispositions are directly related to the manifestation of political culture and economic structure.

According to the correspondence, Japan has a strong cultural inclination to be bureaucratic: strong forces to withhold information (UA), and simultaneously strong forces to seek rents (M). The same holds (to a lesser degree) for countries such as Mexico, Belgium, Greece and Italy. The political system fitting these conditions is bureaucratic: strong principals, relatively weak agents and a political capture by

Figure 2

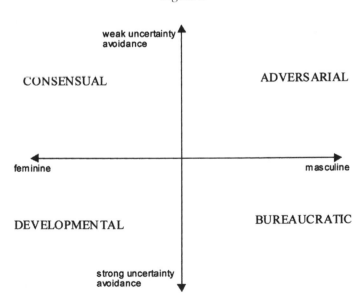

way of collusion under imperfect information. Balanced rents and transfers are key components of this bureaucratic capture.

On the other extreme, the northern European countries are characterized by a cultural inclination towards a "consensual state," typically based on mutual consent, middle ground and common interest. People are hardly inclined to withhold information (avoid uncertainty) nor to seek rents. This results in a "soft" political system, characterized by compromise decision making. Political capture is realized by way of collective agreement under relatively perfect information. In essence, regulatory capture is reversed, as interest groups are to actively participate in the decision process ("participatory capture"). Agents are captured to commit themselves to accept the finally resulting social welfare.

The various Anglo-Saxon political systems are adversarial. Conflicts are fought out, preferably in public and one-on-one. This means a strongly competitive environment, characterized by a culture that tolerates and encourages masculine, opportunistic behavior. Politics often revolves around "playing out" adversarial opponents. The basic assumption is almost by definition the self-maximizing, self-interested agent. And policy making is determined by classic regulatory capture. Excessive rent seeking is controlled by legal conditions. The risks are accepted as an unavoidable feature of the system.

Finally, the third quadrant of the cultural coordinates may be labeled "developmental" in terms of the political system. Uncertainty avoidance entails a far from perfect flow of information, but the relatively feminine culture stands for a limited inclination to seek rents. The combination provides ground for relatively benevolent autocrats that respect the feminine preference of the people. The principals can capture the agents by providing a seemingly "good" state that appeals to the solidarity principles (note that information is scarce).

Hofstede's sample regrettably does not include the eastern European countries, but in this respect strong correlations may be expected between the UA- and M-scores and the success of the recent free market and democratization initiatives. The Baltic states, Hungary, Poland and the Czech Republic are probably not very uncertainty avoidant (and possibly quite feminine). Rumania, Bulgaria, Russia and several other former Soviet states are probably strongly uncertainty avoidant (and quite masculine).

IV

Political Culture and Economic Structure: The Case of Japan

IN THIS SECTION we discuss the Japanese case of political culture and economic structure. The case illustrates the value of the framework that describes the nature of the state, and it can be closely linked to the U.S. case, often wrongfully labeled the "Consensual State."

The mistaken notion of the "Developmental State" as *the model* of the "Japanese system" emanates—in our view—from the works of two foreign observers of Japan: Reischauer (1977, 1988) and Vogel (1979). The academic, diplomat and advisor Reischauer established his reputation as one of the most vocal foreign observers of Japan in a number of early books on Japan and U.S.-Japanese relations (Reischauer 1946, 1958, 1965). Probably his most influential work has been the 1977 volume entitled *The Japanese* (revised and updated in 1988). In this book he wrote: "Political corruption is not widespread in Japan" (1977:309), later observing that constantly repeated "cries of corruption" did emanate from the Japanese public, but that "foreigners" did not understand what they meant (1988:283). In the revised and updated version of his book published in 1988, Reischauer changed this to "Political corruption is less widespread in Japan than in many other countries, and, is probably less than in local government in the United States" (1988:283). He wrote this *after* Tanaka had built and institutionalized the "Construction State" (1973–1982) and only a year before Noboru Takeshita and his successor were forced to resign the premiership of Japan due to scandals (in 1989).

Vogel, in his book *Japan as No. 1* (1979), brought forth the idea that consensus in the Japanese system emanates from the "higher interests" of politics and politicians rather than from the collusive rent seeking of politicians, industrialists and bureaucrats. It is not surprising that the myth of the Developmental State sprang from such fertile *misrepresentations* of the realities of the Japanese system.

We now turn to a brief description of the main characteristics of the

Developmental State model in order to enable its operationalization in a welfare function approach and to counterpoint it to the characteristics of the Bureaucratic State model, which we claim represents the *realities* of Japanese political culture and economic policy making. While much has been written over the past decade about the Developmental State, a *coherent* theory does not exist regarding it. Rather, a number of *prescriptive* ideas have been put forward by various authors to describe its characteristics (Amsden 1989; Best 1990; Wade 1990; Cowling and Sudgen 1992). These range from outright support of the use of government economic policy—especially industrial policy—to intensive and purposeful *direction* of the market economy into development channels considered "correct" by bureaucrats *cum* indicative planners. These ideas propose that *activities* of the Japanese Developmental State have been organized around the notion of economic development and especially industrial development. However, recently there has been a backlash against the Developmental State model, with Chan, Clark and Lam desiring to go beyond it in the East Asian case (Chan et al. 1998), and Fine even declaring it "dead" (Fine 1999).

Now, in the view of those observers who support the Developmental State description of the Japanese system, Japan's industrial development was led by government action, with industrial policy by bureaucratic "administrative guidance" on the one hand, and compromise between bureaucrats and industrialists on the other. In this view, targeted export-oriented strategic industries were fruitfully promoted while declining industries were accordingly fruitfully designated for protection (Nester 1990:167–170 and 1991:29). According to this model, allocation of investment resources in Japan were administered and guided by the government, whose relationship with the private sector was governed by the recognition of common interest. Economic policy making in the Developmental State model, then, was the result of a process whereby the market mechanism is channeled in *specific* directions by the closely linked public and private sector and the intense involvement of the government in the market activities (Leftwich 1995). Leftwich also noted that such a state would "concentrate considerable power, authority, autonomy and competence in the central political and bureaucratic institutions of the state, notably their economic bureaucracies" (1995:420). In terms of the model, the outcome of this was, as Onis notes, "institutionalized public-private cooperation in the process of economic policy formulation and implementation (1991:119).

What the Developmental State model leaves out is the Japanese reality regarding resource allocation and its outcome. There is structural corruption, represented by a rent-seeking bureaucracy acting in collusion with rent-seeking politicians and rent-seeking industrialists. The latter forge what the Japanese term *kozo oshoku*, or structural corruption. This structural corruption is so extensive and inbuilt that it neither inhibits nor dishonors the extant system. Rather, it becomes the system, at least under Tanaka and his Construction State (Johnson 1995: Chap. 9).

In Japan, resources were allocated and transferred to the private sector via the Fiscal Loan and Investment Program (FLIP), which provided funds to public agencies and corporations and that, in turn, lent funds to the private sector. Thus, in effect, all Japanese companies had direct or indirect access to FLIP resources (Ito 1992:120–121). It was the political masters of the Japanese bureaucrats—not mentioned in the Developmental State model of the Japanese system—who determined where FLIP resources would be invested. This took place in collusion with the beneficiaries of the resources, the industrialists and the bureaucrats whose "administrative guidance" directed the resources to their targets at the behest of the politicians. This is the core of the Japanese system of structural corruption (*kozo oshoku*) that characterized the implementation of Developmental State economic policies and that turned the Japanese case into one best described by the Bureaucratic State.

Mohiro Hosokawa—the man whose election in 1993 broke the LDP hegemony for the first time in almost four decades—used the term "Bureaucratic State" to describe the Japanese system in a 1992 political manifesto (Hosokawa 1993). The Bureaucratic State model, as it applies to Japan, emanates from the Public Choice approach, in which self-maximizing state elites (bureaucrats) constitute a specific interest group, and in which their autonomous actions in conjunction with politicians result not only in a misallocation of resources, but in *malevolent state action* (e.g., Tanaka's Construction State as described above). The outcome of the Bureaucratic State model is perhaps reflected best in the welfare function that exhibits what we call bureaucratic capture, to be discussed below.

Interestingly enough, it was Veblen, in his article "The Opportunity of Japan" (1915), who noted that even in the "New Japan"—that is, Japan after the Meiji Restoration of 1868—the bureaucratic ethos of "Old Japan" was still dominant. At first glance, it could be said that in 1915 Veblen saw this in a positive light, similar to the Development State theorists over half a century later, for he noted that the "new" Japanese Imperial bureaucracy was still highly motivated by a feudal type fealty and code of honor, and that this, combined with the efficiency provided by modern technology, would lead to a strong Japan.

However, it was Veblen's very stress on the core of this feudalistic spirit, fealty and honor (prestige), that provides the reason for the downfall of the successor to the pre–World War II Imperial bureaucracy, that is, the state bureaucracy of post–World War II Japan. In his recent introduction to the Japanese bureaucracy, Takashi (1997) cites a number of Japanese authors regarding the mind set and ethos of Japanese bureaucrats and the institutions they forged. Among these authors was Gotoda, who in his book *Sei to kan* (*Politics and the Bureaucracy*, 1994) wrote

> If bureaucratic institutions are to achieve their objectives, they must have the people's trust. But somewhere along the line trust and prestige have traded places; objectives have become secondary to prestige and face. . . . Putting means before ends is not the only reason for bureaucrat's obsession with prestige. From the Meiji era (1868–1912) until the end of World War II they were in the position of exercising sovereignty. The relationship between bureaucrat and citizen was that of ruler and subject. In short, until the end of the war Japan's bureaucrats, as "agents of the emperor," were the superintendents of imperial sovereignty. Today, however, this relationship has been reversed. . . . This role reversal took place almost 50 years ago, yet bureaucrats have had a hard time changing their mind-set . . . . (cited in Takashi 1997:3).

Another Japanese observer, Uekusa, has noted the linkage between the functioning of bureaucrats and the failure of economic policy, calling it the problem of bureaucratic "privatization" of economic policy in Japan:

> The bureaucracy is supposed to function as an organization of public servants, but it has turned into a set of institutions that serve themselves. In ef-

fect, economic policy has become "privatized." The biggest objective of each of the ministries and agencies of the central government is to maximize its own authority. Each of them wants to secure as many affiliated organizations as possible, so as to provide comfortable jobs for its retiring members. And it wants to maximize its own discretionary powers and the size of the budget appropriations over which it can exercise a high degree of discretionary authority. Economic policy, which is supposed to be conducted for the sake of the people of the nation, has ended up becoming a tool for the furthering of narrow bureaucratic interests. (Uekusa 1998:4)

But let us leave the last word on this matter to another Japanese observer, Sakaiya (1998), who in his article "The Myth of the Competent Bureaucrat" notes that "Japanese bureaucrats today demonstrate the three worst kinds of incompetence"—that is, their "inability to forecast trends and developments," "their lack of administrative ability," and "their ethical decay" (1998:5, 7). So much for the contribution of the bureaucracy to the Developmental State model explanation in the Japanese case.

In the U.S. case, the nature of the interaction between bureaucrats, politicians and interest groups leads one *beyond* the notion of consensus, cooperation and the search for the "middle ground" (the "Consensual State"). It leads to a model of partisanship, conflict and rent seeking on the part of these groups (the "Adversarial State"), with a commensurate welfare function reflecting bureaucratic behavior, which has been termed "regulatory capture." It is to the welfare functions and their implications that we now turn.

V

Economic Structure and Policy: Regulatory and Bureaucratic Capture

IN THIS SECTION, we will first present the regulatory capture model as it applies to the U.S. case (the "Adversarial State"). We will then expand its welfare function to represent the Developmental State and finally the Bureaucratic State as it exemplifies the Japanese system characterized by bureaucratic capture. We utilize the regulatory capture model because in our view it comes closest to reflecting a Public Choice interpretation of administrative guidance and is thus applicable in the U.S. and the Japanese case.

Perhaps the most clear agency-theoretic approach to regulatory capture is that of Laffont and Tirole (1991, 1993). Their model is comprised of a three-tier hierarchy, ranging from the level of the firm through the agency to Congress, with a two-tiered regulatory structure consisting of an agency (the "supervisor") and Congress (the "principal"). The firm is accordingly the final agent (1991:1092–1095). While Laffont and Tirole do deal with multiple interest groups (1991:1105ff), their approach is still less realistic—albeit more formal—than, for example, that of Chubb (1983). According to Chubb, *change in the "sovereign political environment" produces change in the relations within the regulatory model*, such as change in presidential administration (Chubb 1983:195). Such changes are *not* taken into account by Laffont and Tirole; making their approach essentially static.

As we will show below, the Laffont and Tirole model can be extended to include change over time in the nature of the agency. It allows for a possible convergence or divergence of interests between the principal (Congress) and the agency.

Before proceeding to extend the Laffont and Tirole model, however, a caveat is necessary. The caveat stated by Laffont and Tirole is that their model may admit alternative interpretations. In particular, it allows for the interpretation that the "agency" represents the coalition of a government agency and the members of the relevant congressional oversight committee, and that "Congress" represents the rest of the legislature (1991:1094). Correspondingly, a change in "regulation" may mean a change from a colluding agency that hides information from Congress to protect firms, to an agency that tells the truth (or that at least does not collude with the firms or other interest groups (1991:1096, 1102–1103, 1106).

The static Laffont-Tirole model proceeds as follows. Assume a possible set of alternative regulatory policies S and an initial behavioral model of the regulated industrial or financial complex $X(s)$, which predicts the behavior of the complex as a whole and the components of it as a function of the regulatory policy s adopted by the regulatory agency. The agency, for its part, does not only choose a regulatory policy $s \in S$, but also a regulatory stance or position vis-à-vis the principal and the interest groups (agents). This involves choosing to tell the truth to the principals regarding, for example, costs including externalities of the projects it promotes and/or regulates, or, alternately, choosing to hide such information and collude with the agents in the complex.

Laffont and Tirole (1991:1095) specify a cost parameter β with high or low values, the realization of which is known by the agents in the complex. The agency collects information about the cost parameter β, getting a signal σ from the agents, directly or indirectly, which is either equal to the true value of β or empty ∅. If the agency gets a signal, Laffont and Tirole assume σ = β, the true value. If the agency learns nothing, σ = ∅. According to Laffont and Tirole, *the signal is hard evidence in the sense that the agency is able to reveal "the actual value of β ('true cost') to the principal"* (1991:1096). We may assume that the agents (producers, consumer groups) know what signal the agency receives or we may assume that *when the agency has an incentive to collude, it can freely disclose the signal (back to that interest group)* (1991:1096, note 15, our emphasis). The probability of the agency's learning the true value of β can be thought of as entirely determined by the budget for investigation (1991:1096). On this basis, they conclude, "the agency reports r ∈ {σ, ∅} to Congress. If the agency has learned nothing, it can only say so (r = ∅). If it has learned the truth (σ = β), it can either tell the truth (r = β), or, it can claim its search for information was unfruitful (r = ∅)" (1991:1096)

This being the case, we can extend the L-T approach in the following manner. Let us specify a welfare function of the form W = (X(s), s, r, e_p). *X(s)* is a behavioral model of the regulated complex (industrial, financial), predicting the behavior of the complex as a whole (and of its components). This is a function of the regulatory policy *s* and stance *r*, as adopted by the regulatory agency. The regulatory policy *s* is an element of the possible set of alternative regulatory policies *S*. The *r* is the vector of possible signals to disclose by the agency (received information regarding cost). And e_p is the vector of elements in the "sovereign political environment," Congress and its oversight committees, the President, the budgeting agency and the courts. The object of the agency is to *choose* the regulatory *policy s* and regulatory *stance* r ∈ {σ, ∅}, so as to maximize *W* contingent on e_p *over time*.

Following Laffont and Tirole, collusion occurs when the agency has an incentive to hide information from elements in the sovereign political environment, which can arise only if the retention of information benefits the firms and the agency (1991:1102–1103). According to the welfare function as specified, it seems logical that the larger the number of elements in e_p—for example, congressional oversight committees—the higher the potential price paid by the agency if it decides to hide cost information in order to protect or benefit firms. Intuition suggests that the larger e_p, the smaller the incentive to hide information. Alternatively, the larger e_p, the more information must be supplied by the agency at its own expense and/or that of the firms if it decides to tell the truth. In either case, there will be a potential or actual budget constraint on information dissemination, both negative and positive (including the penalties for being found out).

The agency's decision will be a function of the cost (political and budget penalties) of hiding information versus the opportunity costs of telling the truth. This being so, intuition further suggests that the larger e_p, the higher the probability that r = β and the agency will decide to tell the truth and cooperate with beneficiaries and cost-bearing agents alike. Indeed, the addition of what Chubb called the "presidential constraint" (1983:119) expands the political environment in both scope and time frame, from the static "Congress" of the Laffont and Tirole vintage, to the dynamic "sovereign political environment," e_p.

We can now further develop the extended L-T approach regarding regulatory capture by including a relational parameter that represents what we see as the linkage between Laffont and Tirole's "captured" cost vector and what we call the "non-captured" cost vector, the "true" cost in Laffont-Tirole terms.

Let us now specify a welfare function of the form

$$W = (X(s), s, r^*/r, e_p)$$

X(s) again is the "behavioral model" of the regulated complex, which predicts the behavior of the complex as a whole and the components of it as a function of the regulatory policy *s* adopted by the regulatory agency. *r* is the Laffont-Tirole *captured* "vector of signals and information regarding cost" that the agency obtains from the firms and that it provides to the principals. If σ is not equal to β, then *r* is *captured,* but as σ approaches β the degree of capture decreases. The *r** is the non-captured vector of signals and information regarding β, such that, as σ approaches β, *r* approaches *r**. When σ = β, r = r* and the cost vector is not captured (at all).

In this setting, the object of the agency is to choose regulatory *policy* s $\in$ S and *stance* r/r* $\in$ {σ, $\varnothing$}, so as to maximize *W* contingent on e_p. In the case of some agencies, however, in retrospect *W* is not maximized, as the stance they take regarding the cost vectors actually only maximizes the gap between *r* and *r**.

A welfare function representing the Developmental State model may now be counterpointed to that of the Bureaucratic State and bureaucratic capture. The extended L-T model (including the relational parameter *r/r**) can be applied. Theoretically, if only administrative guidance prevails, there may be regulatory capture of a benign form, where *r* may be captured, but *r* still approaches *r** and positive welfare results.

The Japanese reality, however, is described by another solution. Bureaucratic withholding and concealment of information from superiors or the public at large may actually be the behavioral norm—especially if the information is damaging to certain interest groups (firms, politicians) or to the bureaucrats themselves. According to Japanese observers, this seems to be the case (Kazuo 1996; Takashi 1996; Yomiuri Shimbun 1996).

If this is the case, the basic L-T model must be revised as follows before applying its extension. The L-T "cost parameter" β remains specified with low or high values. The realization is known by the firms in the complex (e.g., in the case of financial institutions such as banks, credit and loan activities). The bureaucrats collect information or get a signal σ about β directly or indirectly from the firms. If the bureaucrats learn the "true" value of β, "the signal is hard evidence," and the bureaucrat is able to reveal the actual value of β (true cost) to the principal (superiors, political masters). In other words, if $\sigma = \beta$, the L-T model assumes that interest groups (firms, politicians) can learn what signal the bureaucrat receives. However in the Japanese case, they cannot. They can only trust.

Now, let us return to the Developmental State model welfare function. As specified above, this is the same as the extended L-T model with the relational parameter *r**/*r* . But in Japan, as noted above, information is concealed or withheld because of bureaucratic capture, i.e., collusion between bureaucrats, firms and politicians. *W* is usually not maximized, and thus a possible Developmental State model breaks down. Indeed, the best and most costly example of this is the outcome of the financial "bubble" in Japan, which, due to bureaucratic concealment and withholding of information, reached the extreme cost it did, with consequences that are still felt today, almost a decade after the bubble burst. Another example, with human cost, is that of atomic energy, but more about this in Section VI below.

With regard to the Adversarial State, the extended L-T approach as developed above is most applicable to explain the regulatory capture that characterizes it. In the case of the Consensual State, on the other hand, participatory capture occurs, as described in Section III above—in other words, a reversal of regulatory capture. In terms of the extended L-T model, government agencies deliberately provide information to an interest group or groups so as to encourage their active participation in the decision-making process, thereby capturing them to committing themselves to politically accept or support the social welfare that finally results.

VI

Case Study: Atomic Energy in Japan and the United States

PERHAPS THE MOST significant example of the analytical efficacy of our proposed approach can be seen in the case of atomic power. Less than a decade ago, Japan's nuclear program was expanding rapidly, resulting in about a third of its electricity being currently produced by atomic energy. In the past five years or so, not only has its nuclear program slowed down, but there has been a movement away from putting all its energy investment into nuclear power research and development. In this section we will first briefly outline the reasons for the rise and slowdown of the Japanese nuclear program. We will then compare the Japanese case to what happened in the United States, based upon some of the aspects of the agency-theoretic perspective developed above.

To the casual observer, it may seem ironic that Japan would develop an extensive nuclear program. But only a decade after atomic bombs destroyed Hiroshima and Nagasaki, Japan initiated a program of atomic energy development after the Diet (or Japanese Parliament) enacted the 1955 Atomic Energy Law. That Japan would opt for a program of nuclear power development is neither surprising nor ironic to the astute observer, for Japan was always energy deficient, dependent upon external sources of energy supply. The 1955 law set up the Japanese Atomic Energy Commission and the Nuclear Safety Commission. The former was responsible for long-term planning, rather than the regulation of nuclear energy, which became the responsibility of the Ministry of International Trade and Industry (MITI); the latter was responsible for monitoring the enforcement of safety regulations, which were actually voluntary and *not* compulsory (Kondo 1994:17; Lowinger and Hinman 1994:54). In 1968, the Power Reactor and Fuel Development Corporation (PNC) was also established by the Japanese government to develop advanced power reactors and nuclear fuel-cycle technology.

When OPEC 1 occurred in 1973, almost 80 percent of Japan's energy needs were supplied by imported oil. Over the decade 1965–1975, Japan's electric utilities imported Light Water Reactors (LWRs) from the United States, and by 1975, 12 atomic energy power plants were on line, supplying over 6 percent of electricity demand. In 1979, OPEC 2 again shocked Japanese industry. In order to reach some degree of freedom from oil imports, the nuclear energy and liquified natural gas programs were expanded, so that by 1985 oil imports had declined to less than 60 percent of Japan's energy needs. By the 1991 Gulf War oil shock, 40 commercial nuclear plants were in operation, supplying about 27 percent of total electricity generation, with another eight plants under construction and four in the planning stage.

However, as early as 1989, nuclear accidents started to affect public opinion in Japan apart from the environmentalists, who had opposed the nuclear program from the start. The first incident, in 1989, occurred when a recirculation pump disintegrated at a nuclear power station owned and operated by Tokyo Electric Power. This got wide media coverage and brought about anti-nuclear protests. The second serious incident took place in February 1991 and has been described by Japanese commentators as the country's worst nuclear accident up until that time. While this incident did not involve any large scale external release of radioactivity, both a steam generation tube rupture and a pressure valve malfunction caused the first justified activation of an emergency core cooling system in the history of Japan's nuclear power program. These accidents resulted in increased opposition to the program not only from national anti-nuclear groups but also from rural residents and local authorities regarding the siting of nuclear power plants.

More recent serious accidents, however, have called the entire Japanese nuclear program into question. In April 1997 a major leak of radioactive tritium from an advanced thermal reactor occurred. About 30 hours passed before local authorities were told about it by the PNC. Not only had there been an attempt to cover up errors made by the PNC, but only a few days later it admitted that 11 "minor leaks" had occurred at this reactor over the previous three years. Only a month before, in March 1997, an explosion caused by a fire at a PNC nuclear fuel plant had resulted in Japan's most serious *actual* nuclear accident, with some 40 workers exposed to radiation. The PNC reactor was temporarily shut down. This plant will be closed until at least 2001; and if people in the surrounding region are found to have been affected by radiation, the level of that accident will be upgraded from 3 to 4 on the international scale of nuclear accidents (Chernobyl scored 7; Three Mile Island, 5).

These accidents, however, pale in comparison to the potential disaster that almost occurred in December 1995 at the PNC's Monju Liquid Metal Fast Breeder Reactor (LMFBR). Molten sodium burst out of the cooling circuits at the Monju LMFBR and almost exploded. Although no radiation was released, the near-explosion could have blown up the plutonium-fueled reactor; a disaster that would have paralleled that at Chernobyl. Before committing suicide, the PNC safety officer on duty at the time disclosed that the PNC *itself* had delayed reporting the leak to the local authorities by an hour and that the videotape of the accident eventually released to the media had been heavily edited. Moreover, the reactor had been slowly shut down *manually* instead of immediately by automatic (manual override) shutdown mechanisms. Since then, this reactor has remained shut down and will probably never be re-opened. Indeed, it was the Japanese Prime Minister himself that intervened and ordered the shutdown after the PNC cover up was disclosed (Young 1998:73–78).

In contrast, the 1979 Three Mile Island nuclear accident in the United States was investigated by a Presidential Commission. Its report focused criticisms upon what it saw as the central problems in the U.S. nuclear program, among which were information flow and dissemination. However, that the Commission did not stress that "regulatory bodies" in the United States should have been a clearinghouse for such an information flow and dissemination of crucial real-time analysis was, it would seem, because "in the United States, the relations between the nuclear industry and the regulatory bodies have frequently been characterized as confrontational and antagonistic" (Lowinger and Hinman 1994:55).

Now, in theory, the centralized and collaborative nature of nuclear regulation in Japan should promote information flow, and as Fort and Hallagan note, "recent changes at the U.S. NRC have been directed at copying some aspects of the regulatory process in Japan" (1994:217). But, despite its decentralization and confrontational nature, the *present* U.S. system actually promotes a degree of openness *previously unknown* (i.e., under the Atomic Energy Commission and the Congressional Joint Committee on Atomic Energy) and *virtually absent* in Japan. And, as we will show below, it is this *only recent* "confrontational and antagonistic" position taken by the "regulatory bodies" that has prevented the United States from proceeding along the slippery slope that now characterizes Japan's nuclear program and the repeated cover-ups of its major nuclear accidents. In order to understand why there is a gap between theory and practice in the Japanese case, we must briefly survey the structure of Japan's nuclear regulatory system and contrast it with that in the United States It is to this that we now turn.

In Japan, there is considerable stress on voluntary compliance with nuclear regulations, which are less strict in the critical plant operating stage. This stress on voluntary compliance is because of three factors. The first is that MITI extensively reviews plans during the initial licensing stage. The second is that compliance with regulations in Japan is essentially *self-administered* due to the fact that MITI "has great confidence in the utilities' voluntary assurance system" (Lowinger and Hinman 1994:54; Fort and Hallagan 1994:209). The third and perhaps most significant factor is that, as Lowinger and Hinman observe, "the

Japanese nuclear regulatory system as a whole (and MITI in particular) is concerned with energy security and the stability of energy supply system . . . the various components of the nuclear industry collaborate and share information. . . . " Moreover, "because of shared basic values and a long history of close collaboration" they "have jointly and *often behind the scenes* arrived at . . . solutions to . . . problems" (1994:55, our emphasis). And it is the reasons for this "behind the scenes" collaboration that must be analyzed here, based upon the gap between theory and practice in the case of Japanese nuclear regulation. First of all, while Japan's Diet was, in theory, based upon an "open" multi-party parliamentary system, in practice, it acquired a centralized Byzantine-like nature based upon a party-political machine (the long-ruling Liberal Democratic Party or LDP) that was essentially unresponsive to changing or competing interests and changes in the composition of interest groups. The desire of LDP beneficiaries—such as the Japanese nuclear-industrial complex—were facilitated by governmental organizations with which they were closely linked. What occurred in Japan, therefore, was that the centralized government agencies regulating nuclear power, MITI and NSC (Nuclear Safety Commission), simply collaborated on safety issues to the benefit of the Japanese nuclear-industrial complex (Fort and Hallagan 1994:204–206). Second, Japan's parliamentary and regulatory structures were not only centraslized, but the nature of the domestic power interests—industries and utilities—was also monolithic and uncompetitive. Moreover, the concentration of utilities—via excluding entry—in Japan by MITI was paralleled by the concentration of the nuclear-industrial complex under the aegis of MITI by the Diet (essentially, the LDP). Thus, *given* that MITI's nuclear regulatory activities were *"consistent with the goals of the Diet"* (our emphasis), not only did this limit the "number of competing producer interest groups" but also *assured that the interests of the nuclear-industrial complex were met, including subsidized capital for nuclear power generation from the government-financed Japan Development Bank*, which reached almost one-third of nuclear construction costs in Japan (Fort and Hallagan 1994:208–211).

Finally, even though there was—and still is—growing public opposition to nuclear power in Japan, this did not translate into party political platforms or bring about change in nuclear legislation in the Diet as late as the mid-1990s. Indeed, as Fort and Hallagan observe, it very well could be that "if rising public anti-nuclear sentiment is to matter in Japan, *it must be in the context of the utility company-MITI technocracy* [our emphasis]." Moreover, as they put it "given MITI's *modus operandi* . . . [and] past proclivities, based upon the form of government in the Diet . . . the power company cartel would be *managed* quite tightly by MITI, *to the benefit of the cartel members and the electoral fortunes of members of the Diet*" (1994:213, our emphasis).

This being the case, it is not surprising that behind the scenes collaboration took place. Nor is it surprising —based upon the extension of the Laffont-Tirole model developed above—that the Japanese nuclear program has indeed exhibited a slowdown recently, when one takes into consideration penalties for lying and increased environmental protest due to ever more serious nuclear accidents. It is to this explanation that we now briefly turn. *Before* the spate of serious nuclear accidents, the principal-agency-agent model operated on the levels of the Diet as *principal*, MITI and NCS as main regulatory *agencies* and elements in the nuclear-industrial complex, such as the PNC and nuclear power-based utilities as *agents*; this *without* the entry of national environmental groups and their political supporters into the regulatory model. *After* the Japanese nuclear accidents, the penalties for lying and *repeated* cover-ups on the one hand, and the influence of these environmental groups and their supporters on the other, enter the extended L-T model via changes in the parameters and the need for the additional twist developed above regarding regulatory capture in the Japanese case, that is, bureaucratic capture.

In the U.S. case, on the other hand, the *representative* and adversarial form of government exhibits much more openness to competing interests. Indeed, in light of the congressional committee and sub-committee structure, it would seem that Congress has, in effect, almost maximized access to the policy-making process. Thus, when compared to the system in Japan, the United States exhibits what could be termed "dynamic accommodation," especially in terms of *recent* nuclear regulation. Moreover, in the United States not only do federal-level agencies, such as the Department of Energy and Nuclear Regulatory Commission, have input into the nuclear regulatory process, but state and local commissions and environmental bodies also provide input (Fort and Hallagan 1994:205–206). Indeed, there are fifty public utility commissions (PUCs) in the United States—one per state—versus only one in Japan—MITI—even though Japanese local government is based upon prefectures. This contrasts the centralized and monolithic form of government in Japan against the representative, albeit, adversarial form in the United States Fort and Hallagan hypothesize that "the only difference between the U.S. and Japanese nuclear power industries might be the politics of cartel management for the latter. The result would be that Japanese nuclear power has grown primarily as a result of maintaining the economic health and welfare of power companies in Japan" (1994:217). If this is indeed the case, then the extended L-T model presented above must be further developed to include a parameter to express the welfare of the power companies. Indeed, in Japan up to the present, and in the United States in the past, the nuclear regulatory agencies and bureaucrats (MITI in Japan; AEC in the United States) maximized the "economic health and welfare of power companies" and *not overall welfare that should have emanated from the regulatory policy and regulatory stance adopted* (Young 1998:96).

VII

Discussion

UNTIL NOW, economists have overlooked the importance of political culture and its effect upon economic structure and policy making. In this paper, we have shown that national and political culture—as manifested in the combination of the dimensions of national culture as outlined above with the sovereign political environment and the behavioral characteristics of bureaucrats—is directly linked not only with rent-seeking activities but also with asymmetric information provision and the capture of economic policy making by government agents. To this end, we have extended the Laffont-Tirole model and enabled its extension to cover four types of "capture" in economic policy making. In evaluating the extended model, it was shown that regulatory capture is truly incentive-compatible only if one assumes that government agents are self-maximizing.

The extended model was then applied to Japan. It was shown that the extended model explains not only bureaucratic behavior but also the breakdown of the mythical Development State approach, the bureaucratic capture that actually represents the Japanese case, and its implications in the case of atomic energy and its regulation by organizations such as MITI. Now, some observers of Japan would perhaps object to our approach and claim that the successes and failures of institutions such as MITI emanate from industrial economics and are not linked to the system or political and national culture as such, but more to the specific conditions of market structure, barriers of entry/exit, needs of brokerage and so on or, alternatively, to domination ostensibly *in turn* by politicians, bureaucrats and business groups (e.g., Callon 1995; Kikkawa 1995a, 1995b). *But it is these specific Japanese conditions and the very nature of the Japanese principals (politicians and bureaucrats) and agents (business) emanating from a particular political culture that are the reasons for, in Porter's terms, what "went wrong" in Japan* (Porter and Takeuchi 1999:67).

Summing up, we have tried to link cultural variation and variation in political systems in order to assess whether cultural predispositions are related to the manifestations of political and economic structure. The case of Japan was considered in detail in order to illustrate the efficacy of the Bureaucratic State alternative against the conventional Developmental State approach. The Laffont-Tirole model of regulatory capture was extended in order to highlight the relationship between and effect of cultural predisposition upon behavior in the political-economic sphere of interaction between principals and agents, and the notion of bureaucratic capture was also introduced here. Finally, the case of atomic energy in Japan and the United States was studied to assess the efficacy of the extended L-T model in its bureaucratic capture form and to explain differences in the behavior of both principals and agents in the respective cases as well as the differences in outcomes when nuclear incidents occurred.

In our view, further investigation is warranted to examine whether the extended Laffont-Tirole model we have presented in this paper can be applied to explain additional cases of the collapse of economic policy making due to its capture.

References

Abrams, B. and Lewis, K. (1995). "Cultural and Institutional Determinants of Economic Growth," *Public Choice* 83: 3–4, June, pp. 273–89.

Amsden, A. (1989). *Asia's Next Giant.* New York: Oxford University Press.

Best, M. (1990). *The New Competition.* Cambridge: Polity Press.

Callon, S. (1995). *Divided Sun: MITI and the Breakdown of Japanese High-Tech Industrial Policy, 1975–1993.* Stanford: Stanford University Press.

Chan, S., Clark, C. and Lam, D. (1998). *Beyond the Developmental State: East Asia's Political Economies Reconsidered.* London: Macmillan.

Chubb, J. (1983). *Interest Groups and the Bureaucracy.* Stanford: Stanford University Press.

Cowling, K. and Sudgen, R. (eds.) (1992). *Current Issues in Industrial Economic Strategy.* Manchester, UK: Manchester University Press.

Drucker, P. (1998). "Defending Japanese Bureaucrats," *Foreign Affairs,* 77: 5, September/ October, pp. 68–80.

Eccleston, B. (1989). *State and Society in Post-War Japan.* Cambridge, UK: Polity Press.

Fine, B. (1999). "The Development State is Dead—Long Live Social Capital?," *Development and Change* 30: 1, January, pp. 1–19.

Fort, R. and Hallagan, W. (1994). "Nuclear Power in the United States and Japan: Economic versus Political Explanations," in Lowinger, T. and Hinman, G. (eds.), *Nuclear Power at the Crossroads: Challenges and Prospects for the Twenty-First Century,* pp. 191–218. Boulder, CO: ICEED.

Grief, A. (1994). "Cultural Beliefs and the Organization of Society: A Historical and Theoretical Reflection on Collectivist and Individualist Societies," *Journal of Political Economy,* 102: 5, pp. 912–50.

Hofstede, G. (1980). *Culture's Consequences: International Differences in Work-related Values.* Beverly Hills: Sage.

———. (1991). *Cultures and Organizations: Software of the Mind.* London: Macmillan.

Hosokawa, M. (1993). *The Time to Act is Now: Thoughts for a New Japan.* Tokyo: NTT Mediascope.

Inglehart, R. (1997). *Modernization and Postmodernization: Cultural, Economic and Political Change in 43 Societies.* Princeton, NJ: Princeton University Press.

Ito, T. (1992). *The Japanese Economy.* Cambridge, MA: MIT Press.

Johnson, C. (1982). *MITI and the Japanese Miracle: The Growth of Industrial Policy, 1925–197.* Stanford: Stanford University Press.

———. (1995). *Japan: Who Governs? The Rise of the Developmental State.* New York: Norton.

Kazuo, U. (1996). "A Reform Proposal for Financial Administration," *Japan Echo,* 23:3, Autumn, pp. 62–65.

Kikkawa, T. (1995a). "The Formation and Function of Enterprise Groups," *Business History*, 37:2, April, pp. 44–53.

———. (1995b). "Enterprise Groups, Industrial Associations, and the Government: The Case of the Petrochemical Industry in Japan," *Business History*, 37: 3, July, pp. 89–110.

Kondo, S. (1994). "Japanese Policy for Nuclear Energy Development and Utilization toward the Twenty-First Century," in Lowinger, T. and Hinman, G. (eds.), *Nuclear Power at the Crossroads: Challenges and Prospects for the Twenty-First Century*, pp. 11–32. Boulder, CO: ICEED.

Laffont, J. and Tirole, J. (1991). "The Politics of Government Decision-Making; A Theory of Regulatory Capture," *Quarterly Journal of Economics*, 106, pp. 1089–1127.

———. (1993). *A Theory of Incentives in Procurement and Regulation*, Chapter 11, pp. 475–514. Cambridge, MA: MIT Press.

Leftwich, A. (1995). "Bringing Politics Back: Towards a Model of the Developmental State," *Journal of Development Studies*, 31: 3, pp. 400–27.

Lowinger, T. and Hinman, G. (1994). "A Comparative Study of Nuclear Safety Regulation and Safety Performance in Japan and the United States," in Lowinger, T. and Hinman, G. (eds.), *Nuclear Power at the Crossroads: Challenges and Prospects for the Twenty-First Century*, pp. 49–66. Boulder, CO: ICEED.

Meijaard, J. (1998). *Decision-Making in Research and Development: A Comparative Study of the Netherlands and the United States*. Amsterdam: Thela Thesis.

Nester, W. (1990). *Japan's Growing Power over East Asia and the World Economy*. London: Macmillan.

———. (1991). *Japanese Industrial Targeting*. London: Macmillan.

Olson, M. (1965). *The Logic of Collective Action*. Cambridge, MA: Harvard University Press.

Onis, Z. (1991). "The Logic of the Developmental State," *Comparative Politics,*, October, pp. 109–126.

Ozawa, T. (1993). "Foreign Direct Investment and Structural Transformation: Japan as a Recycler of Market and Industry," *Business and the Contemporary World* 5: 2, pp. 129–150.

Porter, M. and Takeuchi, H. (1999). "Fixing What Really Ails Japan," *Foreign Affairs*, 78: 3, May/June, pp. 66–81.

Reischauer, E. ([1946] 1958). *Japan: Past and Present*. New York: Knopf.

———. (1965). *The United States and Japan*. Cambridge, MA: Harvard University. Press.

———. (1977). *The Japanese*. Cambridge, MA: Harvard University, Belknap Press.

———. (1988). *The Japanese Today: Change and Continuity*. Cambridge, MA: Harvard University, Belknap Press.

Ryuichiro, M. (1996). "Why Bureaucrats Don't Serve the Public Interest," *Japan Echo,* 23: 3, Autumn, pp. 10–14.

Sakaiya, T. (1998). "The Myth of the Competent Bureaucrat," *Japan Echo,* 25: 1, February, pp. 1–10.

Sawyer, M. (1992). "Reflections on the Nature and Role of Industrial Policy," *Metroeconomica:* 43.

Sayle, M. (1998). "The Social Contradictions of Japanese Capitalism," *Atlantic Monthly,* 281: 6, June, pp. 84–94.

Seiichiro, S.(1997). "Don't Expect a Big Bang from MOF," *Japan Echo,* 24: 3, August, p. 27.

Stigler, G. (1971). "The Economic Theory of Regulation," *Bell Journal of Economics,* 2, pp. 3–21.

Takashi, M. (1996). "Reforming the Bureaucracy," *Japan Echo,* 23: 3, Autumn, pp. 6–9.

———— . (1997). "The Japanese Bureaucracy," *Japan Echo,* 24 (Special Issue), pp. 1–10.

Trentmann, F. (1998). "Political Culture and Political Economy," *Review of International Political Economy,* 5: 2, Summer, pp. 217–51.

Uekusa, K. (1998). "Structural Reform for Economic Policy Making," *Japan Echo,* 25: 5, October, pp. 1–6.

Veblen. T. (1898). "Why Economics is not an Evolutionary Science," *Quarterly Journal of Economics,* July, pp. 373–397.

———— . (1904). *Theory of Business Enterprise.* New York: Scribners.

———— . (1906). "The Place of Science in Modern Civilization," *American Journal of Sociology,* March, pp. 585–609.

———— . (1915). "The Opportunity of Japan," *Journal of Race Development,* July, pp. 23–28.

Vogel, E. (1979). *Japan as No. 1: Lesson's for America.* Cambridge, MA: Harvard University Press.

Wade, R. (1990). *Governing the Market.* Princeton, NJ: Princeton University Press.

Wildavsky, A. (1994). "Why Self Interest Means Less Outside of a Social Context: Cultural Contributions to a Theory of Rational Choices," *Journal of Theoretical Politics,* 6: 2, April, pp. 131–59.

Wildavsky, A. et al. (1990). *Cultural Theory.* Boulder, CO: Westview Press.

Yomiuri Shimbun (1996). Constitutional Studies Group, "Proposal for Reorganizing the Cabinet and Administration," *Japan Echo,* 23: 3, Autumn, pp. 25–31.

Young, W. (1998). *Atomic Energy Costing.* Boston: Kluwer.

PART VII

New Perspectives on Transition Economies: Africa

American Journal of Economics and Sociology, Vol. 61, No. 1 (January, 2002).

Political Instability and Economic Growth

Implications of Coup Events in Sub-Saharan Africa

By AUGUSTIN KWASI FOSU*

ABSTRACT. The study examines the differential roles of various elite political instability (PI) events—successful coups d'etat, abortive coups, or coup plots—in the growth of Sub-Saharan Africa. It analyzes World Bank economic statistics and data on the incidence of coups d'etat for 31 countries in a cross-country augmented production function framework that incorporates PI events as well as labor and capital as arguments. It finds that abortive coups, rather than successful coups, had the greatest adverse impact on economic growth over the 1960–1986 period. Coup plots were also observed to be growth-inhibiting. This deleterious "direct" effect of PI is observed to be channeled via the deterioration in the marginal productivity of capital, regardless of coup event. While abortive coups negatively influenced economic growth monotonically, however, the impacts of successful coups and coup plots appeared to be non-monotonic: negative generally but positive at very low levels of investment.

I

Introduction

THE GENERALLY DISMAL African economic growth record during the post-colonial period has been accorded plenty of attention in the de-

* The author is Director of Research, African Economic Research Consortium, Nairobi, Kenya; and Professor of Economics (on leave), Oakland University, Michigan, U.S.A. Part of the research for the study was conducted while he was Visiting Associate Professor, University of Rochester, New York. The author gratefully acknowledges comments by E. N. Botsas, O. Izraeli, and anonymous referees, as well as grant support from the Oakland University Research Committee and the School of Business Administration. The author's recent published research includes work on implications of various factors for growth in developing economies, with special emphasis on Sub-Saharan Africa: external debt, export composition, and instabilities. Other recent published research is on labor economics of racial and gender groups in the United States: the role of anti-discrimination measures for the occupational and earnings advancement of African-American men and women, and the labor force participation of women.

American Journal of Economics and Sociology, Vol. 61, No. 1 (January, 2002).

velopment literature as well as in the popular press. At the same time, there is an emerging consensus in the literature that institutional factors are major determinants of economic growth. One such variable that has been given special attention is political instability (PI), measured as the incidence of coups d'etat, which is generally observed to be adverse to growth (e.g., Londregan and Poole 1990; Barro 1991, 1996; Fosu 1992; Alesina et al. 1996; and Easterly and Levine 1997).

PI has been found to be a particularly important culprit in the observed low growth of African economies. For example, Fosu (1992) finds the "direct" adverse effect of PI in Sub-Saharan Africa (SSA) to be as much as 33 percent of the GDP growth over the 1960–1986 period. This finding is based on a PI index of the frequencies of "abortive" coups and "plots," as well as "successful" coups (McGowan and Johnson 1984).[1] The present paper examines the extent to which these three forms of PI events may exert differential impacts on economic growth.

Assessing the relative importance of the various facets of coups is important for three related reasons. First, it should shed light on the appropriate weights for the PI index. For example, McGowan and Johnson assume that successful coups were the most destabilizing, followed by attempted coups, and then coup plots. Thus they, rather arbitrarily, assigned respective weights of 5, 3, and 1. Are these weights supportable by the empirical evidence, or are there better empirically defensible weights? Second, evidence on the comparative importance of these different forms of coups would permit a relatively accurate prediction of the implications of a given coup event for economic growth.

Third, as Table 1 indicates, the composition of coup events varied substantially across countries over the 1958–1986 period. For example, concentrating on nations that experienced at least two types of coup events, Liberia's coup incidence was primarily plots, whereas about two-thirds of Niger's and Zambia's coup frequencies were abortive. Meanwhile, as many as one-half of the coup incidents were successful for several of the countries: Benin, Burkina Faso, Burundi, Nigeria, and Rwanda. Thus, if the implications of PI for economic growth vary by coup event, there would appear to be different consequences for various countries, depending on their respective historical patterns of coups.

Table 1

Relative Frequencies of Coup Events in Sub-Saharan Africa, 1958–1986

Country	ACOUPS	CPLOTS	SCOUPS
Benin	0.25	0.25	0.50
Botswana	0	0	0
Burkina Faso	0.10	0.40	0.50
Burundi	0.16	0.33	0.50
Cameroon	0.50	0.50	0
Central African Republic	0.38	0.25	0.38
Chad	0.50	0.25	0.25
Congo	0.45	0.27	0.27
Cote d'Ivoire	0	1.00	0
Ethiopia	0.17	0.75	0.08
Ghana	0.25	0.54	0.21
Kenya	0.33	0.67	0
Lesotho	0	0	1.00
Liberia	0.15	0.77	0.08
Madagascar	0.33	0.33	0.33
Malawi	0	1.00	0
Mali	0	0.80	0.20
Mauritania	0.11	0.56	0.33
Mauritius	0	0	0
Niger	0.66	0.17	0.17
Nigeria	0.10	0.40	0.50
Rwanda	0.50	0	0.50
Senegal	1.00	0	0
Sierra Leone	0.17	0.50	0.33
Somalia	0.29	0.57	0.14
Sudan	0.32	0.54	0.13
Togo	0	0.67	0.33
Uganda	0.43	0.29	0.29
Zaire	0.10	0.70	0.20
Zambia	0.67	0.33	0
Zimbabwe	0.50	0.50	0

ACOUPS, CPLOTS, and SCOUPS are abortive coups, coup plots, and successful coups, respectively. Rows may not sum to unity due to rounding; they sum to zero where there are zero events for each category. The list of countries shown here is the sample used in the study. See the text for details of definitions of variables and data sources.

II

Theoretical Discussion

THE THEORETICAL RATIONALE underlying why "elite" PI—the forceful removal, or attempt or plot to remove, from office those in leadership positions in a given country (Morrison and Stevenson 1971)—may be economically deleterious is well discussed in the literature (e.g., Alesina et al. 1996; Fosu 1992). PI is hypothesized to destabilize economic rules of resource allocation governing effort and expected reward. Such destabilization would likely reduce the efficiency of the production process and, hence, economic growth (Fosu 1992). Kuznets, for example, writes: "Clearly some minimum political stability is necessary if members of the economic society are to plan ahead and be assured of a relatively stable relation between their contribution to economic activity and their rewards" (1966:451). There might, however, be differential impacts of the various forms of PI events measuring this political stability.

Since a successful coup tends to put the stamp of a new regime on a given country, it portends the greatest likelihood of actual changes in the economic rules of operation. New (military) governments that seize executive power must justify their *raison d'etre*. The African historical coup incidence record is replete with accounts of emerging military coup leaders decreeing new rules such as debt abrogation, cancellation of previous currency devaluations, and reinstitution of government subsidies. Such policies usually favor the politically weighty elite, including the military. While politically palatable in the short run, however, these policies can have disastrous long-run economic consequences.

By virtue of their power base, military governments might actually be better equipped than their civilian counterparts in implementing economic reforms. However, such altruistic motives are likely to be supplanted, sooner or later, by the rational political objective to satisfy their respective constituencies, which may differ even among military governments. In effect, rules governing rewards from resource allocation are likely to vary with the frequency of military takeovers. By potentially changing the rules of economic operation, successful coups d'etat are likely to engender uncertainties in long-term decision making and, hence, be associated with economic destabilization and decline (Fosu 1992).

Abortive coups may intensify the uncertainty of the political and economic atmosphere, as the existing government usually resorts to harsh measures to deal with the perpetrators of an abortive coup. These measures normally include declarations of states of emergency and suspensions of freedom, as well as property confiscation, imprisonment, and even executions of the accused. Though some of these measures may also accompany a successful coup, they are likely to be more severe in the case of an abortive one, as the threatened government seeks to insulate itself, usually through harsh retaliatory and repressive measures, against any further coup attempts. Such actions combined with the highly charged political atmosphere accompanying failed coups would probably generate a great deal of uncertainty and cloud investment decisions. Indeed, threatened governments would be reluctant to undertake economic reforms such as currency devaluation that may portend long-run economic benefits but be fraught with short-run political dangers. Thus, a higher level of economic destabilization and decline is likely to accompany a larger frequency of abortive coups.

Coup plots probably have similar but less intensified effects as failed coups. Threatened governments usually retaliate against the accused plotters; however, since no actual attempts have been carried out, such retaliatory actions are unlikely to be as severe. Indeed, *reported* plots need not be reflective of the likelihood with which an actual coup might occur. They could instead be used as a pretext by an existing government to demonstrate that it is adept and in control. Nonetheless, a high frequency of coup plots could signal increased uncertainty in the economic environment and, hence, inhibit economic activity.

Coup events are likely to adversely influence both the levels and productivities of the production inputs. "Direct" effects on output are channelled via deteriorations in the efficiency of production, whereas "indirect" impacts would be through reductions in input levels (Fosu 1992). Employing a dichotomous variable based on the McGowan-Johnson PI index involving all the three PI events, Fosu (1992) uncovers a large direct, but weak indirect, effect of PI for SSA. In the light of this finding, the present study concentrates on the direct impact and examines the extent to which it differs according to the type of coup event.

III

The Model

FOLLOWING FOSU (1992), we postulate the following augmented production function:

$$Q' = a_0 + a_1 L' + a_2 K' + a_3 X' + a_4 P \tag{1}$$

where Q', L', K', and X' are the growth rates of output, labor, capital, and exports, respectively; P is a measure of PI. The coefficients a_i (i = 0, 1, 2, 3, 4) are the marginal effects or "productivities" of the respective variables. However, since exports are also produced, we additionally specify a PI-augmented export production function:

$$X' = b_0 + b_1 L' + b_2 K' + b_3 P \tag{2}$$

Incorporating equation (2) into (1) yields the following reduced-form PI-augmented production function:

$$Q' = c_0 + c_1 L' + c_2 K' + c_3 P \tag{3}$$

where $c_0 = a_0 + a_3 b_0$; $c_1 = a_1 + a_3 b_1$; $c_2 = a_2 + a_3 b_2$; and $c_3 = a_4 + a_3 b_3$. Thus the coefficients in equation (3) reflect the effects of the respective variables through exports as well.[2]

For the current study, we are especially interested in the coefficient of P that measures the PI impact. The above discussion suggests that c_3 will be negative. However, c_3 may vary with coup event: abortive, successful, or plot. In general, the relative importance of a given coup event appears to be an empirical question. For example, would the probable rule changes accompanying a successful coup be more or less economically destabilizing than the heightened uncertainty that might accompany a failed coup? In addition, how severe would be the economic destabilization resulting from the uncertainty engendered by a coup plot?

The pattern of the effect of PI might also be coup-type dependent. Using a dichotomous classification of the sample into "high" and "low" PI groups, Fosu (1992), for example, finds that the PI effect is non-monotonic: positive at very low levels of the production inputs, though negative generally. How does this pattern differ by coup event? To examine this phenomenon, we similarly assume that the marginal productivities of the production inputs depend on PI.[3] Permitting the possibility that the PI-growth relationship may not be discontinuous, however, the PI-marginal productivity function is expressed here as:

$$a_i = a_{i1} + a_{i2}P, i = 1, 2 \qquad (4)$$

$$b_i = b_{i1} + b_{i2}P, i = 1, 2 \qquad (5)$$

where a_{i1} and b_{i1} measure the independent effects of L' (i = 1) and K'(i = 2) on output and exports, respectively, which are positive under the neoclassical model; a_{i2} and b_{i2} are the effects of P on the impacts of L' (i = 1) and K' (i = 2) on output and exports, respectively, and are expected to be negative according to the above discussion.

Incorporating equations (4) and (5) into equations (1) and (2) and rearranging terms, we arrive at the following estimable model (with an appended error term u):

$$Q' = c_0 + c_{11}L' + c_{12}P^*L' + c_{21}K' + c_{22}P^*K' + c_3P + u \qquad (6)$$

where $c_{ij} = a_{ij} + a_3b_{ij}$; i, j = 1, 2. The effect of P on output growth can now be written as:

$$d = c_3 + c_{12}L' + c_{22}K' \qquad (7)$$

That is, the impact of PI on economic growth depends on the growth levels of the production inputs; c_3 is the independent effect of PI on output growth, while c_{12} and c_{22} are the respective PI impacts through the growths of labor and capital.

Since a_{i2} and b_{i2} are negative, and a_3, the export effect on output, is positive, the coefficients of L' and K' in equation (7) are negative. However, the sign of c_3 in equation (7), the effect of P when L' and K' are zero, is generally unknown. It is quite conceivable, however, that c_3 would be non-negative; that is, a given coup event need not worsen the economic growth of a nation already experiencing dismal conditions of extremely low labor and capital growths. Nevertheless, at sufficiently large levels of L' and K', the overall PI effect, d, is negative. Furthermore, this adverse impact of PI increases with L' and K', due to the tendency of PI to reduce the marginal "productivities" of the production inputs.

IV

Estimation and Results

THE DATA USED to estimate equation (6) consist of World Bank economic data on Q', L', and K' and unpublished data on coup incidence. The economic data are mean annual growth rates of the respective variables over the 1960–1986 period for each country and are derived from various issues of *World Development Report* and *World Tables*. Q' and L' are measured as the growth rates of GDP and labor force, respectively. Following Ram (1985) and Fosu (1990), for example, K' is represented by gross domestic investment as a percentage of GDP.[4] The sample used here is shown in Table 1; it is limited to 31 Sub-Saharan African countries by the availability of the economic data over the sample period.

The source of the PI data is McGowan (1986), who compiles the intervention events primarily from several issues of *Keesing's Contemporary Archives*, *Africa Research Bulletin*, and the *New York Times*. The data comprise the frequencies of successful coups d'etat, attempted coups, and reported plots to overthrow existing governments over the 1958–1986 period. This database is particularly unique in that it provides information on all these three types of coup events.[5] Means and standard deviations of the coup frequencies, as well as those of the economic data, are provided in Table 2.

Equation (6) and restricted versions of it are estimated using Ordinary Least Squares (OLS); the results are presented in Table 3. We first consider the appropriateness of using OLS in the estimation. In particular, given the cross-sectional nature of the present study, heteroscedasticity constitutes a potential problem in that it can distort the precision of the estimates. Reported in Table 3, therefore, is the Bartlett likelihood ratio statistic, B, in order to provide a test for possible misspecification. This test statistic suggests, however, that there is

Table 2

Coup Event and Economic Growth in Sub-Saharan Africa, 1960–1986 Summary Statistics of the Basic Regression Variables

Variable	Mean	Std. Dev.
Q'	3.36	1.84
L'	2.20	0.56
K'	18.61	6.08
P: ACOUPS	1.84	1.92
SCOUPS	1.81	1.78
CPLOTS	3.42	3.46

The variables Q' and L' are the mean percent annual growth rates of GDP and the labor force, respectively; K' is the mean gross domestic investment as a percentage of GDP; ACOUPS, SCOUPS, and CPLOTS are the respective frequencies of abortive coups, successful coups, and coup plots. For details of definitions of variables and data sources, see the text.

no evidence of heteroscedasticity in any of the estimated equations,[6] thus providing some justification for the use of OLS here.

The "basic neoclassical equation" that includes only labor and capital as arguments is presented as equation A.1 in Table 3. The PI-*augmented* models are shown under categories B, C, and D, where PI is measured by the respective frequencies of abortive coups (ACOUPS), successful coups (SCOUPS), and coup plots (CPLOTS).

According to the adjusted R^2 and SEE in Table 3, the PI-augmented models provide better goodness of fit than does the basic neoclassical model for all measures of PI. This outcome suggests that PI is not inconsequential for growth for SSA, as others have previously observed (e.g., Fosu 1992). However, several coefficients in the fully specified model (equation [.1] in each PI category) are only weakly significant, if at all, suggesting that some of the variables might be superfluous. Specifically, restricting the interactive effect of PI through labor to zero improves the goodness of fit (compare equations [.1] and [.3] for each PI category in Table 3). In contrast, constraining the coefficient of the capital interactive variable to zero reduces the model's fit (equation

Table 3

Coup Event and Economic Growth in Sub-Saharan Africa, 1960–1986

Eqn.	Const.	L'	K'	P	P*L'	P*K'	Adj.R²	SEE	B
A. Basic Neoclassical Equation									
(A.1)	−1.21	.790 (1.55)	.153[a] (3.24)	—	—	—	.346	1.49	.548
B. P = ACOUPS									
(B.1)	−1.50	.659 (1.02)	.213[a] (3.02)	.690 (0.77)	−.162 (0.52)	−.038[c] (1.83)	.474	1.34	.163
(B.2)	−.089	.860[c] (1.84)	.118[b] (2.59)	−.342[b] (2.49)	—	—	.449	1.37	.400
(B.3)	−1.02	.456 (0.90)	.214[a] (3.08)	.270 (0.73)	—	−.036[c] (1.78)	.490	1.32	.159
(B.4)	−.549	.619 (1.38)	.173[a] (4.15)	—	—	−.022[a] (3.08)	.499	1.31	.243
C. P = SCOUPS									
(C.1)	−2.21	.306 (0.43)	.280[a] (3.21)	1.32 (1.56)	−.207 (0.63)	−.062[c] (1.97)	.413	1.41	.220
(C.2)	−.317	.607 (1.15)	.145[a] (3.08)	−.197 (1.21)	—	—	.357	1.48	.377

Regression Results (absolute t values in parentheses)

						Adj.R²	SEE	B
(C.3)	−1.82	.044 (0.77)	.292ᵃ (3.49)	.923 (1.65)	—	−.064ᵇ (2.08)	.426	1.40	.206
(C.4)	−.358	.409 (0.76)	.178ᵃ (3.72)	—	—	−.015ᶜ (1.75)	.391	1.44	.277
D. P = CPLOTS									
(D.1)	−1.31	.221 (0.25)	.256ᵃ (3.55)	.108 (0.18)	−.119 (0.40)	−.031ᵇ (2.20)	.435	1.39	.362
(D.2)	−.536	.787 (1.57)	.137ᵃ (2.88)	−.113 (1.41)	—	—	.432	1.47	.487
(D.3)	−1.77	.517 (1.08)	.244ᵃ (2.78)	.332 (1.59)	—	−.029ᵇ (2.27)	.453	1.36	.285
(D.4)	−.712	.692 (1.44)	.169ᵃ (3.75)	—	—	−.010ᵇ (2.17)	.422	1.40	.366

Notes: The dependent variable is Q', measured as the mean annual percent growth rate of GDP; L' is the average percent growth rate of the labor force; K' denotes the mean gross domestic investment as a percentage of GDP; P is a measure of (elite) political instability, measured as the frequency of abortive coups (ACOUPS), successful coups (SCOUPS), or coup plots (CPLOTS). For details of the definitions of variables and data sources, see the text. Adj.R² and SEE are the usual regression statistics; B is the Bartlett likelihood ratio statistic to test for heteroscedasticity. The sample size is 31.

ᵃ Significant at the .01 two-sided level.

ᵇ Significant at the .05 two-sided level.

ᶜ Significant at the .10 two-sided level.

[.2] versus equation [.3] in each category). It appears, therefore, that labor productivity is little affected by PI, whereas, as predicted above, PI adversely influences capital productivity.

It is interesting to note, furthermore, that while the coefficient of the PI variable, P, is negative in the basic equation for each coup event category (B.2, C.2, and D.2 of Table 3), as expected, it is statistically significant only for ACOUPS. This relatively simple specification suggests, then, that the adverse effect of ACOUPS is most pronounced. Meanwhile, the coefficient of the capital interactive variable, p*k, is negative and significant in each specification. Thus it appears that the "direct" adverse impact of PI is transmitted through a deterioration in capital productivity, irrespective of the PI measure used here.

On the basis of goodness of fit (adjusted R^2 and SEE), the "best" model where PI is measured by ACOUPS is equation B.4 of Table 3, which restricts the coefficient of P to zero. It seems then that an abortive coup engenders a monotonically negative effect of PI via a deterioration in capital productivity.

In contrast, the "best" model in the case of SCOUPS and CPLOTS is the third equation, C.3 and D.3 in Table 3, respectively, where the coefficient of P is not restricted to zero. Although the estimated effect of P is only weakly significant in either case, it is positive, and the goodness of fit of the model improves when P is included (the third versus fourth equation, respectively). Thus, a successful coup or coup plot may be associated with an increase in output growth when the investment ratio (GDI/Q) is sufficiently low. A possible explanation of this finding is that when economic conditions are very dismal, as exemplified by low investment rates for example, a coup incident may actually help to improve the expectations and economic conditions of the people, at least initially (Fosu 1992:836).

The threshold value of the investment variable is 14.4 percent (i.e., .923/.064) and 11.4 percent (i.e., .332/.029) for SCOUPS and CPLOTS, respectively. In other words, on average, the growth rate of a country with an investment/GDP ratio of less than 14.4 percent could be enhanced by a successful coup, whereas a coup plot could be growth-enhancing for a ratio less than 11.4 percent.

Only in five out of the 31 countries in the sample was the investment ratio less than 11.4 percent and, therefore, small enough for the positive effect of CPLOTS to occur. These nations are Burundi, Chad, Ethiopia, Ghana, and Uganda. Furthermore, only nine countries would satisfy the condition of a beneficial impact of a successful coup: Burundi, Chad, Ethiopia, Ghana, Rwanda, Sierra Leone, Somalia, Sudan, and Uganda.[7]

Why might the effect of PI be monotonically negative through ACOUPS but non-monotonic in the case of SCOUPS and CPLOTS? One possible explanation is that, under depressed economic conditions, an attempted coup that fails is unlikely to ameliorate the negative expectations associated with such conditions, so that no positive expectations are generated. In contrast, a successful coup may engender the anticipation that the economic woes will probably improve, or the coup could effect an actual change in the status quo. Such improved expectations or change can be a stimulus to growth.

The interpretation is a little harder in the case of CPLOTS, however. Since there is no actual change in regimes, it is difficult to argue that there will be improved expectations or that the rules of operation will change for the better. Nevertheless, the signal provided by the evidence that others are plotting to overthrow the regime presumed to be responsible for the gloomy economic conditions (investment ratio of about 11 percent or less!) might foster positive expectations. This is to be contrasted with the ACOUPS case where there is an actual failure in the coup attempt, thus forestalling any positive expectations.

The results in Table 3 further indicate that an abortive coup reduced GDP growth by an average of .41 of a percentage point per year. The respective reduction rates were .27 and .21 for SCOUPS and CPLOTS.[8] Thus, on average, an abortive coup tends to be the most growth-inhibiting, followed by a successful coup and, very closely, by a coup plot.[9]

Further Empirical Evidence

The above empirical results are based on estimating the PI-growth relationship separately for the different coup events. A question, therefore, arises of possible omitted-variable problems associated with the estimation. For example, if the various events are correlated, as they are in the present case, then a given PI event might reflect as well the

effects of the other omitted PI variables. At the same time, unfortunately, the three types of PI seem more correlated among themselves
than with output growth.[10] Hence, there is the potential problem of
severe multicollinearity when all the PI variables are included in a single model. That might reduce both the precision of the estimates and
the ability to separate out the independent effects of the various PI
events.

Nonetheless, equation (6) is re-estimated, treating P as a vector of
the three PI events, and using the idiosyncratic patterns observed for
the various events in Table 3. The results are reported below as (absolute value of the t ratio in parentheses):

$$Q' = -1.83 + .192L' + (.309 - .0220AC - .0135SC - .0294CP)K'$$
$$(1.35) \quad (0.38) \quad (4.17) \quad (2.80) \quad \quad (0.38) \quad \quad (2.02)$$
$$+.196SC + .431CP$$
$$(0.311) \quad (1.73)$$
$$\text{Adj. } R^2 = 0.574, \text{ SEE} = 1.22 \tag{8}$$

where AC, SC, and CP are the respective frequencies of abortive coups
(ACOUPS), successful coups (SCOUPS), and coup plots (CPLOTS);
and the remaining variables are as previously defined (see Table 3).

It is reassuring that the results presented in equation (8) generally
confirm the earlier findings. In particular, ACOUPS appears to be the
dominant PI variable. It exhibits a significant negative coefficient interactively with K' (at the .01 two-tailed level). In addition, note that the
coefficient of (interactive) ACOUPS is remarkably similar to the one
earlier obtained when it was the sole PI variable (see equation [B.4],
Table 3). Thus, the estimated effect of ACOUPS appears quite robust.
While the coefficients of the SCOUPS and CPLOTS remain negative,
however, only that of CPLOTS is significant.

To provide a more complete discussion of the empirical results, Table 4 reports as "partial effects" and "partial elasticities" the respective
independent impacts of the three coup events. These estimates are derived from the results of equation (8), so that for each PI variable the
impacts of the remaining events are controlled. Compared with the
earlier estimates in Table 3, note that the effect of SCOUPS falls rather

Table 4

Independent Effects of Coup Events

Variable[1]	Partial Effect[2]	Partial Elasticity[3]
ACOUPS	−0.409	0.224
SCOUPS	−0.055	0.030
CPLOTS	−0.116	0.118

[1]The variables are as defined in Table 3.

[2]Calculated as $c_{22}K' + c_3P$, where all symbols are as defined in equation (6) of the text; the estimated coefficients are given in equation (8); and K' is computed at the sample mean. For ACOUPS, SCOUPS, and CPLOTS, we have, respectively: $-0.0220(18.6)$, $-0.0135(18.6) + 0.196$, and $-0.0294(18.6) + 0.431$.

[3]Calculated as bP/Q', where b is the respective absolute value of the "partial effect" of P, as computed in the first column in the table. P and Q' are PI and output growth, respectively (see Table 3); they are estimated at their respective sample means.

precipitously and is actually insignificant.[11] The impact of CPLOTS also diminishes;[12] unlike the case of SCOUPS, however, it is statistically significant, and its diminution is less dramatic.

Whether the "partial effects" or "partial elasticities" are used, it is apparent from Table 4 that the deleterious effect of ACOUPS is the largest. However, unlike the estimates in Table 3 where each event was entered separately as the sole PI variable, Table 4 indicates that CPLOTS exercises a greater impact than SCOUPS. It is further observed that when all the PI events are included together in the model (equation [8]), the goodness of fit, as measured by the SEE and adjusted R^2, improves substantially over those specifications where the PI variables are entered separately. In particular, note that the goodness of fit of equation (8) exceeds that for the model containing ACOUPS alone (equation [B.4], Table 3). Thus SCOUPS and CPLOTS are not extraneous, notwithstanding the superiority of ACOUPS in the growth equation. Given the relatively high collinearity among the PI events,[13] however, these "independent" effects of the PI events from equation (8) should be interpreted with some caution. Through their collinearity, the various events apparently exhibit reinforcing effects, which may not lend themselves to a clean separation intended in equation (8). Thus the current results should be viewed together with those in Table 3.

V

Summary and Conclusion

THE CURRENT STUDY has examined the extent to which the various coup events of political instability (PI) afflicting the developing economies of Sub-Saharan Africa (SSA) during the post-colonial period—"successful" coups (SCOUPS), "abortive" coups (ACOUPS), and coup "plots" (CPLOTS)—might have differentially influenced economic growth. Although these coup events tend to be positively correlated, they have exhibited composition differences across nations over the post-colonial sample period. Thus, information regarding differences in their impacts should, at least, aid in determining appropriate weights for an index of the severity of elite political instability.

A PI-augmented production function, accounting for the growth levels of capital and labor inputs, was first estimated separately using the three PI events. ACOUPS was observed to exercise the largest adverse effect on GDP growth, followed by SCOUPS, and then closely by CPLOTS.

The model was then re-estimated with all the three PI events together. Again, ACOUPS was found to exert the highest negative impact on growth. The effect of CPLOTS was also negative and significant. Though negative, the impact of SCOUPS was, however, observed to be insignificant.

The above findings contrast with the hypothesis underlying previous research that SCOUPS would be the most economically destabilizing (McGowan and Johnson 1984). They also call into question the rationale behind the tendency in the literature to employ SCOUPS as the measure of PI (e.g., Alesina et al. 1996).

The study further uncovers, for all three coup events, that the above effects were transmitted via the deterioration in the marginal productivity of capital attributable to PI. In addition, while the impact of ACOUPS was monotonically negative, that of CPLOTS, and possibly SCOUPS, tended to be positive initially at very low levels of investment, but with increasingly negative effects at higher investment levels.

The above results suggest that, despite some similarities, there are substantial differences in the impacts of the various forms of coup events. In particular, ACOUPS is by far the most growth-inhibiting among the three forms of coup events examined here. On average, however, all the three forms of PI events appear to have been deleterious to economic growth. Even in those cases where a successful coup would be harmless or growth-enhancing, undertaking it might not be desirable, since the probability of an attempted coup becoming successful is estimated at only 50 percent.[14] What the findings here suggest, instead, is that a mechanism for a peaceful transition of regimes would be most preferable.

Notes

1. A "successful" coup d'etat entails a forceful and unlawful change of the present government, usually by the military; "abortive" coups are such efforts that fail. A "plot" is said to exist if there is an official announcement by the existing regime that a conspiracy to forcefully change the government has been detected.

2. One advantage of this reduced-form specification is that it avoids a possible problem of high collinearity between X and P. For example, Fosu (1992: 834) finds substantial correlation between these two variables.

3. The rationale behind this assumption is that PI is likely to generate a sub-optimal investment portfolio. For example, PI may render short-term projects preferable to longer-term ones that may actually be more productive, due to a rise in the discousnt rate attributable to PI.

4. Expressing capital formation as a proportion of GDP is now rather standard in the literature. For justification see, for instance, Fosu (1990, footnote 11) and Ram (1985, footnote 6). Note that using this measure also converts the coefficient of the capital variable to a marginal product of capital.

5. For example, Alesina et al. (1996) use actual and not potential coups in their analysis, and Barro (1991) does not distinguish between the different forms of coups. For a more detailed description of the PI data used here, see McGowan and Johnson (1984) and Fosu (1992).

6. The Bartlett statistic is distributed as chi-square with (c–1) degrees of freedom, where *c* represents the number of groups formed from the sample to evaluate the uniformity of the variance of the error term. With *c* equal to 3 in the present sample, then, there are 2 degrees of freedom associated with B,

and we fail to reject the null hypothesis of homoscedasticity at any reasonable significance level. For details see, for example, Kmenta (1986:297–298).

7. Interestingly, it is these same nine countries that met a similar threshold involving capital and exports based upon a dichotomous PI classification constructed from all the three forms of PI (Fosu 1992:835). This consistency is, of course, not totally unexpected, since the McGowan-Johnson (M-W) index forming the basis of the PI binary variable was weighted most heavily by SCOUPS. (The M-W weights were 5, 3, and 1 for SCOUPS, ACOUPS, and CPLOTS, respectively.)

8. These statistics are computed from the "best" equations: B.4, C.3, and D.3 of Table 3, respectively, using the appropriate variant of equation (7) and a sample mean investment/GDP ratio of 18.61 percent. For example, in the case of SCOUPS, we have: $0.923 + (-0.064)(18.61) = -0.27$.

9. It is implicitly assumed here that the direction of causality runs from PI to output. Although we have theoretically argued for such a relationship, it might be possible for output to also "cause" PI. The issue of causality is, of course, a very complex one, and a formal test is beyond the scope of the current paper. The present empirical results, however, lead us to believe that reverse causality is unlikely. For example, we have found that the output effect of a coup event was greater for an abortive than for a successful coup or plot. Conversely, if the reverse causality were the case, the impact of output change would be greater for promoting a successful coup or plot than an abortive coup. Such a result appears untenable, however, for whether a coup succeeds or not, for example, would seem to rest on factors that have little to do with output changes.

The above argument is consistent with that of most authors who have written on the subject. They argue that political stability derives from political institutions that change rather slowly; hence PI is determined by institutional, not economic, variables (Cukierman, Edwards, and Tabellini 1992). For example, on a long-term basis, whether a given country would have more or less coup events is likely to depend on the relationship between the military and other institutions of government, regardless of the growth record of the economy.

10. The first-order correlation matrix is (the figures in brackets are the correlation coefficients when the respective PI variables are interacted with K'; see Table 3 for definitions of the variables):

	Q'	ACOUPS	SCOUPS	CPLOTS
Q'	—	−.49 (−.35)	−.36 (−.22)	−.34 (−.24)
ACOUPS		—	.50 (.44)	.54 (.33)
SCOUPS			—	.53 (.43)
CPLOTS				—

11. The partial effect of SCOUPS from equation (8) is -0.055 (see Table 4), compared with -0.267 computable from equation (C.3) of Table 3.

12. The partial effect of CPLOTS from equation (8) is -0.116 (see Table 4), compared with -0.207 computable from equation (D.4), Table 3.

13. Note that the PI variables are much more correlated with each other independently or interactively with respect to K', than each with Q'(see note (10)).

14. This probability is estimated using the sample means of ACOUPS and SCOUPS of 1.84 and 1.81, respectively.

References

Alesina, A., S. Ozler, N. Roubini, and P. Swagel (1996). "Political Instability and Economic Growth," *Journal of Economic Growth*, Vol. 1 (June), pp. 189–211.

Barro, R. J. (1991). "Economic Growth in a Cross-Section of Countries," *Quarterly Journal of Economics* (May), pp. 407–443.

———. (1996). "Democracy and Growth," *Journal of Economic Growth*, Vol. 1, No. 1 (March), pp. 1–27.

Cukierman, A., S. Edwards, and G. Tabellini (1992). "Seignorage and Political Instability," *American Economic Review* (June), pp. 537–555.

Easterly, W., and R. Levine (1997). "Africa's Growth Tragedy: Policies and Ethnic Divisions," Vol. 112, No. 4 (November), pp. 1203–1250.

Fosu, A. K. (1990). "Exports and Economic Growth: The African Case," *World Development*, Vol. 18, No. 6 (June), pp. 831–835.

———. (1992). "Political Instability and Economic Growth: Evidence from Sub-Saharan Africa," *Economic Development and Cultural Change*, Vol. 40, No. 4 (July), pp. 829–841.

Kmenta, J. (1986). *Elements of Econometrics*, 2nd ed. New York: MacMillan.

Kuznets, S. S. (1966). *Modern Economic Growth: Rate, Structure, and Spread.* New Haven, Conn.: Yale University Press.

Londregan, J. B., and K. T. Poole (1990). "Poverty, the Coup Trap, and the Seizure of Executive Power," *World Politics*, Vol. 42, No. 2, pp. 151–183.

McGowan, P. J. (1986). *Intervention Event File.* Tempe, Arizona: Arizona State University, Department of Political Science.

McGowan, P. J., and T. J. Johnson. (1984). "African Military Coups d'Etat and Underdevelopment: A Quantitative Historical Analysis," *Journal of Modern African Studies*, Vol. 22, No. 4, pp. 633–666.

Morrison, D. G., and H. M. Stevenson (1971). "Political Instability in Independent Black Africa: More Dimensions of Conflict Resolution within Nations," *Journal of Conflict Resolution*, Vol. 15 (September), pp. 347–368.

Ram, R. (1985). "Exports and Economic Growth: Some Additional Evidence," *Economic Development and Cultural Change*, vol. 33, no. 2, pp. 415–425.

World Bank. (1988) *World Development Report, 1988.* New York: Oxford University Press.

——— . (1989). *World Tables, 1988–89*. Baltimore, Maryland: Johns Hopkins University Press.

——— . (1991). *World Development Report, 1991*. New York: Oxford University Press.

PART VIII

Radical Criticisms and Reflections

Against the New Economic Imperialism

Some Reflections

By JONATHAN MICHIE, CHRISTINE OUGHTON, AND
FRANK WILKINSON*

ABSTRACT. Classical political economy recognised that what needed analysing, explaining, and acting on was an economic system inextricably linked to the wider political and social systems. Smith and Ricardo, as well as Marx, saw class and the distribution of income as key. Neoclassical economics replaced these social and collective categories with the individual consumer and the marginal product of labour as the fundamental analytical categories—the "political" having been discarded. Yet even one of the founders of neoclassical economics, Alfred Marshall, would barely recognise nor accept what is today presented as economic analysis, ignoring as it does the key industrial and organisational detail underlying production. The "new political economy" claims to incorporate insights from other disciplines. But far from enriching economic analysis, these new strands of theory simply impose the assumptions and methods of neoclassical economics. We argue that this new economic imperialism needs to be replaced with a genuinely multidisciplinary and interdisciplinary approach to analysing economic issues.

* Jonathan Michie is the Sainsbury Professor of Management at Birkbeck College, University of London, London WC1E 7HX: email *j.michie@bbk.ac.uk*. He has published extensively on economic policy issues and edited the *Reader's Guide to Social Sciences* (Fitzroy Dearborn, 2000). Christine Oughton is Reader in Management and Chair of the Department of Management at Birkbeck College, University of London, London WC1E 7HX: email *c.oughton@bbk.ac.uk*. Oughton and Michie are currently running research projects on the impact of globalisation and technological innovation on employment, and on regional innovation strategies. Frank Wilkinson is Reader in Economics at the University of Cambridge and a Visiting Professor in the School of Management and Organizational Psychology at Birkbeck College, University of London: email *f.wilkinson@cbr.cam. ac.uk*. He was a founding editor of the Cambridge Journal of Economics and has published widely on political economy issues, including on the concept of productive systems.

American Journal of Economics and Sociology, Vol. 61, No. 1 (January, 2002).

I

Introduction

THERE WAS DURING THE 1980s and 1990s a counterrevolution—or perhaps more accurately, a counterreformation—in both economic policy
and economic theory. The two developments were inextricably
linked. The restrictive monetary and fiscal policies were in effect a regression to the pre-Keynesian orthodoxies of the 1920s. But they were
justified by new evidence, as well as additional theoretical and policy
work, that sought to promote the theory of monetarism as a guide to
government economic policy. The supposed connection between the
money supply and the price level was presented as a technocratic
economic law. In reality the economic effects of the resulting monetarist policies were far from technical processes. Insofar as they
"worked," this was through, first, their effects on levels of unemployment and, second, the associated legislation that was pursued in various forms within most of the countries that adopted the monetarist
path, including anti-trade-union legislation and privatisation. Together, these political, economic, and social changes helped shift the
balance of power away from organised labour at the macro level, "re-
storing management's right to manage" at the micro level.

This paper argues that the "new political economy" has failed to
analyse these developments. Indeed, it has moved in precisely the
wrong direction, away from what might more justifiably be considered
to be political economy, and instead has adopted an individualistic
and technocratic view of processes that in reality reflect social and political factors, and whose economic component can only be properly
understood by recognising their collective nature.

II

The Counterreformation in Economic Theory

THE SPREAD OF JOB INSECURITY and work intensity in the 1990s, despite
economic recovery and rising employment, is explained by the fact
that the process of work reorganisation and job shedding is now continuous and not just a function of the trade cycle as it might have been
previously. Firms in the private sector have been exposed to substan-

tial trend increases in financial and other pressures resulting from growing demand from customers' requirements for improved products and services at lower prices and from the stock market for higher profits and more capital gains, intensified domestic and foreign competition, industrial concentration, and globalisation. For public sector organisations, privatisation, tight budget constraints, and government pressure to improve quality have had financial effects similar to increasing market pressures.

These processes are being justified and indeed driven by a counterreformation in economic theory. Faced with an inflationary crisis in the 1970s, the conventional economic wisdom—and the policy it informed—reverted to the pre-Keynesian beliefs that money determines prices and the market determines everything else. In industrial countries, especially the English-speaking countries, unemployment and the consequential labour market deregulation and social welfare reforms have shifted the balance of power in favour of capital and against workers. The result has been a growing polarisation of incomes. Concurrently, product and capital market deregulation, privatisation, and the liberalisation of trade have led to an international relocation of production to sources of cheap labour, a multiplication of the size and speed of international capital movements, and a growing concentration of global economic power. Everywhere, governments have been under pressure to scale down the level of their activities and to cut tax in a situation in which, because of growing poverty, demands on government expenditure have been increasing. The response, again especially in English-speaking countries, has been a switch in social welfare away from protecting and toward coercing the unemployed and the poor. Privatisation has changed the ethos in hitherto public provision away from public service and toward gain for shareholders, a switch replicated on behalf of taxpayers in the public sector by managerial reorganisation along private sector lines. The response of government to the resulting decline in standards of services in the newly privatised and what is left of the public sectors is to intensify regulation and monitoring, adding to the pressures that workers there are required to bear.

What explains the neoliberal revival and its tightening grip on policy, given its previous refutation and more recent failure to generate policy results to match its prediction? The Polish economist Kalecki worked along similar lines as Keynes, at the same time but independently. Like Keynes, he demonstrated the flaws in the 1920s' orthodoxy to which neoliberalism has since reverted. Ironically, though, Kalecki would not necessarily have been surprised at governments—and even some economists—reverting to the old discredited orthodoxy. Speculating on the effects of Keynesian policies delivering sustained full employment, he predicted that:

> The workers would "get out of hand" and the "captains of industry" would be anxious to "teach them a lesson". Moreover, the price increases in the up-swing is to the disadvantage of small and big *rentiers* and make them "boom tired". In this situation a powerful block is likely to be formed between big business and the *rentier* interests, and they would probably find more than one economist to declare that the situation was manifestly unsound. The pressure of all these forces, and in particular of big business would most probably induce the Government to return to the orthodox policy of cutting down the budget surplus. (Kalecki 1943:144)

Marx put it more bluntly. He identified 1830 as the watershed, when the middle classes secured power after electoral reform in Britain.

> [This] sounded the knell of scientific bourgeois economics. It was thenceforth no longer a question of whether this or that theorem was true, but whether it was useful to capital or harmful, expedient or inexpedient, in accordance with police regulations or contrary to them. In place of the disinterested inquirers there stepped hired prize fighters; in place of genuine scientific research, the bad conscience and evil intent of the apologetic. (Marx 1873 [1954]:25)

Whether the time frame that Kalecki had in mind for the political reaction against full employment was the generation or so that it actually took is open to question, but the process no doubt occurred. And the "more than one" economist willing to play the role cast by Kalecki has in fact proved too many to enumerate. The process Kalecki depicts is most often thought of in domestic economic terms—giving managers "the right to manage." But similar forces are at work on a global scale, with third world countries being weakened by recession. This political economy of slow growth on a world scale, with powerful interests opposing any return to economic development and full employment, has been highlighted by Ajit Singh (1992). Thus, in a global economy, such processes may be acted out on a global stage, with the advanced capitalist economies having an interest in the weakened power of raw material suppliers, which follows from slow growth.

III

Liberal Economics

LIBERAL ECONOMICS THEREFORE PRESIDES over instability and growing polarisation of wealth and power. The abiding belief of liberal economics is that together the pursuit of self-interests and the spontaneous ordering of the market will generate the greatest happiness for the greatest number. The clearest account of this central belief is to be found in the penultimate paragraph of Chapter 6, *The sale and purchase of labour*, of Volume 1 of Marx's *Capital*:

> This sphere that we are deserting, within whose boundaries the sale and purchase of labour-power goes on, is in fact a very Eden of the innate rights of man. There alone rule Freedom, Equality, Property and Bentham. Freedom, because both buyer and seller of a commodity, say of labour-power, are constrained only by their own free will. They contract as free agents, and the agreement they come to, is but the form in which they give legal expression to their common will. Equality, because each enters into relation with the other, as with a simple owner of commodities, and they exchange equivalent for equivalent. Property, because each enters into relation with the other, as with a simple owner of commodities, and they exchange equivalent for equivalent. Property, because each disposes only of what is his own. And Bentham, because each looks only to himself. The only force that brings them together and puts them in relation with each other, is the selfishness, the gain and the private interests of each. Each looks to himself only, and no one troubles himself about the rest, and just because they do so, do they all, in accordance with the pre-established harmony of things, or under the auspices of an all-shrewd providence, work together to their mutual advantage, for the common weal and in the interest of all. (Marx 1867 [1954]:172)

Adam Smith (1776) identified the market as the driver of productivity-enhancing division of labour and the coordinator of the increasingly specialised parts of the system. He argued that the propensities in human nature to "truck, barter and exchange one thing for another" ([1776] 1976:117) drove the division of labour and therefore the growing dependence of increasingly specialised trades on the production of others. However, these needs were met not "by the benevolence of the butcher, the brewer or the baker," but in exchange where each had "regard for their own interest" (*ibid.*, p. 119). Self-interest thus provides the incentive for specialisation, exchange provides the opportunity and incentive to trade, and the market coordinates these individual production and consumption decisions.[1]

Although he drew heavily on his predecessors, Adam Smith was pivotal in establishing the idea that a central role is played by "the invisible hand" of the market in the efficient coordination and regulation of the operation of individuals relentlessly pursuing their own self-interest. The corollary of this, that combinations are necessarily against the public interest, Smith also popularised:

> People of the same trade seldom meet together, even for merriment and diversion, but the conversation ends in a conspiracy against the public, or in some contrivance to raise prices. (*ibid.*, p. 232)

Therefore, to ensure that markets work effectively, regulation is needed to prevent collective and individual monopolies from operating in restraint of trade. Despite this need, as firms began to increase in size and market domination, economists began to develop theories that extended the idea of the beneficial effects of individuals operating in markets to include large businesses. It came to be argued that large firms emerge because markets offer opportunities to efficient forms of organisations, and that this can result in, or may even require, a degree of market control. Firms grow to dominance, it has been suggested, because of their superior managerial and production organisation, and the economies of their large-scale operation gives them market advantage. Monopoly profits are necessary, theorised Schumpeter, to encourage innovators to develop new products and processes. And, the new institutionalists argue, hierarchical control by large firms provides an efficient coordinating and monitoring alternative to the market when contracts are difficult and costly to enforce (Williamson 1986). Such theories served to broaden the range of benefits provided by the market to include an evolutionary mechanism by which efficient forms of organisation are promoted and the inefficient superseded. And, although large size may be the reward of success, big firms can only survive by generating the operational and dynamic efficiency by which organisations keep their feet in the market-driven "gale of creative destruction."

It is, however, recognised that there are downsides to market dominance. The abuse of power in labour and product markets may have significant distributional effects, the corporate managers might act in their own interests at the expense of shareholders, and the corporate actions may threaten the social and natural environment. Regulation is therefore accepted as necessary to counter such negative externalities[2] and to contain the destructive capabilities of competition. But, caution liberal economists, the urge to regulate must be tempered by the recognition that in the final analysis the market provides the best opportunity for individuals and society. And, while the market concentrates economic power, it also yields important benefits for society in the form of technical progress and economic growth. What is good for business is also good for society, and although dominant firms' excesses require checking, it would check progress if their market opportunities were unduly restricted.

A. Capital Markets

The theory that shareholder value (dividends and share prices) should be the prime objective of corporate managers provides an example of how liberal economic theorising has evolved as a justification for new forms of business organisation. The effect of the introduction of joint stock companies has been to separate owners from control and from the day-to-day activities of the business. This concentrates owners' attention exclusively on financial gain in the form of dividends or of cashing in their shares on the stock market. The ability of shareholders collectively to further their pecuniary interests by disposing of their shares has evolved as a powerful means by which takeovers and mergers can be used to concentrate economic power. This development has been justified on efficiency grounds by hypotheses that stock exchanges operate as efficient markets for corporate control, the means by which shareholders can punish inefficient managers. The managerial pursuit of shareholder value may put at risk the interests of other stakeholders.[3] These stakeholders include employees, suppliers, customers, and communities, all of whose interests might be damaged by the worsening of the terms and conditions of employment, downsizing, plant closure, environmental pollution, and neglect of long-term investment, any of which might be pursued in the interest of meeting shareholder demands.

B. Labour Markets

The perceived threat posed by classical political economy's explanation of the distribution of income in terms of social classes led to the development in the 1880s of the diminishing marginal productivity theory of wages. This theory is based on the idea that as the labour intensity of production increases—that is, as the quantity of labour employed per unit of capital rises—each successive unit of labour adds less to output. The conclusion is therefore that more employment requires lower wages.

In sum, the liberal argument is that the freedom of workers to sell and of capitalists to buy labour in the market ensures that nominal wages equals the value of the marginal product of labour, beyond which point it is no longer profitable for firms to hire more workers. Workers will accept this wage if it at least offsets the marginal disutility of work. The choice individuals have to work and the competition between employers for workers rules out the possibility of exploitation. Exploitation resulting from the existence of a reserve army of unemployed ready and willing to work is ruled out by the denial of the possibility of involuntary unemployment, in the sense of workers being jobless because there is no work for them to do even if they would be prepared to and could accept lower wages.

Keynes argued that as incomes rise, individuals save by an increasing proportion. No mechanism exists whereby the income saved is automatically taken up and invested. The increased propensity to save progressively lowers consumption demand and employment until the reduction in aggregate income squeezes out excess saving. Thus, saving is brought into line with investment, not by the working of the capital market, but by changes in the level of income and employment. The result is involuntary unemployment: the inability of workers to find jobs at, or even below, the going wage because of a shortage of demand for the products or services they could produce. This opens the way for state intervention to regulate the level of effective demand to secure full employment.

With the revival of pre-Keynesian economics has come the new orthodoxy of a labour market clearing wage rate, determined by marginal productivity theory and employability and unemployability as the explanation of joblessness (Michie 1987). The advantages of the theory of diminishing marginal productivity to liberal economics is clear. It delivers stable equilibrium and disposes of the thorny problem of income distribution between competing claimants by linking it to their productivity. The distribution of income between classes does not even arise. The only way the class distribution of income could be addressed within this orthodoxy would be as the result of an aggregation of individuals, each of whose income is determined by his or her marginal productivity. However, these ideas receive no empirical support. In reality, "the pro-cyclical pattern of productivity movements has been solidly established in dozens of empirical studies" (Okun 1981:16), precisely the opposite to that predicted by diminishing marginal productivity theory. This revealed tendency for labour productivity to rise as output increases is readily explained by the fact that the level of efficiency of the operation of plant and machinery rises the closer it is to technically- and organisationally-determined full capacity of operation. Any increase in output beyond full capacity requires investment in new equipment that can be expected to incorporate the latest techniques. This embodied technical change further enhances productivity and is more likely to come into operation when demand and output are growing. This means, as the evidence implies, that there are increasing rather than diminishing returns to labour inputs, so the idea that wages must fall if employment is to rise is a fallacy.

C. Liberal Economics and Employee Subordination

For Marx, the fundamental purpose of capitalist domination in the labour process was exploitation. He did not deny the productivity-enhancing capabilities of capitalism—on the contrary, with given wage levels, increased productivity could boost the rate of exploitation and hence profits.

On leaving this sphere of simple circulation or of exchange of commodities, which furnishes the "Free-trader *Vulgaris*" with his views and ideas, and with the standard by which he judges a society based on capital and wages, we think we can perceive a change in the physiognomy of our *dramatis personae*. He, who before was the money-owner, now strides in front as capitalist; the possessor of labour-power follows as his labourer. The one with an air of importance, smirking, intent on business; the other, timid and holding back, like one who is bringing his own hide to market and has nothing to expect but—a hiding. (Marx 1867 [1954]:172)

The workplace is the palace where surplus value is extracted, aided by unemployment—the reserve army of labour. This prevents competition between capitalists for scarce labour, or the use of labour scarcity by organised labour, from raising real wages or reducing work intensity and hence lowering surplus value—that is, the unpaid labour from which profits derive. More recently, the reserve army of labour has been given a liberal spin. Efficiency wage and insider-outsider theorists argue that unemployment, rather than being a mechanism for extracting additional unpaid labour from workers, serves to counter the transaction costs caused by the rent-extracting, opportunistic[4] behaviour of workers with sufficient bargaining power to prevent the market from working. The reserve army has also reappeared at the "natural" rate of unemployment or the Non-Accelerating Inflation Rate of Unemployment (NAIRU), which is the level necessary to prevent inflationary wage raises.[5]

IV

Human Resource Management and Corporate Performance

ONE OUTCOME OF THESE DEVELOPMENTS was the growth of human resource management (HRM) as a replacement for the traditional industrial relations function designed around conflict management. HRM has been defined as a "set of policies designed to maximise organisational integration, employee commitment, flexibility and the quality of work" (Guest 1987:504), with hard and soft versions identified. Soft HRM aims to release untapped reserves of "human resourcefulness" by increasing employee commitment, participation, and involvement. Hard HRM is designed to maximise economic returns from labour resources by integrating HRM into business strategy. Hard HRM has a broader engineering base and is strongly oriented toward meeting consumer requirements by greater production flexibility and continuous improvement (Appelbaum and Batt 1994).

Ideally, HRM's purpose is to foster a preemptive rather than a reactive approach to operational efficiency, quality control, and process development. This requires shifting accountability for decision making toward the shop floor where production teams share responsibility for identifying and solving problems in the production process as they arise. There is now a considerable body of literature suggesting a positive link between the use of HRM practices and performance, particularly when such methods as flexible work assignments, work teams, skill training, effective communications, and incentive pay schemes are used in combination. Trade union representation has also been shown to have a positive effect.[6]

V

Productive Systems and Creative Competition

THE PARADOX IS THAT in a society that makes a fetish of individualism, everyone is dependent on everyone else. Adam Smith recognised this dependence when he wrote, "In civilised societies," individuals stand "at all times in need of the co-operation and assistance of the great multitudes" ([1776] 1976:118). But he went on to emphasise that these needs could be met by specialisation in production, coordinated by the market. In illustrating this, Smith used the examples of independent artisans, butchers, and bakers, and there is a degree of credibility that they could work in isolation by trading in the markets for their supplies and products. But as labour and capital became increasingly specialised and as the factory system developed, the role of coordination expanded beyond the capability of the market. Wakefield (1835) pinpointed the limitations of the Smithian position in increasingly complex productive systems. He argued that it was not labour that was being divided, but what labour does—its employment.

An important difference between Smith and his critics was that while Smith emphasised the importance of exchange, his critics concentrated attention on production. They were clearly right in emphasising that production is a collective activity. At the technical level, relations of production are necessarily cooperative. At each stage of production, labour, equipment, and materials necessarily work in combination. None can operate without the others, so the failure of any to adequately perform its part lowers the joint product of the whole, an interdependency that extends to technical relations between the different stages of production. Consequently, cooperation between the agents of production (the owners and/or controllers of labour, the means of production, and the different stages of production) is a technical necessity that determines the resource cost and quality of the output of the productive system and hence its competitiveness.

A central feature of the necessary cooperation within productive systems is the sharing of information. This is important in a technical sense to ensure, for example, that all agents of production are equally well informed about the best means of production and that components are designed and produced in such a way as best to fulfill their productive purpose. Success in production will also depend on access to information on the latest products, processes, and forms of organisation. Here, cooperation is important because of the problem-solving benefits of working together and because the sharing of information increases the pace of diffusion and development of new processes and products and hence the pace of technical progress of the productive system. The operational efficiency (that is, the effectiveness of the utilisation of productive resources and the meeting of product specifications) of a productive system depends therefore to an important extent on the generation and transmission of technical information. And its dynamic efficiency (developing and using new technology) requires the generation and diffusion of information on new products and processes and on ways they can be improved. Both operational and dynamic efficiency are critically dependent on cooperation. The question is, how can this best be secured?

In thinking about this question, it is necessary to bring distribution into the discussion. While production is a joint activity, the distribution of its proceeds are indeterminate. Securing agreement on distribution is a social process. But production and distribution are unlikely to be independent; cooperation in production is likely to require agreement on distribution (Wilkinson 1998).

In examining productive systems and the forces operating upon them, it is important to differentiate between the technical and the social relations of production. Technical relations of production are defined as the functional interlinkages between labour, equipment, and materials in the production process and are therefore objective and impersonal associations determined by the technicalities of products and of the methods by which they are produced. The social relations of production are the subjective and personal associations between the agents of production. These create the social network within which the technical relations of production are formed, and within which the productive tasks of labour and the means of production are jointly undertaken. Social relations of production play a central role in determining the effectiveness of technical cooperation and hence operational and dynamic efficiencies.

At the macro level, the social relations of production are structured by the political and legal system. The political and legal system mediates economic relationships by determining the form taken by commercial and employment contracts, setting standards for production, employment, and trade, administering procedures for resolving disputes, regulating private organisations and institutions, determining what constitutes breaches in rules and regulations, and imposing sanctions. These rules, norms, procedures, and sanctions are embedded in company and trade union law, competition policy, labour, product and capital market legislation, and welfare state rules. At the micro level, the social relations include the personnel and industrial relations systems and contractual and other relations with customers and suppliers. In the management of production the social relations of production serve to direct, coordinate, and assert the authority to achieve these objectives. Thus, "economic, social and political forces combine in determining how economies develop . . . the result is a dynamic non-equilibrium process" (Wilkinson 1983:413).

VI

Conclusion

THE DOMINANCE OF NEOCLASSICAL ECONOMICS has overshadowed the development and growth of alternative approaches to economics concerned with analysing, rather than abstracting from, the complexities of economic systems associated with the interaction of economic, historical, social, legal, political, and psychological factors. In recent years there has been a growing recognition that providing satisfactory answers to basic research questions—such as what determines the economic performance of companies or countries—requires the development of an interdisciplinary economics that integrates economic analysis with other social sciences.[7]

This is a welcome development, not to be confused with the "new political economy," which is neither new nor political economy. The new political economy has sought to apply the methods of neoclassical economics in analysing issues that had previously been regarded as falling within the remit of other disciplines. The realism of behavioural assumptions continues to be regarded as being of no analytical consequence, with only the accuracy of a theory's predictions being of any significance.[8] Far from enriching economic analysis, new political economy simply imposes the assumptions and methods of neoclassical economics. This new economic imperialism needs to be replaced with a genuinely multidisciplinary and interdisciplinary approach to analysing economic issues.

Notes

1. However, Adam Smith was far from the naïve free-marketeer that some who quote his name in their support would claim. See Oughton (1990) for a discussion.

2. Externalities are costs not fully accounted for in the price or market system.

3. Stakeholders in an organisation are any individual or group who can affect or is affected by the activities of the organisation.

4. Defined by Williamson as self-seeking with guile.

5. For a critique of these "natural rate" and "NAIRU" theories, see Michie and Wilkinson (1995).

6. For a discussion of the HRM-performance link, of "hard" and "soft" HRM, a review of the evidence of the effect of clustering HRM strategies on company performance, and including in particular the effects of trade unions, see Michie and Sheehan-Quinn (in press).

7. This is argued in detail in Oughton (2001).

8. See Altman (2000), who contrasts this with behavioural economics.

References

Altman, M. (2000). "Behavioural Economics," in *Reader's Guide to the Social Sciences*, edited by J. Michie. London and Chicago: Fitzroy Dearborn Publishers.

Appelbaum E., and R. Batt. (1994). *The New American Workplace: Transforming Work Systems in the United States*. New York: ILR Press.

Guest, D. (1987). "Human Resource Management and Industrial Relations," *Journal of Management Studies* 24(5): 503–521.

Kalecki, M. ([1943] 1971). "Political Aspects of Full Employment," in *Selected Essays on the Dyanmics of the Capitalist Economy*. Cambridge: Cambridge University Press.

Marx, K. (1954a[1867]). *Capital, Volume 1*. London: Lawrence & Wishart.

———. (1954b[1873]). "Afterword," to *Capital, Volume 1*, 2nd German ed. London: Lawrence & Wishart.

Michie, J. (1987). *Wages in the Business Cycle: An Empirical and Methodological Analysis*. London: Frances Pinter.

Michie, J., and M. Sheehan-Quinn. (in press). "Labour 'Flexibility'—Securing Management's Right to Manage Badly?", in *Systems of Production: Markets, Organisations and Performance*, edited by B. Burchell, S. Deakin, J. Michie, and J. Rubery. London: Routledge.

Michie, J., and F. Wilkinson. (1995). "Wages, Government Policy and Unemployment," *Review of Political Economy* 7: 133–149.

Okun, A. M. (1981). *Prices and Quantities: A Macroeconomic Analysis*. Oxford: Basil Blackwell.

Oughton, C. (1990). "Conflict, the allocation of resources and income distribution," in *Conflict in Economics*, edited by Y. Varoufakis and D. Young. London and New York: Harvester Wheatsheaf.

———. (2001). "Interdisciplinary Economics and the Social Sciences," *The Journal of Interdisciplinary Economics* 12: 297–309.

Singh, A. (1992). "The Political Economy of Growth," in *The Economic Legacy: 1979–1992*, edited by J. Michie. London: Academic Press.

Smith, Adam (1974[1776]). *The Wealth of Nations*. Harmondsworth, UK: Penguin.

Wakefield, E. (1835). "Notes," in A. Smith, *An Inquiry into the Nature and Causes of the Wealth of Nations*. London: Knight.

Wilkinson, F. (1983). "Productive Systems," *Cambridge Journal of Economics* 7: 413–429.

———. (1998). *Co-operation, The Organisation of Work and Competitiveness*. ESRC Centre for Business Research, Working Papers No. 85.

Williamson, O. (1986). *Economic Organization*. New York: New York University Press.

Bourgeoisie Out, Expertoisie In

The New Political Economies at Loggerheads

By Donald Clark Hodges and Larry Lustig*

ABSTRACT. Part I of our paper pinpoints the "political" in the new political economies: first, the distinction between political, public, and civic economies that are almost invariably confused; second, the role of power politics, force, and fraud in determining income differentials in the name of market forces. Part II pinpoints the "new" in twentieth-century political economies: first, the emergence of a fourth factor of production in addition to labor, capital, and land, whether identified with organization, knowledge, headwork, education, brainpower, management, or information; second, the subordination of capital to this new factor; third, the formation of a new social class based on its ownership; fourth, the struggle between the owners of capital and the new class for control over decision making and for the lion's share in distribution; fifth, the reliance on government to protect and advance the interests of the new class of professionals; and sixth, the eclipse of the old class struggle between bourgeoisie and proletarians by a new class struggle between managers and managed, executives and exec-utants, "knows" and "know-nots." Part III pinpoints the "loggerheads" or sources of dissension between the "human capital" and post-capitalist variants of the new political economies: first, over whether the expertoisie constitute a new social class or a fraction of the bourgeoisie; second, over whether the new economic order constitutes an advanced stage of capitalism or the advent of a post-capitalist society; and third, whether the "knows" exploit the "know-nots" through their monopoly of economic and political power.

Why "political," why "new," and why "at loggerheads"? Our essay divides into three parts our tentative answers to these questions.

* Donald Clark Hodges is Professor of Philosophy and Affiliate Professor of Political Science at Florida State University. Larry Lustig has been Lecturer in Philosophy and Government-Politics at University of Maryland University College since 1988.

American Journal of Economics and Sociology, Vol. 61, No. 1 (January, 2002).

I.

IN DEFINING THE "POLITICAL" in the new political economies, one should beware of depriving it of autonomy by making it dependent on economic variables. Although there is an economic basis of politics, there is also a political basis of economics.

Harold Lasswell's *Politics: Who Gets What, When, How* provides a corrective to the economic interpretation of politics by demonstrating how the distribution of wealth is conditioned by political factors beyond the ken of most economists. James Burnham's *Managerial Revolution* and Milovan Djilas's *The New Class* also illustrate how differentials in political power contribute to explaining income differentials.[1]

In defining the "political," one must take care not to confuse it with the role political economists assign to government, policy recommendations, and the legislative process. Following Machiavelli instead of Aristotle, the new political science defines "politics" as neither the science nor the art of government, but as the theory and practice of the struggle for power. As Hans Morgenthau sums up the difference between politics, statecraft, and civics: "Domestic and international politics are but two different manifestations of the same phenomenon: the struggle for power." In acting politically one "seeks either to keep power, to increase power, or to demonstrate power" in a show of force aimed at intimidating an enemy.[2]

For political science narrowly interpreted as the science of government, the fundamental distinction is that between the public and the private, the public or national interest as opposed to individual or private interests. When the uniquely political is mistaken for statecraft or the art of government, the public interest becomes the leading concern as if the public as distinct from the private individuals who constitute it led an independent existence with an interest exclusively its own. On scrutiny, the public interest turns out to be a chimera that has precious little to do with the individual patriot's love for his homeland and homefolk. Moreover, the effort to define it hinges on shifting conceptions of the boundaries of the public, of the right of eminent domain, and of the acceptable limits of government interference in the economy.

As for civics, the fundamental distinction is that between getting along with one's neighbors and fellow workers as opposed to being contentious, at odds with everybody, and an outsider. When the uniquely political is swallowed up in civics, the cult of "political correctness" begins to take command. Irreconcilable differences are papered over, not removed. Class antagonisms disappear from view while continuing to fester beneath the surface of the civic culture. Thus "political man" is neither "government man" nor "civic man," not to mention "economic man."

As the intersection of economic and political variables, the science of political economy is laden with conflicts over fundamental issues. But what shall we say about the narrower field of economics, in which political concerns have been deliberately marginalized? Yes, but not altogether eliminated. As the science of the production and distribution of wealth, it includes more than the study of market forces. Not just custom, but also power differentials determine the values assigned to commodities in the process of exchange.

The separation of economics from politics in the expectation of making it scientifically rigorous ended in disaster. Its mathematical models resembled a Platonic heaven unrecognizable in the real world. As E. Ray Canterbery notes in *The Literate Economist*: "Historical perspective puts the lie to any claim that economics is a progressive science—operating like nuclear physics, outside time, and in pursuit of eternal verities." Although mathematics brings rigor to economics, "history prevents it from succumbing to rigor mortis."[3]

The classical statement of the basis of income differentials was formulated over two centuries ago in the wake of the Great French Revolution. In the first communist manifesto on record, *The Manifesto of the Plebeians* (November 1795), François Noël "Gracchus" Babeuf explained income differentials as a result of differences in esteem that custom attaches to different occupations. "A fantastic opinion of this sort," he observed, "leads people to attribute to the work-day of someone who makes a watch twenty times the value of someone who plows a field and grows wheat." As a result, the watch-maker "acquires the patrimony of twenty plowmen."[4]

But do not hold the market responsible for that outcome, he urged. Look behind it to the forces determining public opinion, to the people responsible for manipulating it. Rather than market forces, people of education "have fixed such a high price upon the conceptions of their brains." However, "if the physically strong had been able to keep up with them in regulating the order of things, they would no doubt have established the merit of the arm to be as great as that of the head, and the fatigue of the entire body would have been offered as sufficient compensation for the fatigue of the small part of it that ruminates." Although two centuries old, Babeuf's political interpretation of exchange and distribution has survived among the new political economies.[5]

The role of custom in determining income differentials was later recognized by Marx, if not the role of power differentials behind custom. What he called the "historical and moral element" that enters into the determination of wages he attributed to "the degree of civilization of a country, more particularly to the conditions under which . . . the class of free laborers has been formed."[6] Thus the more comfortable their condition, the higher their wages—as if the former were the underlying cause rather than a supervening one.

As his critics have observed, Marx's theory of exchange-values hinges on a table of equivalences antedating exchange, but also reflecting the relative worth of individuals. Although Marx had an explanation for exploitation under capitalism, it was a narrowly economic one.[7]

War has traditionally been regarded as the sport of kings. It also was and continues to be the highest expression of the political. Force made slavery and a slave economy possible, and later replaced serfdom by free labor under capitalism—as if human livestock were no longer milked. Yet Marxists continue to dispute this thesis. Private property may have preceded the oppressive role of politics in history, just as barter among near equals preceded the capitalist mode of commodity exchange. But to make exchange responsible for increasing inequality instead of the politics of exchange and distribution is to put the cart before the horse.[8]

Marx's *tour de force* was to explain income differentials under capitalism exclusively in terms of the exchange of equivalents. "In other words, even if we exclude all possibility of robbery, force, and fraud . . . the progressive evolution of production and exchange . . . can be explained by purely economic causes; at no point whatever are robbery, force, the state, or political interference of any kind necessary"; that is not why people are exploited and perform servile work as wage-laborers.[9]

Marx was mistaken. Force and fraud underlie the exchange of equivalents without being perceived as such. To be sure, force may no longer take the form of plunder and extortion, and fraud may no longer appear as deliberate imposture and chicanery. Under capitalism they become depersonalized and institutionalized to the point of becoming invisible.

José Miranda, Mexican ex-Jesuit and liberation theologian turned political economist, adds the missing link. What Marx called "primitive capitalist accumulation" based on force has not disappeared. It survives by virtue of its consequences. People without property are compelled to work for another's benefit or starve. People are being fleeced on the fraudulent grounds of "earning a living."[10]

Contrary to Marx, he argues, the politics of surplus value determine the mode of production as well as conversely. The unequal distribution of income compels the working stiff to beg for work like a medieval mendicant seeking alms. While some sweat it out, others loaf and enjoy living.[11] While common laborers sell their labor-power at cost or near-cost as represented by the minimum wage, the educated sell their working capacity at prices far in excess of their individual outlay for expertise. Marx mistakenly assumed that all wage earners were equally exploited regardless of what they earned. He failed to add that, like the capitalist, the brainworker benefits when "what is 'minus' to one is 'plus' to another."[12]

II.

"CAPITAL" WAS THE CORE CONCEPT of nineteenth- and early twentieth-century political economies and of the corresponding politico-economic reality identified with capitalism. The fundamental social relation was widely assumed to be that between the owners of capital and wage-laborers. This is no longer the case. The core concept of the new political economies is one or another equivalent of expertise. The corresponding social relation is that between the expertoisie as owners of this fourth factor, distinct from the classical factors of land, labor, and capital, and a new working class defined by the absence of professional know-how. Increasingly, the expertoisie has displaced the bourgeoisie.

What is expertise? As capital is not simply money, so expertise is not merely professional skill or higher education. *It is the power of education to command a surplus in excess of what it costs the educated.* Expertise is, to follow Marx's idiom for capital, a form of "self-expanding value" at the expense of working stiffs; it is not therefore either identical with, reducible to, or a form of capital, as the loose and misleading notion of "human capital" would suggest.

The *Oxford English Dictionary* defines expertise as advanced knowledge, training, or experience dealing exclusively with a particular subject or practice. Tied to a gainful occupation or career, this specialty becomes a profession. There is no indication that professionals pocket a surplus in excess of the cost of exercising special skills, much less that they get something for nothing. Unlike our definition of expertise, the dictionary definition leaves hidden what the new political economies might be expected to reveal concerning the controlling asset and decisive factor of production in today's economies.

What accounts for the eclipse of the old political economy and the rise of the new? The new political economies are attributable largely to the following: the Roosevelt Revolution, World War II, the ensuing Cold War, the accompanying scientific-technological revolution, and education.

The New Deal planners, according to Robert Reich, wanted a system of industrial coordination that would give authority to professional managers in government and labor. However, New Deal legislation represented a "compromise between the superstructures already in place and the vision of the new national planners." But for the first time during peace the government managers were in charge, and the labor managers got a hearing. A tripartite system came into being, "transcending the disputes that still raged over the relative power of business, labor, and government within the superstructures of management."[13] The closest analogue was the system worked out by the Fascist state in Italy where the government acted as moderator between the claims of business and labor.

John Kenneth Galbraith, a former New Dealer in the Roosevelt administration, is among the few non-Marxist political economists to tie together the theses of a new industrial order indissolubly linked to the state, the replacement of the market by the planning agencies of the modern corporation and big government, the euthanasia of stockholder power in conjunction with the tendency of the corporation to socialize itself, the eclipse of physical capital in relation to professionally trained manpower, and the delegation of decision making to corporate professionals and their staffs. His *New Industrial State* became a landmark in its challenge to the conventional wisdom and in its suggestion that America's new economic order was not fundamentally different from the Soviet Union's in being managed by professionals.[14]

As early as World War I, the intellectual-administrative professional class captured the commanding heights of the economy through its control of the modern corporation. That story, backed with massive statistical data, has been told by Berle and Gardiner C. Means in *The Modern Corporation and Private Property* (1932). But it was not until the New Deal (1933–1939) that the new class of professionals also captured the government.

It was not the vast array of New Deal social legislation and alphabetical agencies and commissions alone that launched America's new economic order and that eventually made possible the new political economies as retrospective and descriptive accounts rather than merely projected scenarios of the nature of post-capitalist society. Variously described as government planning, collectivism, state capitalism, and national socialism, the new order had Mars for its midwife.

World War II and the accompanying rise in the prestige and power of the administrators of war and related professionals led James Burnham in 1943 to revise his 1941 depiction of America's new order to provide a leading role for professional soldiers. Throughout most of the capitalist era they had played a decidedly secondary role. Not until World War II did war managers rise to the rank of civilian managers in determining national policy. Thus to the other managerial elites—"the production executives and organizers of the industrial process, officials trained in the manipulation of the great labor organizations, and the administrators, bureau chiefs, and commissars developed in the executive branch"—he added the graduates of America's various military academies and war colleges.[15]

The Cold War was the road to pre-eminence of professional managers, professional bureaucrats in the federal government, and the professional military—at the expense of the propertied interests. Big military budgets made possible by the permanent threat of war translated into bigger salaries all around. Following World War II and the Korean War, full employment and the expansion of the wage surplus made the professional class the principal beneficiary as well as the driving force of the knowledge society. In response to the technological demands of a high-tech war and the scientific-technical revolution that enabled America to prevail over the Axis powers, the quality as well as quantity of employment broke all records. High-paid as well as high-skilled jobs enabled the country to cross the threshold from managerial capitalism, in which managers still functioned largely as agents of capitalists, to corporate socialism, in which managers functioned as the senior partners of the monied interests.

Education also played a key role. More than 20 million veterans had their skills upgraded after Congress passed the Servicemen's Readjustment Act, the first G.I. Bill, during Roosevelt's fourth term in office. Designed for veterans of World War II, it was followed during President Truman's Fair Deal by a second G.I. Bill covering veterans of the Korean War.

Peter Drucker noted in his *Post-Capitalist Society* (1993) that the 1944 G.I. Bill of Rights "signaled the shift to the knowledge society," an event even more important than the invention of the computer in giving every veteran of World War II the money to attend university. Professionals mushroomed through the pores of the old society, replacing Marx's bourgeoisie and proletarians—the fundamental classes of capitalist society—with the fundamental "classes of post-capitalist society . . . knowledge workers and service workers."[16]

As Theodore Schultz noted more than three decades before Drucker's 1993 book appeared, "Investment in education has risen at a rapid rate and by itself may well account for a substantial part of the otherwise unexplained rise in earnings." Fritz Machlup's statistics on the explosive growth in size and earning power of the class of professionals are part and parcel of the story of the transition from a nineteenth-century republic of moneybags to a twentieth-century republic of experts. "In 1940," he writes, "a total of 10,573,000 knowledge-producing workers were employed and earned a total of $15,120 million. . . . In 1958, there were 20,497,000 employed, earning $89,960 million."[17] That's a multiple of two in numbers of knowledge workers alongside a multiple of six in the aggregate income of those workers.

The combined effect of the above historical-economic factors was the displacement of capital to a subordinate position in the economy, the emergence of expertise as the driving force of the new economy, the relegation of the political economy of capital to an earlier historical era, and the corresponding emergence of the new political economies of expertise, whether as champions or as critics of America's new social and economic order. Given this reality, it is more than a little ironic to find both establishment and Marxist political economists competing in support of an obsolete theory of capitalism, the one group so as to defend capitalism, the other so as to critique it.

In sum, what is new about twentieth century political economies is the concept of expertise, whether in the name of "intelligence," "information," "knowledge," "education," "human capital," "intellectual capital," "brainpower," "management," "organization," or "professionalism." They arose in response to a new economic order both in the making and as fully realized. Since the economic world is not what it used to be, it is understandable that political economies have also changed. What Marxists call bourgeois political economy or the "political economy of property" has been displaced not by a "political economy of labor," however, but by the political economies of the expertoisie.[18]

III.

WHILE THE NEW POLITICAL ECONOMIES AGREE about the displacement of physical capital by expertise, they disagree in their depictions of the new economic order. They disagree, first, over whether the new economic order is an advanced stage of capitalism or a post-capitalist political economy. Second, they disagree over the presence or absence of exploitation under the new order.

The emergence of expertise in the twentieth century has been accompanied by the appearance of apologists of the new order who defend the theory of human capital, according to which expertise is in effect the latest form taken by capital in the latter's ongoing and presumably progressive development. In 1950 Johannes Alasco asserted that the age of intellectual capitalism was upon us and, since the 1960s, Theodore Schultz's theory of human capital has figured prominently in the mainstream version of the political economy of expertise.

Alasco expected the owners of knowledge "to continue the ventures of their predecessors, the owners of industrial equipment." He believed the new class would be just as restless and ambitious as the old in seeking opportunities for the profitable use of its particular capital. "It will attempt to revolutionize the Western world for this sole purpose: its own personal profit"—in the form of privileged salaries.[19]

Alasco claimed that the main conflict of the twentieth century was not that between bourgeois and proletarians, but one between stockholders and professionals, or between finance capitalism and intellectual capitalism, to see which would become the decisive asset of the economy: money or knowledge. He characterized the possessors of knowledge as people motivated by a passion for building, while the monied interests were bent only on consuming the fruits of the past.

Schultz's theory of human capital as the key to modernization makes a similar case for education by tracing the increasing importance of knowledge over traditional forms of capital through the twentieth century. Much of the popularity of his work in the halls of academe can be traced to his inflating of the cost of expertise and corresponding suggestion that the salaries of professional workers need also to be inflated so as to make the acquisition of human capital a sound business proposition.[20]

MIT professor of economics and Democratic party neoliberal ideologue Lester Thurow challenges Schultz's assumption that education is not only the best public but also the best private investment. The owners of human capital, he argues, are not capitalists, and the investments in knowledge required to generate new brainpower industries are mainly public instead of private. Around the globe, the achievement of even semiliteracy on a national scale has required a publicly financed, compulsory education system. Yet, as Thurow notes, that violates every principle of capitalism as it means giving away what could be sold![21]

Thurow persists in using the term "human capital" even as he argues that a hard-nosed capitalist would seldom make an investment therein. One is left to wonder what sort of capitalism it is when capitalist enterprises do not own the human capital of their employees. The era of brainpower Thurow identifies with the dominance of human capital, but the capital that is human bears little resemblance to that owned by capitalists. With brainpower becoming the decisive factor, observes the MIT economist, the capitalism with a future is the one that relies on the public sector to make investments in education that the capitalists cannot be counted on to make. Capitalism can survive only in a mixed economy, and that mix is increasingly in favor of the owners of human capital at the expense of capitalists. With capitalism's increasing dependence on human capital and brainpower industries along with an obsolete ideology of instant gratification, capitalism can only survive if it undergoes a profound metamorphosis.[22] But that implies a radical change in substance. So why call the new order capitalist? Virtually every social system is a mixed economy, and in each case the proper name for it is that of the dominant partner in the mix.

Alasco and Gouldner both understand the struggle between capitalists and owners of human or intellectual capital to be the main struggle of the twentieth century; they also see that struggle as one between two forms of capitalism. That is partly because they are seduced by the language of "human capital," "cultural capital," "intellectual capital," etc., and partly because of their overly broad definition of capital. For Alasco, "anything which can be defined in terms of legal ownership and may become a source of income" is capital. For Gouldner, "Anything is capital that serves as the basis of enforceable claims to the private appropriation of incomes legitimated for their contribution to the production of economic valuables or wealth."[23] Either definition will serve to legitimate extension of the meaning of capitalism both backward and forward in time to include "feudal capitalism," in which land is the controlling asset, as well as "intellectual capitalism," in which expertise is the controlling asset. Since slaves also fit under the heading "capital," we may as well speak of "slave capitalism." On this road, the terms "capital" and "capitalism" lose their historical specificity.

Marx assigned to labor the task of swallowing expertise. Today, non-Marxist political economists go to the other extreme of swallowing labor in the name of human, intellectual, or knowledge capital. Both parties make the same mistake in not recognizing expertise as an independent, fourth factor of production having the same status as land, labor, and capital. The main difference is that the theory of intellectual capital—in the hands, for example, of Alvin Gouldner—acknowledges the existence of a new class corresponding to the ownership of intellectual capital, whereas the Marxist theory of intellectual labor denies that its owners constitute anything more than an upper stratum of the proletariat.

The most credible way out of this impasse is to acknowledge expertise as a fourth and independent factor of production. Its owners, tied to a professional position, are the members of the corresponding class of experts or professionals—the expertoisie. They are thus neither a stratum of the capitalist class nor a stratum of the so-called working class. They are a class in and for themselves as the history of their relation to labor and capital in America through the twentieth century clearly indicates.

The thesis that professionals are on the road to class power or have already arrived there is in large measure conceded. What has not been conceded is, first, that their newly won pre-eminence constitutes a revolution, not a further stage, evolution, or metamorphosis of capitalism, and second, that they constitute a new exploiting class. The second claim is especially controversial because it runs counter to the self-image and the material interests of professionals.

The antagonists on this second issue line up as follows. In the camp of those who ignore the possibility that labor might be exploited were Berle and Means, Burnham, Schumpeter, Chandler, Reich, Thurow, Stewart, John Kenneth Galbraith, and Schultz's prevailing school of "human capital." On the opposite side were Machajski, Nomad, Rizzi, Castoriadis, Djilas, Bazelon, Gouldner, Drucker, James K. Galbraith, and Hodges, all critics of Marxist political economy, albeit deeply or partly influenced by it.[24]

The new political economies are at loggerheads because there are sizeable economic interests at stake when it comes to any dissection of the political-economic workings of the Information Age. The champions of the class of professionals in the United States during the years of the Great Depression offered themselves as defenders of the common working man. But with the consolidation of their rule, they switched sides from defenders of the welfare state to proponents of trickle-down and other theories designed of, by, and for professionals.

The antagonisms internal to and the patterns of development characteristic of capitalism convinced Marx that this social order was not the end of history But his polarization thesis, that the development of capitalism is the polarization of the whole of society into two great classes, bourgeoisie and proletariat, led him to suppose that post-capitalist society would be a non-exploitive one.

In short, Marx was seduced by Hegelian dialectics into reasoning that slavery ends with the annihilation of the class of slaveowners; that serfdom ends with the annihilation of the class of landed aristocrats; and that capitalism ends with the annihilation of the class of capitalists. That means also, in the first case, no slaves; in the second, no serfs; and in the third, no wage-laborers. Ironically, history proved more dialectical than Marx imagined when his celebrated working class split into two—a class of unskilled and semiskilled working stiffs, and a class of professionals—and when the latter class displaced the bourgeoisie as the new ruling class at the expense of both capital and labor.

Class antagonisms in post-capitalist society can hardly be seen let alone understood without a radical recasting of Marx's model. But as that model is virtually the only theory of exploitation under capitalism, the failure to recast it means leaving the field entirely in the hands of those who disclaim the presence of exploitation in post-capitalist societies.[25]

Notes

1. See Lasswell 1965:13, 15, 17–20; Burnham 1941:112–138 (on the economy of managerial society); and Djilas1957:103–123 (on the economy of the new class).

2. Lasswell 1965:13 and Morgenthau 1967:36. For the definition of politics as the struggle for power, see also Loewenstein 1957:3–6.

3. Canterbery 1995:2, 3.

4. Babeuf 1964:64. The greater part of Babeuf's defense from the trial at Vendôme in February–May 1797 was taken verbatim from his *Manifesto of the Plebeians.*

5. *Ibid.,* p. 65, cited in quotes from Babeuf's *Manifesto.*

6. Marx n.d.:190.
7. Miranda 1972:42–43, 106.
8. Engels 1959:223, 224–225.
9. *Ibid.,* p. 226. See also *Capital*, pp. 180–181, 195.
10. Miranda 1972:106, 121.
11. *Ibid.,* pp. 63, 64.
12. *Ibid.,* p. 101; and *Capital*, p. 181.
13. Reich 1984:99, 100.
14. Galbraith 1971:389 and 1975:2–4, 115, 314–315, 391, 394–395, 403.
15. Burnham 1943:258, 261, 262.
16. Drucker 1993:3, 5, 6.
17. Schultz 1970:163, 164; and Machlup 1962:392.
18. Marx 1978:517.
19. Alasco 1950:103–104.
20. Schultz 1981:61, 63.
21. Thurow 1996:49, 132.
22. *Ibid.,* pp. 49–50, 133.
23. Alasco 1950:104; and Gouldner 1979:23, 24–25.
24. See the discussion of each in Hodges 2000:20–54, 123–151.
25. For a detailed explanation of exploitation by the expertoisie in the former Soviet Union and an effort to measure its mass and rate in the U.S. economy after World War II, see Hodges's trilogy on political economy: *The Bureaucratization of Socialism* (1981), pp. 18–38, 62–76; *America's New Economic Order* (1996), pp. 50–82; and *Class Politics in the Information Age* (2000), pp. 55–75, 99–122.

References

Alasco, Johannes. (1950). *Intellectual Capitalism*. New York: World University Press.
Babeuf, François Noël "Gracchus." (1964). "Excerpt from the Trial of Babeuf," in *Socialist Thought: A Documentary History*, edited by Albert Fried and Ronald Sanders. Garden City, NY: Anchor.
Burnham, James. (1941). *The Managerial Revolution: What Is Happening in the World*. New York: John Day.
———. (1943). *The Machiavellians*. New York: John Day.
Canterbery, E. Ray. (1995). *The Literate Economist: A Brief History of Economics*. New York: HarperCollins.
Djilas, Milovan. (1957). *The New Class: An Analysis of the Communist System*. New York: Praeger.
Drucker, Peter F. (1993). *Post-Capitalist Society*. New York: Harper Business.
Engels, Frederick. ([1878] 1959). *Anti-Dühring: Herr Eugen Dühring's Revolution in Science*, 2nd ed. Moscow: Foreign Languages Publishing House.

Fried, Albert, and Ronald Sanders (eds.). (1964). *Socialist Thought: A Documentary History*. Garden City, NY: Anchor.

Galbraith, John Kenneth. (1971). *The New Industrial State*, rev. ed. Boston: Houghton Mifflin.

———. (1975). *Economics and the Public Purpose*. New York: New American Library.

Gouldner, Alvin W. (1979). *The Future of Intellectuals and the Rise of the New Class*. New York: Continuum.

Hodges, Donald Clark. (1981). *The Bureaucratization of Socialism*. Amherst, MA: University of Massachusetts Press.

———. (1996). *America's New Economic Order*. Aldershot, UK: Avebury.

———. (2000). *Class Politics in the Information Age*. Urbana and Chicago: University of Illinois Press.

Lasswell, Harold. (1965). *Politics: Who Gets What, When, How*. Cleveland, OH: Meridian.

Loewenstein, Karl. (1957). *Political Power and the Governmental Process*. Chicago: University of Chicago Press.

MacEwan, Arthur, and Thomas E. Weisskopf (eds.) (1970). *Perspectives on the Economic Problem: A Book of Readings in Political Economy*. Englewood Cliffs, NJ: Prentice-Hall.

Machlup, Fritz. (1962). *The Production and Distribution of Knowledge in the United States*. Princeton, NJ: Princeton University Press.

Marx, Karl. (n.d.). *Capital: A Critique of Political Economy*, Vol. 1, trans. by Samuel Moore and Edward Aveling, edited by Frederick Engels and revised by Ernest Untermann. New York: Modern Library.

———. (1978). "Inaugural Address of the Working Men's International Association," in *The Marx-Engels Reader*, edited by Robert C. Tucker. New York: Norton.

Miranda, José P. (1972). *Marx en México: plusvalía y política*. Mexico D.F.: Siglo XXI.

Morgenthau, Hans. (1967). *Politics Among Nations: The Struggle for Power and Peace*, 4th ed. New York: Knopf.

Reich, Robert. (1984). *The Next American Frontier*. New York: Penguin.

Schultz, Theodore W. (1970). "Investment in Human Capital" in *Perspectives on the Economic Problem: A Book of Readings in Political Economy*, edited by Arthur MacEwan and Thomas E. Weisskopf. Englewood Cliffs, NJ: Prentice-Hall.

———. (1981). *Investing in People: The Economics of Population Quality*. Berkeley: University of California Press.

Thurow, Lester C. (1996). *The Future of Capitalism*. New York: Penguin.

Index

Action, economic, Weber's definition of, 171
Actors, place in economic sociology, 162
Africa, transition economies, 329–348
  Coup events in Sub-Saharan Africa, 329–348
Alchian, A. A., 33, 234–236
Allocative outcomes, constitutional economics, 106–111
Arrow's impossibility theorem, 196
Asia, transition economies, 279–326
  China, 279–293
    corruption in, root of, 280–285
    formal model, 286–287
    free market economy, 287–288
    market economy with privilege, 288–290
    socialist market economy, 289
    two-part tariff, 290–293
  Japan, Laffont-Tirole model extended to, 301–326
    atomic energy, case study, 316–322
    culture, dimensions of, 302–305
    economic structure, 307–311
    political culture, 305–307
    regulatory and bureaucratic capture, 311–316
Atomic energy, Japan vs. United States, 316–322
Austrian school perspectives, 161–214
  Hayek, polity, society, and economy in, 161–191
    Critique of new political economy from perspective of, 193–211
    Knowledge-oriented research program, 201–210

  Weberian approach of, 173–176
  Mises, polity, society, and economy in, 161–191
    Weberian approach of, 173–176
  Embeddedness
    analytic narrative grounded in, examples of, 176–181
    single, problem of, 165–167, 169
    Weber's conception of, 167–170
  Scientism and knowledge, 193–211
  Weber, polity, society, and economy in, 161–191
    embeddedness conception, 167–170
    understanding, concept of, 170–173

Babeuf, F. N., 369
Backhaus, Jüergen, 3, 9, 59
Bahamas, pirate culture of, 180
Baltics, transition economy of, 233–257
Becker, Gary, 163
Belarus, transition economy of, 233–257
Benin, coup events in, 331
Bergson, Abram, 26, 39
Boettke, Peter J., 5, 9, 161
Botswana, coup events in, 331
Bourgeoisie vs. expertoisie, 367–381
Bribery, China, 285, 291
Burkina Faso, coup events in, 331
Burundi, coup events in, 331
Butler, Bishop, 16

Cameroon, coup events in, 331
Canterbery, E. Ray, 369

American Journal of Economics and Sociology, Vol. 61, No. 1 (January, 2002).
© 2002 American Journal of Economics and Sociology, Inc.